# MARKETS NOT CAPITALISM

## individualist anarchism against bosses, inequality, corporate power, and structural poverty

**Edited by Gary Chartier & Charles W. Johnson**

ISBN 978-1-57027-242-4

Gary Chartier and Charles W. Johnson
*Markets Not Capitalism: Individualist Anarchism against Bosses, Inequality,
Corporate Power, and Structural Poverty*
Includes bibliographic references
1. Economics – philosophy. 2. Socialism. 3. Capitalism. 4. Anarchism. I.
Title II. Johnson, Charles W. III. Chartier, Gary


Cover image based on an image by Walter Baxter.

Released by Minor Compositions, London / New York / Port Watson
Minor Compositions is a series of interventions & provocations drawing
from autonomous politics, avant-garde aesthetics, and the revolutions of
everyday life.

Minor Compositions is an imprint of Autonomedia
www.minorcompositions.info | info@minorcompositions.info


Distributed by Autonomedia
PO Box 568 Williamsburgh Station
Brooklyn, NY 11211

Phone/fax: 718-963-0568
www.autonomedia.org
info@autonomedia.org

*In memory of*
*Karl Hess*

# CONTENTS

## Part Eight
Freed-Market Regulation: Social Activism and
   Spontaneous Order

# ACKNOWLEDGEMENTS

This book has been a labor of love on the part of many people.

Our comrades at the Center for a Stateless Society – including Brad Spangler, Roderick T. Long, Kevin Carson, Charles W. Johnson, Sheldon Richman, Chris Lempa, Joseph R. Stromberg, James Tuttle, Roman Pearah, Anna O. Morgenstern, Tom Knapp, Darian Worden, David S. D'Amato, Tennyson McCalla, Mike Gogulski, Stacy Litz, Ross Kenyon, Matt Gold, Mariana Evica, Rocco Stanzione, Wendy McElroy, and Stephan Kinsella – deserve our ongoing thanks for, among other things, the stimulation they have provided for this and other projects. We are particularly grateful to Roderick for proposing an April 2010 Association of Private Enterprise Education symposium with the title "Free Market Anti-Capitalism?" in which a number of us participated along with our friend Steven Horwitz, that provided the initial impetus for work on the project.

Alex Cockburn, Bill Kauffman, Sean Gabb, and Ken MacLeod deserve our thanks for their willingness to endorse the book. We are also grateful to Stevphen Shukaitis of Minor Compositions and Autonomedia for his continued support. More broadly, we appreciate Autonomedia's willingness to release a potentially controversial project like this one. We are very much aware of the ambivalence members of the Autonomedia collective and some of Autonomedia's constituents feel regarding arguments featured in the book, and of course we understand that all those associated with the press reserve the right to disagree profoundly with us. At the same time, we appreciate and share their hope that the book will both prompt productive conversation within the anarchist milieu and facilitate the redirection in a more positive and liberatory direction of the "libertarian populism" currently attracting attention in the United States. We are very pleased by the collective's willingness to accept us as fellow leftists and fellow opponents of corporate privilege, even as some if its members view our proposed solutions with pronounced skepticism. Similarly, we are thankful for rapid, appealing, eye-catching work to the book's designer, who, deeply uncomfortable with some aspects of the book's content, asked not to be identified as associated with the project.

Charles would like to extend special thanks to Sheldon Richman, Tennyson McCalla, and James Tuttle, for encouragement, helpful suggestions, and for immensely helpful support to the many disparate projects that came together in this book; to his comrades and interlocutors – Abe, Kelly, Kaleb, Mitch, Rachel, Nicole, Bobby, Irina and Joanna – from Vegas Anarchist Cafe and Living Without Borders; and for debts far too great to account – in the making of this book, and for everything else besides – to his teacher, Roderick T. Long; his father, Paul M. Johnson; and his beloved companion, Laura Breitenbeck. Without them, none of this would have been possible.

On Gary's part, thanks are due to the usual suspects: Elenor Webb, Jeffrey Cassidy, Annette Bryson, Aena Prakash, Alexander Lian, Andrew Howe, Angela Keaton, Anne-Marie Pearson, Bart Willruth, Carole Pateman, Craig R. Kinzer, David B. Hoppe, David R. Larson, Deborah K. Dunn, Donna Carlson, Ellen Hubbell, Eva Pascal, Fritz Guy, Heather Ferguson, Jan M. Holden, Jesse Leamon, Joel Sandefur, John Elder, John Thomas, Julio C. Muñoz, Kenneth A. Dickey, Lawrence T. Geraty, Less Antman, Ligia Radoias, Maria Zlateva, Michael Orlando, Nabil Abu-Assal, Patricia Cabrera, Robert E. Rustad, Jr., Ronel Harvey, Ruth E. E. Burke, Sel J. Hwahng, W. Kent Rogers, and Wonil Kim. He especially appreciates the moral and logistical support Elenor provided as work on the book was completed. As usual, John Thomas ensured that La Sierra University's School of Business was a congenial place in which to work on a scholarly project of this nature.

We've dedicated *Markets Not Capitalism* to Karl Hess – a gentle, insightful, graceful, articulate, and passionate believer in freedom, decentralization, and peaceful, voluntary cooperation. Karl bridged the gap between the Old Right and the New Left, powerfully indicted the political status quo, and provided a compelling and unsettling model of life outside the state's clutches. Flawed like everyone else, he was nonetheless good and decent, embodying the commitment to human liberation we seek to foster with this book.

We thank publishers of copyrighted material for reprint permission.

# INTRODUCTION

**M**ARKET ANARCHISTS BELIEVE IN MARKET EXCHANGE, NOT IN ECONOMIC PRIVILEGE. THEY believe in free markets, not in capitalism. What makes them *anarchists* is their belief in a fully *free and consensual society* – a society in which order is achieved not through legal force or political government, but through free agreements and voluntary cooperation on a basis of equality. What makes them *market* anarchists is their recognition of free market exchange as a vital medium for peacefully anarchic social order. But the markets they envision are not like the privilege-riddled "markets" we see around us today. Markets laboring under government and capitalism are pervaded by persistent poverty, ecological destruction, radical inequalities of wealth, and concentrated power in the hands of corporations, bosses, and landlords. The consensus view is that exploitation – whether of human beings or of nature – is simply the natural result of markets left unleashed. The consensus view holds that private property, competitive pressure, and the profit motive must – whether for good or for ill – inevitably lead to capitalistic wage labor, to the concentration of wealth and social power in the hands of a select class, or to business practices based on growth at all costs and the devil take the hindmost.

Market anarchists dissent. They argue that economic privilege is a real and pervasive social problem, but that the problem is not a problem of private property, competition, or profits *per se*. It is not a problem of *the market form* but of markets *deformed* – deformed by the long shadow of historical injustices and the ongoing, continuous exercise of legal privilege on behalf of capital. The market anarchist tradition is radically pro-market and anticapitalist – reflecting its consistent concern with the deeply *political* character of corporate power, the dependence of economic elites on the tolerance or active support of the state, the permeable barriers between political and economic elites, and the cultural embeddedness of hierarchies established and maintained by state-perpetrated and state-sanctioned violence.

## THE MARKET FORM

This book is intended as an extended introduction to the economic and social theory of left-wing market anarchism. Market anarchism is a radically individualist and anticapitalist social movement. Like other anarchists, market anarchists are radical advocates of individual liberty and mutual consent in every aspect of social life – thus rejecting all forms of domination and government as invasions against liberty and violations of human dignity. The market anarchists' distinct contribution to anarchist thought is their analysis of the market form as a core component of a thoroughly free and equal society – their understanding of the revolutionary possibilities inherent in market relationships freed from government and capitalistic privilege, and their insights into the structures of political privilege and control that deform actually-existing markets and uphold exploitation in spite of the naturally equilibrating tendencies of market processes. Since they insist on so sharp a distinction between the market form as such and the economic features of actually-existing capitalism, it is important to carefully distinguish the key features of markets as market anarchists understand them. The social relationships that market anarchists explicitly defend, and hope to free from all forms of government control, are relationships based on:

1. **ownership of property,** especially *decentralized individual* ownership, not only of personal possessions but also of land, homes, natural resources, tools, and capital goods;

2. **contract and voluntary exchange** of goods and services, by individuals or groups, on the expectation of mutual benefit;

3. **free competition** among all buyers and sellers – in price, quality, and all other aspects of exchange – without *ex ante* restraints or burdensome barriers to entry;

4. **entrepreneurial discovery,** undertaken not only to compete in existing markets but also in order to discover and develop new opportunities for economic or social benefit; and

5. **spontaneous order,** recognized as a significant and positive coordinating force – in which decentralized negotiations, exchanges, and entrepreneurship converge to produce large-scale coordination without, or *beyond the capacity of,* any deliberate plans or explicit common blueprints for social or economic development.

Market anarchists do not limit ownership to possession, or to common or collective ownerhip, although they do not exclude these kinds of ownership either; they insist on the importance of contract and market exchange, and on profit-motivated free competition and entrepreneurship; and they not only tolerate but celebrate the unplanned, spontaneous coordation that Marxists deride as the "social anarchy of production." But left-wing market anarchists are also radically anticapitalist, and they absolutely reject the belief – common to both the anti-market Left and the pro-capitalist Right – that these five features of the market form must entail a social order of bosses, landlords, centralized corporations, class exploitation, cut-throat business dealings, immiserated workers, structural poverty, or large-scale economic inequality. They insist, instead, on five distinctive claims about markets, freedom, and privilege:

- **The centrifugal tendency of markets:** market anarchists see freed markets, under conditions of free competition, as tending to *diffuse* wealth and *dissolve* fortunes – with a centrifugal effect on incomes, property-titles, land, and access to capital – rather than *concentrating* it in the hands of a socioeconomic elite. Market anarchists recognize no *de jure* limits on the extent or kind of wealth that any one person might amass; but they believe that market and social realities will impose much more rigorous *de facto* pressures against massive inequalities of wealth than any *de jure* constraint could achieve.

- **The radical possibilities of market social activism:** market anarchists also see freed markets as a space not only for profit-driven commerce, but also as spaces for social experimentation and hard-driving grassroots activism. They envision "market forces" as including not only the pursuit of narrowly financial gain or maximizing returns to investors, but also the appeal of solidarity, mutuality and sustainability. "Market processes" can – and ought to – include conscious, coordinated efforts to raise consciousness, change economic behavior, and address issues of economic equality and social justice through nonviolent direct action.

- **The rejection of *statist-quo* economic relations:** market anarchists sharply distinguish between the defense of the market form and apologetics for actually-existing distributions of wealth and class divisions, since these distributions and divisions hardly emerged as the result of unfettered markets, but rather from the governed, regimented, and privilege-ridden markets that exist today; they see actually-existing distributions of wealth and class divisions as serious and genuine social problems, but not as problems with the market form itself; these are not *market* problems but *ownership problems* and *coordination problems*.

- **The regressiveness of regulation:** market anarchists see *coordination problems* – problems with an unnatural, destructive, politically-imposed interruption of the free operation of exchange and competition – as the result of continuous, ongoing legal privilege for incumbent capitalists and other well-entrenched economic interests, imposed at the expense of small-scale competitors and the working class.

- **Dispossession and rectification:** market anarchists see economic privilege as partly the result of serious *ownership problems* – problems with an unnatural, destructive, politically-imposed maldistribution of property titles – produced by the history of political dispossession and expropriation inflicted worldwide by means of war, colonialism, segregation, nationalization and kleptocracy. Markets are not viewed as being maximally free so long as they are darkened by the shadow of mass robbery or the denial of ownership; and they emphasize the importance of reasonable rectification of past injustices – including grassroots, anti-corporate, anti-neoliberal approaches to the "privatization" of state-controlled resources; processes for restitution to identifiable victims of injustice; and revolutionary expropriation of property fraudulently claimed by the state and state-entitled monopolists.

## THE MARKET ANARCHIST TRADITION

Early anarchist thinkers such as Josiah Warren and Pierre-Joseph Proudhon emphasized the positive, socially harmonizing features of market relationships when they were conducted within a context of equality – with Proudhon, for example, writing that social revolution would abolish the "system of laws" and "principle of authority," to replace them with the "system of contracts"[1].

Drawing on Warren's and Proudhon's use of contract and exchange for models of social mutuality, distinctive strands of market anarchism have emerged repeatedly within the broad anarchist tradition, punctuated by crises, collapses, interregnums and resurgences. The history is complex but it can be roughly divided into three major periods represented in this text – (i) a "first wave," represented mainly by "individualist anarchists" and "mutualists" such as Benjamin Tucker, Voltairine de Cleyre, and Dyer Lum, and occupying roughly the period from the American Civil War to 1917;[2] (ii) a

---

1   See "Organization of Economic Forces," *General Idea of the Revolution in the Nineteenth Century*, ch. 3 (37-58), in this volume.

2   The exact differences between "individualists" and "mutualists" during the first wave were hardly ever cut and dried; many writers (such as Tucker) used each word at different times to refer to their own position. However, a few

"second wave," coinciding with the radicalization of formerly pro-capitalist American libertarians and the resurgence of anarchism as a family of social movements during the radicalism of the 1960s and 1970s; and (iii) a "third wave," developing as a dissident strand within the anarchist milieu of the 1990s and the post-Seattle movement of the new millennium.

In spite of discontinuities and differences, each wave has typically revived the literature of the earlier waves and drawn explicitly on its themes; what has, in general, united them is their defense of market relationships and their particular emphasis on the revolutionary possibilities inherent in the market form, when it is – to the extent that it is – liberated from legal and social institutions of privilege.

The anticapitalism of the "first wave" individualists was obvious to them and to many of their contemporaries. Benjamin Tucker famously argued that four monopolies, or clusters of state-guaranteed privileges, were responsible for the power of the corporate elite – the patent monopoly, the effective monopoly created by the state's distribution of arbitrarily engrossed land to the politically favored and its protection of unjust land titles, the money and credit monopoly, and the monopolistic privileges conferred by tariffs. The economically powerful depended on these monopolies; eliminate them, and the power of the elite would dissolve.

Tucker was committed to the cause of justice for workers in conflict with contemporary capitalists and he clearly identified with the burgeon-

---

differences might be sketched between those who were *most frequently* called "individualists," such as Tucker or Yarros, and those who were most frequently called "mutualists," such as Dyer Lum, Clarence Swartz, or the European followers of Proudhon—in particular, that while both supported the emancipation of workers and ensuring that all workers had access to capital, the "mutualists" tended to emphasize the specific importance of worker-owned co-operatives and direct worker ownership over the means of production, while "individualists" tended to emphasize that under conditions of equal freedom, workers would settle on whatever arrangements of ownership made most sense under the circumstances.

Complicating matters, "mutualism" is now retrospectively used, in the twenty-first century, to refer to most anti-capitalist market anarchists, or specifically to those (like Kevin Carson) who differ from the so-called "Lockean" position on land ownership—who believe that land ownership can be based only on personal occupancy and use, ruling out absentee landlordship as undesirable and unworthy of legal protection. "Mutualists" in this sense of the term includes both those who were most frequently called "individualists" during the first wave (such as Tucker) and those who were most frequently called "mutualists" (such as Lum).

ing socialist movement. But he argued against Marx and other socialists that market relationships could be fruitful and non-exploitative *provided* that the market-distorting privileges conferred by the four monopolies were eliminated.

The radicalism of Tucker and his compatriots and that of the strand of anarchism they birthed was arguably less apparent after the breaking of the first wave than it was to their contemporaries. Perhaps in part this is because of their disputes with representatives of other anarchist tendencies, whose criticisms of their views have influenced the perceptions of later anarchists. It is also, unavoidably, a consequence of the identification of many of their twentieth-century descendants with the right wing of the libertarian movement and thus as apologists for the corporate elite and its social dominance.

Though there were honorable exceptions, twentieth-century market-oriented libertarians frequently lionized corporate titans, ignored or rationalized the abuse of workers, and trivialized or embraced economic and social hierarchy. While many endorsed the critique of the state and of state-secured privilege offered by Tucker and his fellow individualists, they often overlooked or rejected the radical implications of the earlier individualists' class-based analysis of structural injustice. There were, in short, few vocal enthusiasts for the individualists' brand of anticapitalism in the early-to-mid-twentieth century.

The most radical fringe of the market-oriented strand of the libertarian movement – represented by thinkers like Murray Rothbard and Roy Childs – generally embraced, not the anticapitalist economics of individualism and mutualism, but a position its advocates described as "anarcho-capitalism." The future free society they envisioned was a market society – but one in which market relationships were little changed from business as usual and the end of state control was imagined as freeing business to do much what it had been doing before, rather than unleashing competing forms of economic organization, which might radically transform market forms from the bottom up.

But in the "second wave" of the 1960s, the family of anarchist social movements – revived by antiauthoritarian and countercultural strands of the New Left – and the antiwar radicals among the libertarians began to re-discover and republish the works of the mutualists and the other individualists. "Anarcho-capitalists" such as Rothbard and Childs began to question libertarianism's historical alliance with the Right, and to abandon defenses of big business and actually-existing capitalism in favor of a more consistent left-wing market anarchism. Perhaps the most visible and dramatic example was Karl Hess's embrace of the New Left radicalism, and his abandonment of "capitalist" economics in favor of small-scale, community-based, non-capitalist markets. By 1975, the former Goldwater speechwriter declared, "I have lost my faith in capitalism" and "I resist this capitalist nation-state," observing that he had "turn[ed] from the religion of capitalism."[3]

The "second wave" was followed by a second trough, for anarchism broadly and market anarchism in particular. By the later 1970s and the 1980s, the anticapitalist tendency among market-oriented libertarians had largely dissipated or been shouted down by the mainstreaming pro-capitalist politics of well-funded "libertarian" institutions like the Cato Institute and the leadership of the Libertarian Party. But with the end of the Cold War, the realignment of longstanding political coalitions, and the public coming-out of a third wave anarchist movement in the 1990s, the intellectual, social stages were set for today's resurgence of anticapitalist market anarchism.

By the beginning of twenty-first century, anticapitalist descendants of the individualists had grown in number, influence, and visibility. They shared the early individualists' conviction that markets need not in principle be exploitative. At the same time, they elaborated and defended a distinctively libertarian version of class analysis that extended Tucker's list of monopolies and highlighted the intersection of state-secured privilege with systematic past and ongoing dispossession and with a range of issues of ecology, culture, and interpersonal power relations. They emphasized the fact that, while genuinely liberated – *freed* – markets could be empowering, market transactions that occurred in contexts misshapen by past and ongoing injustice were, not surprisingly, debilitating and oppressive. But the problem, the new individualists (like their predecessors) insisted, lay not with markets but rather with *capitalism* – with social dominance by economic elites secured by the state. The solution, then, was the abolition of capitalism through the elimination of legal privileges, including the privileges required for the protection of title to stolen and engrossed assets.

The new individualists have been equally critical of explicitly statist conservatives and progressives and of market-oriented libertarians on the right who use the rhetoric of freedom to legitimate corporate privilege. Their

---

3    To be sure, while Hess's social attitudes do not seem to have changed substantially after he made these statements, he became less wedded to the *language* of anti-capitalism; he published *Capitalism for Kids: Growing Up to Be Your Own Boss* in 1986. But there is no reason to doubt that what Hess meant by "capitalism" here was what contemporary left-wing market anarchists mean when they talk about peaceful, voluntary exchange in a genuinely freed market, rather than what he had rejected in 1975. Certainly, as the book's subtitle suggests, he had no intention of steering young readers into careers as corporate drones.

aggressive criticism of this sort of "vulgar libertarianism" has emphasized that existing economic relationships are shot through with injustice from top to bottom and that calls for freedom can readily be used to mask attempts to preserve the freedom of elites to retain wealth acquired through state-tolerated or state-perpetrated violence and state-guaranteed privilege.

## THE NATURAL HABITAT OF THE MARKET ANARCHIST

This book would not have been possible without the Internet. The reader of *Markets Not Capitalism* will quickly notice that many of the articles do not read quite like chapters in an ordinary book. Many of them are short. Many of them begin in the middle of a dialogue – one of the most frequent opening phrases is "In a recent issue of such-and-such, so-and-so said that…" The contemporary articles often originally appeared online, as posts to a weblog; they refer frequently to past posts or pre-existing discussions, and often criticize on or elaborate comments made by other authors in other venues. While the articles have been reformatted for print, many still read very distinctly like the blog posts that they once were.

But this is not merely an artifact of Internet-based social networks. The history of the individualist and mutualist tradition is largely a history of ephemeral publications, short-lived presses, self-published pamphlets, and small radical papers. The most famous is certainly Benjamin Tucker's *Liberty* (1881-1908), but also includes such publications as Hugh Pentecost's *Twentieth Century* (1888-1898), as well as "second wave" market anarchist journals such as *Left and Right* (1965-1968) and *Libertarian Forum* (1969-1984). All these publications were short and published frequently; their articles were typically critical rather than comprehensive, idiosyncratic rather than technical in approach and tone. Long-standing, far-reaching debates between papers, correspondents, and the surrounding movement were constant sources of material; where a specific interlocutor was not available for some of these articles, the author might, as in de Cleyre and Slobodinsky's "The Individualist and the Communist: A Dialogue," go so far as to invent one. The most famous book-length work from the "first wave" – Tucker's *Instead of a Book, by a Man Too Busy to Write One* (1893) – is simply a collection of short articles from *Liberty*, the majority of which are clearly themselves replies to questions and arguments posed by *Liberty's* readers or fellow journal editors. The critical exchanges read very much like those one might encounter today on Blogger or WordPress sites – because, of course, today's blog is merely a new technological form taken by the small, independent press.

The independent, dialogue-based small press has provided a natural habitat for market anarchist writing to flourish – whereas liberal and Marxist writing found their most distinctive habitats in declarations, manifestos, and intricate, comprehensive treatises. Why this might be the case is a large question, worth exploring far beyond what the limits of this preface might allow. However, it may be worth noting that market anarchism has more or less always emerged as a *critical* and *experimental* project – on the radical fringes of social movements (whether the Owenite movement, the freethought movement, the labor movement, the American market-oriented libertarian movement, or the counterglobalization movement and the associated social anarchist milieu).

Market anarchism aims to draw out social truths not by dogmatizing or laying down the law, but rather by allowing as far as possible for the free interplay of ideas and social forces, by looking for the unintended consequences of accepted ideas, by engagement in an open-ended process of experimentation and discovery that permits the constant testing of both ideas and institutions against competitors and bottom-line reality.

The revolutionary anarchist and mutualist Dyer D. Lum (1839-1893) wrote in "The Economics of Anarchy" that a defining feature of market anarchy was the "plasticity" of social and economic arrangements as opposed to the "rigidity" of either statist domination or communist economic schemes. The substance of market anarchist ideas has arguably shaped the form in which market anarchist writers feel most at home expressing them. Or perhaps, conversely, the *form* of the writing may even be what has often made the *substance* possible: it may be that market anarchist ideas most naturally take shape in the course of dialogue rather than disquisition, in the act of critical give-and-take rather than one-sided monologue. The value of spontaneity, exploratory engagement, and the rigors of the competitive test may be as essential to the formation of market anarchist ideas in writing as they are to the implementation of those ideas in the world at large.

If so, then these articles must be read with the awareness that they have, to a certain extent, been lifted out of their natural environment. There are longer, sustained treatments of the topics they address, but most articles were originally contributions to longstanding, ongoing projects, and took place in the course of wide-ranging debates. We have collected them in a printed anthology to do a service to the student, the researcher, and anyone else who is curious about alternative approaches in free market economics and anarchist social thought. But they are best understood not as identifying the end of the subject, or even really the beginning, but rather as offering an invitation to dive in *in medias res*, to see left-wing market anarchist ideas emerging from the dialogical process itself – and to participate in the ongoing conversation.

## WHAT'S IN IT

With these articles, we seek to help unearth a tradition of radical dissent that arguably deserves greater attention. But we hope that they will prove to be of more than historical interest. Our goal is to offer detailed analyses of key issues related to power and resistance, provide a basis for conversation between individualist anarchists and representatives of other anarchist tendencies, and clearly undermine the self-serving corporatist apologetics, and the claim to the "libertarian" label, of defenders of conventionally pro-capitalist "vulgar libertarianism."

The book collects essays from the late nineteenth century to the present, organized into eight parts.[4]

Part One, "The Problem of Deformed Markets," introduces the central theme of the text: the political deformation that distorts, obliterates, or perverts the naturally positive and mutual relationships characteristic of markets, and the naturally productive and harmonizing role of market forces such as competition, trade, and the division of labor, into the alienating, exploitative structure of state capitalism. In "The Freed Market," William Gillis shows how a simple change of tense can make all the difference in clarifying the difference between market anarchy and statist capitalism. In "State Socialism and Anarchism," Benjamin Tucker explains why a market-oriented variety of anarchism can be understood as part of the socialist tradition, provided the role of privilege in bringing about the evils against which socialists rightly protest is understood. In excerpts taken from his *General Idea of the Revolution in the Nineteenth Century*, Proudhon argues that competition, division of labor, commerce, contract, and property – economic forces which are, today, forces driving exploitation, alienation and poverty – can be transfigured by the revolutionary dissolution of political privilege, and the replacement of the authoritarian "system of laws" by the mutual "system of contracts."[5] In "Markets Freed from Capitalism,"

---

4    We have sought throughout these essays to standardize reference style and in some cases to correct, expand, or update references. In at least one case, we have also corrected a quotation.

5    In selecting passages from Proudhon's nuanced and immensely challenging work, we must acknowledge—and indeed insist—that we have not presented anything like the whole of Proudhon's social and economic thought, or even the entirety of his thought about economic forces, contracts, and property. Rather, we have attempted to identify and present a particular *strand* within the tapestry of Proudhon's thought, and, in particular, to present the strand which was best understood by and most influential on the work of later market anarchists, such as Benjamin Tucker or Dyer Lum—with such themes as the mutuality of contract, the deformation of markets by privilege, and the

Charles Johnson examines the political mechanisms and structures of privilege by which government misshapes markets, constructs state capitalism, and foists fetishized forms of exchange into social spaces where they are not wanted; and examines the importance of envisioning the revolutionary transformation of markets without capitalistic inequalities.

Part Two, "Identities and Isms," collects careful reflections by individualist anarchists on the desirability, undesirability, and significance of multiple identities: "capitalist," "socialist," "libertarian," "individualist," "communist." In "Armies that Overlap" and "Socialism: What It Is," Benjamin Tucker argues that the socialist call for worker autonomy and the end of capitalist privilege is not a violation of market principles; it is against privilege that socialists fight, and that need not mean a fight against market exchange. In "Advocates of Freed Markets Should Oppose Capitalism" and "What *Laissez Faire*?," Gary Chartier and Sheldon Richman argue that right wing market-oriented libertarians' romance with capitalism is profoundly mistaken and that the rejection of capitalism is not only compatible with but, indeed, *required by* support for genuinely freed markets. In "Market Anarchism as Stigmergic Socialism" and "Socialist Ends, Market Means," Brad Spangler and Gary Chartier argue more aggressively that the market-oriented anarchism of the individualists is, as Tucker made clear, not only anticapitalist but part of the *socialist* tradition. In "The Individualist and the Communist," and the follow-up essay, "A Glance at Communism," Rosa Slobodinsky and Voltairine de Cleyre explain why two varieties of anarchism can be thought of as pursuing similar goals using different means. (The individualist in Slobodinsky and de Cleyre's imagined dialogue accepts the label "capitalist" for the sake of argument, but takes a position unequivocally opposed to capitalist privilege.) Charles Johnson's "Libertarianism through Thick and Thin" explains why a narrowly conceived anti-statism fails to capture the emancipatory potential of libertarianism, and lays the groundwork for arguments designed to link opposition to state power with challenges to such other forms of hierarchy as subordination in the workplace and patriarchal gender relations.

Part Three, "Ownership," enters an open debate among market anarchists, individualist anarchists, and mutualists: the nature and justification of property. Individualists and mutualists have a broad, end-of-the-day

---

transfiguration of property, competition, and exchange in markets liberated from hierarchy. In these passages Proudhon should, to an extent, be read as "Tucker's Proudhon" or "the mutualists' Proudhon;" there are other Proudhons to be found (the Communards' Proudhon, Kropotkin's Proudhon, the syndicalists' Proudhon . . .), and the real thinker himself must be recognized as someone quite as important as, and far more intricate than, any of these.

agreement on the question of ownership – they view *actually-existing* property titles as shot through with privilege and injustice, but argue in favor of free social arrangements in which decentralized individual ownership – cured of the disease of privilege and political dispossession – will play an important role. But within that broad, end-of-the-day agreement there is an intense and complicated dialogue over justifications for property as well as the details of how it ought to be recognized and how far it might extend. In this section we aim to offer a series of unconventional defenses of property rights from some of the major perspectives repersented in the debate – unconventional both in their foundations and in their implications for the kinds of "property" that might characterize markets freed radically from capitalist privilege. In "A Plea for Public Property," the individualist anarchist Roderick Long defends a natural-rights justification for individual property rights – and shows that, given the arguments he uses to defend such rights, it follows that a fully freed market must include space for the commons and genuinely public property, owned neither by the state nor by private owners, but rather by the "unorganized public" that enjoys its use. In "From Whence Do Property Titles Arise?" the market anarchist William Gillis begins with a sympathetic exploration of anarchist communism and ends with a utilitarian defense of a strong form of private property, derived from considerations of economic calculation. In "The Gift Economy of Property," the mutualist Shawn Wilbur re-examines Proudhon's approach to property and commerce, and asks whether the social anarchist conception of the gift economy and the gift of mutual recognition might not provide a subversive sort of foundation for an economy of ownership and equal exchange, which challenges both conventional natural-rights accounts and utilitarian understandings of property. In "Fairness and Possession," Gary Chartier offers an alternative market-anarchist defense of possessory rights rooted in a natural-law approach, shaped by the Golden Rule and a fundamental appeal to principles of fairness, taken in tandem with a set of truisms about human behavior and the human situation. Finally, in "The Libertarian Case against Intellectual Property Rights," Roderick Long turns to an important question of application, challenging capitalists' frequent assertions of ownership over *ideas* through copyrights and patents; "intellectual property rights," Long argues, are not genuine labor-based property rights, but instead coercive, monopolistic claims on the minds and tangible property of others.

Part Four, "Corporate Power and Labor Solidarity," brings together articles on big business, bosses, workers, and the extent to which the concentration of economic power and inequality in the labor market depend on large-scale privileges conferred repeatedly and persistently by the state on corporations and capitalists. In "Corporations versus the Market, or Whip Conflation Now," Roderick Long lays out the problem of "conflation" or "vulgar libertarianism" – in which patterns of corporate ownership and common business practices propped up by state intervention are confusedly defended as if they were the outcome of free market processes. In "Does Competition Mean War?" and "Economic Calculation in the Corporate Commonwealth," Benjamin Tucker and Kevin Carson each show how market competition and profit motives, typically invoked to try to defend the interests of large corporations, would actually dissolve their fortunes and free markets from their grip in the absence of legal protections for over-centralized business models. Roy Childs's "Big Business and the Rise of American Statism" takes a step back into history, emphasizing that the growth of state power in American history cannot be seen as a counterweight to the growth of corporate power because it has largely been *driven by* the corporate interests of politically-connected robber barons. Thus also Roderick Long demonstrates, in "Regulation: The Cause, Not the Cure, of the Financial Crisis," that it was not "unregulated finance markets" but a long history of unaccountable, government-insulated finance capitalism which produced the financial and economic collapse of the last half-decade. In "Industrial Economics," "Labor Struggle in a Free Market," and "Should Labor Be Paid or Not?" Dyer Lum, Kevin Carson, and Benjamin Tucker consider the foremost alternative to corporate power: not a political solution or a regulatory state, but radical free market labor solidarity, wildcat unionism, and, ultimately, worker ownership of the means of production.

Part Five, "Neoliberalism, Privatization, and Redistribution," considers the pseudo-market politics of neoliberal "market" reforms, and considers how a *radical* defense of free markets, private property, and the "de-statification" of the economy might call for dramatically different approaches from either state progressivism, or corporate "liberalization" and subsidized capitalist "development." In "Free Market Reforms and the Reduction of Statism," Kevin Carson underscores the importance of understanding just how particular legal, social, and political structures are interconnected and what the net effect of altering each would be on the dismantling of the state. In "Free Trade is Fair Trade," Joe Peacott of the Boston Anarchist Drinking Brigade looks at the radical possibilities of a world truly without economic borders, and the political fraud of government-managed, corporate-subsidizing "free trade" agreements. In "Two Words on 'Privatization,'" Charles Johnson disentangles two senses of "privatization" – on the one hand, genuine efforts to devolve control of politically-confiscated resources from government back to civil society, and on the other the kind of corporate-driven "privatization" routinely inflicted on developing countries, which amounts to little more than the outsourcing of government monopolies. Finally, in "Where are the Specifics?" and "Confiscation and the Homestead Principle," Karl Hess and Murray Rothbard look at the radical implications of anarchistic property rights, and argue that the emergence of freed markets calls for a radically different model of "privatization:" worker occupations of many large businesses and institutions, and revolutionary expropriation of the means of production.

Part Six, "Inequality and Social Safety Nets," asks whether freed markets would sustain large-scale inequalities of wealth, and how, with the abolition of all forms of government, including government welfare, economic crises and poverty might still be addressed through authentically *social* safety nets – that is, through grassroots mutual aid. Jeremy Weiland's "Let the Free Market Eat the Rich" begins by discussing "economic entropy" and the doom of accumulated fortunes in freed markets; he shows how economic relationships genuinely free from privilege can, and naturally will tend to, undermine the wealth and power consolidated in a capitalist society. Joe Peacott's "Individualism and Inequality" considers how capitalism depends on economic inequality, and how market anarchy would confine or destroy such inequality; he goes on to ask how the end of destructive, systemic inequalities might relate to smaller-scale, more everyday forms of social inequality. Roderick Long's "How Government Solved the Health Care Crisis" and Joe Peacott's "The Poverty of the Welfare State" discuss ways in which statist welfare programs destory social power while fostering state power, and suggest that the form of social power working people have repeatedly used to gain control over their own health care costs and provide security for each other in hard times – grassroots networks of worker-run mutual aid associations – can provide positive alternatives to statist welfare systems in a flourishing free market.

Part Seven, "Barriers to Entry and Fixed Costs of Living," examines how capitalist economic relations have depended on the forced immiseration of the poor, and the systematic burning out of alternatives to wage labor and rent. One of the most effective means is to make workers artificially desperate by means of a sort of ratchet effect – simultaneously boosting fixed costs of living and destroying opportunities for making a living outside of the cash-wage economy. The ratchet effect has been exerted by means of government-granted monopolies that drive up the costs of pervasive, everyday goods; large-scale land theft and engrosssment that bolster rents and deprive workers of opportunities to support themselves on their own terms; and government regulation in the interest of socioeconomic cleansing. In "How 'Intellectual Property' Impedes Competition," Kevin Carson looks at the large-scale structural ripple effects of pervasive monopoly rents in the transmission and expression of ideas in culture, medicine, and technology. In "English Enclosures and Soviet Collectivization," Joseph R. Stromberg shows how the state, whatever its explicit ideology, can foster what he suggestively identifies as an "anti-peasant mode of development." In "The American Land Question," Stromberg shows that massive land theft and engrossment have distorted economic relationships in the United States since before the colonial period. In "Health Care as Radical Monopoly," Carson explains in detail how the cost, accessibility, and flexibility of health care are profoundly limited by the state's action on behalf of multiple groups on whom it deliberately or inadvertently confers legal privileges. "Scratching By," by Charles Johnson, is a devastating indictment of the regulatory state's role in the creation and perpetuation of poverty.

Part Eight, "Freed-Market Regulation: Social Activism and Spontaneous Order," looks at ways in which the social order achieved in a market society freed from capitalist domination would ensure productive and mutual cooperation, and live up to a reasonable ideal of social justice, without coercive regulation by a state. Where other sections have demonstrated *negatively* that social and economic privileges often depend on background legal coercion, and that removing legal coercion will undermine or eliminate unjust privilege, this section focuses on potential social problems within the market form, and the *positive* means by which those problems might be addressed without the use of aggressive force. In "Regulation Red Herring," Sheldon Richman discusses the importance of *spontaneous order* as an organizing and harmonizing force in markets, and a natural form of market "regulation" based on mutual human relationships instead of political domination. In "We Are Market Forces," Charles Johnson develops the same point and emphasizes the possibility not only of unplanned orders, but also of *consensual social activism* within freed markets: from the individualists' radical anticapitalist perspective, the world of *markets* is much more extensive than the world of *commercial transactions*, and incorporates all of the voluntary, cooperative actions in which people can engage – including those designed to restrain or otherwise respond to non-violent but morally objectionable conduct on the part of other people or organizations. In "Platonic Productivity," Roderick Long considers the question of gender wage gaps, arguing that even in a fully freed market sexist discrimination might continue to be a serious social and economic problem, one which conscious social activism could be needed to address. In "Libertarianism and Anti-Racism," Sheldon Richman encourages market anarchists to consider the nonviolent sit-in movement against segregated lunch counters in the American South as a historical model for precisely this sort of freed-market social activism. Mary Ruwart's "Aggression and the Environment," from her book *Healing Our World*, and Charles Johnson's "The Clean Water Act versus Clean Water" continue developing this the theme by examining ways in which capitalist privilege, rather than free-market profit motives, encourage environmental destruction and the anti-environmental ethic of limitless "growth" at all costs – and in which, in freed markets, community activists would be far freer to use market pressure and direct action to preserve the environment and heal the damage already inflicted by ecologically unsustainable corporate capitalism. In "Context-Keeping and Community Organizing," Sheldon Richman provides a strong defense and synthetic overview of the possibility of freed market grassroots social activism.

The individualist anarchist tendency is alive and well. *Markets Not Capitalism* offers a window onto this tendency's history and highlights its potential contribution to the global anticapitalist movement. We seek in this book to stimulate a thriving conversation among libertarians of all varieties, as well as those with other political commitments, about the most fruitful path toward human liberation. We are confident that individualist anarchist insights into the liberatory potential of markets without capitalism can enrich that conversation, and we encourage you to join it.

GARY CHARTIER   CHARLES W. JOHNSON
*La Sierra University*   *Molinari Institute*

# PART ONE

-------------

## The Problem of Deformed Markets

# 1

*Human Iterations* (n.p., July 31, 2007) <http://williamgillis.blogspot. com/2007/07/freed-market-one-of- tactics-ive-taken.html> (Aug. 10, 2011)

# THE FREED MARKET

## WILLIAM GILLIS
## (2007)

ONE OF THE TACTICS I'VE TAKEN UP IN THE ANARCHIST ECONOMICS WARS IS TO REFER to our modern corporatist/mercantilist/lovecraftian mix of economic systems as "Kapitalism" and when referencing Ancaps go out of my way to use "Anarcho"-Capitalist and Anarcho-"Capitalist" as distinct labels.

These have proved decent if not pretty effective ways of kicking a wedge into their thinking and forcing a degree of nuance into the discussion. But they're distinctions primarily aimed at the willfully ignorant bullying Reds who – while certainly annoying – are nowhere near as atrocious as the out-and-out Vulgar Libertarians. The corporate apologists who actually approve of the modern cesspit the Reds call "Capitalism." You know the ones. The contrarian brats who consider Somalia a utopia. The ones that fit the Reds' stereotypes so hardcore that all intelligence is immediately sucked into an event horizon of *"poor people obviously deserve to starve to death, screw 'em"* and *"yeah, well after The Revolution we'll put your family in death camps and expropriate all your stuff."*

Well, by blessed typo I've stumbled across a very effective counter to them. Instead of referring to the behavior and dynamics of the free market, I refer instead to *"a freed market."*

You'd be surprised how much of a difference a change of tense can make. "Free market" makes it sound like such a thing already exists and thus passively perpetuates the Red myth that Corporatism and wanton accumulation of Kapital are the natural consequences of free association and competition between individuals. (It is not.)

But "freed" has an element of distance and, whatsmore, a degree of action to it. It becomes so much easier to state things like: Freed markets don't have corporations. A freed market naturally equalizes wealth. Social hierarchy is by definition inefficient and this is particularly evident in freed markets.

It moves us out of the present tense and into the theoretical realm of "after the revolution," where like the Reds we can still use present day examples to back theory, but we're not tied into implicitly defending every horror in today's market. It's easier to pick out separate mechanics in the market and make distinctions. Also, have I mentioned that it makes an implicit call to action?

I don't know if anyone else has stumbled over this before, but it's been useful and I felt I should share.

# 2

*Instead of a Book By A Man Too Busy to
Write One: A Fragmentary Exposition of
Philosophical Anarchism* (New York. Tucker
1897) 1-18.

# STATE SOCIALISM AND ANARCHISM
## How Far They Agree, and Wherein They Differ

### BENJAMIN R. TUCKER
### (1888)

PROBABLY NO AGITATION HAS EVER ATTAINED THE MAGNITUDE, EITHER IN THE NUMBER OF its recruits or the area of its influence, which has been attained by Modern Socialism, and at the same time been so little understood and so misunderstood, not only by the hostile and the indifferent, but by the friendly, and even by the great mass of its adherents themselves. This unfortunate and highly dangerous state of things is due partly to the fact that the human relationships which this movement – if anything so chaotic can be called a movement – aims to transform, involve no special class or classes, but literally all mankind; partly to the fact that these relationships are infinitely more varied and complex in their nature than those with which any special reform has ever been called upon to deal; and partly to the fact that the great moulding forces of society, the channels of information and enlightenment, are well-nigh exclusively under the control of those whose immediate pecuniary interests are antagonistic to the bottom claim of Socialism that labor should be put in possession of its own.

Almost the only persons who may be said to comprehend even approximately the significance, principles, and purposes of Socialism are the chief leaders of the extreme wings of the Socialistic forces, and perhaps a few of the money kings themselves. It is a subject of which it has lately become quite the fashion for preacher, professor, and penny-a-liner to treat, and, for the most part, woeful work they have made with it, exciting the derision and pity of those competent to judge. That those prominent in the intermediate Socialistic divisions do not fully understand what they are about is evident from the positions they occupy. If they did; if they were consistent, logical thinkers; if they were what the French call consequent men – their reasoning faculties would long since have driven them to one extreme or the other.

For it is a curious fact that the two extremes of the vast army now under consideration, though united, as has been hinted above, by the common claim that labor shall be put in possession of its own, are more diametrically opposed to each other in their fundamental principles of social action and their methods of reaching the ends aimed at than either is to their common enemy, the existing society. They are based on two principles the history of whose conflict is almost equivalent to the history of the world since man came into it; and all intermediate parties, including that of the upholders of the existing society, are based upon a compromise between them. It is clear, then, that any intelligent, deep-rooted opposition to the prevailing order of things must come from one or the other of these extremes, for anything from any other source, far from being revolutionary in character, could be only in the nature of such superficial modification as would be utterly unable to concentrate upon itself the degree of attention and interest now bestowed upon Modern Socialism.

The two principles referred to are **AUTHORITY** and **LIBERTY**, and the names of the two schools of Socialistic thought which fully and unreservedly represent one or the other of them are, respectively, State Socialism and Anarchism. Whoso knows what these two schools want and how they propose to get it understands the Socialistic movement. For, just as it has been said that there is no half-way house between Rome and Reason, so it may be said that there is no half-way house between State Socialism and Anarchism. There are, in fact, two currents steadily flowing from the center of the Socialistic forces which are concentrating them on the left and on the right; and, if Socialism is to prevail, it is among the possibilities that, after this movement of separation has been completed and the existing order have been crushed out between the two camps, the ultimate and bitterer conflict will be still to come. In that case all the eight-hour men, all the trades-unionists, all the Knights of Labor, all the land nationalizationists, all the greenbackers, and, in short, all the members of the thousand and one different battalions belonging to the great army of Labor, will have deserted their old posts, and, these being arrayed on the one side and the other, the great battle will begin. What a final victory for the State Socialists will mean, and what a final victory for the Anarchists will mean, it is the purpose of this paper to briefly state.

To do this intelligently, however, I must first describe the ground common to both, the features that make Socialists of each of them.

The economic principles of Modern Socialism are a logical deduction from the principle laid down by Adam Smith in the early chapters of his *Wealth of Nations*, namely, that labor is the true measure of price. But Adam Smith, after stating this principle most clearly and concisely, immediately abandoned all further consideration of it to devote himself to showing what actually does measure price, and how, therefore, wealth is at present distributed. Since his day nearly all the political economists have followed his example by confining their function to the description of society as it is, in its industrial and commercial phases. Socialism, on the contrary, extends its function to the description of society as it should be, and the discovery of the means of making it what it should be. Half a century or more after Smith enunciated the principle above stated, Socialism picked it up where he had dropped it, and in following it to its logical conclusions, made it the basis of a new economic philosophy.

This seems to have been done independently by three different men, of three different nationalities, in three different languages: Josiah Warren, an American; Pierre J. Proudhon, a Frenchman; Karl Marx, a German Jew. That Warren and Proudhon arrived at their conclusions singly and unaided is certain; but whether Marx was not largely indebted to Proudhon for his economic ideas is questionable. However this may be, Marx's presentation of the ideas was in so many respects peculiarly his own that he is fairly entitled to the credit of originality. That the work of this interesting trio should have been done so nearly simultaneously would seem to indicate that Socialism was in the air, and that the time was ripe and the conditions favorable for the appearance of this new school of thought. So far as priority of time is concerned, the credit seems to belong to Warren, the American – a fact which should be noted by the stump orators who are so fond of declaiming against Socialism as an imported article. Of the purest revolutionary blood, too, this Warren, for he descended from the Warren who fell at Bunker Hill.

From Smith's principle that labor is the true measure of price – or, as Warren phrased it, that cost is the proper limit of price – these three men made the following deductions: that the natural wage of labor is its product; that this wage, or product, is the only just source of income (leaving out, of course, gift, inheritance, etc.); that all who derive income from any other source abstract it directly or indirectly from the natural and just wage of labor; that this abstracting process generally takes one of three forms – interest, rent, and profit; that these three constitute the trinity of usury, and are simply different methods of levying tribute for the use of capital; that, capital being simply stored-up labor which has already received its pay in full, its use ought to be gratuitous, on the principle that labor is the only basis of price; that the lender of capital is entitled to its return intact, and nothing more; that the only reason why the banker, the stockholder, the landlord, the manufacturer, and the merchant are able to exact usury from labor lies in the fact that they are backed by legal privilege, or monopoly; and that the only way to secure labor the enjoyment of its entire product, or natural wage, is to strike down monopoly.

It must not be inferred that either Warren, Proudhon, or Marx used exactly this phraseology, or followed exactly this line of thought, but it indicates definitely enough the fundamental ground taken by all three, and their substantial thought up to the limit to which they went in common. And, lest I may be accused of stating the positions and arguments of these men incorrectly, it may be well to say in advance that I have viewed them broadly, and that, for the purpose of sharp, vivid, and emphatic comparison and contrast, I have taken considerable liberty with their thought by rearranging it in an order, and often in a phraseology, of my own, but, I am satisfied, without, in so doing, misrepresenting them in any essential particular.

It was at this point – the necessity of striking down monopoly – that came the parting of their ways. Here the road forked. They found that they must turn either to the right or to the left – follow either the path of Authority or the path of Liberty. Marx went one way; Warren and Proudhon the other. Thus were born State Socialism and Anarchism.

First, then, State Socialism, which may be described as *the doctrine that all the affairs of men should be managed by the government, regardless of individual choice.*

Marx, its founder, concluded that the only way to abolish the class monopolies was to centralize and consolidate all industrial and commercial interests, all productive and distributive agencies, in one vast monopoly in the hands of the State. The government must become banker, manufacturer, farmer, carrier, and merchant, and in these capacities must suffer no competition. Land, tools, and all instruments of production must be wrested from individual hands, and made the property of the collectivity. To the individual can belong only the products to be consumed, not the means of producing them. A man may own his clothes and his food, but not the sewing machine which makes his shirts or the spade which digs his potatoes. Product and capital are essentially different things; the former belongs to individuals, the latter to society. Society must seize the capital which belongs to it, by the ballot if it can, by revolution if it must. Once in possession of it, it must administer it on the majority principle, though its organ, the State, utilize it in production and distribution, fix all prices by the amount of labor involved, and employ the whole people in its workshops, farms, stores, etc. The nation must be transformed into a vast bureaucracy, and every individual into a State official. Everything must be done on the cost principle, the people having no motive to make a profit out of themselves. Individuals not being allowed to own capital, no one can employ another, or even himself. Every man will be a wage-receiver, and the State the only wage-payer. He who will not work for the State must starve, or, more likely, go to prison. All freedom of trade must disappear. Competition must be utterly wiped out. All industrial and commercial activity must be centered in one vast, enormous, all-inclusive monopoly. The remedy for *monopolies* is MONOPOLY.

Such is the economic programme of State Socialism as adopted from Karl Marx. The history of its growth and progress cannot be told here. In this country the parties that uphold it are known as the Socialistic Labor Party, which pretends to follow Karl Marx; the Nationalists, who follow Karl Marx filtered through Edward Bellamy; and the Christian Socialists, who follow Karl Marx filtered through Jesus Christ.

What other applications this principle of Authority, once adopted in the economic sphere, will develop is very evident. It means the absolute control by the majority of all individual conduct. The right of such control is already admitted by the State Socialists, though they maintain that, as a matter of fact, the individual would be allowed a much larger liberty than he now enjoys. But he would only be allowed it; he could not claim it as his own. There would be no foundation of society upon a guaranteed equality of the largest possible liberty. Such liberty as might exist would exist by sufferance and could be taken away at any moment. Constitutional guarantees would be of no avail. There would be but one article in the constitution of a State Socialistic country: "The right of the majority is absolute."

The claim of the State Socialists, however, that this right would not be exercised in matters pertaining to the individual in the more intimate and private relations of his life is not borne out by the history of governments. It has ever been the tendency of power to add to itself, to enlarge its sphere, to encroach beyond the limits set for it; and where the habit of resisting such encroachment is not fostered, and the individual is not taught to be jealous of his rights, individuality gradually disappears and the government or State becomes the all-in-all. Control naturally accompanies responsibility. Under the system of State Socialism, therefore, which holds the community responsible for the health, wealth, and wisdom of the individual, it is evident that the community, through its majority expression, will insist more and more in prescribing the conditions of health, wealth, and wisdom, thus impairing and finally destroying individual independence and with it all sense of individual responsibility.

Whatever, then, the State Socialists may claim or disclaim, their system, if adopted, is doomed to end in a State religion, to the expense of which all must contribute and at the altar of which all must kneel; a State school of medicine, by whose practitioners the sick must invariably be treated; a State system of hygiene, prescribing what all must and must not eat, drink, wear, and do; a State code of morals, which will not content itself with punishing crime, but will prohibit what the majority decide to be vice; a State system of instruction, which will do away with all private schools, academies, and colleges; a State nursery, in which all children must be brought up in common at the public expense; and, finally, a State family, with an attempt at stirpiculture, or scientific breeding, in which no man and woman will be allowed to have children if the State prohibits them and no man and woman can refuse to have children if the State orders them. Thus will Authority achieve its acme and Monopoly be carried to its highest power.

Such is the ideal of the logical State Socialist, such the goal which lies at the end of the road that Karl Marx took. Let us now follow the fortunes of Warren and Proudhon, who took the other road – the road of Liberty.

This brings us to Anarchism, which may be described as *the doctrine that all the affairs of men should be managed by individuals or voluntary associations, and that the State should be abolished.*

When Warren and Proudhon, in prosecuting their search for justice to labor, came face to face with the obstacle of class monopolies, they saw that these monopolies rested upon Authority, and concluded that the thing to be done was, not to strengthen this Authority and thus make monopoly universal, but to utterly uproot Authority and give full sway to the opposite principle, Liberty, by making competition, the antithesis of monopoly, universal. They saw in competition the great leveler of prices to the labor cost of production. In this they agreed with the political economists. They query then naturally presented itself why all prices do not fall to labor cost; where there is any room for incomes acquired otherwise than by labor; in a word, why the usurer, the receiver of interest, rent, and profit, exists. The answer was found in the present one-sidedness of competition. It was discovered that capital had so manipulated legislation that unlimited competition is allowed in supplying productive labor, thus keeping wages down to the starvation point, or as near it as practicable; that a great deal of competition is allowed in supplying distributive labor, or the labor of the mercantile classes, thus keeping, not the prices of goods, but the merchants' actual profits on them down to a point somewhat approximating equitable wages for the merchants' work; but that almost no competition at all is allowed in supplying capital, upon the aid of which both productive and distributive labor are dependent for their power of achievement, thus keeping the rate of interest on money and of house-rent and ground-rent at as high a point as the necessities of the people will bear.

On discovering this, Warren and Proudhon charged the political economists with being afraid of their own doctrine. The Manchester men were accused of being inconsistent. The believed in liberty to compete with the laborer in order to reduce his wages, but not in liberty to compete with the capitalist in order to reduce his usury. *Laissez Faire* was very good sauce for the goose, labor, but was very poor sauce for the gander, capital. But how to correct this inconsistency, how to serve this gander with this sauce, how to put capital at the service of business men and laborers at cost, or free of usury – that was the problem.

Marx, as we have seen, solved it by declaring capital to be a different thing from product, and maintaining that it belonged to society and should be seized by society and employed for the benefit of all alike. Proudhon scoffed at this distinction between capital and product. He maintained that capital and product are not different kinds of wealth, but simply alternate conditions or functions of the same wealth; that all wealth undergoes an incessant transformation from capital into product and from product back into capital, the process repeating itself interminably; that capital and product are purely social terms; that what is product to one man immediately becomes capital to another, and vice versa; that if there were but one person in the world, all wealth would be to him at once capital and product; that the fruit of A's toil is his product, which, when sold to B, becomes B's capital (unless B is an unproductive consumer, in which case it is merely wasted wealth, outside the view of social economy); that a steam-engine is just as much product as a coat, and that a coat is just as much capital as a steam-engine; and that the same laws of equity govern the possession of the one that govern the possession of the other.

For these and other reasons Proudhon and Warren found themselves unable to sanction any such plan as the seizure of capital by society. But, though opposed to socializing the ownership of capital, they aimed nevertheless to socialize its effects by making its use beneficial to all instead of a means of impoverishing the many to enrich the few. And when the light burst in upon them, they saw that this could be done by subjecting capital to the natural law of competition, thus bringing the price of its own use down to cost – that is, to nothing beyond the expenses incidental to handling and transferring it. So they raised the banner of Absolute Free Trade; free trade at home, as well as with foreign countries; the logical carrying out of the Manchester doctrine; *laissez faire* the universal rule. Under this banner they began their fight upon monopolies, whether the all-inclusive monopoly of the State Socialists, or the various class monopolies that now prevail.

Of the latter they distinguished four of principal importance: the money monopoly, the land monopoly, the tariff monopoly, and the patent monopoly.

First in the importance of its evil influence they considered the money monopoly, which consists of the privilege given by the government to certain individuals, or to individuals holding certain kinds of property, of issuing the circulating medium, a privilege which is now enforced in this country by a national tax of ten percent, upon all other persons who attempt to furnish a circulating medium, and by State laws making it a criminal offense to issue notes as currency. It is claimed that the holders of this privilege control the rate of interest, the rate of rent of houses and buildings, and the prices of goods – the first directly, and the second and third indirectly. For, say Proudhon and Warren, if the business of banking were made free to all, more and more persons would enter into it until the competition should become sharp enough to reduce the price of lending money to the labor cost, which statistics show to be less than three-fourths of once per cent. In that case the thousands of people who are now deterred from going into business by the ruinously high rates which they must pay for capital with which to start and carry on business will find their difficulties removed. If they have property which they do not desire to convert into money by sale, a bank will take it as collateral for a loan of a certain proportion of its market value at less than one percent discount. If they have no property, but are industrious, honest, and capable, they will generally be able to get their individual notes endorsed by a sufficient number of known and solvent parties; and on such business paper they will be able to get a loan at a bank on similarly favorable terms. Thus interest will fall at a blow. The banks will really not be lending capital at all, but will be doing business on the capital of their customers, the business consisting in an exchange of the known and widely available credits of the banks for the unknown and unavailable, but equality good, credits of the customers and a charge therefor of less than one percent, not as interest for the use of capital, but as pay for the labor of running the banks. This facility of acquiring capital will give an unheard of impetus to business, and consequently create an unprecedented demand for labor – a demand which will always be in excess of the supply, directly to the contrary of the present condition of the labor market. Then will be seen and exemplification of the worlds of Richard Cobden that, when two laborers are after one employer, wages fall, but when two employers are after one laborer, wages rise. Labor will then be in a position to dictate its wages, and will thus secure its natural wage, its entire product. Thus the same blow that strikes interest down will send wages up. But this is not all. Down will go profits also. For merchants, instead of buying at high prices on credit, will borrow money of the banks at less than one per cent, buy at low prices for cash, and correspondingly reduce the prices of their goods to their customers. And with the rest will go house-rent. For no one who can borrow capital at one per cent. with which to build a house of his own will consent to pay rent to a landlord at a higher rate than that. Such is the vast claim made by Proudhon and Warren as to the results of the simple abolition of the money monopoly.

Second in importance comes the land monopoly, the evil effects of which are seen principally in exclusively agricultural countries, like Ireland. This monopoly consists in the enforcement by government of land titles which do not rest upon personal occupancy and cultivation. It was obvious to Warren and Proudhon that, as soon as individualists should no longer be protected by their fellows in anything but personal occupancy and cultivation of land, ground rent would disappear, and so usury have one less leg to stand on. Their followers of today are disposed to modify this claim to the extent of admitting that the very small fraction of ground rent which rests, not on monopoly, but on superiority of soil or site, will continue to exist for a time and perhaps forever, though tending constantly to a minimum under conditions of freedom. But the inequality of soils which gives rise to the economic rent of land, like the inequality of human skill which gives rise to the economic rent of ability, is not a cause for serious alarm even to the most thorough opponent of usury, as its nature is not that of a germ from which other and graver inequalities may spring, but rather that of a decaying branch which may finally wither and fall.

Third, the tariff monopoly, which consists in fostering production at high prices and under unfavorable conditions by visiting with the penalty of taxation those who patronize production at low prices and under favorable conditions. The evil to which this monopoly gives rise might more properly be called *mis*usury than usury, because it compels labor to pay, not exactly for the use of capital, but rather for the misuse of capital. The abolition of this monopoly would result in a great reduction in the prices of all articles taxed, and this saving to the laborers who consume these articles would be another step toward securing to the laborer his natural wage, his entire product. Proudhon admitted, however, that to abolish this monopoly before abolishing the money monopoly would be a cruel and disastrous police, first, because the evil of scarcity of money, created by the money monopoly, would be intensified by the flow of money out of the country which would be involved in an excess of imports over exports, and, second, because that fraction of the laborers of the country which is now employed in the protected industries would be turned adrift to face starvation without the benefit of the insatiable demand for labor which a competitive money system would create. Free trade in money at home, making money and work abundant, was insisted upon by Proudhon as a prior condition of free trade in goods with foreign countries.

Fourth, the patent monopoly, which consists in protecting inventors and authors against competition for a period long enough to enable them to extort from the people a reward enormously in excess of the labor measure of their services – in other words, in giving certain people a right of property for a term of years in laws and facts of Nature, and the power to exact tribute from others for the use of this natural wealth, which should be open to all. The abolition of this monopoly would fill its beneficiaries with a wholesome fear of competition which would cause them to be satisfied with pay for their services equal to that which other laborers get for theirs, and to secure it by placing their products and works on the market at the outset at prices so low that their lines of business would be no more tempting to competitors than any other lines.

The development of the economic programme which consists in the destruction of these monopolies and the substitution for them of the freest competition led its authors to a perception of the fact that all their thought rested upon a very fundamental principle, the freedom of the individual, his right of sovereignty over himself, his products, and his affairs, and of rebellion against the dictation of external authority. Just as the idea of taking capital away from individuals and giving it to the government started Marx in a path which ends in making the government everything and the individual nothing, so the idea of taking capital away from government-protected monopolies and putting it within easy reach of all individuals started Warren and Proudhon in a path which ends in making the individual everything and the government nothing. If the individual has a right to govern himself, all external government is tyranny. Hence the necessity of abolishing the State. This was the logical conclusion to which Warren and Proudhon were forced, and it became the fundamental article of their political philosophy. It is the doctrine which Proudhon named Anarchism, a word derived from the Greek, and meaning, not necessarily absence of order, as is generally supposed, but an absence of rule. The Anarchists are simply unterrified Jeffersonian Democrats. They believe that "the best government is that which governs least," and that that which governs least is no government at all. Even the simple police function of protecting person and property they deny to governments supported by compulsory taxation. Protection they look upon as a thing to be secured, as long as it is necessary, by voluntary association and cooperation for self-defence, or as a commodity to be purchased, like any other commodity, of those who offer the best article at the lowest price. In their view it is in itself an invasion of the individual to compel him to pay for or suffer a protection against invasion that he has not asked for and does not desire. And they further claim that protection will become a drug in the market, after poverty and consequently crime have disappeared through the realization of their economic programme. Compulsory taxation is to them the life-principle of all the monopolies, and passive, but organized, resistance to the tax- collector they contemplate, when the proper time comes, as one of the most effective methods of accomplishing their purposes.

Their attitude on this is a key to their attitude on all other questions of a political or social nature. In religion they are atheistic as far as their own opinions are concerned, for they look upon divine authority and the religious sanction of morality as the chief pretexts put forward by the privileged classes for the exercise of human authority. "If God exists," said Proudhon, "he is man's enemy." And in contrast to Voltaire's famous epigram, "If God did not exist, it would be necessary to invent him," the great Russian Nihilist, Mikhail Bakunin, placed this antithetical proposition: "If God existed, it would be necessary to abolish him." But although, viewing the divine hierarchy as a contradiction of Anarchy, they do not believe in it, the Anarchists none the less firmly believe in the liberty to believe in it. Any denial of religious freedom they squarely oppose.

Upholding thus the right of every individual to be or select his own priest, they likewise uphold his right to be or select his own doctor. No monopoly in theology, no monopoly in medicine. Competition everywhere and always; spiritual advice and medical advice alike to stand or fall on their own merits. And not only in medicine, but in hygiene, must this principle of liberty be followed. The individual may decide for himself not only what to do to get well, but what to do to keep well. No external power must dictate to him what he must and must not eat, drink, wear, or do.

Nor does the Anarchistic scheme furnish any code of morals to be imposed upon the individual. "Mind your own business" is its only moral law. Interference with another's business is a crime and the only crime, and as such may properly be resisted. In accordance with this view the Anarchists look upon attempts to arbitrarily suppress vice as in themselves crimes. They believe liberty and the resultant social well-being to be a sure cure for all the vices. But they recognize the right of the drunkard, the gambler, the rake, and the harlot to live their lives until they shall freely choose to abandon them.

In the matter of the maintenance and rearing of children the Anarchists would neither institute the communistic nursery which the State Socialists favor nor keep the communistic school system which now prevails. The nurse and the teacher, like the doctor and the preacher, must be selected voluntarily, and their services must be paid for by those who patronize them. Parental rights must not be taken away, and parental responsibilities must not be foisted upon others.

Even in so delicate a matter as that of the relations of the sexes the Anarchists do not shrink from the application of their principle. They acknowledge and defend the right of any man and woman, or any men and women, to love each other for as long or as short a time as they can, will, or may. To them legal marriage and legal divorce are equal absurdities. They look forward to a time when every individual, whether man or woman, shall be self-supporting, and when each shall have an independent home of his or her own, whether it be a separate house or rooms in a house with others; when the love relations between these independent individuals shall be as varied as are individual inclinations and attractions; and when the children born of these relations shall belong exclusively to the mothers until old enough to belong to themselves.

Such are the main features of the Anarchistic social ideal. There is wide difference of opinion among those who hold it as to the best method of obtaining it. Time forbids the treatment of that phase of the subject here. I will simply call attention to the fact that it is an ideal utterly inconsistent with that of those Communists who falsely call themselves Anarchists while at the same time advocating a regime of Archism fully as despotic as that of the State Socialists themselves. And it is an ideal that can be as little advanced by Prince Kropotkin as retarded by the brooms of those Mrs. Partingtons of the bench who sentence them to prison; an ideal which the martyrs of Chicago did far more to help by their glorious death upon the gallows for the common cause of Socialism than by their unfortunate advocacy during their lives, in the name of Anarchism, of force as a revolutionary agent and authority as a safeguard of the new social order. The Anarchists believe in liberty both as an end and means, and are hostile to anything that antagonizes it.

I should not undertake to summarize this altogether too summary exposition of Socialism from the standpoint of Anarchism, did I not find the task already accomplished for me by a Brilliant French journalist and historian, Ernest Lesigne, in the form of a series of crisp antithesis; by reading which to you as a conclusion of this lecture I hope to deepen the impression which it has been my endeavor to make.

"There are two Socialisms.

One is communistic, the other solidaritarian.

One is dictatorial, the other libertarian.

One is metaphysical, the other positive.

One is dogmatic, the other scientific.

One is emotional, the other reflective.

One is destructive, the other constructive.

Both are in pursuit of the greatest possible welfare for all.

One aims to establish happiness for all, the other to enable each to be happy in his own way.

The first regards the State as a society sui generis, of an especial essence, the product of a sort of divine right outside of and above all society, with special rights and able to exact special obediences; the second considers the State as an association like any other, generally managed worse than others.

The first proclaims the sovereignty of the State, the second recognizes no sort of sovereign.

One wishes all monopolies to be held by the State; the other wishes the abolition of all monopolies.

One wishes the governed class to become the governing class; the other wishes the disappearance of classes.

Both declare that the existing state of things cannot last.

The first considers revolutions as the indispensable agent of evolutions; the second teaches that repression alone turns evolutions into revolution.

The first has faith in a cataclysm.

The second knows that social progress will result from the free play of individual efforts.

Both understand that we are entering upon a new historic phase.

One wishes that there should be none but proletaires.

The other wishes that there should be no more proletaires.

The first wishes to take everything away from everybody.

The second wishes to leave each in possession of its own.

The one wishes to expropriate everybody.

The other wishes everybody to be a proprietor.

The first says: 'Do as the government wishes.'

The second says: 'Do as you wish yourself.'

The former threatens with despotism.

The latter promises liberty.

The former makes the citizen the subject of the State.

The latter makes the State the employee of the citizen.

One proclaims that labor pains will be necessary to the birth of a new world.

The other declares that real progress will not cause suffering to any one.

The first has confidence in social war.

The other believes only in the works of peace.

One aspires to command, to regulate, to legislate.

The other wishes to attain the minimum of command, of regulation, of legislation.

One would be followed by the most atrocious of reactions.

The other opens unlimited horizons to progress.

The first will fail; the other will succeed.

Both desire equality.

One by lowering heads that are too high.

The other by raising heads that are too low.

One sees equality under a common yoke.

The other will secure equality in complete liberty.

One is intolerant, the other tolerant.

One frightens, the other reassures.

The first wishes to instruct everybody.

The second wishes to enable everybody to instruct himself.

The first wishes to support everybody.

The second wishes to enable everybody to support himself.

One says:

The land to the State

The mine to the State

The tool to the State

The product to the State

The other says:

The land to the cultivator.

The mine to the miner.

The tool to the laborer.

The product to the producer.

There are only these two Socialisms.

One is the infancy of Socialism; the other is its manhood.

One is already the past; the other is the future.

One will give place to the other.

Today each of us must choose for the one or the other of these
two Socialisms, or else confess that he is not a Socialist."

Excerpted. Trans. John Beverly Robinson
(London: Freedom 1923 [1851]).

# 3

# GENERAL IDEA OF THE REVOLUTION IN THE NINETEENTH CENTURY

## PIERRE-JOSEPH PROUDHON
## (1851)

### IS THERE SUFFICIENT REASON FOR REVOLUTION IN THE NINETEENTH CENTURY?

*Chaos of economic forces. Tendency of society toward poverty.*

I CALL CERTAIN PRINCIPLES OF ACTION *ECONOMIC FORCES*, SUCH AS THE DIVISION OF LAbor, Competition, Collective Force, Exchange, Credit, Property, etc., which are to Labor and to Wealth what the distinction of classes, the representative system, monarchical heredity, administrative centralization, the judicial hierarchy, etc., are to the State.

If these forces are held in equilibrium, subject to the laws which are proper to them, and which do not depend in any way upon the arbitrary will of man, Labor can be organized, and comfort for all guaranteed. If, on the other hand, they are left without direction and without counterpoise,

Labor is in a condition of chaos; the useful effects of the economic forces is mingled with an equal quantity of injurious effects; the deficit balances the profit; Society, in so far as it is the theatre, the agent, or the subject of production, circulation, and consumption, is in a condition of increasing suffering.

Up to now, it does not appear that order in a society can be conceived except under one of these two forms, the political and the industrial; between which, moreover, there is fundamental contradiction.

The chaos of industrial forces, the struggle which they maintain with the government system, which is the only obstacle to their organization, and which they cannot reconcile themselves with nor merge themselves in, is the real, profound cause of the unrest which disturbs French society...

Everybody has heard of the *division of labor.*

It consists of the distribution of the hand work of a given industry in such a manner that each person performs always the same operation, or a small number of operations, so that the product, instead of being the integral product of one workman, is the joint product of a large number.

According to Adam Smith, who first demonstrated this law scientifically, and all the other economists, the division of labor is the most powerful lever of modern industry. To it principally must be attributed the superiority of civilized peoples to savage peoples. Without division of labor, the use of machines would not have gone beyond the most ancient and most common utensils: the miracles of machinery and of steam would never have been revealed to us; progress would have been closed to society; the French Revolution itself, lacking an outlet, would have been but a sterile revolt; it could have accomplished nothing. But, on the other hand, by division of labor, the product of labor mounts to tenfold, a hundredfold, political economy rises to the height of a philosophy, the intellectual level of nations is continually raised. The first thing that should attract the attention of the legislator is the separation of industrial functions – the division of labor – in a society founded upon hatred of the feudal and warlike order, and destined in consequence to organize itself for work and peace.

It was not done thus. This economic force was left to all the overturns caused by chance and by interest. The division of labor, becoming always more minute, and remaining without counterpoise, the workman has been given [over] to a more and more degrading subjection to machinery. That is the effect of the division of labor when it is applied as practised in our days, not only to make industry incomparably more productive, but at the same time to deprive the worker, in mind and body, of all the wealth which it creates for the capitalist and the speculator... All the economists are in accord as to this fact, one of the most serious which the science has to announce; and, if they do not insist upon it with the vehemence which they habitually use in their polemics... it is because they cannot believe that this perversion of the greatest of economic forces can be avoided.

So the greater the division of labor and the power of machines, the less the intelligence and skill of hand of the worker. But the more the value of the worker falls and the demand for labor diminishes, the lower are wages and the greater is poverty. And it is not a few hundreds of men but millions, who are the victims of this economic perturbation...

Philanthropic conservatives, admirers of ancient customs, charge the industrial system with this anomaly. They want to go back to the feudal-farming period. I say that it is not industry that is at fault, but economic chaos: I maintain that the principle has been distorted, that there is disorganization of forces, and that to this we must attribute the fatal tendency with which society is carried away.

Another example.

*Competition*, next to the division of labor, is one of the most powerful factors of industry; and at the same time one of the most valuable guaranties. Partly for the sake of it, the first revolution was brought about. The workmen's unions, established at Paris some years since, have recently given it a new sanction by establishing among themselves piece work, and abandoning, after their experience of it, the absurd idea of the equality of wages. Competition is moreover the law of the market, the spice of the trade, the salt of labor. To suppress competition is to suppress liberty itself; it is to begin the restoration of the old order from below, in replacing labor by the rule of favoritism and abuse, of which '89 rid us.

Yet competition, lacking legal forms and superior regulating intelligence, has been perverted in turn, like the division of labor. In it, as in the latter, there is perversion of principle, chaos and a tendency toward evil. This will appear beyond doubt if we remember that of the thirty-six million souls who compose the French nation, at least ten millions are wage workers, to whom competition is forbidden, for whom there is nothing but to struggle among themselves for their meagre stipend.

Thus that competition, which, as thought in '89, should be a general right, is today a matter of exceptional privilege: only they whose capital permits them to become heads of business concerns may exercise their competitive rights.

The result is that competition... instead of democratizing industry, aiding the workman, guaranteeing the honesty of trade, has ended in building up a mercantile and land aristocracy, a thousand times more rapacious than the old aristocracy of the nobility. Through competition all the profits of production go to capital; the consumer, without suspecting the frauds of commerce, is fleeced by the speculator, and the condition of the workers is made more and more precarious... Competition ought to make us more and more equal and free; and instead it subordinates us one to the other, and makes the worker more and more a slave! This is a perversion of the principle, a forgetfulness of the law. These are not mere accidents; they are a whole system of misfortunes.

Let us cite one more example.

Of all economic forces, the most vital, in a society reconstructed for industry by revolution, is *credit*. The proprietary, industrial, trading business world knows this well: all its efforts since '89 have tended, at the bottom, toward only these two things, peace and credit...

In a nation devoted to labor, credit is what blood is to an animal, the means of nutrition, life itself. It cannot be interrupted without danger to the social body. If there is a single institution which should have appealed before all others to our legislators, after the abolition of feudal privileges and the levelling of classes, assuredly it is credit. Yet not one of our pompous declarations of right, not one of our constitutions, so long drawn out, not one of these has mentioned it at all. Credit, like the division of labor, the use of machinery and competition, has been left to itself; even the **FINANCIAL** power, far greater than that of the executive, legislative and judicial, has never had the honor of mention in our various charters... After the Revolution as before it, credit got along as best it could; or rather, as it pleased the largest holders of coin...

What has been the result of this incredible negligence?

In the first place, forestalling and usury being practised upon coin by preference, coin being at the same time the tool of industrial transactions and the rarest of merchandise, and consequently the safest and most profitable, dealing in money was rapidly concentrated in the hands of a few monopolists, whose fortress is the Bank.

Thereupon the Country and the State were made the vassals of a coalition of capitalists.

Thanks to the tax imposed by this bankocracy upon all industrial and agricultural industry, property has already been mortgaged for two billion dollars, and the State for more than one billion...

Property, fleeced by the Bank, has been obliged to follow the same course in its relations with industry, to become a usurer in turn toward labor; thus farm rent and house rent have reached a prohibitive rate, which drives the cultivator from the field and the workman from his home.

So much so that today they whose labor has created everything cannot buy their own products, nor obtain furniture, nor own a habitation, nor ever say: This house, this garden, this vine, this field, are mine.

On the contrary, it is an economic necessity, in the present system of credit, and with the growing disorganization of industrial forces, that the poor man, working harder and harder, should be always poorer, and that the rich man, without working, always richer…

Some utopians attack competition; others refuse to accept the division of labor and the whole industrial order; the workingmen, in their crass ignorance, blame machinery. No one, to this day, has thought of denying the utility and legitimacy of credit; nevertheless it is incontestable that the perversion of credit is the most active cause of the poverty of the masses. Were it not for this, the deplorable effects of the division of labor, of the employment of machinery, of competition, would scarcely be felt at all, would not even exist. Is it not evident that the tendency of society is towards poverty, not through the depravity of men, but through the disorder of its own elementary principles?…

### Anomaly of Government. Tendency toward Tyranny and Corruption.

… What is the principle which rules existing society? *Each by himself, each for himself. God and* **LUCK** *for all.* Privilege, resulting from luck, from a commercial turn, from any of the gambling methods which the chaotic condition of industry furnishes, is then a providential thing, which everybody must respect.

On the other hand, what is the function of Government? To protect and defend each one in his person, his industry, his property. But if by the necessity of things, property, riches, comfort, all go on one side, poverty on the other, it is clear that Government is made for the defence of the rich against the poor. For the perfecting of this state of affairs, it is necessary that what exists should be defined and consecrated by *law:* that is precisely what Power wants…

What does the system demand?

That the capitalistic feudalism shall be maintained in the enjoyment of its rights; that the preponderance of capital over labor shall be increased; that the parasite class shall be reinforced, if possible, by providing for it everywhere hangers-on, through the aid of public functions, and as recruits if necessary, and that large properties shall be gradually reestablished, and the proprietors ennobled;… finally, that everything shall be attached to the surpeme patronage of the State – charities, recompenses, pensions, awards, concessions, exploitations, authorizations, positions, titles, privileges, ministerial offices, stock companies, municipal administrations, etc., etc…

Through these three ministries, that of agriculture and commerce, that of public works, and that of the interior, through the taxes of consumption and through the custom house, the Government keeps its hand on all that comes and goes, all that is produced and consumed, on all the business of individuals, towns and provinces; it maintains the tendency of society toward the impoverishment of the masses, the subordinating of the laborers, and the always growing preponderance of parasite offices. Through the police, it watches the enemies of the system; through the courts, it condemns and represses them; through the army it crushes them; through public institutions it distributes, in such proportions as suit it, knowledge and ignorance; through the Church it puts to sleep any protest in the hearts of men; through the finances it defrays the cost of this vast conspiracy at the expense of workers...

Liberty, equality, progress, with all their oratorical consequences, are written in the text of the constitutions and the laws; there is no vestige of them in the institutions... [T]he abuses have changed the face which they bore before '89, to assume a different form of organization; they have diminished neither in number nor gravity. On account of our being engrossed with politics, we have lost sight of social economy... All minds being bewitched with politics, Society turns in a circle of mistakes, driving capital to a still more crushing agglomeration, the State to an extension of its prerogatives that is more and more tyrannical, the laboring class to an irreparable decline, physically, morally and intellectually...

In place of this governmental, feudal and military rule, imitated from that of the former kings, the new edifice of industrial institutions must be built; in place of this materialist centralization which absorbs all the political power, we must create the intellectual and liberal centralization of economic forces...

## SOCIAL LIQUIDATION.

To deduce the organizing principle of the Revolution, the idea at once economic and legal of *reciprocity* and of *contract*, taking account of the difficulties and opposition which this deduction must encounter, whether on the part of revolutionary sects, parties or societies, or from the reactionaries and defenders of the *statu quo*; to expound the totality of these reforms and new institutions, wherein labor finds its guaranty, property its limit, commerce its balance, and government its farewell; that is to tell, from the intellectual point of view, the story of the Revolution...

Two producers have the right to promise each other, and to guarantee reciprocally for, the sale or exchange of their respective products, agreeing upon the articles and the prices...

The same promise of reciprocal sale or exchange, under the same legal conditions, may exist among an unlimited number of producers: it will be the same contract, repeated an unlimited number of times.

French citizens have the right to agree, and, if desired, to club together for the establishment of bakeries, butchery shops, grocery stores, etc., which will guarantee them the sale and exchange, at a reduced price, and of good quality, of bread, meat, and all articles of consumption, which the present mercantile chaos gives them of light weight, adulterated, and at an exorbitant price. For this purpose the *Housekeeper* was founded, a society for the mutual insurance of a just price and honest exchange of products.

By the same rule, citizens have the right to found, for their common advantage, a Bank, with such capital as they choose, for the purpose of obtaining at a low price the currency that is indispensable in their transactions, and to compete with individual privileged banks. In agreeing among themselves with this object, they will only be making use of the right which is guaranteed to them by the principle of the freedom of commerce...

Thus a Bank of Discount may be a public establishment, and to found it there is needed neither association, nor fraternity, nor obligation, nor State intervention; only a reciprocal promise for sale or exchange is needed; in a word, a simple contract.

This settled, I say that not only may a Bank of Discount be a public establishment, but that such a bank is needed. Here is the proof:

The Bank of France was founded, *with Governmental privilege*, by a company of stockholders, with a capital of $18,000,000. The specie at present buried in its vaults amounts to about $120,000,000. Thus five-sixths of this specie which has accumulated in the vaults of the Bank, by the substitution of paper for metal in general circulation, is the property of the citizens. Therefore the Bank, by the nature of its mechanism, which consists in using capital which does not belong to it, ought to be a public institution.

Another cause of this accumulation of specie is the **GRATUITOUS** privilege which the Bank of France has obtained from the State of issuing notes against the specie of which it is the depositary. So, as every privilege is public property, the Bank of France, by its privilege alone, tends to become a public institution.

The privilege of issuing bank notes, and of gradually displacing coin by paper in the circulation, has for its immediate result, on the one hand, to give to the stockholders of the Bank an amount of interest far in excess of that due to their capital; on the other, to maintain the price of money at a high rate, to the great profit of the class of bankers and money-lenders, but to the great detriment of producers, manufacturers, merchants, consumers of every kind who make use of currency. This excess of interest paid to stockholders, and the rise in the rates for money, both the result of the desire which Power has always had to make itself agreeable to the rich, capitalistic class, are unjust, they cannot last forever; therefore the

Bank, by the illegitimacy of its privileges, is doomed to become a public establishment.

... The present rate of interest on money at the Bank is 4 percent; which means 5, 6, 7, 8 and 9 percent. at other bankers, who almost alone have the privilege of discounting at the Bank.

Well, as this interest belongs to the public, the public will be able to reduce it at will to 3, 2, 1, ½ and ¼ percent., according to whether it is found to be of greater advantage to draw a large revenue from the Bank, or to carry on business at a lower cost.

Let this course of reduction, for however small an amount, once be entered upon... then, I assert, the social tendency in all that concerns the price of money and discount, throughout the whole territory of the Republic, will be immediately changed, ipso facto, and that this simple change will cause the Country to pass from the present capitalistic and governmental system to a revolutionary system.

Ah! is anything so terrible as a revolution?

... If I desire to pay no interest to the Bank, it is because interest is in my eyes a governmental, feudal practice, from which we shall never be able to escape of the Bank of the Country becomes a Bank of the State. For a long time Socialism has dreamed of a State Bank, State Credit, revenues and profits of the State; all which means the democratic and social consecration of the spoliation principle, robbery of the worker, in the name, with the example, and under the patronage of the Republic. Place the Bank of the People in the hands of the Government, and, under the pretext of saving for the State the profits of discount in place of new taxes, new sinecures, huge pickings, unheard of waste will be created at the expense of the People: usury, parasitism and privilege will again be favored. No, no, I want no State, not even for a servant; I reject government, even direct government; I see in all these inventions only pretexts for parasitism and refuges for idlers...

Let us take up this great question of property, the source of such intolerable pretensions, and of such ridiculous fears. The Revolution has two things to accomplish about property, its dissolution and its reconstitution. I shall address myself first to its dissolution, and begin with buildings.

If by the above described measures, property in buildings were relieved of mortgages; if the owners and builders found capital at a low price, the former for the buildings they wanted to put up, the latter for the purchase of materials; it would follow, in the first place, that the cost of construction would diminish considerably, and that old buildings could be cheaply and advantageously repaired; and furthermore, that a drop in the rental of buildings would be perceived.

On the other hand, as capital could no longer be invested with advantage in government securities and in banks, capitalists would be led to seek investments in real estate, especially in buildings, which are always more productive than land. There would thereupon occur in this matter also an increase of competition; the supply of buildings would tend to outrun the demand, and the rentals would fall still lower.

It would fall so much the more as the reduction of interest collected by the Bank, and paid to the creditors of the State was greater; and if, as I propose, the interest of money were fixed at zero, the returns of capital invested in buildings would soon be zero also.

Then, as the rental of buildings is composed of but three factors, the reimbursement of the capital spent in their construction, the keeping up of the building and the taxes, a lease would cease to be a *loan for use* and would become a sale by the builder to the tenant.

Finally, as speculation would no longer seek buildings as an investment, but only as an object of industry, the purely legal relation of landlord and tenant, which the Roman law has transmitted to us, would give place to a purely commercial relation between the seller and the tenant: there would be the same relation, and in consequence the same law, the same jurisdiction, as between the forwarder of a package and the consignee. In a word, house rent, losing its feudal character, would become an **ACT OF COMMERCE**...

The right of property, so honorable in its origin, when that origin is none other than labor, has become in Paris, and in most cities, an improper and immoral instrument of speculation in the dwelling places of citizens. Speculation in bread and food of prime necessity is punished as a misdemeanor, sometimes as a crime: is it more permissible to speculate in the habitations of the people?...

Through the land the plundering of man began, and in the land it has rooted its foundations. The land is the fortress of the modern capitalist, as it was the citadel of feudalism, and of the ancient patriciate. Finally, it is the land which gives authority to the governmental principle, an ever-renewed strength, whenever the popular Hercules overthrows the giant.

To-day the stronghold, attacked upon all the secret points of its bastions, is about to fall before us, as fell, at the sound of Joshua's trumpets, the walls of Jericho. The machine which is able to overthrow the ramparts has been found; it is not my invention; it has been invented by property itself...

Suppose that the proprietors, no longer waiting for the Government to act, but taking their affairs into their own hands, follow the example of the workmen's associations, and get together to found a Bank by subscription, or mutual guaranty... Nothing is easier than to apply to the repurchase of land the mechanism of this system of credit, which is usually regarded only as a protection against excessive interest, and an instrument for the conversion of mortgages...

With the Land Bank the farmer is released; it is the proprietor who is caught... Thus what we call farm rent, left to us by Roman tyranny and feudal usurpation, hangs only by a thread, the organization of a bank, demanded even by property itself. It has been demonstrated that the land tends to return to the hands that cultivate it, and that farm rent, like house rent, like the interest of mortgages, is but an improper speculation, which shows the disorder and anomaly of the present economic system.

Whatever may be the conditions of this Bank... whatever be the rate of charge for its services, however small its issues, it can be calculated in how many years the soil will be delivered from the parasitism which sucks it dry, while strangling the cultivator.

And when once the revolutionary machine shall have released the soil, and agriculture shall have become free, feudal exploitation can never reëstablish itself. Property may then be sold, bought, circulated, divided or united, anything; the ball and chain of the old serfdom will never be dragged again; property will have lost its fundamental vices, it will be transfigured. It will no longer be the same thing. Still, let us continue to call it by its ancient name, so dear to the heart of man, so agreeable to the ear of the peasant, **PROPERTY**.

## ORGANIZATION OF ECONOMIC FORCES.

... When I agree with one or more of my fellow citizens for any object whatever, it is clear that my own will is my law; it is I myself, who, in fulfilling my obligation, am my own government.

Therefore if I could make a contract with all, as I can with some; if all could renew it among themselves, if each group of citizens, as a town, county, province, corporation, company, etc., formed by a like contract, and considered as a moral person, could thereafter, and always by a similar contract, agree with every and all other groups, it would be the same as if my own will were multiplied to infinity. I should be sure that the law thus made on all questions in the Republic, from millions of different initiatives, would never be anything but my law; and if this new order of things were called government, it would be my government.

Thus the principle of contract, far more than that of authority, would bring about the union of producers, centralize their forces, and assure the unity and solidarity of their interests.

The *system of contracts*, substituted for the *system of laws*, would constitute the true government of the man and of the citizen; the true sovereignty of the people, the **REPUBLIC**.

For the contract is Liberty, the first term of the republican motto: we have demonstrated this superabundantly in our studies on the principle of authority and on social liquidation. I am not free when I depend upon another for my work, my wages, or the measure of my rights and duties; whether that other be called the Majority or Society. No more am I free, either in my sovereignty or in my action, when I am compelled by another to revise my law, were that other the most skilful and most just of arbiters. I am no more at all free when I am forced to give myself a representative to govern me, even if he were my most devoted servant.

The Contract is Equality, in its profound and spiritual essence. Does this man believe himself my equal; does he not take the attitude of my master and exploiter, who demands from me more than it suits me to furnish, and has no intention of returning it to me; who says that I am incapable of making my own law, and expects me to submit to his?

The contract is Fraternity, because it identifies all interests, unifies all divergences, resolves all contradictions, and in consequence, give wings to the feelings of goodwill and kindness, which are crushed by economic chaos, the government of representatives, alien law.

The contract, finally, is order, since it is the organization of economic forces, instead of the alienation of liberties, the sacrifice of rights, the subordination of wills.

Let us give an idea of this organism; after liquidation, reconstruction; after the thesis and antithesis, the synthesis.

### Credit.

The organization of credit is three-quarters done by the winding up of the privileged and usurious banks, and their conversion into a National Bank of circulation and loan, at ½, ¼, or ⅛ percent. It remains only to establish branches of the Bank, wherever necessary, and to gradually retire specie from circulation, depriving gold and silver of their privilege as money.

As for *personal credit*, it is not for the National Bank to have to do with it; it is with the workingmen's unions, and the farming and industrial societies, that personal credit should be exercised.

### Property.

I have shown above how property, repurchased by the house rent or ground rent, would come back to the tenant farmer and house tenant. It remains for me to show, especially in relation to property in land, the organizing power of the principle which we have invoked to bring about this conversion...

I have been obliged to conclude that the hypothesis of [State ownership and] general farm tenancy did not contain the solution that I sought; and that, after having settled for the land, it would be necessary to seriously consider reassigning it in full sovereignty to the worker, because, without that, neither his pride as a citizen nor his rights as a producer could be satisfied...

Make of this idea, apparently quite negative, and which at first seemed a mere fancy, for the need of the cause – make of it a positive, general, fixed rule, and property becomes constituted. It will receive its organization, its rules, its police, its sanction. It will have fulfilled the Idea beneath it, its charter for all and accepted by all, in a single clause; whence all the rest is deducible by the light of common sense.

With this simple contract, protected, consolidated and guaranteed by the commercial and agricultural association, you may, without the slightest apprehension, permit the proprietor to sell, transmit, alienate, circulate, his property at will. Property in land, under this new system, property deprived of rent, delivered from its chains and cured of its leprosy, is in the hands of the proprietor like a five franc piece or a bank note in the hands of the bearer. It is worth so much, neither more nor less, it can neither gain nor lose in value by changing hands; it is no longer subject to depreciation; above all, it has lost that fatal power of accumulation which it had, not in itself, but through the ancient prejudice in favor of caste and nobility which attached to it.

Thus from the point of view of equality of conditions, of the guarantee of labor and of public security, property in land cannot cause the slightest perturbation to social economy: it has lost its vicious character; there remain to be seen the good qualities which it must have acquired. It is to this that I call the attention of my readers, notably of the Communist, whom I beg to weigh well the difference between association, that is to say, government, and contract.

### Division of Labor, Collective Forces, Machines, Workingmen's Associations

... Agricultural labor, resting on this basis, appears in its natural dignity. Of all occupations it is the most noble, the most healthful, from the point of view of morals and health, and as intellectual exercise, the most encyclopaedic. From all these considerations, agricultural labor is the one which least requires the societary form; we may say even more strongly, which most energetically rejects it. Never have peasants been seen to form a society for the cultivation of their fields; never will they be seen to do so. The only relations of unity and solidarity which can exist among farm workers, the only centralization of which rural industry is susceptible, is that which we have pointed out which results from compensation for economic rent, mutual insurance, and, most of all, from abolishing rent, which makes accumulation of land, parcelling out of the soil, serfdom of the peasant, dissipation of inheritances, forever impossible.

It is otherwise with certain industries, which require the combined employment of a large number of workers, a vast array of machines and hands, and, to make use of a technical expression, a great division of labor, and in consequence a high concentration of power. In such cases, workman is necessarily subordinate to workman, man dependent on man. The producer is no longer, as in the fields, a sovereign and free father of a family; it is a collectivity. Railroads, mines, factories, are examples.

In such cases, it is one of two things; either the workman, necessarily a piece-worker, will be simply the employee of the proprietor-capitalist-promoter; or he will participate in the chances of loss or gain of the establishment, he will have a voice in the council, in a word, he will become an associate.

In the first case the workman is subordinated, exploited: his permanent condition is one of obedience and poverty. In the second case he resumes his dignity as a man and citizen, he may aspire to comfort, he forms a part of the producing organization, of which he was before but the slave; as, in the town, he forms a part of the sovereign power, of which he was before but the subject.

Thus we need not hesitate, for we have no choice. In cases in which production requires great division of labor, and a considerable collective force, it is necessary to form an **ASSOCIATION** among the workers in this industry; because without that, they would remain related as subordinates and superiors, and there would ensue two industrial castes of masters and wage-workers, which is repugnant to a free and democratic society.

Such therefore is the rule that we must lay down, if we wish to conduct the Revolution intelligently.

Every industry, operation or enterprise, which by its nature requires the employment of a large number of workmen of different specialties, is destined to become a society or a company of workers...

But where the product can be obtained by the action of an individual or a family, without the co-operation of special abilities, there is no opportunity for association. Association not being called for by the nature of the work, cannot be profitable nor of long continuance...

I do not consider as falling within the logical class of division of labor nor of collective force the innumerable small shops which are found in all trades, and which seem to me the effect of the preference of the individuals who conduct them, rather than the organic result of a combination of forces. Anybody who is capable of cutting out and sewing up a pair of shoes can get a license, open a shop, and hang out a sign, *"So-and-So, Manufacturing Shoe Merchant,"* although there may be only himself behind his counter. If a companion, who prefers journeyman's wages to running the risk of starting in business, joins with the first, one will call himself the employer, the other, the hired man; in fact, they are completely equal and completely free...

But when the enterprise requires the combined aid of several industries, professions, special trades; when from this combination springs a new product, that could not be made by any individual, a combination in which man fits in with man as wheel with wheel; the whole group of workers forms a machine, like the fitting of the parts of a clock or a locomotive; then, indeed, the conditions are no longer the same. Who could arrogate the right to exploit such a body of slaves? Who would be daring enough to take one man for a hammer, another for a spade, this one for a hook, that one for a lever?...

The industry to be carried on, the work to be accomplished, are the common and undivided property of all those who take part therein: the granting of franchises for mines and railroads to companies of stockholders, who plunder the bodies and souls of the wage-workers, is a betrayal of power, a violation of the rights of the public, an outrage upon human dignity and personality...

The cultivator had been bent under feudal servitude through rent and mortgages. He is freed by the land bank, and, above all, by the right of the user to the property. The land, vast in extent and in depth, becomes the basis of equality.

In the same way the wage-worker of the great industries, had been crushed into a condition worse than that of the slave, by the loss of the advantage of collective force. But by the recognition of his right to the profit from this force, of which he is the producer, he resumes his dignity, he regains comfort; the great industries, terrible engines of aristocracy and pauperism, become, in their turn, one of the principal organs of liberty and public prosperity...

By participation in losses and gains, by the graded scale of pay, and the successive promotion to all grades and positions, the collective force, which is a product of the community, ceases to be a source of profit to a small number of managers and speculators: it becomes the property of all the workers. At the same time, by a broad education, by the obligation of apprenticeship, and by the co-operation of all who take part in the collective work, the division of labor can no longer be a cause of degradation for the workman: it is, on the contrary, the means of his education and the pledge of his security...

### Constitution of Value. Organization of Low Prices.

If commerce or exchange, carried on after a fashion, is already, by its inherit merit, a producer of wealth; if, for this reason, it has been practised always and by all the nations of the globe; if, in consequence, we must consider it as an economic force; it is not the less true, and it springs from the very notion of exchange, that commerce ought to be so much the more profitable if sales and purchases are made at the lowest and most just price; that is to say, if the products that are exchanged can be furnished in greater abundance and in more exact proportion...

[C]ertain economists have nevertheless aspired to erect into a law this mercantile disorder and commercial disturbance. They see in it a principle as sacred as that of the family or of labor. The school of Say, sold out to English and native capitalism... has for ten years past seemed to exist only to protect and applaud the execrable work of the monopolists of money and necessaries, deepening more and more the obscurity of a science naturally difficult and full of complications...

Everybody knows that from the earliest period **EXCHANGE** has been separated into two elementary operations, *Sale* and *Purchase*. Money is the universal commodity, the tally, which serves to connect the two operations, and to complete the exchange...

According to what we have just said, Sale will be genuine, normal, fair, from the point of view of economic justice and of value, if it is made at a *just price*, as far as human calculation permits this to be established...

But, unfortunately for humanity, things are not done so in commerce. The *price* of things is not proportionate to their **VALUE**: it is larger or smaller according to an influence which justice condemns, but the existing economic chaos excuses – Usury.

Usury is the arbitrary factor in commerce. Inasmuch as, under the present system, the producer has no guarantee that he can exchange his product, nor the merchant any certainty of reselling, each one endeavors to pass off his merchandise at the highest possible price, in order to obtain by the excess of profit the security of which labor and exchange fail sufficiently to assure him. The profit thus obtained in excess of the cost, including the wages of the seller, is called Increase. Increase – theft – is therefore compensation for insecurity.

Everybody being given to Increase, there is reciprocal falsehood in all relations, and universal deceit, by common consent, as to the value of things. [ … ]

This is what the Revolution proposes.

Since there is a universal tacit agreement among all producers and traders to take from each other increase for their products or services, to work in the dark in their dealings, to play a sharp game; in a word, to take each other by surprise by all the tricks of trade; why should there not as well be a universal and tacit agreement to renounce increase, that is to say, to sell and pay at the only just price, which is the average cost?

… What will surprise more than one reader, and what seems at first sight contradictory, is that a *just price*, like any sort of service or guarantee, must be **PAID FOR**: the low price of merchandise, like the merchandise itself, must have its recompense: without this premium offered to the merchant, the just price becomes impossible, the low price a chimaera…

If the dealer usually refuses to sell his goods at cost, it is, on the one hand, because he has no certainty of selling enough to secure him an income; on the other, because he has no guarantee that he will obtain like treatment for his purchases.

Without this double guarantee, sale at a just price, the same as sale below the market price, is impossible: the only cases in which it occurs arise from failures and liquidations.

Do you wish then to obtain goods at a just price, to gain the advantage of a low price, to practise a truth-telling commerce, to assure equality in exchange?

You must offer the merchant a sufficient guarantee.

This guarantee may take various forms: perhaps the consumers, who wish to have the benefit of a just price, are producers themselves, and will obligate themselves in turn to sell their products to the dealer on like terms, as is done among the different Parisian associations; perhaps the consumers will content themselves, without any reciprocal arrangements, with assuring the retailer of a premium, the interest, for example, of his capital, or a fixed bonus, or a sale large enough to assure him of a revenue. This is what is generally done by the butchers' associations, and by the *Housekeeper* society, of which we have already spoken.

… When, by the liquidation of debts, the organization of credit, the deprivation of the power of increase of money, the limitation of property, the establishment of workingmen's associations and the use of a just price, the tendency to raising of prices shall have been definitely replaced by a tendency to lower them, and the fluctuations of the market by a normal commercial rate; when general consent shall have brought this great about-face of the sphere of trade, then Value, at once the most ideal and most real of things, may be said to have been constituted, and will express at any moment, for every kind of product, the true relation of Labor and Wealth, while preserving its mobility through the eternal progress of industry.

The constitution of Value solves the problem of competition and that of the rights of Invention; as the organization of workmen's associations solves that of collective force and of the division of labor. I can merely indicate at this moment these consequences of the main theorem; their development would take too much space in a philosophical review of the Revolution...

### Foreign Commerce. Balance of Imports and Exports

By the suppression of custom houses, the Revolution, according to theory, and regardless of all military and diplomatic influences, will spread from France abroad, extend over Europe, and afterwards over the world.

To suppress our custom houses is in truth to organize foreign trade as we have organized domestic trade... In the matter of the tariff, as in everything else, the *statu quo*, indicated by rising prices, is reaction; progress, indicated by falling prices, is the Revolution... As for me, I, who oppose the free traders because they favor interest, while they demand the abolition of tariffs – I should favor lowering the tariff from the moment that interest fell; and if interest were done away with, or even lowered to ¼ or ½ percent., I should be in favor of free trade... Free trade would then become equal exchange, the diversity of interests among nations would gradually result in unity of interest, and the day would dawn when war would cease among nations, as would lawsuits among individuals, from lack of litigable matter and absence of cause for conflict...

## ABSORPTION OF GOVERNMENT BY THE ECONOMIC ORGANISM

Given:

Man, *The Family*, **SOCIETY**.

An individual, sexual and social being, endowed with reason, love and conscience, capable of learning by experience, of perfecting himself by reflection, and of earning his living by work.

The problem is to so organize the powers of this being, that he may remain always at peace with himself, and may extract from Nature, which is given to him, the largest possible amount of well-being.

We know how previous generations have solved it... This system... may be called the system of order by authority... [I]t is desirable, in order to convince the mind to set alongside each other the fundamental ideas of, on the one hand, the politico-religious system... on the other hand, the economic system.

Government, then, that is to say, Church and State indivisibly united, has for its dogmas:

1. The original perversity of human nature;
2. The inevitable inequality of fortunes;
3. The permanency of quarrels and wars;
4. The irremediability of poverty.

Whence it is deduced:

The necessity of government, of obedience, of resignation, and of faith.

These principles admitted, as they still are, almost universally, the forms of authority are already settled. They are:

a) The division of the people into classes or castes, subordinate to one another; graduated to form a pyramid, at the top of which appears, like the Divinity upon his altar, like the king upon his throne, **AUTHORITY**;
b) Administrative centralization;
c) Judicial hierarchy;
d) Police;
e) Worship.

... What is the aim of this organization?

To maintain *order* in society, by consecrating and sanctifying obedience of the citizen to the State, subordination of the poor and to the rich, of the common people to the upper class, of the worker to the idler, of the layman to the priest, of the business man to the soldier...

Beneath the governmental machinery, in the shadow of political institutions, out of the sight of statesmen and priests, society is producing its own organism, slowly and silently; and constructing a new order, the expression of its vitality and autonomy, and the denial of the old politics, as well as of the old religion.

This organization, which is as essential to society as it is incompatible with the present system, has the following principles:

1. The indefinite perfectibility of the individual and of the race;
2. The honorableness of work;
3. The equality of fortunes;
4. The identity of interests;
5. The end of antagonisms;
6. The universality of comfort;
7. The sovereignty of reason;
8. The absolute liberty of the man and of the citizen.

I mention below its principal forms of activity:

a) Division of labor, through which classification of the People by **IN-DUSTRIES** replaces classification by *caste*;

b) Collective power, the principle of **WORKMEN'S ASSOCIA-TIONS**, in place of *armies*;

c) Commerce, the concrete form of **CONTRACT**, which takes the place of *Law*;

d) Equality in exchange;

e) Competition;

f) Credit, which turns upon **INTERESTS**, as the governmental hierarchy turns upon *Obedience*;

g) The equilibrium of values and of properties.

The old system, standing on Authority and Faith, was essentially based on *Divine Right*. The principle of the sovereignty of the People, introduced later, did not change its nature… The sovereignty of the People has been, is I may say so, for a century past, but a skirmishing line for Liberty… The new system, based upon the spontaneous practice of industry, in accordance with individual and social reason, is the system of *Human Right*. Opposed to arbitrary command, essentially objective, it permits neither parties nor sects; it is complete in itself, and allows neither restriction nor separation.

There is no fusion possible between the political and economic systems, between the system of laws and the system of contracts; one or the other must be chosen.

… But to live without government, to abolish all authority, absolutely and unreservedly, to set up pure *anarchy*, seems to them ridiculous and inconceivable, a plot against the Republic and against the nation. What will these people who talk of abolishing government put in place of it? they ask.

We have no trouble in answering.

It is industrial organization that we will put in place of government, as we have just shown.

In place of laws, we will put contracts. – No more laws voted by a majority, nor even unanimously; each citizen, each town, each industrial union, makes its own laws.

In place of political powers, we will put economic forces.

In place of the ancient classes of nobles, burghers, and peasants, or of business men and working men, we will put the general titles and special departments of industry: Agriculture, Manufacture, Commerce, etc.

In place of public force, we will put collective force.

In place of standing armies, we will put industrial associations.

In place of police, we will put identity of interests.

In place of political centralization, we will put economic centralization.

Do you see now how there can be order without functionaries, a profound and wholly intellectual unity?

You, who cannot conceive of unity without a whole apparatus of legislators, prosecutors, attorneys-general, custom house officers, policemen, you have never known what real unity is! What you call unity and centralization is nothing but perpetual chaos, serving as a basis for endless tyranny; it is the advancing of the chaotic condition of social forces as an argument for despotism – a despotism which is really the cause of the chaos...

We have shown that the industrial system is the harmony of interests resulting from social liquidation, free currency and credit, the organization of economic forces, and the constitution of value and property.

When that is accomplished, what use will there be any more for government; what use punishment; what use judicial power? The **CONTRACT** solves all problems. The producer deals with the consumer, the member with his society, the farmer with his township, the township with the province, the province with the State...

The secret of this equalizing of the citizen and the State, as well as of the believer and the priest, the plaintiff and the judge, lies in the economic equation which we have hereinbefore made, by the abolition of capitalist interest between the worker and the employer, the farmer and the proprietor. Do away with this last remnant of the ancient slavery by the reciprocity of obligations, and both citizens and communities will have no need of the intervention of the State to carry on their business, take care of their property, build their ports, bridges, quays, canals, roads, establish markets, transact their litigation, instruct, direct, control, censor their agents, perform any acts of supervision or police, any more than they will need its aid in offering their adoration to the Most High, or in judging their criminals and putting it out of their power to do injury, supposing that the removal of motive does not bring the cessation of crime.

... The Revolution would be vain if it were not contagious: it would perish, even in France, if it failed to become universal. Everybody is convinced of that. The least enthusiastic spirits do not believe it necessary for revolutionary France to interfere among other nations by force of arms: it will be enough for her to support, by her example and her encouragement, any effort of the people of foreign nations to follow her example.

What then is the Revolution, completed abroad as well as at home?

Capitalistic and proprietary exploitation stopped everywhere, the wage system abolished, equal and just exchange guaranteed, value constituted, cheapness assured, the principle of protection changed, and the markets of the world opened to the producers of all nations; consequently the barrier struck down, the ancient law of nations replaced by commercial agreements; police, judiciary administration, everywhere committed to the hands of the workers; the economic organization replacing the governmental and military system in the colonies as well as in the great cities; finally, the free and universal commingling of races under the law of contract only: that is the Revolution.

Understand once for all: the most characteristic, the most decisive result of the Revolution is, after having organized labor and property, to do away with political centralization, in a word, with the State... The kings may sharpen their swords for their last campaign. The Revolution in the Nineteenth Century has for its supreme task, not so much the overthrow of their dynasties, as the destruction to the last root of their institution. Born as they are to war, educated for war, supported by war, domestic and foreign, of what use can they be in a society of labor and peace? Henceforth there can be no more purpose in war than in refusal to disarm. Universal brotherhood being established upon a sure foundation, there is nothing for the representatives of despotism to do but to take their leave...

As for those who, after the departure of kings, still dream of consulates, of presidencies, of dictatorships, of marshalships, of admiralties and of ambassadorships, they also will do well to retire. The Revolution, having no need for their services, can dispense with their talents. The people no longer want this coin of monarchy: they understand that, whatever phraseology is used, feudal system, governmental system, military system, parliamentary system, system of police, laws and tribunals, and system of exploitation, corruption, lying and poverty, are all synonymous. Finally they know that in doing away with rent and interest, the last remnants of the old slavery, the Revolution, at one blow, does away with the sword of the executioner, the blade of justice, the club of the policeman, the gauge of the customs officer, the erasing knife of the bureaucrat, all those insignia of government which young Liberty grinds beneath her heel...

## EPILOGUE

The fundamental, decisive idea of this Revolution is it not this: **NO MORE AUTHORITY**, neither in the Church, nor in the State, nor in land, nor in money?

No more Authority! That means something we have never seen, something we have never understood; the harmony of the interest of one with the interest of all; the identity of collective sovereignty and individual sovereignty.

No more Authority! That means debts paid, servitude abolished, mortgages lifted, rents reimbursed, the expense of worship, justice, and the State suppressed; free credit, equal exchange, free association, regulated value, education, work, property, domicile, low price, guaranteed: no more antagonism, no more war, no more centralization, no more governments, no more priests. Is not that Society emerged from its shell and walking upright?

No more Authority! That is to say further: free contract in place of arbitrary law; voluntary transactions in place of the control of the State; equitable and reciprocal justice in place of sovereign and distributive justice; rational instead of revealed morals; equilibrium of forces instead of equilibrium of powers; economic unity in place of political centralization. Once more, I ask, is not this what I may venture to call a complete reversal, a turn-over, a Revolution?

# 4

# MARKETS FREED FROM CAPITALISM

## CHARLES W. JOHNSON
## (2010)

L ET'S TALK ABOUT THE STRUCTURE AND MECHANISMS OF STATE CAPITALISM. I MEAN HOW, IN everyday economic life, the *political structure* of corporate privilege tends to produce, and sustain, the *material conditions* of the bosses' economy – how, to use Gary Chartier's threefold distinction,[1] capitalism2 promotes capitalism3 – and how freed markets would abolish the one and run the other into the ground. Most of my remarks here will be broadly historical and economic in character – although necessarily of a sketchy or programmatic sort, given the size of the topic and the constraints of the space. So consider this a guide to directions for inquiry and discussion; an attempt to show you briefly where key landmarks of the free market anticapitalist analysis are at, rather than an attempt at a full guided tour. I think it important to at least sketch out the map because the chief obstacle that free market anticapitalists confront in explaining our position is not so much a matter of correcting particular mistakes in political principles, or economic analysis – although there *are* particular mistakes we hope to address and correct. It is more a matter of convincing our conversation partners to make a sort of *aspect-shift*, to adopt a new point of view from which to see the political-economic *gestalt*.

---

1    Gary Chartier, "Advocates of Freed Markets Should Oppose Capitalism," ch. 9 (107-117) in this book.

The need for this shift is pressing because – with apologies to Shulamith Firestone[2] – the political economy of state capitalism is so deep as to be invisible. Or it may appear to be a superficial set of interventions, a problem that can be solved by a few legal reforms, or perhaps the elimination of bail-outs and the occasional export subsidy, while preserving more or less intact the basic recognizable patterns of capitalistic business as usual. The free market anticapitalist holds there is something deeper, and more pervasive, at stake than the sort of surface level policy debates to which pro-capitalist libertarians too often limit their discussions. A fully freed market means the liberation of vital command posts in the economy, reclaiming them from points of state control to nexuses of market and social entrepreneurship – transformations from which a market would emerge that would look profoundly different from anything we have now. That so profound a change cannot easily fit into traditional categories of thought, e.g. "libertarian" or "left-wing," "laissez-faire" or "socialist," "entrepreneurial" or "anticapitalist," is not because these categories do not apply but because they are not big enough: radically free markets burst through them. If there were another word more all-embracing than *revolutionary*, we would use it.

## TWO MEANINGS OF "MARKETS"

In order to get clear on the topic in a conversation about "Free Market Anticapitalism," the obvious points where clarification may be needed are going to be the meaning of *capitalism*, the meaning of *markets*, and the meaning of *freedom* in the market context. Left-libertarians and market anarchists have spent a lot of time, and raised a lot of controversy talking about the *first* topic – whether "capitalism" is really a good name for the sort of thing that we want, the importance of distinguishing markets from actually-existing capitalism, and the possibility of disentangling multiple senses of "capitalism." There's been a lot of argument about that, but for the moment I would like to pass that question by, in order to focus on the less frequently discussed side of our distinction – not the meaning of "capitalism," but the different strands of meaning within the term *"market."* The meaning of the term is obviously central to any free *market* economics; but I would argue that there are at least *two* distinct senses in which the term is commonly used:

- **Markets as free exchange:** when libertarians talk about markets, or especially about *"the* market," singular, we often mean to pick

---

2    See Shulamith Firestone, *The Dialectic of Sex: The Case for Feminist Revolution* (New York: Farrar 2003) 3.

out the *sum of all voluntary exchanges*[3] – any economic order based, to the extent that it is based, on principles of personal ownership of property, consensual exchange, free association, and the freedom to engage in peaceful competition and entrepreneurial discovery.

- **Markets as the cash nexus:** but we often also use the term in a different sense – to refer to a particular *form* of acquiring and exchanging property – that is, to refer to commerce and *quid pro quo* exchanges, relatively impersonal social relationships on a paying basis, typically mediated by currency or by financial instruments denominated in units of currency.

These two senses are interrelated. When they take place within the context of a system of *free exchange,* the social relationships based on the *cash nexus* – producing, buying, and selling at market prices, saving money for future use, investing money in productive enterprises, and the like have all positive, even essential, role in a flourishing free society. I do not intend to argue that these will disappear in a society of equal freedom; but I do intend to argue that they may not look like what you expect them to look like, if your picture of commercial relationships is taken from commerce under the conditions of corporate capitalism. Commerce under capitalism does have many of the exploitative and alienating features that critics on the Left accuse "private enterprise" or "market society" of having. But not because of the enterprise, or because of the market. The problem with commerce under capitalism is *capitalism*, and without it, *both* freed-market exchange and cash-nexus commerce will take on a wholly different character.

To see how they might come together, we must first attend to how they come apart. However often they may be linked in fact, free exchange and the cash nexus are distinguishable in concept. Markets in the first sense

---

3    Pro-capitalist economists have often suggested such a broad understanding of "markets," even if they have not fully understood, or were not willing to fully draw out, its implications. For example, Murray Rothbard, "Toward a Reconstruction of Utility and Welfare Economics" (Ludwig von Mises Institute, 2002) <http://mises.org/rothbard/toward.pdf> (March 13, 2011) writes that "The free market is the name for the array of *all the voluntary exchanges that take place in the world*" (29-9). Ludwig von Mises, *Human Action: A Treatise on Economic Principles*, scholars ed. (Auburn, AL Mises 1998), writes that "There is in the operation of the market no compulsion and coercion… Each man [*sic*] is free; nobody is subject to a despot. Of his [*sic*] own accord the individual integrates himself [*sic*] into the cooperative system… The market is not a place, a thing or a collective entity. The market is a process, actuated by the interplay of the actions of the various individuals cooperating under the division of labor" (158).

(the sum of all voluntary exchanges) *include* the cash nexus – but also *much more than* the cash nexus. If a "freed market" is the sum of all voluntary exchanges, then family sharing takes place within a freed market; charity is part of a freed market; gifts are part of a freed market; informal exchange and barter are all part of a freed market. Similarly, while markets-as-free-exchange may include "capitalistic" arrangements – so long as they are consensual – they also encompass far more than that. There is nothing in a freed market that *prohibits* wage labor, rent, corporate jobs, or corporate insurance. But a freed market also encompasses alternative arrangements – including many that clearly have nothing to do with employer-employee relationships or corporate management, and which fit awkwardly, at best, with *any* conventional meaning of the term "capitalism:" worker ownership and consumer co-ops are part of the market; grassroots mutual aid associations and community free clinics are part of the market; so are voluntary labor unions, consensual communes, narrower or broader experiments with gift economies, and countless other alternatives to the prevailing corporate-capitalist *status quo*. To focus on the specific act of *exchange* may even be a bit misleading; it might be more suggestive, and less misleading, to describe a fully freed market, in this sense, as **the space of maximal consensually-sustained social experimentation**.

The question, then, is whether, when people are free to experiment with any and every peaceful means of making a living, the sort of mutualistic alternatives that I've mentioned might take on an increased role in the economy, or whether the prevailing capitalistic forms would continue to predominate as they currently do. To be sure, the capitalistic arrangements predominate *now* – most of the viable ways to make a living are capitalist jobs; most people either rent their home from a landlord or "own" it only so long as they keep up with monthly bills to a bank; large, centralized management predominates in companies and corporations predominate in providing credit, insurance, health care, and virtually all capital and consumer goods. Productive enterprises are almost all commercial enterprises, commercial enterprises are predominantly large-scale, centralized corporate enterprises, and corporate enterprises are controlled by a select, relatively small, socially privileged class of managers and financiers. Inequalities in wealth and income are vast, and the vast inequalities have profound social effects.

But of course the fact that capitalistic arrangements predominate *now* is no reason to conclude that "the market has spoken," or that capitalistic concentrations of wealth are a basic tendency of free-market exchange. It might be a reason to think that *if* the predominance of capitalistic arrangements were the product of revealed preferences in a free market; but since we don't at present *have* a free market, it will, at the very least, take some further investigation – in order to determine whether those capitalistic alternatives prevail *in spite of* the unfreedom of actually-existing markets, or if they prevail, in part, *because* of that unfreedom.

First, let us take this lesson and apply it to *the market as cash nexus*. The cash nexus does not exhaust the forms of voluntary exchange and economic experimentation that might emerge within a freed market. But, more than that, a cash nexus may exist, and may be expansive and important to economic life, *whether or not it* operates under conditions of genuine individual freedom. Markets in our first, voluntary-exchange sense exist where people really are free to produce and exchange – "free market," in the voluntary-exchange sense of "market," is really a tautology, and where there is no free exchange, there is no market order. But a "market" in the cash-nexus sense may be either free or unfree; cash exchanges are still cash exchanges, whether they are regulated, restricted, subsidized, taxed, mandated, or otherwise constrained by government action.

Any discussion of the cash nexus in the real world – of the everyday "market institutions," economic relationships, and financial arrangements that we have to deal with in this governmental economy – needs to take account not only of the ways in which government *limits* or *prohibits* market activity, but also the ways in which government, rather than erasing markets, *creates* new **rigged markets** – points of exchange, cash nexuses which would be smaller, or less important, or radically different in character, or simply would not exist at all, but for the intervention of the state. Libertarians often speak of market exchange and government allocation as cleanly separate spheres, as if they were two balloons, set one next to the other, in a closed box, so that when you blow one of them up, the other has to shrink to the same extent. That's true enough about *markets as social experimentation* – to the extent you put in political processes, you take out voluntary relationships. But the relationship between *cash-nexus exchange* and government allocation is really more like two plants growing next to each other. When one gets bigger, it may overshadow the other, and stunt its growth. But they also climb each other, shape each other, and each may even cause some parts of the other plant to grow far more than if they had not had the support.

Market anarchists must be clear, when we speak about the growth of "markets" and their role in social life, whether we are referring to *markets as free exchange*, or *markets as a cash nexus*. Both have a valuable role to play, but the kind of value they offer, and the conditions and context within which they have that value, depends on which we mean. For a principled anti-statist, the growth of "markets" as *spaces for consensual social experimen-*

*tation* is always a liberating development – but these social experiments may be mediated by the cash-nexus, or may be mediated by entirely different social relationships, and may look nothing like conventional business or commerce. The growth of "markets" as cash-nexus exchanges, on the other hand, may be liberating *or* violating, and its value must depend entirely on the context within which it arises – whether those relationships come about through the free interplay of social forces, or through the direct or indirect ripple-effects of government force and coercive creation of rigged markets. Forms of interaction that are positive and productive in the context of free exchange easily become instruments of alienation and exploitation when coercive government forces them on unwilling participants, or shoves them into areas of our lives where we don't need or want them.

## RIGGED MARKETS, CAPTIVE MARKETS, AND CAPITALISTIC BUSINESS AS USUAL

When market anarchists carefully distinguish the broad meaning of "markets" (as *voluntary social experimentation*) and the narrow meaning, and connotations, of "markets" *as the cash nexus*, this underlines the need to look not only at the ways in which *voluntary* exchange may be confined or erased, but also the ways in which *cash* exchange – and the sorts of human relationships and social mediation that go along with it – may be locked out *or* locked in – held back from people *or* foisted on them.

For anticapitalist market anarchists, there are at least three specific mechanisms we might mention that shove people into rigged markets – mechanisms that are especially pervasive and especially important to the overall structure of actually-existing markets – mechanisms by which incumbent big businesses, and capitalistic arrangements broadly, benefit from rigged markets, at the expense of workers, consumers, taxpayers, and mutualistic alternatives to the statist quo. These three are:

1. **Government monopolies and cartels:** in which government penalties directly suppress competition or erect effective barriers to entry against newcomers or substitute goods and services;

2. **Regressive redistribution:** in which property is directly seized from ordinary workers by government expropriation, and transferred to economically powerful beneficiaries, in the form of tax-funded subsidies and corporate welfare, taxpayer-backed sweetheart loans, the widespread use of eminent domain to seize property from small owners and transfer it to big commercial developers,[4] etc.; and

---

4    For the most famous recent case of such "eminent domain abuse," see *Kelo*

3. **Captive markets:** in which demand for a good is created, or artificially ratcheted up, by government coercion – which can mean a direct mandate with penalties inflicted on those who do not buy in; or a situation in which market actors are driven into a market on artificially disadvantageous terms as an indirect (perhaps even unintended) ripple-effect of prior government interventions.

As an easy example of a directly-imposed captive market, consider the demand for corporate car insurance. When state governments mandate that every driver to purchase and maintain car insurance from bureaucratically-approved insurance companies, they necessarily shrink the scope of voluntary exchange, but they also dramatically *bulk up* a *particular, fetishized form* of cash exchange – by creating a new bill that everyone is forced to pay, and a select class of incumbent companies with easy access to a steady stream of customers, many of whom might not pay for their "services" but for the threat of fines and arrest. The space of social experimentation contracts, but the cash nexus fattens on what government has killed.

As an example of an *indirectly*-imposed captive market, consider the demand for professionally-certified accountants. CPAs perform a useful service, but it's a service that far fewer people, and indeed far fewer businesses, would need, except for the fact that they need help coping with the documentation and paperwork requirements that government tax codes impose. A CPA is essentially someone trained in dealing with financial complexity, but finances are much more complex than they would be in a free society precisely because of government taxation and the bizarre requirements and perverse incentives that tend to make things much more complex than

v. *New London*, 545 U.S. 469 (2005). City government used eminent domain to condemn and seize the houses of Susette Kelo and many other small homeowners in New London, Connecticut, to hand the real estate over to a wealthy private developer. The developer intended to bulldoze the houses and replace them with "developments" for his own profit and for the benefit of the Fortune 500 drug company Pfizer Inc. The Court backed the city government, holding they could take any home, and transfer it to any private party, so long as a government-sponsored "economic development" plan indicated that it would increase government's tax revenues. *Kelo* drew widespread attention to the issue, but similar seizures and transfers, mostly targeted against the neighborhoods of racial minorities, immigrants, and the urban poor, had been widely practiced for decades, under the heading of "Urban Renewal." Cf. Mindy Fullilove, *Root Shock: How Tearing Up City Neighborhoods Hurts America and What We Can Do About It* (New York: Random 2005), and Dick M. Carpenter and John K. Ross, *Victimizing the Vulnerable: The Demographics of Eminent Domain Abuse* (Arlington, VA: Institute for Justice 2007).

they would otherwise be. Although government has no special interest in benefiting the bottom line of CPAs, it is nevertheless the case that CPAs are able to get far more business, and at a far higher rate, than they would in a market without income tax, payroll tax, capital gains tax, property tax, sales tax, use tax, and the myriad other taxes that demand specialized expertise in accounting and interpretation of legal requirements.

With these three mechanisms in sight, a quick way to gloss the free-market anticapitalist thesis is this: we hold that many of the recognizable patterns of capitalist economics result from the fact that certain key markets – importantly, the labor market, housing rental market, insurance and financial markets, and other key markets are rigged markets. And In particular, that they are often indirectly-created captive markets, and that the extent to which these needs are met through through conventionally commercial relationships under the heading of the cash nexus – rather than being met through other, possibly radically different sorts of social relationships, like co-ops, homesteading, sweat equity, informal exchange, loosely reciprocal gift economies, grassroots mutual aid networks, and other mutualistic alternatives – has little to do with people's underlying desires or preferences, and a great deal to do with the constraints placed on the expression of those desires or preferences. Commercial relationships and the cash nexus grow fat because working-class folks in need of houses or jobs are driven into a market where they are systematically stripped of resources and alternatives, where they are constantly faced by artificially high costs, and where they are generally constrained to negotiate with incumbent market players who have been placed in an artificially advantageous position over them through continuous, repeated and pervasive government interventions in the incumbents' favor.[5]

## TUCKER'S BIG FOUR AND THE MANY MONOPOLIES

It may be unusual for claims like this to be associated with advocates for the market freedom. "Free-market economics" is generally assumed to be the province of "pro-business" politicians and the economic Right. It is usually state liberals, Progressives, Social Democrats and economic radicals who are expected to argue that people in their roles as workers, tenants, or consumers are shoved into alienating relationships and exploitative transac-

---

5    See also Charles W. Johnson, "Scratching By: How Government Creates Poverty As We Know It," *The Freeman: Ideas on Liberty* 57.10 (Dec. 2007): 33-8 (Foundation for Economic Education, 2007) <http://www.thefreemanonline.org/featured/scratching-by-how-government-creates-poverty-as-we-know-it/> (Jan. 2, 2010).

tions – that they are systematically deprived of more humane alternatives and suffer because they are left to bargain, at a tremendous disadvantage, with bosses, banks, landlords, and big, faceless corporations. But while I agree that this is a radical – indeed, a *socialistic* position – I deny that there is anything reactionary, Right wing, or "pro-business" about the ideal of freed markets. Indeed, it is freed market relationships which provide the most incisive, vibrant, and fruitful basis for socialist ideals of economic justice, worker emancipation, and grassroots solidarity. Anticapitalist claims like the ones I have just made may be rarely heard among vulgar "free enterprise" apologists now, but they are hardly unusual in the long view of libertarian history.

Before the mid-20th century, when American libertarians entangled themselves in conservative coalitions against the New Deal and Soviet Communism, "free market" thinkers largely saw themselves as liberals or radicals, not as conservatives. Libertarian writers, from Smith to Bastiat to Spencer, had little interest in tailoring their politics to conservative or "pro-business" measurements. They frequently identified capitalists, and their protectionist policies, as among the most dangerous enemies of free exchange and property rights. The most radical among them were the mutualists and individualist Anarchists, among them Benjamin Tucker, Dyer Lum, Victor Yarros, and Voltairine de Cleyre. Tucker, the individualist editor of *Liberty*, wrote in 1888[6] that his Anarchism called for "Absolute Free Trade… *laissez faire* the universal rule;" but all the while he described this doctrine of complete *laissez faire* and free competition a form of *"Anarchistic socialism."* For Tucker, of course, "socialism" could not mean government ownership of the means of production (that was "State Socialism," which Tucker opposed root and branch); what he meant, rather, was *workers' control over the conditions of their labor* – opposition to actually-existing economic inequalities, capitalist labor relations, and the exploitative practices of big businesses supported by state privilege. For Tucker, the surest way to dismantle capitalist privilege was to knock through the political privileges which shield it, and to expose it, unprotected, to the full range of competing enterprises – including mutualistic enterprise of, for, and by freed workers – that genuinely freed exchange would allow.

In order to make clear what those privileges were and how they rigged markets in favor of capitalistic big business, Tucker identified and analyzed of four great areas where government intervention artificially created or encouraged "class monopolies" – concentrating wealth and access to factors of production into the hands of a politically-select class insulated from

---

6    Benjamin R. Tucker, "State Socialism and Anarchism: How Far They Agree and herein They Differ," ch. 2 (21-35) of this book.

competition, and prohibiting workers from organizing mutualistic alternatives. The Big Four monopolies Tucker identified as central to the Gilded Age economy were:[7]

1. **The Land Monopoly:** government concentration of ownership of land and natural resources through the enforcement of legally-fabricated land titles (such as preferential land grants to politically-connected speculators, or literally feudal land claims in Europe).

   Since Tucker, the land monopoly, already key to the Gilded Age economy, has radically expanded – with the frequent nationalization of mineral and fossil fuel resources throughout, and the emergence of local zoning codes, complex housing construction codes, land-use restrictions, "Urban Renewal," for-profit eminent domain and municipal "development" rackets, and a host of local policies intended to keep real estate prices high and permanently rising. In a freed market, land ownership would be based entirely on labor-based homesteading and consensual transfer, rather than on military conquest, titles of nobility, sweetheart "development" deals, or eminent domain seizures, and land would tend (*ceteris paribus*) to be more widely distributed, with more small individual ownership, dramatically less expensive, with more ownership free and clear, and could as easily be based on "sweat equity" and the homesteading of unused land, without the need for any commercial cash exchange.[8]

2. **The Money Monopoly:** government control over the money supply, artificially limiting the issue of money and credit to a government-approved banking cartel. Tucker saw this not only as a source of monopoly profits for the incumbent banks, but also the source of the concentration of capital (and hence economic ownership) in the hands of a select business class: credit and access to capital were artificially restricted to those large, established businesses which the large, established banks preferred to deal with, while government-imposed specie requirements, capitalization requirements, and penalties on the circulation of alternative currencies, suppressed competition

7   Tucker (1888). For a contemporary discussion, see also Part 2 of Kevin Carson's *Studies in Mutualist Political Economy* (Charleston, SC: BookSurge 2007).

8   See also Charles Johnson, "Scratching By," ch. 41 (377-384), in this volume, along with Charles Johnson, "Urban Homesteading," *Rad Geek People's Daily* (n.p., Nov. 16, 2007) <http://radgeek.com/gt/2007/11/16/urban_home-steading> (March 13, 2011); Charles Johnson, "Enclosure Comes to Los Angeles" (n.p., June 15, 2006) <http://radgeek.com/gt/2006/06/14/enclo-sure_comes> (March 13, 2011).

from mutual credit associations, labor notes, land banks, and other means by which workers might be able to pool their own resources and access credit on more advantageous terms than those offered by commercial banks.

Tucker, in 1888, was writing about the Money Monopoly before the Federal Reserve or the conversion to a pure fiat currency, before the SEC, FDIC, TARP, Fannie, Freddie, IMF, World Bank, banking holidays, bailouts, "Too Big To Fail," and the myriad other means by which government has insulated big bankers and financiers from market consequences, often at direct taxpayer expense, and erected regulatory barriers to entry which insulate politically-approved business models from market competition. Perhaps just as importantly, in light of recent political debates, is the extent to which regulation and industry cartelization has also turned *insurance*, as well as credit, savings and investment, into a new arm of the money monopoly, with government-rigged markets directly mandating the purchase of corporate car insurance and corporate health insurance, and crowding out or shutting down the non-corporate, grassroots forms of mutual aid that could provide alternative means for securing against catastrophic expenses.

3. **The Patent Monopoly:** government grants of monopoly privileges to patent-holders and copyright holders. Tucker argued that patents and copyrights did not represent a legitimate private property claim for their holders, since it did not protect any tangible property that the patent-holder could be deprived of, but rather prohibited other market actors from peacefully using their own tangible property to offer a good or service that imitated or duplicated the product being offered by the holder of the so-called "Intellectual Property."

These prohibitions, enforced with the explicit purpose of suppressing market competition and ratcheting up prices, in order to secure a long period of monopoly profits for the IP-holder, have only dramatically escalated since Tucker's day, as the growth in the media industry, the technology industry, and scientific innovation have made politically-granted control over the *information economy* a linchpin of corporate power, with monopoly profits on "IP" now constituting more or less the entire business model of Fortune 500 companies like General Electric, Pfizer, Microsoft, or Disney. These IP monopolists have insisted on the need for nearly-unlimited government power, extending to every corner of the globe, to insulate their privileged assets from peaceful free market competition, and as a result of their legislative influence, typical copyright terms have doubled or quadrupled in length, legal sanctions have only gotten harsher, and, to crown all, mandates for massive, internationally-synchronized expansions in copyright and patent protections are now standard features embedded in neoliberal "free trade" agreements such as NAFTA, CAFTA, and KORUS FTA.

4. **The Protectionist Monopoly:** Tucker identified the protectionist tariff as a "monopoly," in the sense that it artificially protected politically-favored domestic producers from foreign competition: the tax on imports was explicitly intended to make goods more expensive for consumers when they came from the other side of a government border, thus allowing domestic producers stay in business while selling their wares at higher prices and lower quality than they could in the face of unfettered competition. Besides protecting the bottom line of domestic capitalists, protectionist monopoly also inflicted artificially high costs of living on the working class, due to the ratcheting up of the costs of consumer goods.

Of the Big Four, the Protectionist Monopoly has seen the most reconfiguration and realignment since Tucker's day; with the rise of Multi-National Corporations and political pressure in favor of neoliberal "free trade" agreements,[9] the tariff has declined noticeably in political and economic importance since the 1880s. However, tariffs remain a distorting force within limited domains (for example, the United States and European countries still maintain high tariffs on many imported agricultural goods). Moreover, the specific *mecha-*

---

9    These agreements do not actually represent "free trade;" they represent a *shift* in coercive trade barriers, not a reduction in them. While they reduce tariff rates in some industries, neoliberal "free trade" agreements typically include massive, coordinated *increases* in patent and copyright monopolies. They also are typically accompanied by the large-scale use of government-to-government loans, government land seizures, government-financed infrastructure "development" projects, and government-granted monopolies to privateering multinational corporations, carried out through multi-government alliances such as the International Monetary Fund and the World Bank. See Joe Peacott, "Free Trade *is* Fair Trade," ch. 29 (279-282), in this volume; Kevin Carson, "Free Market Reforms and the Reduction of Statism," ch. 28 (273-278), in this volume; and Charles Johnson, "'Two Words on 'Privatization,'" ch. 30 (283-288), in this volume. See also Shawn Wilbur, "Whatever Happened to (the Discourse on) Neoliberalism?," *Two Gun Mutualism & the Golden Rule* (n.p., Oct. 3, 2008) <http://libertarian-labyrinth.blogspot.com/2008/10/what-ever-happened-to-discourse-on.html> (March 13, 2011).

*nism* of import *tariffs* was much less important, for Tucker's purposes, than the overarching aim of *protecting connected incumbents from foreign competition*. In the 1880s, that meant the protectionist tariff. In the 2010s, it means a vast and complicated network of import tariffs on incoming foreign goods, *export subsidies* to outgoing domestic goods, the political manipulation of fiat currency exchange rates, and other methods for political control of the balance of international trade.

As I've tried to indicate, Tucker's Big Four remain pervasive, and at least three of those four have in fact dramatically expanded their scope and invasiveness since Tucker originally described them. But besides the expansion, and intensification, of Tucker's Four, the past century has seen the proliferation and metastatic spread of government regulatory bodies intended to re-structure markets and monitor and regiment economic transactions. If we were to try to make a similar list of all the major ways in which local, state, federal and foreign governments now intervene to protect incumbent interests and place barriers to entry against potential competitors, there's no knowing how many monopolies we'd be dealing in; but I think that there are at least five new major monopolies, in addition to Tucker's original four, and a sixth structural factor, which are worthy of special notice for their pervasiveness and importance to the overall structure of the state-regulated economy.

First, the **agribusiness monopoly:** since the New Deal, an extensive system of government cartels, USDA regulatory burdens, subsidies to *artificially increase* prices for sale in American markets, more subsidies to *artificially lower* prices for export to foreign markets, surplus buy-up programs,[10] irrigation projects, Farm-to-Market road building projects, government technical support for more mechanized and capital-intensive forms of farming, along with many other similar measures, have all converged to ratchet up food prices for consumers, to make importing and exporting produce over tremendous distances artificially attractive, to distort agricultural production towards the vegetable and animal products that can most successfully attract subsidies and government support projects, to favor large-scale monocrop cultivation over smaller-scale farming, and generally to concentrate agriculture into factory farming and industrialized agribusiness.

Second, there is the **security monopoly:** government has always ex-

---

10     In particular, the USDA's massive buy-up programs for school lunches and the military, which keep prices high and profoundly skew the agricultural markets, by encouraging the overproduction of, and providing a guaranteed captive market-of-last-resort for, low-grade meat, potatoes, dairy, and other factory-farmed commodity cash crops.

ercised a monopoly on force within its territory, but since the 1880s, government has massively expanded the size of standing military forces, paramilitary police forces, and "security" and "intelligence" agencies. The past century has, thus, seen the creation of a gigantic industry full of monopsonistic rigged markets, catering to the needs of government "security" forces and with an flourishing ecosystem of nominally "private" companies that subsist largely or entirely on tax-funded government contracts – contracts which, because they are tax funded, are coercively financed by captive workers, but controlled by government legislators and agencies. In addition to companies like Lockheed-Martin, General Dynamics, Raytheon, DynCorp, Blackwater/Xe Services, and the rest of the "military industrial complex," the security monopoly also includes the growing number of companies, such as Taser,[11] American Science & Engineering,[12] or Wackenhut/GEO Group,[13] which cater primarily to government police forces and other "Homeland Security" agencies. War taxes, police taxes or prison taxes represent a massive diversion of blood, sweat, tears and toil from peaceful workers into a parallel, violent economy controlled by government contracts and politically-connected corporations.

Third, we must account for the **infrastructure monopoly:** that is, federal, state, or local government monopolization, tax subsidies, and allocation of access to transportation infrastructure. Government builds roads and rails and airports, with extensive tax subsidies and resources allocated to government infrastructure on the basis of political pull. In addition, government cartelizes and heavily regulates local mass transit and long-distance travel, with policies tightly restricting competition and entry into taxi, bus, rail, subway, shipping, and airline transportation. These subsidies to particular forms of long-distance transportation and long-haul freight shipping provide monopoly profits to the cartelized providers. They also provide a tax-supported business opportunity for agribusiness and for big-box retailers like Wal-Mart, whose business models are enabled by, and dependent on, government subsidies to road-building and maintenance, and the resulting artificially low costs of long-haul trucking.

Fourth, there is the **communications monopoly:** just as government control of transportation and physical infrastructure has benefited incumbent, centralized corporations in retail and distribution, incumbent tele-

---

11  Manufacturer of widely-used mobile electrical torture devices for government police forces.

12  Manufacturer of widely-used "backscatter" sexual assault devices for the Transportation Security Administration.

13  Manufacturer of widely-used tax-funded corporate-run prisons for several state governments.

communications and media companies (from Viacom to AT&T to Comcast) have been able to build empires in part because access to broadcast bandwidth has been restricted and politically allocated through the FCC, while access to cable, telephone, and fiber-optic bandwidth has been tightly controlled and restricted through monopoly concessions on laying cable and fiber, which local governments' have generally granted as a monopoly to one established company for each major transmission medium.

Fifth, we might add **regulatory protectionism:** the proliferation of commercial regulations, government bureaucracy and red tape, business license fees, byzantine tax codes, government-enforced professional licensure cartels and fees (for everything from taxi-driving to hair braiding to interior design)[14] – all of which, cumulatively, tend to benefit established businesses at the expense of new upstarts, to protect those who can afford the fees and lawyers and accountants necessary to meet the requirements from competition by those who cannot, and generally to the poor out of enterpreneurial opportunities, independent professions and more autonomous alternatives to conventional wage labor.

In addition to these five new monopolies, we might also mention the structural effects of **mass criminalization, incarceration, and deportation** of socially or economically marginalized people. Activist libertarians have often condemned, on a moral or political level, the government's War on Drugs, or Border Apartheid, or other government efforts to criminalize the poor and subject them to imprisonment for victimless crimes. As well they should – these government "wars" are nothing more than massive violence and cruelty directed against innocent people. But there has not yet been enough recognition of the *structural, economic* by-products of government policies which confine, dispossess, terrorize, and stigmatize minorities, immigrants, and the poor generally. These policies lock one out of every three African-American men in a cage, often for years at a time, take away years of their working life, expose their homes, cars and money to police forfeiture proceedings, subject them to humiliating, sub-minimum wage prison labor (often outsourced to politically-connected corporations), and permanently stigmatize them as they try to reenter the labor market and civil society. These polices which constantly threaten undocumented immigrants with the threat of arrest, imprisonment, and exile from their homes and livelihoods, cutting them off from nearly all opportunities outside of immediate cash wages and exhausting under-the-table manual labor; locking away opportunities for education behind proof-of-residency requirements; and putting them constantly at the mercy of bosses, coworkers, landlords and neighbors who can threat-

14   See Johnson, "Scratching By."

en to turn them in and have them deported for retaliation, leverage, or simply for the sake of employee turnover. Such a massive system of government violence, dispossession, and constraint on livelihoods is sure to have massive impacts on the conditions under which many poor and legally-vulnerable people enter into labor markets, housing markets, and all other areas of economic life.

## WHAT ABOUT THEM POOR OL' BOSSES? WHAT ABOUT GAINS FROM TRADE AND ECONOMIES OF SCALE?

I've spent a fair amount of time discussing the general thesis that the cash-nexus is artificially expanded, and forcibly deformed, into the patterns of actually-existing capitalism, by means of government privilege to big players; and discussing the many monopolies (once the Big Four; now the Big Ten, at least) that provide some of the most pervasive and intense points of force that dispossess working people, favor big, centralized forms of business, and coercively favor capitalistic, formalized, commercialized uses of resources over non-commercialized alternatives.[15] One of the objections which may have occurred to you by now is that government intervention in the economy goes in *more than one direction*. It may be true that the monopolies Tucker and I have named tend to benefit entrenched players and conventionally capitalistic arrangements. But what about government regulations that benefit poor people (such as government welfare schemes), small players (such as, say, Small Business Administration loans), or which are supposed to regulate and control the business practices of large-scale, concentrated forms of enterprise (such as health-and-safety regulations or antitrust legislation)?

But, first, this kind of response seems to suggest an unjustified faith in the efficacy of government regulation and welfare state programs to achieve their stated ends. In fact, as I've already suggested, much of the "progressive" regulatory structure, supposedly aimed at curbing big business, has mainly served to *cartelize* big business, and to create large fixed costs which tend to drive out potential competitors from the rigged markets in which they have entrenched themselves. Historical work by Gabriel Kolko[16] and Butler

---

15    For more on the last point, see Charles Johnson, "Three Notes for the Critics of the Critics of Apologists for Wal-Mart," *Rad Geek People's Daily* (n.p., April 25, 2009) <http://radgeek.com/gt/2009/04/25/three_notes/> (June 16, 2010).

16    Gabriel Kolko, *The Triumph of Conservatism: A Reinterpretation of American*

Shaffer[17] has, I think, convincingly shown that these regulatory measures mainly served to rigidify the positions of existing market incumbents, and to bail out failing cartelists, so as to prevent freedom from "disrupting" a well-regulated market. Nor was this, generally, an accident; these measures were, most often, passed at the behest of the incumbent companies which hoped to see their competitors squashed by the compliance costs. There are good apriori reasons – from the public choice analysis of the incentives faced by politically-appointed regulators – to believe that such regulatory efforts will *always* be highly prone to capture by the concentrated interests of market incumbents, to be wielded against the dispersed interests of consumers, workers, and would-be start-up competitors.

Second, it is important to keep in mind questions of priority and scale. While I object to SBA loans, OSHA, antitrust legislation, social welfare programs, and other government interventions as much as any other free marketeer, I think that in this age of trillion-dollar bank bailouts it ought to be clear that, even if government is putting its finger on both sides of the scale, one finger is pushing down a lot harder than the other.[18]

You may also be concerned that I have had so little to say, so far, about some of the conventional explanations that free market economists have offered for the efficiency and scalability of capitalistic arrangements – arguments based, for example, on the division of labor, or on economies of scale, or the gains from trade. But *I am not denying* the value of either the division of labor, or gains from trade; I am suggesting that labor and trade might be organized along different lines than they are currently organized, in alternative forms of specialization and trade such as co-ops, worker-managed firms, or independent contracting, with comparatively less centralization of decision-making, less hierarchy, less management, and, in many cases, more trade and entrepreneurial independence among the workers involved. Centralized, capitalistic forms of organization are only one sort of cash nexus among many others. And the cash nexus itself is only one way of facilitating a division of labor and a mutually-beneficial exchange can take

*History*, 1900-1916 (New York: Free 1963)

17  Butler Shaffer, *In Restraint of Trade: The Business Campaign against Competition, 1918-1938* (Lewisburg, PA: Bucknell University Press 1997).

18  A few years back, I received a $600 check from the United States Department of the Treasury, during the tax rebate program, supposedly for the sake of economic recovery. At about the same time, AIG received an $85,000,000,000 check from the United States Department of the Treasury, also supposedly for the sake of economy recovery. But it would strain credulity to say that this means that bail-out capitalism is subsidizing the little guy *just like* how it subsidizes entrenched corporate players.

place; returning to the broader sense of "markets" as a space of social experimentation, there are all kinds of other social experiments, not necessarily based on *quid pro quo* exchanges or on cash media, that provide places for people to meet, work and swap. If the Big Ten and the Many Monopolies prove anything, it is that there are numerous areas of life in which people are not choosing to divide their labor or make trades through the medium of corporate commerce. There are many areas of life where they would rather not be spending much or any money at all, but are shoved into doing so, and shoved into doing so with a boss, landlord, or faceless corporation, when a freed market would allow them to divide their labor in other ways, trade for other things, or trade for what they need by means other than an invoice and cash on the barrelhead.

It is also common to point to economies of scale as an economic reason for believing that large, centralized corporations, industrial agribusiness, *et cetera* would survive even without the government subsidies and monopolies they currently enjoy, so long as they had a market arena to compete in. But while I'd hardly deny the importance of economies of scale, I think it is important to remember that economies of scale represent a trade-off between gains and losses. There are *dis*economies of scale, just as there are economies of scale – as scale increases, so do the costs of communication and management within the larger workforce, the costs of maintaining heavier equipment, the difficulty of accounting and efficiently allocating resources as more transactions are internalized within the firm, and the difficulty of regearing such a large mechanism to respond to new challenges from new competitors and changing market conditions.[19]

The question is not whether or not there are economies of scale; there are, and there is also a point at which the economies of scale are outweighed by the diseconomies. The question is where that point is; and whether, in a free market, the equilibrium point would tend to shift towards smaller scales, or towards larger scales. When government monopolies and rigged markets artificially encourage large, consolidated, bureaucratic forms of organization – organizations which can better afford the high fixed costs imposed by regulatory requirements, can better lobby for subsidies, can better capture regulatory bodies and use them to advance their own interests, etc. – that shifts the balance by forcing up the rewards of scale. When the same measures punish small competitors in favor of market incumbents, and especially when it punishes informal, small-scale community or personal uses of scarce resources, in favor of formalized commercial uses,

---

19     For a detailed discussion of the diseconomies of scale, see Kevin A. Carson, "Economic Calculation in the Corporate Commonwealth," ch. 22 (213-222), in this volume.

government forcibly pushes the diseconomies of scale down, by suppressing competitors who might eat the eggs of the political-economic dinosaurs. In both cases, the most pervasive and far-reaching forms of government economic intervention tend to deform economic life towards formalization, commercialization, consolidation, hyperthyroidal scale and the complex hierarchy that's needed to manage it. Not because these things are naturally demanded by economies of scale, but rather because they grow out of control when the costs of scale are socialized and the competitive pressures and alternatives burned out by government monopoly.

## IS THIS ALL JUST A SEMANTIC DEBATE?

When market anarchists come out for "free markets," but against "capitalism," when they suggest that it's important not to use the term "capitalism" to describe the system that we are for, and fit out their position with the rhetorical and social identity of the radical Left, conventionally pro-capitalist libertarians often charge that the market anarchists are just playing with words, or trying to "change the vocabulary of our [*sic*] message" in a misguided "ploy" to "appeal to people who do not share our [*sic*] economic views."[20] There is not much to say to that, except to ask just who wrote this "message" we are supposed to be sharing with the economic Right, and to point out that the use of "capitalism," in any case, really is more complicated than that. There are several meanings attached to the word, which have coexisted historically. Those meanings are often conflated and confused with each other, and capitalism1, the peculiar technical use of the term by "pro-capitalist" libertarians to refer strictly to free markets – free markets in the very broadest sense, markets as spaces of unbounded social experimentation) is only one historical use among many, neither the original use[21] nor the use that's most

---

20  Jackson Reeves, letter to Walter Block, qtd. Walter Block and Jackson Reeves, "'Capitalism' Yesterday, 'Capitalism' Today, 'Capitalism' Tomorrow, 'Capitalism' Forever," *LewRockwell.Com* (Center for Libertarian Studies, March 26, 2010) <http://www .lewrockwell.com/block/block154.html> (June 16, 2010). The letter was in response to some recent anticapitalist sentiments aired by Sheldon Richman.

21  "Capitalism," or "*capitalisme*," first appears as a term used to describe a political-economy *system* of production in French radical literature of the mid-19th century; prior to that the term was simply used to refer to the line of work that capitalists were in—that is, making money by lending money at interest, by investing in other people's businesses, or by personally owning capital and hiring labor to work it. The original uses of the term had nothing in particular to do with free markets in the factors of production. Louis

commonly used today.[22] Free market anticapitalists aren't trying to change anything; we're using the word "capitalism" in a perfectly traditional and reasonable sense, straight out of ordinary language, when we use it to describe the political privileges we're against (capitalism2) and the nasty structural consequences of those privileges (capitalism3).

But the worry at this point may be whether it's even worth it to fight over that particular patch of ground. To be sure, equivocal uses and conflation of terms is a bad thing – it's important to distinguish the different meanings of "capitalism," to be clear on what we mean, and to get clear what our interlocutors mean, when we use the term. But once you've done the distinguishing, is it worth spending any great effort on arguing about the label "capitalism," rather than just breaking out the subscripts where necessary and moving on? If the argument about "capitalism" has helped draw out some of the economic and historical points that I've been concentrating on in these remarks, then that may be of some genuine use to libertarian dialogue. But once those points are drawn out, aren't *they* the important thing, not the terminological dispute? And aren't they something that nominally pro-"capitalist" libertarians would also immediately object to, if asked? All libertarians, even nominally pro-"capitalist" libertarians, oppose corporate welfare, government monopolies, regulatory cartels, and markets rigged in favor of big business. So why worry so much about the terminology?

I certainly sympathize with the impulse; if I have to choose between debates about the word "capitalism" and debates over the state-corporatist interventions I've been discussing, I think the latter is always going to be a lot more important. When we try to understand what other people say about markets or capitalism, considerations of charity absolutely call for this kind of approach – when a libertarian writer praises "capitalism," *meaning freed markets*, or when a libertarian writer *condemns "capitalism,"* meaning corporatist privilege or boss economies, then the best thing to do is just take them on their own terms and interpret their argument accordingly.

But there's a lot to argue about here that's not just about labels, and it's

---

Blanc, in *Organisation du Travail*, defined "capitalisme" as "the appropriation of capital by some to the exclusion of others," and when Proudhon, who was in favor of free markets, wrote of "capitalisme" in *La Guerre et la Paix*, he defined it as an "Economic and social regime in which capital, the source of income, does not generally belong to those who make it work through their labour." Depending on the details of what one means by "appropriation" and "exclusion," Blanc's usage may refer to capitalism2 or capitalism3. Proudhon's definition is clearly a reference to capitalism3.

22   Michael Moore's recent film, *Capitalism: A Love Story*, is not about free markets; it's about the bail-outs.

not always clear that that's something that "we all" readily agree on. What about when it's not clear that the writer has really consistently held onto the distinction between free markets and actually-existing capitalism?[23] What about when we're not just talking about single positions on isolated policy proposals, but talking about the bigger picture of how it all works – not just the individual pieces but the gestalt picture that they form when fitted together? When, that is, it really starts to matter not only how a writer would answer a list of questions if asked, but also *which questions she thinks to ask in the first place* – which features of the situation immediately come to mind for analysis and criticism, and which features are kept left as afterthoughts? This raises the question of *paradigm cases*, of what sorts of examples we take as typical, or characteristic, or especially illustrative of what freed markets would be and how they would work.

When we're looking at the broader picture, at how political and economic structures play off of each other, we're talking about a structure that has a foreground and a background – more important and less important features. And one of the important questions is not just what may be encompassed by the *verbal definitions* given for our terminology, but also what sorts of *paradigm cases* for markets and voluntary society the terminology might suggest, and whether the cases it suggests really are good paradigm cases – whether they reveal something important about free societies, or whether they conceal or obscure it. Identifying a free market position with "capitalism" – even if you are absolutely clear that you just mean capitalism1, theoretically including all kinds of market exchange and voluntary social experimentation outside the cash nexus – offers a particular *picture* of what's important about and characteristic of a free society, and that picture tends to obscure a lot more than it reveals.

When we *picture* freed-market activity, what does it look like? Is our model something that looks a lot like business as usual, with a few changes here and there around the edges? Or something radically different, or radically *beyond* anything that currently prevails in this rigidified, monopolized market. Do we conceive of and explain markets on the model of a *commer-*

---

23    For examples, see the critical discussion in Roderick Long, "Corporations Versus the Market; or, Whip Conflation Now," ch. 20 (201-210), in this volume; Kevin Carson, "Vulgar Libertarianism, Neoliberalism, and Corporate Welfare: A Compendium of Posts," *Mutualist Blog: Free Market Anticapitalism* (n.p., Sep. 9, 2006) <http://mutualist.blogspot.com/2006/09/vulgar-libertarianism-neoliberalism.html> (March 13, 2011); Charles Johnson, "El pueblo unido jamás será vencido!" *Rad Geek People's Daily* (n.p., March 23, 2005) <http://radgeek.com/gt/2005/03/23/el_pueblo> (March 13, 2011); etc.

*cial strip mall:* sanitized, centralized, regimented, officious, and dominated by a few powerful proprietors and their short list of favored partners, to whom everyone else relates as either an employee or a consumer? Or do we instead look at the revolutionary potential of truly free markets to *make things messy* – how markets, without the pervasive control of state licensure requirements, regulation, inspections, paperwork, taxes, "fees," and the rest, so often look more like traditional image of a bazaar: decentralized, diverse, informal, flexible, pervaded by haggling, a gathering for *social* intercourse just as much as stereotypical commerce, and all of it kept together by the spontaneous order of countless small-time independent operators, who quickly and easily shift between the roles of customer, merchant, leisure-seeker, independent laborer, and more besides?[24]

When "markets" are associated with a term like "capitalism," which is *historically* so closely attached to workplace hierarchy and big business, and a term which is so *linguistically* connected with the business of professional capitalists (that is, people in the business of renting out accumulated capital), this naturally influences the kind of examples that come to mind, fetishizing the business of professionalized capitalists at the expense of more informal and simply non-commercial forms of ownership, experimentation and exchange. It tends to rig the understanding of "markets" towards an exclusive focus on the cash nexus; and it tends to rig the understanding of *the cash nexus* towards an exclusive focus on the most comfortably capitalistic – hierarchical, centralized, formalized and "businesslike" – sorts of enterprises, as if these were so many features of the natural landscape in a market, rather than the visible results of concerted government force.

Freeing the freed market from the banner of "capitalism," on the other hand, and identifying markets with the *opposition* to mercantile privilege, to the expropriation of labor, and to the resulting concentrations of wealth in the hands of a select class, brings a whole new set of considerations and examples into the foreground. These new paradigm cases for "free markets" are deeply important if they encourage a wider and richer conception of what's in a market, a conception which doesn't just *theoretically* include mutualistic alternatives and social experimentation outside the cash nexus (as some sort of bare possibility or marginal phenomenon), but actually *encourages* us to envision "markets" pervaded by these forms of free association and exchange, to see how non-capitalist and non-commercial experi-

---

24    The images of the strip mall and the bazaar are taken from my concluding paragraph in "Scratching By." Those images were inspired by and modified from Eric Raymond's use of "The Cathedral and the Bazaar" to explain and defend hacker culture and open-source software.

mentation might take on a prominent, even *explosive* role in an economy freed from the rigged markets and many monopolies of state-supported corporate capitalism.

The free market anticapitalist holds that it's precisely *because* of those rigged markets that we have the strip mall rather than the bazaar, and precisely because we have the strip mall rather than the bazaar that so many working-class folks find themselves on the skids, trapped in precarious arrangements, at the mercy of bosses, landlords, bill-collectors and insurance adjusters, reeling from sky-high medical bills or endless rent and debt, confronted by faceless corporations, hypercommercialized society, and a cold, desperate struggle to scrape by in a highly rigidified capitalists' market.

Since this cruel predicament is so central to how most people experience "the market" in everyday life, it's vital for market anarchists to clearly mark out the different, positive, disruptive possibilities markets offer for a liberated civil society. The social problem is not the fact of *market exchange* but rather the *deformation* of market exchange by hierarchy and political privilege. We must show what commerce might look like without capitalism, and what markets might look like when commercial dealings are only one kind of dealing among many, chosen where they the most positive and pleasant way to take care of things, not where they are foisted on us by grim necessity. Our words must be revolutionary words; and our banners must not be banners that bury radical alternatives underneath conservatism and privilege. They must be banners that honestly and bravely hold out the promise of radical social and economic transformation.

# PART TWO

------------

## Identities and Isms

# 5

*BradSpangler.Com* (n.p., Sep. 15, 2006)
<http://bradspangler.com/blog/ar-
chives/473> (Aug. 22, 2011).

# MARKET ANARCHISM AS STIGMERGIC SOCIALISM

## BRAD SPANGLER
## (2006)

T HE WIKIPEDIA ENTRY ON MARKET ANARCHISM HAS BEEN EVER SO SLIGHTLY BUGGING ME
for a while, but I've not been able to lay my finger upon the matter of
precisely why until now.

> Market anarchism is a philosophy opposing the state and fa-
> voring trade of private property in markets. Market anarchists
> include mutualists and anarcho-capitalists.
>
> Market anarchists include mutualists (such as Proudhon)
> and some individualist anarchists (such as Tucker), who sup-
> ported a market economy and a system of possession based
> upon labour and use. As a result of their adherence to the labor
> theory of value, they oppose profit.
>
> The term "market anarchism" is also used to describe an-
> archo-capitalism, a theory which supports a market economy,
> but unlike mutualism, does not have a labor theory of value.

As a result, it has no opposition to profit.

Agorism might be considered a branch of anarcho-capitalism or individualist anarchism/mutualism. It might be considered an attempt to reconcile anarcho-capitalism with individualist anarchism and even the rest of libertarian socialism
where possible.

After thinking about this a great deal, I've come to the conclusion that
the above exaggerates the differences between anarcho-capitalism and
mutualism as *ideologies*, but not necessarily as *movements* – an important
distinction to make. As a result, I'd like to review why I believe anarcho-
capitalism is, in some ways, incorrectly named and why this, in turn, has
resulted in an anarcho-capitalist movement consisting of a large number of
deviationists insufficient in their adherence to their own stated principles.

Once again, we must explore the various definitions of capitalism and
socialism to see why. Why, for instance, is mutualism considered "socialism" while the Rothbardian strain of market anarchist thought is "capitalism"? To understand, let's first examine the anarcho-capitalist movement as
a whole.

There are two sharply divided strands of thought within anarcho-capitalism, based on the stated rationale for a market anarchist society – the
natural law/natural rights thought of Murray Rothbard and the utilitarianism of David Friedman. To understand the differences between the two and
why they matter, let's look at Rothbard's "Do You Hate The State?"[1]

The essay explains in Rothbards own words that genuine Rothbardians
are motivated by a passion for pure and simple justice. The state and its allies are understood to be a criminal gang – an ongoing system of theft, oppression, slavery and murder. The thought of the Friedmanites, by contrast,
is a mere intellectual discourse upon what would maximise total prosperity
in a society. Utilitarianism is an academic exercise suitable for economics
textbooks. Such studies are to be welcomed to the extent that they make
justice (i.e. anarchy) more appealing to the amoral and boost our own
confidence in the workability – but to substitute utilitarianism for natural
rights theory within anarcho-capitalism is to quite literally sell out ethical
principle for a mess of pottage.

For whereas the natural-rights libertarian seeking morality and
justice cleaves militantly to pure principle, the utilitarian only
values liberty as an ad hoc expedient. And since expediency

---

1    Murray N. Rothbard, "Do You Hate the State?," *Libertarian Forum* 10.7
     (July 1977): 1+.

can and does shift with the wind, it will become easy for the utilitarian in his cool calculus of cost and benefit to plump for statism in ad hoc case after case, and thus to give principle away.

Under a strictly utiliatrian view, then, one loses sight of who the enemy is. Those who unfairly benefit from plunder, as an aggregate, will never willingly give up on it.

As an aside, the Anarchist FAQ touches on this matter, while insufficiently illuminating it. In a criticism of Friedmanite utilitarianism, Rothbard explains the problem of utilitarianism lacking an anti-state theory of property (unlike his own natural law approach). The FAQ offers an out of context excerpt from a passage that appears to give the impression that Rothbard was arguing in favor of tyranny, when in fact he was doing the exact opposite (in highlighting the shortcomings of the utilitarian approach). From the FAQ:

> Even worse, the possibility that private property can result in worse violations of individual freedom (at least of workers) than the state of its citizens was implicitly acknowledged by Rothbard. He uses as a hypothetical example a country whose King is threatened by a rising "libertarian" movement. The King responses by "employ[ing] a cunning stratagem," namely he "proclaims his government to be dissolved, but just before doing so he arbitrarily parcels out the entire land area of his kingdom to the 'ownership' of himself and his relatives." Rather than taxes, his subjects now pay rent and he can "regulate to regulate the lives of all the people who presume to live on" his property as he sees fit. Rothbard then asks:
> "Now what should be the reply of the libertarian rebels to this pert challenge? If they are consistent utilitarians, they must bow to this subterfuge, and resign themselves to living under a regime no less despotic than the one they had been battling for so long. Perhaps, indeed, more despotic, for now the king and his relatives can claim for themselves the libertarians' very principle of the absolute right of private property, an absoluteness which they might not have dared to claim before." [Op. Cit., pp. 54-5]
> So not only does the property owner have the same monopoly of power over a given area as the state, it is more despotic as it is based on the "absolute right of private property"!

And remember, Rothbard is arguing in favour of "anarcho"-capitalism"…

The passage mirrors a passage making the same point in *For a New Liberty*:

> Let us illustrate with a hypothetical example. Suppose that libertarian agitation and pressure has escalated to such a point that the government and its various branches are ready to abdicate. But they engineer a cunning ruse. Just before the government of New York state abdicates it passes a law turning over the entire territorial area of New York to become the private property of the Rockefeller family. The Massachusetts legislature does the same for the Kennedy family. And so on for each state. The government could then abdicate and decree the abolition of taxes and coercive legislation, but the victorious libertarians would now be confronted with a dilemma. Do they recognize the new property titles as legitimately private property? The utilitarians, who have no theory of justice in property rights, would, if they were consistent with their acceptance of given property titles as decreed by government, have to accept a new social order in which fifty new satraps would be collecting taxes in the form of unilaterally imposed "rent." The point is that only natural-rights libertarians, only those libertarians who have a theory of justice in property titles that does not depend on government decree, could be in a position to scoff at the new rulers' claims to have private property in the territory of the country, and to rebuff these claims as invalid.

So, that part of the Anarchist FAQ critique would appear to lead to an inaccurate perception of what Rothbard was arguing for. It applies to Friedman's version of anarcho-capitalism, and Rothbard was the one who first pointed it out – long before the Anarchist FAQ was even around.

In fact, Rothbard's natural law theory very much laid an alternative foundation for understanding of why the distribution of property under existing capitalism is unjust – because the so-called "property" of the plutocracy is typically unjustly acquired. Natural law theory and the resulting radically anti-state Rothbardian take on Lockean principles of property can potentially be expanded upon to offer a framework for the revolutionary anti-State redistribution of property – in that state granted title to property is often a fraudulent perk of the political class.

> The only genuine refutation of the Marxian case for revolution, then, is that capitalists' property is just rather than unjust, and that therefore its seizure by workers or by anyone else would in itself be unjust and criminal. But this means that we must enter into the question of the justice of property claims, and it means further that we cannot get away with the easy luxury of trying to refute revolutionary claims by arbitrarily placing the mantle of "justice" upon any and all existing property titles. Such an act will scarcely convince people who believe that they or others are being grievously oppressed and permanently aggressed against. But this also means that we must be prepared to discover cases in the world where violent expropriation of existing property titles will be morally justified, because these titles are themselves unjust and criminal.

Refer also to Rothbard's "Confiscation and the Homestead Principle." In it, he makes the case for anarcho-syndicalist style worker takeover of large enterprises that have become mammoth concentrations of capital because of markets being skewed in favor of the corporation by government favoritism. I believe he only retreated from this position because he did not see a clear path to revolution and did not trust the state to redistribute property in an ethical manner. Yet if the matter of who defines the bounds of property rights is handled in a de-statized manner with open registries for proerty claims that must stand up to popular approval if those claims will be of actual use in resolving disputes in a market anarchist "court" (i.e arbitration) system, such can and should be an organic component of market anarchist revolutionary strategy of the sort Konkin envisioned.

Compare the above with the matter of why mutualism is considered "socialism." Mutualism is considered "socialism" because of its foundation on the labor theory of value. Socialism, however, has never been a mere intellectual discourse upon why the labor theory of value was supposedly a superior line of academic thought. Socialism is not and never has been a "club." Socialists have always been motivated by a passion for social justice as best they understand it – which naturally implies that understanding is capable of being raised to a greater degree of accuracy and sophistication. The labor theory of value previously provided the chosen theoretical understanding for why and how the lower classes in society were systematically robbed by the upper classes. That understanding of existing capitalist society as systematic theft (oppression) and speculation about how to achieve a more just society has, I contend, always been the defining quality of all earnest socialists.

It is my contention that Rothbardian anarcho-capitalism is misnamed because it is actually a variety of socialism, in that it offers an alternative understanding of existing capitalism (or any other variety of statism) as systematic theft from the lower classes and envisions a more just society without that oppression. Rather than depending upon the the labor theory of value to understand this systematic theft, Rothbardian market anarchism utilizes natural law theory and Lockean principles of property and self-ownership taken to their logical extreme as an alternative framework for understanding and combating oppression.

I'll say it – although his cultural roots in the Old Right would, if he were still alive, admittedly cause him fits to be characterized as such, Murray Rothbard was a visionary socialist. The inconsistencies in Rothbardian thought derive from Rothbard's failure to fully develope libertarian class theory and a theory of revolution – work that was largely completed within the Rothbardian tradition by Konkin.

Because the market anarchist society would be one in which the matter of systematic theft has been addressed and rectified, market anarchism (with the exception of Friedmanite utilitarian anarcho-capitalism) is best understood a new variety of socialism – a stigmergic socialism. Stigmergy is a fancy word for systems in which a natural order emerges from the individual choices made by the autonomous components of a collective within the sphere of their own self-sovereignty. To the extent coercion skews markets by distorting the decisions of those autonomous components (individual people), it ought to be seen that a truly free market (a completely stigmergic economic system) necessarily implies anarchy, and that any authentic collectivism is necessarily delineated in its bounds by the the natural rights of the individuals composing the collective.

In conclusion, lack of adherence to the labor theory of value does not mean Rothbardian market anarchists are not socialist. The labor theory of value served as an attempted illumination of the systematic theft the lower classes have always suffered from under statism. Rothbard's natural law theory and radically anti-state version of Lockean property rights theory serves the same role.

I would suggest, as I have before, that no anarchism is 'capitalist' if capitalism is understood as the status quo and that it is oppressive in an economic sense as a result of the monopolization of capital.

Rothbardian market anarchism as a body of theory, particularly as contextually modified by Konkin's theories of revolution and class, *answers* the social question (i.e. it addresses the problem of 'capitalism') and is therefore just as much a part of the libertarian socialist tradition as Tuckerite/Proudhonian mutualism. In some ways, it's very nearly the same thing explained with different rhetoric.

- Abolition of state granted privilege? Check.
- Labor-based ownership rights? Check.
- Redistribution of property as a result of the above? Check. (An unavoidable consequence of the rise of a non-state system of law not beholden to fake grants of title to politically favored interests).

We're socialists. Get over it.

In fact, it could even be argued that we're "redder" in the sense that having a theory of revolution that Tucker and Proudhon never had makes us a tad more insurrectionary. Anarcho-socialism is a misnomer. Anarchism (all of anarchism) *is* libertarian socialism.

Anarcho-socialism is a misnomer. Anarchism (all of anarchism) is libertarian socialism.

The argument that anarcho-capitalism is not anarchism because it's "capitalist" is shown to be wrong once capitalism is properly understood as state driven monopolization of capital. Rothbardian market anarchism is socialism because it meets the most basic (and original) definition of socialism – attempting to answer "the social question." (It's actually anti-capitalist, and therefore misnamed.)

Most of what we've come to see as indicators of socialist thought (hostility to markets & true [labor-based] property rights, pro-state authority – are actually indicative of a subset of socialist thought that gained influence. The labor theory of value was simply the leading edge of economic theory at the time in the 1800's. Now it's subjective value theory and the Austrian school generally. We're still answering the social question. Our answer is simple: free the market!

## 6

*Liberty* 6.6 (March 8, 1890): 4.

# ARMIES THAT OVERLAP

## *BENJAMIN R. TUCKER*
## *(1890)*

OF LATE THE *TWENTIETH CENTURY* HAS BEEN DOING A GOOD DEAL IN THE WAY OF definition. Now, definition is very particular business, and it seems to me that it is not always performed with due care in the *Twentieth Century* office.

Take this, for instance: A Socialist is one who believes that each industry should be coordinated for the mutual benefit of all concerned under a government by physical force.

It is true that writers of reputation have given definitions of Socialism not differing in any essential from the foregoing – among others, General Walker. But it has been elaborately proven in these columns that General Walker is utterly at sea when he talks about either Socialism or Anarchism. As a matter of fact this definition is fundamentally faulty, and correctly defines only State Socialism.

An analogous definition in another sphere would be this: Religion is belief in the Messiahship of Jesus. Supposing this to be a correct definition of the Christian religion, nonetheless it is manifestly incorrect as a definition of religion itself. The fact that Christianity has overshadowed all other forms of religion in this part of the world gives it no right to a monopoly of the religious idea. Similarly, the fact that State Socialism during the last decade or two has overshadowed other forms of Socialism gives it no right to a monopoly of the Socialistic idea.

Socialism, as such, implies neither liberty nor authority. The word itself implies nothing more than harmonious relationship. In fact, it is so broad a term that it is difficult of definition. I certainly lay claim to no special authority or competence in the matter. I simply maintain that the word Socialism having been applied for years, by common usage and consent, as a generic term to various schools of thought and opinion, those who try to define it are bound to seek the common element of all these schools and make it stand for that, and have no business to make it represent the specific nature of any one of them. The *Twentieth Century* definition will not stand this test at all.

Perhaps here is one that satisfies it: Socialism is the belief that progress is mainly to be effected by acting upon man through his environment rather than through man upon his environemnt.

I fancy that this will be criticised as too general, and I am inclined to accept the criticism. It manifestly includes all who have any title to be called Socialists, but possibly it does not exclude all who have no such title.

Let us narrow it a little: Socialism is the belief that the next important step in progress is a change in man's environment of an economic character that shall include the abolition of every privilege whereby the holder of wealth acquires an anti-social power to compel tribute.

I doubt not that this definition can be much improved, and suggestions looking to that end will be interesting; but it is at least an attempt to cover all the forms of protest against the existing usurious economic system. I have always considered myself a member of the great body of Socialists, and I object to being read out of it or defined out of it by General Walker, Mr. Pentecost, or anybody else, simply because I am not a follower of Karl Marx.

Take now another *Twentieth Century* definition – that of Anarchism. I have not the number of the paper in which it was given, and cannot quote it exactly. But it certainly made belief in co-operation an essential of Anarchism. This is as erroneous as the definition of Socialism. Co-operation is no more an essential of Anarchism than force is of Socialism. The fact that the majority of Anarchists believe in co-operation is not what makes them Anarchists, just as the fact that the majority of Socialists believe in force is not what makes them Socialists. Socialism is neither for nor against liberty; Anarchism is for liberty, and neither for nor against anything else. Anarchy is the mother of co-operation – yes, just as liberty is the mother of order; but, as a matter of definition, liberty is not order nor is Anarchism cooperation.

I define Anarchism as the belief in the greatest amount of liberty compatible with equality of liberty; or, in other words, as the belief in every liberty except the liberty to invade.

It will be observed that, according to the *Twentieth Century* definitions, Socialism excludes Anarchists, while, according to Liberty's definitions, a Socialist may or may not be an Anarchist, and an Anarchist may or may not be a Socialist. Relaxing scientific exactness, it may be said, briefly and broadly, that Socialism is a battle with usury and that Anarchism is a battle with authority. The two armies – Socialism and Anarchism – are neither coextensive nor exclusive; but they overlap. The right wing of one is the left wing of the other. The virtue and superiority of the Anarchistic Socialist – or Socialistic Anarchist, as he may prefer to call himself – lies in the fact that he fights in the wing that is common to both. Of course there is a sense in which every Anarchist may be said to be a Socialist virtually, inasmuch as usury rests on authority, and to destroy the latter is to destroy the former. But it scarcely seems proper to give the name Socialist to one who is such unconsciously, neither desiring, intending, nor knowing it.

## 7

*The Twentieth Century* 6.15 (June 18,
1891): 3-6.

# THE INDIVIDUALIST AND THE COMMUNIST
## A Dialogue

## ROSA SLOBODINSKY AND VOLTAIRINE DE CLEYRE
## (1891)

INDIVIDUALIST: "OUR HOST IS ENGAGED AND REQUESTS THAT I INTRODUCE MYSELF TO — I BEG YOUR pardon, sir, but have I not the pleasure of meeting the Communist speaker who addressed the meeting on Blank street last evening?"

**Communist:** "Your face seems familiar to me, too."

**Indv.:** "Doubtless you may have seen me there, or at some kindred place. I am glad at the opportunity to talk with you as your speech proved you to be somewhat of a thinker. Perhaps – "

**Com.:** "Ah, indeed, I recognize you now. You are the apostle of capitalistic Anarchism!"

**Indv.:** "Capitalistic Anarchism? Oh, yes, if you choose to call it so. Names are indifferent to me; I am not afraid of bugaboos. Let it be so, then, capitalistic Anarchism."

**Com.:** "Well, I will listen to you. I don't think your arguments will have much effect, however. With which member of your Holy Trinity will you begin: free land, free money, or free competition?"

**Indv.:** "Whichever you prefer."

**Com.:** "Then free competition. Why do you make that demand? Isn't competition free now ?"

**Indv.:** "No. But one of the three factors in production is free. Laborers are free to compete among themselves, and so are capitalists to a certain extent. But between laborers and capitalists there is no competition whatever, because through governmental privilege granted to capital, whence the volume of the currency and the rate of interest is regulated, the owners of it are enabled to keep the laborers dependent on them for employment, so making the condition of wage-subjection perpetual. So long as one man, or class of men, are able to prevent others from working for themselves because they cannot obtain the means of production or capitalize their own products, so long those others are not free to compete freely with those to whom privilege gives the means. For instance, can you see any competition between the farmer and his hired man? Don't you think he would prefer to work for himself? Why does the farmer employ him? Is it not to make some profit from his labor? And does the hired man give him that profit out of pure good nature? Would he not rather have the full product of his labor at his own disposal?"

**Com.:** "And what of that? What does that prove?"

**Indv.:** "I am coming to that directly. Now, does this relation between the farmer and his man in any way resemble a cooperative affair between equals, free to compete, but choosing to work together for mutual benefit? You know it does not. Can't you see that since the hired man does not willingly resign a large share of his product to his employer (and it is out of human nature to say he does), there must be something which forces him to do it? Can't you see that the necessity of an employer is forced upon him by his lack of ability to command the means of production? He cannot employ himself, therefore he must sell his labor at a disadvantage to him who controls the land and capital. Hence he is not free to compete with his employer any more than a prisoner is free to compete with his jailer for fresh air.

**Com.:** "Well, I admit that much. Certainly the employee cannot compete with his employer."

**Indv.:** "Then you admit that there is not free competition in the present state of society. In other words, you admit that the laboring class are not free to compete with the holders of capital, because they have not, and cannot get, the means of production. Now for your 'what of that?' It follows that if they had access to land and opportunity to capitalize the product of their labor they would either employ themselves, or, if employed by others, their wages, or remuneration, would rise to the full product of their toil, since no one would work for another for less than he could obtain by working for himself."

**Com.:** "But your object is identical with that of Communism! Why all this to convince me that the means of production must be taken from the hands of the few and given to all? Communists believe that; it is precisely what we are fighting for."

**Indv.:** "You misunderstand me if you think we wish to take from or give to any one. We have no scheme for regulating distribution. We substitute nothing, make no plans. We trust to the unfailing balance of supply and demand. We say that with equal opportunity to produce, the division of product will necessarily approach equitable distribution, but we have no method of 'enacting' such equalization."

**Com.:** "But will not some be strong and skillful, others weak and un-skillful? Will not one-deprive the other because he is more shrewd?"

**Indv.:** "Impossible! Have I not just shown you that the reason one man controls another's manner of living is because he controls the opportunities to produce? He does this through a special governmental privilege. Now, if this privilege is abolished, land becomes free, and ability to capitalize products removing interest, and one man is stronger or shrewder than another, he nevertheless can make no profit from that other's labor, because he cannot stop him from employing himself. The cause of subjection is removed."

**Com.:** "*You* call that equality! That one man shall have more than others simply because he is stronger or smarter? Your system is no better than the present. What are we struggling against but that very inequality in people's possessions?"

**Indv.:** "But what is equality? Does equality mean that I shall enjoy what you have produced? By no means. Equality simply means the freedom of every individual to develop all his being, without hindrance from another, be he stronger or weaker."

**Com.:** "What! You will have the weak person suffer because he is weak? He may need as much, or more, than a strong one, but if he is not able to produce it what becomes of his equality?"

**Indv.:** "I have nothing against your dividing your product with the weaker man if you desire to do so."

**Com.:** "There you are with charity again. Communism wants no charity."

**Indv.:** I have often marveled on the singularity of Communistic mathematics. My act you call charity, our act is not charity. If one person does a kind act you stigmatize it; if one plus one, summed up and called a commune, does the same thing, you laud it. By some species of alchemy akin to the transmutation of metals, the arsenic of charity becomes the gold of justice! Strange calculation! Can you not see that you are running from a bugaboo again? You change the name, but the character of an action is not altered by the number of people participating in it."

**Com.:** "But it is not the same action. For me to assist you out of pity is the charity of superior possession to the inferior. But to base society upon the principle: 'From each according to his capacity, and to each according to his needs' is not charity in any sense."

**Indv.:** "That is a finer discrimination than logic can find any basis for. But suppose that, for the present, we drop the discussion of charity, which is really a minor point, as a further discussion will show."

**Com.:** "But I say it is very important. See! Here are two workmen. One can make five pair of shoes a day; the other, perhaps, not more than three. According to you, the less rapid workmen will be deprived of the enjoyments of life, or at any rate will not be able to get as much as the other, because of a natural inability, a thing not his fault, to produce as much as his competitor."

**Indv.:** "It is true that under our present conditions, there are such differences in productive power. But these, to a large extent, would be annihilated by the development of machinery and the ability to use it in the absence of privilege. Today the majority of trade-people are working at uncongenial occupations. Why? Because they have neither the chance for finding out for what they are adapted, nor the opportunity of devoting themselves to it if they had. They would starve to death while searching; or, finding it, would only bear the disappointment of being kept outside the ranks of an already overcrowded pathway of life. Trades are, by force of circumstances, what formerly they were by law, matters of inheritance. I am a tailor because by father was a tailor, and it was easier for him to introduce me to that mode of making a living than any other, although I have no special adaptation for it. But postulating equal chances, that is free access and non-interest bearing capital, when a man finds himself unable to make shoes as well or as rapidly as his co-worker, he would speedily seek a more congenial occupation."

**Com.:** "And he will be traveling from one trade to another like a tramp after lodgings!"

**Indv.:** "Oh no; his lodgings will be secure! When you admitted that competition is not now free, did I not say to you that when it becomes so, one of two things must happen: either the laborer will employ himself, or the contractor must pay him the full value of his product. The result would be increased demand for labor. Able to employ himself, the producer will get the full measure of his production, whether working independently, by contract, or cooperatively, since the competition of opportunities, if I may so present it, would destroy the possibility of profits. With the reward of labor raised to its entire result, a higher standard of living will necessarily follow; people will want more in proportion to their intellectual development; with the gratification of desires come new wants, all of which guarantees constant labor-demand. Therefore, even your trades-tramp will be sure of his existence.

"But you must consider further that the business of changing trades is no longer the difficult affair it was formerly. Years ago, a mechanic, or laborer, was expected to serve from four to seven years' apprenticeship. No one was a thorough workman until he knew all the various departments of his trade. Today the whole system of production is revolutionized. Men become specialists. A shoemaker, for instance, spends his days in sewing one particular seam. The result is great rapidity and proficiency in a comparatively short apace of time. No great amount of strength or skill is required; the machine furnishes both. Now, you will readily see that, even supposing an individual changes his vocation half a dozen times, he will not travel very long before he finds that to which he is adapted, and in which he can successfully compete with others."

**Com.:** "But admitting this, don't you believe there will always be some who can produce more than their brothers? What is to prevent their obtaining advantages over the less fortunate?"

**Indv.:** "Certainly I do believe there are such differences in ability, but that they will lead to the iniquity you fear I deny. Suppose A does produce more than B, does he in anyway injure the latter so long as he does not prevent B from applying his own labor to exploit nature, with equal facilities as himself, either by self-employment or by contract with others?'"

**Com.:** "Is that what you call right? Will that produce mutual fellowship among human beings? When I see that you are enjoying things which I cannot hope to get, what think you will be my feelings toward you? Shall I not envy and hate you, as the poor do the rich today."

**Indv.:** "Why, will you hate a man because he has finer eyes or better health than you? Do you want to demolish a person's manuscript because he excels you in penmanship? Would you cut the extra length from Samson's hair, and divide it around equally among al short-haired people? Will you share a slice from the poet's genius and put it in the common storehouse so everybody can go and take some? If there happened to be a handsome woman in your neighborhood who devotes her smiles to your brother, shall you get angry and insist that they be 'distributed according to the needs' of the Commune? The differences in natural ability are not, in freedom, great enough to injure any one or disturb the social equilibrium. No one man can produce more than three others; and even granting that much you can see that it would never create the chasm which lies between Vanderbilt and the switchman on his tracks."

**Com.:** "But in establishing equal justice, Communism would prevent even the possibility of injustice."

**Indv.:** "Is it justice to take from talent to reward incompetency? Is it justice to virtually say that the tool is not to the toiler, nor the product to the producer, but to others? Is it justice to rob toil of incentive? The justice you seek lies not in such injustice, where material equality could only be attained at the dead level of mediocrity. As freedom of contract enlarges, the nobler sentiments and sympathies invariably widen. With freedom of access to land and to capital, no glaring inequality in distribution could result. No workman rises far above or sinks much below the average day's labor. Nothing but the power to enslave through controlling opportunity to utilize labor force could ever create such wide differences as we now witness."

**Com.:** "Then you hold that your system will practically result in the same equality Communism demands. Yet, granting that, it will take a hundred years, or a thousand, perhaps, to bring it about. Meanwhile people are starving. Communism doesn't propose to wait. It proposes to adjust things here and now; to arrange matters more equitably while we are here to see it, and not wait till the sweet impossible sometime that our great, great grand children may see the dawn of. Why can't you join in with us and help us to do something?"

**Indv.:** "Yea, we hold that comparative equality will obtain, but pre-arrangement, institution, 'direction' can never bring the desired result – free society. Waving the point that any arrangement is a blow at progress, it really is an impossible thing to do. Thoughts, like things, grow. You cannot jump from the germ to perfect tree in a moment. No system of society can be instituted today which will apply to the demands of the future; that, under freedom will adjust itself. This is the essential difference between Communism and cooperation. The one fixes, adjusts, arranges things, and tends to the rigidity which characterizes the cast off shells of past societies; the other trusts to the unfailing survival of the fittest, and the broadening of human sympathies with freedom; the surety that that which is in the line of progress tending toward the industrial ideal, will, in a free field, obtain by force of its superior attraction. Now, you must admit, either that there will be under freedom, different social arrangements in different societies, some Communistic, others quite the reverse, and that competition will necessarily rise between them, leaving to results to determine which is the best, or you must crush competition, institute Communism, deny freedom, and fly in the face of progress. What the world needs, my friend, is not new methods of instituting things, but abolition of restrictions upon opportunity."

## 8

*The Twentieth Century* 9.9 (Sep. 1, 1892):
10-11.

# A GLANCE AT COMMUNISM

## VOLTAIRINE DE CLEYRE
## (1893)

"Cast thy bread upon the waters,
Find it after many days."

TWO YEARS AGO, IN A LITTLE UPTOWN PARLOR, THE HOME OF A PHILADELPHIA WEAVER, a group of inquirers after truth were wont to assemble bi-weekly for the discussion of "Communism vs. Individualism." There were generally present some fifteen Communists and five or six Individualists. Let it be here admitted that while all were earnestly seeking truth, each side was pretty thoroughly convinced that the other was searching in the wrong direction, and as near as I am able to ascertain we are all of the same opinion still. However, in the course of a year some crumbs of the bread floated into sight in the shape of a dialogue presenting the substance of those discussions, which appeared in the *Twentieth Century*.[1] Many more days again passed, and now a new fragment, in the shape of a criticism of the dialogue by M. Zametkin in the *People* of July 17, drifts in with the tide.

---

1    See Voltairine de Cleyre and Rosa Slobodinsky, "The Individualist and the Communist: A Dialogue," ch. 7 (97-102), in this volume.

In attempting a brief reply to this criticism I do not presume to answer for my co-writer, Miss Slobodinsky. Being an Individualist of the ex-quoted stamp myself, I am in nowise authorized to speak for the "school." That is the advantage I possess over my critic. Individualism (without quotes) may very comfortably be interpreted as a general name for persons bound to agree upon only one thing, which is that they are not bound to agree on anything else. But when one adds Communist one begins to represent a creed common to a good many others; and if one doesn't represent it correctly, one must immediately recant or – be excommunicated. I suspect the arguments presented by "the imaginary Communist," which were really a condensation of those given by fifteen actual Communists in the discussions before mentioned, would be deemed heretical by Mr. Zametkin (in which case he must take to quotation marks), for it is well known that Communism itself has two individuals within its folds known as the State Communist and the Free Communist. Now, my friends, of whom the imaginary Communist was a composite, and who will be much surprised to learn on good Communistic authority that they are only straw men, belong to the latter variety sometimes called Anarchist-Communists. An Anarchist-Communist is a person who is a man first and a Communist afterward. He generally gets into a great many irreconcilable situations at once, believes that property and competition must die yet admits he has no authority to kill them, contends for equality and in the same breath denies its possibility, hates charity and yet wishes to make society one vast Sheltering Arms, and, in short, very generally rides two horses going in opposite directions at the same time. He is not usually amenable to logic; but he has a heart forty or fifty times too large for nineteenth century environments, and in my opinion is worth just that many cold logicians who examine society as a naturalist does a beetle, and impale it on their syllogisms in the same manner as the Emperor Domitian impaled flies on a bodkin for his own amusement. Besides, a free Communist when driven into a corner always holds to freedom first. The State Communist, on the other hand, is logical. He believes in authority, and says so. He ridicules a freedom for the individual which he believes inimical to the interests of the majority. He cries: "Down with property and competition," and means it. For the one he prescribes "take it" and for the other "suppress it." That is very frank.

Now to the "one point" of criticism, viz: the ill-adjustment of supply to demand in the case of free competition, resulting in a deficiency once in a thousand cases, and over-production the rest of the time – either of which is bad economy. Communism, I infer, would create a general supervisory board, with branch offices everywhere, which should proceed with a general kind of census-taking regarding the demand for every possible product of manufacture, of agriculture, of lumber, of minerals, for every improvement in education, amusement or religion. "Madam, about how many balls do your boys lose annually over the neighbors' fence? How many buttons do your little girls tear off their frocks? Sir, how many bottles of beer do you stow away in your cellar weekly for Sunday use? Miss, have you a lover? If so, how often do you write him, and how many sheets of paper do you use for each letter? How many gallons of oil do you use in the parlor lamp when you sit up late? This is not intended as personal, but merely to obtain correct statistics upon which to base next year's output of balls, buttons: beer, paper, oil, etc. Mr. Storekeeper, show me your books, that the government may make sure you sell no more than the prescribed quantity. Mr. Gatekeeper, how many people were admitted to the Zoological Garden last week? Two thousand? At the present ratio of increase the government will supply a new animal in six months. Mr. Preacher, your audiences are decreasing. We must inquire into the matter. If the demand is not sufficient, we must abolish you." Just what means would be taken by the Commune in case of a natural deficiency, as, for instance, the partial failure of the West Pennsylvania gas wells, to compel the obstreperous element to yield the "prescribed quantity," I can only conjecture. It might officially order an invention to take the place of the required commodity. Failing this, I do not know what plan would be adopted to preserve the equivalence of labor costs in exchange and have everybody satisfied. Omniscience, however, might provide a way. The competitive law is that the price of a shortened commodity goes up. Free competition would prevent artificial shortening; but if nature went into the business the commodity would certainly exact a premium in exchange, until some substitute had diminished the demand for it. "Ah," cries Communism, "injustice." To whom? "The fellows who were robbed in exchange." And you, what will you do? Exchange labor equivalents to the first comers, and let the rest go without? But what then becomes of the equal right of the others, who may have been very anxious to give more in this last case where is the injustice? As our critic observes, however, deficiency is not the greatest trouble, especially natural deficiency. The main thing is, must we be licensed, protected, regulated, labeled, taxed, confiscated, spied upon, and generally meddled with, in order that correct statistics may be obtained and a "quantity prescribed;" or may we trust to the producers to look out for their own interests sufficiently to avoid understocked and overstocked markets? Whether we may expect provision and order from those concerned, or be condemned to accept a governmental bill of fare from those not concerned. For my part, sooner than have a meddlesome bureaucracy sniffing around in my kitchen, my laundry, my dining room, my study, to find out what I eat, what I wear, how my table is set, how many times I wash myself, how many books I have, whether my pictures are "moral" or "immoral," what I waste, etc., ad nauseam, after the manner of ancient Peru and Egypt, I had rather a few thousand cabbages should rot, even if they happened to be my cabbages.

It is possible I might learn something from that.

*Philadelphia, Pa.*

# 9

(Tulsa, OK. Tulsa Alliance of the Libertarian Left 2011).

# ADVOCATES OF FREED MARKETS SHOULD OPPOSE CAPITALISM

*GARY CHARTIER*
*(2010)*

## I. INTRODUCTION

DEFENDERS OF FREED MARKETS HAVE GOOD REASON TO IDENTIFY THEIR POSITION AS A species of "anticapitalism."[1] To explain why, I distinguish three potential meanings of "capitalism" before suggesting that people committed to freed markets should oppose capitalism in my second and third senses. Then, I offer reasons for using "capitalism" to tag some of the social arrangements to which freed-market advocates should object.

---

1  For "*freed* markets," see William Gillis, "The Freed Market," ch. 1 (19-20), in this volume; for "free market anticapitalism," see Kevin A. Carson, *Mutualist Blog: Free Market Anticapitalism* (n.p.) <http://mutualist .blogspot.com> (Dec. 31, 2009).

## II. THREE SENSES OF "CAPITALISM"

There are at least three distinguishable senses of "capitalism":[2]

captalism₁    an economic system that features personal property rights and voluntary exchanges of goods and services

capitalism₂    an economic system that features a symbiotic relationship between big business and government

capitalism₃    rule – of workplaces, society, and (if there is one) the state – by *capitalists* (that is, by a relatively small number of people who control investable wealth and the means of production)[3]

Capitalism₁ just *is* a freed market; so if "anticapitalism" meant opposition to captalism₁, "free-market anticapitalism" would be oxymoronic. But proponents of free-market anticapitalism aren't opposed to capitalism₁; in-

---

2    Cp. Charles Johnson, "Anarquistas por La Causa," *Rad Geek People's Daily* (n.p., March 31, 2005) <http://radgeek.com/gt/2005/03/31/anarquistas_por/> (Dec. 31, 2009); Roderick T. Long, "POOTMOP Redux," *Austro-Athenian Empire* (n.p., June 22, 2009) <http://aaeblog.com/2009/06/22/pootmop-redux/> (Dec. 31, 2009); Fred Foldvary, "When Will Michael Moore Nail Land Speculators?," *The Progress Report* (n.p., Oct. 19, 2009) <http://www.progress.org/2009/fold635.htm> (Jan. 18, 2010). "Capitalism" in Johnson's third sense refers to "boss-directed labor," while Long's parallel expression, "capitalism-2," denotes "control of the means of production by someone other than the workers—i.e., by capitalist owners." Foldvary's parallel proposal is "exploitation of labor by the big owners of capital." I am inclined to think that many of those who employ "capitalism" in the pejorative sense intend it to encompass the dominance by capitalists of all social institutions, and not just workplaces, though they doubtless see societal dominance and workplace dominance as connected. At any rate, supposing that they do may provide a slender justification for distinguishing my typology from the ones offered by Johnson, Long, and Foldvary. For an earlier discussion by a libertarian of the inherently ambiguous character of "capitalism," see Clarence B. Carson, "Capitalism: Yes and No," *The Freeman: Ideas on Liberty* 35.2 (Feb. 1985): 75-82 (Foundation for Economic Education) <http://www.thefreemanonline.org/columns/capitalism-yes-and-no> (March 12, 2010); thanks to Sheldon Richman for bringing this article to my attention.

3    While capitalism₂ obtains whenever business and the state are in bed together, under capitalism₃ business is clearly on top.

stead, they object either to capitalism$_2$ or to both capitalism$_2$ and capitalism$_3$.[4]

Many people seem to employ definitions that combine elements from these distinct senses of "capitalism." Both enthusiasts for and critics of capitalism seem too often to mean by the word something like "an economic system that features personal property rights and voluntary exchanges of goods and services – and *therefore, predictably*, also rule by capitalists." But there's good reason to challenge the assumption that dominance by a small number of wealthy people is in any sense a likely feature of a freed market. Such dominance, I suggest, is probable only when force and fraud *impede* economic freedom.

## III. WHY CAPITALISM$_2$ AND CAPITALISM$_3$ ARE INCONSISTENT WITH FREED-MARKET PRINCIPLES

*A. Introduction*

Capitalism$_2$ and capitalism$_3$ are both inconsistent with freed-market principles: capitalism$_2$ because it involves direct interference with market freedom, capitalism$_3$ because it depends on such interference – both past and ongoing – and because it flies in the face of the general commitment to freedom that underlies support for market freedom in particular.

---

4    It is unclear when "capitalism" was first employed (the *Oxford English Dictionary* identifies William Makepeace Thackeray as the earliest user of the term: see *The Newcomes: Memoirs of a Most Respectable Family*, 2 vols. [London: Bradbury 1854–5] 2:75). By contrast, "capitalist" as a pejorative has an older history, appearing at least as early as 1792, and figuring repeatedly in the work of the free-market socialist Thomas Hodgskin: see, *e.g.*, *Popular Political Economy: Four Lectures Delivered at the London Mechanics Institution* (London: Tait 1827) 5, 51-2, 120, 121, 126, 138, 171 ("greedy capitalists"!), 238-40, 243, 245-9, 253-7, 265; *The Natural and Artificial Right of Property Contrasted: A Series of Letters, Addressed without Permission to H. Brougham, Esq. M.P. F.R.S.* (London: Steil 1832) 15, 44, 53, 54, 67, 87, 97-101, 134-5, 150, 155, 180. The pejorative use occurs nearly eighty times throughout the thirty-odd pages of Hodgskin's *Labour Defended against the Claims of Capital, or, The Unproductiveness of Capital Proved* (London: Knight 1825). It is also possible to find "capitalist" employed in less-than-flattering ways by another noted classical liberal: see John Taylor, *Tyranny Unmasked* (Washington: Davis 1822).

### B. Capitalism₂ Involves Direct Interference with Market Freedom

Capitalism$_2$ is clearly inconsistent with captalism$_1$, and so with a freed market. Under capitalism$_2$, politicians interfere with personal property rights and voluntary exchanges of goods and services to enrich themselves and their constituents, *and* big businesses influence politicians in order to foster interference with personal property rights and voluntary exchanges to enrich themselves and their allies.

### C. Capitalism₃ Depends on Past and Ongoing Interference with Market Freedom

There are three ways in which capitalism$_3$ might be understood to be inconsistent with captalism$_1$, and so with a freed market. The first depends on a plausible, even if contestable, view of the operation of markets. Call this view Markets Undermine Privilege (MUP). According to MUP, in a freed market, absent the kinds of privileges afforded the (usually well-connected) beneficiaries of state power under capitalism$_2$, wealth would be widely distributed and large, hierarchical businesses would prove inefficient and wouldn't survive.

Both because most people don't like working in hierarchical work environments and because flatter, more nimble organizations would be much more viable than large, clunky ones without government support for big businesses, most people in a freed market would work as independent contractors or in partnerships or cooperatives. There would be far fewer large businesses, those that still existed likely wouldn't be as large as today's corporate behemoths, and societal wealth would be widely dispersed among a vast number of small firms.

Other kinds of privileges for the politically well connected that tend to make and keep people poor – think occupational licensure and zoning laws, for instance – would be absent from a freed market.[5] So ordinary people, even ones at the bottom of the economic ladder, would be more likely to enjoy a level of economic security that would make it possible for them to opt out of employment in unpleasant working environments, including big businesses. And because a free society wouldn't feature a government with the supposed right, much less the capacity, to interfere with personal

---

5   For a devastating critique of rules—often supported by politicians beholden to wealthy and well connected people who expect to benefit from them—that systematically make and keep people poor, see Charles Johnson, "Scratching By: How Government Creates Poverty As We Know It," *The Freeman: Ideas on Liberty* 57.10 (Dec. 2007): 33-8 (Foundation for Economic Education) <http://www.thefreemanonline.org/featured/scratching-by-how-government-creates-poverty-as-we-know-it> (Jan. 2, 2010).

property rights and voluntary exchanges, those who occupy the top of the social ladder in capitalism$_3$ wouldn't be able to manipulate politicians to gain and maintain wealth and power in a freed market, so the ownership of the means of production wouldn't be concentrated in a few hands.

In addition to ongoing interference with market freedom, MUP suggests that capitalism$_3$ would not be possible without past acts of injustice on a grand scale. And there *is* extensive evidence of massive interference with property rights and market freedom, interference that has led to the impoverishment of huge numbers of people, in England, the United States, and elsewhere.[6] Freed-market advocates should thus object to capitalism$_3$ because capitalists are *able* to rule only in virtue of large-scale, state-sanctioned violations of legitimate property rights.

### D. Support for Capitalism$_3$ is Inconsistent with Support for the Underlying Logic of Freedom

Capitalism$_3$ might also be understood to be inconsistent with captalism$_1$ in light of the underlying logic of support for freed markets. No doubt some people favor personal property rights and voluntary exchanges – captalism$_1$ – for their own sake, without trying to integrate support for captalism$_1$ into a broader understanding of human life and social interaction. For others, however, support for captalism$_1$ reflects an underlying principle of respect for personal autonomy and dignity. Those who take this view – advocates of what I'll call Comprehensive Liberty (CL) – want to see people free to develop and flourish as they choose, in accordance with their own preferences (provided they don't aggress against others). Proponents of CL value not just freedom from aggression, but also freedom from the kind of social pressure people can exert because they or others have engaged in or benefited from aggression, *as well as* freedom from non-aggressive but unreasonable – perhaps petty, arbitrary – social pressure that constrains people's options and their capacities to shape their lives as they like.

Valuing different kinds of freedom emphatically isn't the same as approving the same kinds of remedies for assaults on these different kinds of freedom. While most advocates of CL aren't pacifists, they don't want to see

---

6    Cp. Albert Jay Nock, *Our Enemy the State* (New York: Morrow 1935); Kevin A. Carson, "The Subsidy of History," *The Freeman: Ideas on Liberty* 58.5 (June 2008): 33-8 (Foundation for Economic Education) <http://www.thefreemanonline.org/featured/the-subsidy-of-history> (Dec. 31, 2009); Joseph R. Stromberg, "The American Land Question," *The Freeman: Ideas on Liberty* 59.6 (July-Aug. 2009): 33-8 (Foundation for Economic Education) <http://www.thefreemanonline.org/featured/the-american-land-question> (Dec. 31, 2009).

arguments settled at gunpoint; they unequivocally oppose aggressive violence. So they don't suppose that petty indignities warrant violent responses. At the same time, though, they recognize that it makes no sense to favor
freedom as a general value while treating non-violent assaults on people's
freedom as trivial. (Thus, they favor a range of non-violent responses to
such assaults, including public shaming, blacklisting, striking, protesting,
withholding voluntary certifications, and boycotting.)[7]

CL provides, then, a further reason to oppose capitalism$_3$. Most people
committed to CL find MUP very plausible, and thus will be inclined to think
of capitalism3 as a product of capitalism$_2$. But the understanding of freedom
as a multi-dimensional value that can be subject to assaults both violent and
non-violent provides good reason to oppose capitalism$_3$ even if – as is most
unlikely – it were to occur in complete isolation from capitalism$_2$.

### E. Conclusion

Capitalism$_2$ and capitalism$_3$ are both inconsistent with freed-market
principles: capitalism$_2$ because it involves direct interference with market
freedom, capitalism$_3$ because it depends on such interference – both past
and ongoing – and because it flies in the face of the general commitment to
freedom that underlies support for market freedom in particular.

## IV. WHY FREED-MARKET ADVOCATES SHOULD CALL THE SYSTEM THEY OPPOSE "CAPITALISM"

Given the contradictory meanings of "capitalism," perhaps sensible people should avoid using it at all. But "words are known by the company they
keep";[8] so, while they certainly shouldn't use it as a tag for the system they
favor, there are good reasons for advocates of freed markets, especially those
committed to CL, to use this word for what they oppose.[9]

---

7    Cp. Charles Johnson, "Libertarianism through Thick and Thin," *Rad Geek
     People's Daily* (n.p., Oct. 3, 2008) <http://www.radgeek.com/gt/2008/10/03/
     libertarianism_through> (Dec. 31, 2009); Kerry Howley, "We're All Cultural
     Libertarians," *Reason* (Reason Foundation, Nov. 2009) <http://www.reason.
     com/archives/2009/10/20/are-property-rights-enough> (Dec. 31, 2009).

8    I became acquainted with this phrase thanks to Nicholas Lash, *Believing
     Three Ways in One God: A Reading of the Apostles' Creed* (Notre Dame, IN:
     University of Notre Dame Press 1992); see, *e.g.*, 12. But it appears, I have
     subsequently discovered, to have a legal provenance and to be a rough trans-
     lation of the Latin phrase *noscitur a sociis*.

9    To be sure, proponents of freed markets, and so of captalism$_1$, could obvi-

1. *To Emphasize the Specific Undesirability of Capitalism$_3$.* Labels like "state capitalism" and "corporatism" capture what is wrong with capitalism$_2$, but they don't quite get at the problem with capitalism$_3$. Even if, as seems plausible, rule by capitalists requires a political explanation – an explanation in terms of the independent misbehavior of politicians and of the manipulation of politicians by business leaders[10] – it is worth objecting to rule by big business in addition to challenging business-government symbiosis. To the extent that those who own and lead big businesses are often labeled "capitalists," identifying what proponents of freedom oppose as "capitalism" helps appropriately to highlight their critique of capitalism$_3$.

2. *To Differentiate Proponents of Freed Markets from Vulgar Market Enthusiasts.* The "capitalist" banner is often waved enthusiastically by people who seem inclined to confuse support for freed markets with support for capitalism$_2$ and capitalism$_3$ – perhaps ignoring the reality or the problematic nature of both, perhaps even celebrating capitalism$_3$ as appropriate in light of the purportedly admirable characters of business titans. Opposing "capitalism" helps to ensure that advocates of freed markets are not confused with these vulgar proponents of freedom-for-the-power-elite.

3. *To Emphasize That the Freed Market Really is an Unknown Ideal.* Similarly, given the frequency with which the contemporary economic order in Western societies is labeled "capitalism," anyone who acknowledges

---

ously refer to capitalism$_2$, at least, as "state capitalism," "corporate capitalism," "actually existing capitalism," or "corporatism." But doing so wouldn't make clear their opposition to capitalism$_3$.

10 See, *e.g.*, Roderick T. Long, "Toward a Libertarian Theory of Class," *Social Philosophy and Policy* 15.2 (Sum. 1998): 303-49; Tom G. Palmer, "Classical Liberalism, Marxism, and the Conflict of Classes: The Classical Liberal Theory of Class Conflict," *Realizing Freedom: Libertarian Theory, History, and Practice* (Washington: Cato 2009) 255-76; Wally Conger, *Agorist Class Theory: A Left Libertarian Approach to Class Conflict Analysis* (n.p., n.d.) (Agorism.info, n.d.) <http://www.agorism.info/AgoristClassTheory.pdf> (Jan. 18, 2010); Kevin A. Carson, "Another Free-for-All: Libertarian Class Analysis, Organized Labor, Etc.," *Mutualist Blog: Free-Market Anticapitalism* (n.p., Jan 26, 2006) <http://www.mutualist.blogspot.com/2006/01/another-free-for-all-libertarian-class.html> (Jan. 18, 2010); Sheldon Richman, "Class Struggle Rightly Conceived," *The Goal Is Freedom* (Foundation for Economic Education, July 13, 2007) <http://www.fee.org/articles/in-brief/the-goal-is-freedom-class-struggle-rightly-conceived> (Jan. 18, 2010); Walter E. Grinder and John Hagel, "Toward a Theory of State Capitalism: Ultimate Decision Making and Class Structure," *Journal of Libertarian Studies* 1.1 (1977): 59-79.

the vast gap between ideals of freedom and an economic reality distorted by privilege and misshapen by past acts of violent dispossession will have good reason to oppose what is commonly called capitalism, rather than embracing it.

4. *To Challenge a Conception of the Market Economy that Treats Capital as More Fundamental than Labor.* Multiple factors of production – notably including labor – contribute to the operation of a market economy. To refer to such an economy as "capitalist" is to imply, incorrectly, that capital plays the most central role in a market economy and that the "capitalist," the absenteee owner of investable wealth, is ultimately more important than the people who are the sources of labor. Advocates of freed-markets should reject this inaccurate view.[11]

5. *To Reclaim "Socialism" for Freed-Market Radicals.* "Capitalism" and "socialism" are characteristically seen as forming an oppositional pair. But it was precisely the "socialist" label that a radical proponent of freed markets, Benjamin Tucker, owned at the time when these terms were being passionately debated and defined.[12] Tucker clearly saw no conflict between his intense commitment to freed markets and his membership of the First International. That's because he understood socialism as a matter of liberating workers from oppression by aristocrats and business executives, and he – plausibly – believed that ending the privileges conferred on economic elites by the state would be the most effective – and safest – way of achieving socialism's liberating goal. Opposing capitalism helps to underscore the important place of radicals like Tucker in the contemporary freedom movement's lineage and to provide today's advocates of freedom with a persua-

---

11 See Kevin A. Carson, "Capitalism: A Good Word for a Bad Thing," *Center for a Stateless Society* (Center for a Stateless Society, Mar. 6, 2010) <http://www.c4ss.org/content/1992> (Mar. 6, 2010).

12 See Benjamin R. Tucker, "State Socialism and Anarchism: How Far They Agree and Wherein They Differ," *Instead of a Book: By a Man Too Busy to Write One* (New York: Tucker 1897) (Fair-Use.Org, n.d.) <http://www.fair-use.org/benjamin-tucker/instead-of-a-book> (Dec. 31, 2009). Cp. Kevin A. Carson, "Socialist Definitional Free-for-All: Part II," *Mutualist Blog: Free Market Anticapitalism* (n.p., Dec. 8, 2005) <http://www.mutualist.blogspot.com/2005/12/socialist-definitional-free-for-all_08.html> (Dec. 31, 2009); Brad Spangler, "Re-Stating the Point: Rothbardian Socialism," *BradSpangler. Com* (n.p., Oct. 10, 2009) <http://bradspangler.com/blog/archives/1458> (Dec. 31, 2009); Gary Chartier, *Socialist Ends, Market Means: 5 Essays* (Tulsa, OK: Tulsa Alliance of the Libertarian Left 2009) (Center for a Stateless Society, Aug. 31, 2009) <http://c4ss.org/wp-content/uploads/2009/08/Garychartier_forprint_binding.pdf> (Dec. 31, 2009).

sive rationale for capturing the socialist label from *state* socialists. (This is especially appropriate because advocates of freedom believe that society – connected people cooperating freely and voluntarily – rather than the state should be seen as the source of solutions to human problems. Thus, they can reasonably be said to favor *social*ism not as a kind of, but as an alternative to, *stat*ism.)[13] Embracing anticapitalism underscores the fact that freed markets offer a way of achieving socialist goals – fostering the empowerment of workers and the wide dispersion of ownership *of* and control *over* the means of production – using market means.[14]

6. *To Express Solidarity with Workers.* If MUP is correct, the ability of big business – "capital" – to maximize the satisfaction of its preferences more fully than workers are able to maximize the satisfaction of theirs is a function of business-state symbiosis that is inconsistent with freed-market principles. And, as a matter of support for CL, there is often further reason to side with workers when they are being pushed around, even non-aggressively. To the extent that the bosses workers oppose are often called "capital*ists*," so that "anticapital*ism*" seems like a natural tag for their opposition to these bosses, and to the extent that freed markets – by contrast with capitalism$_2$ and capitalism$_3$ – would dramatically increase the opportunities for workers simultaneously to shape the contours of their own lives and to experience significantly greater prosperity and economic security, embracing "anticapitalism" is a way of clearly signaling solidarity with workers.[15]

7. *To Identify with the Legitimate Concerns of the Global Anticapitalist Movement.* Owning "anticapitalism" is also a way, more broadly, of identifying with ordinary people around the world who express their opposition to imperialism, the increasing power in their lives of multinational

---

13    Thanks to Sheldon Richman for helping me to see this point.

14    Alex Tabarrok, "Rename Capitalism Socialism?" *Marginal Revolution* (n.p., Jan. 25, 2010) <http://www.marginalrevolution.com/marginalrevolution/2010/01/rename-capitalism-socialism.html> (Feb. 3, 2010), maintains: "capitalism is a truly *social* system, a system that unites the world in cooperation, peace and trade. Thus, if all were tabula rasa socialism might be a good name for capitalism. But that boat has sailed." It seems to me that Tabarrok misses the point of the argument about "capitalism," which is precisely whether what is regularly labeled "capitalism" by the majority of the people in the world really is "a truly social system . . . that unites the world in cooperation, peace and trade."

15    Cp. Sheldon Richman, "Workers of the World Unite for a Free Market," *The Freeman: Ideas on Liberty* (Foundation for Economic Education, Dec. 18, 2009) <http://www.thefreemanonline.org/tgif/workers-of-the-world-unite> (Dec. 31, 2009).

corporations, and their own growing economic vulnerability by naming their enemy as "capitalism." Perhaps some of them endorse inaccurate theoretical accounts of their circumstances in accordance with which it really is a freed-market system – captalism$_1$ – that should be understood as lying behind what they oppose. But for many of them, objecting to "capitalism" doesn't really mean opposing freed markets; it means using a convenient label provided by social critics who are prepared – as advocates of freedom too often regrettably are not – to stand with them in challenging the forces that seem bent on misshaping their lives and those of others. Advocates of freedom have a golden opportunity to build common ground with these people, agreeing with them about the wrongness of many of the circumstances they confront while providing a freedom-based *explanation of* their circumstances and *remedy for* the attendant problems.[16]

## V. CONCLUSION

Thirty-five years ago, Karl Hess wrote: "I have lost my faith in capitalism" and "I resist this capitalist nation-state," observing that he had "turn[ed] from the religion of capitalism."[17] Distinguishing three senses

---

16  "'If you were to ask, "What is anarchism?" we would all disagree,' said Vlad Bliffet, a member of the collective that organized the . . . [2010 Los Angeles Anarchist Bookfair]. While most anarchists agree on the basic principle that the world would be better without hierarchy and without capitalism, he said, they have competing theories on how to achieve that change" (Kate Linthicum, "Book Fair Draws an Array of Anarchists," *LATimes.Com* [*Los Angeles Times*, Jan. 25, 2010] <http://www.latimes.com/news/local/la-me-anarchists25-2010jan25,0,3735605.story?track=rss> [Jan. 27, 2010]). Given the focus on opposition to real-world hierarchy, I suspect, without evidence, that Bliffet's primary objection was not to capitalism as a system of ownership and exchange in the abstract—capitalism$_1$—but rather to social dominance by capitalists—capitalism$_3$. The failure to see this point will tend to impede an otherwise natural alliance focused on issues ranging from war to torture to surveillance to drugs to freedom of speech to corporatism to bailouts to decentralization to the reach of the administrative state.

17  Karl Hess, *Dear America* (New York: Morrow 1975) 3, 5. Even more bluntly, Hess writes: "What I have learned about corporate capitalism, roughly, is that it is an act of theft, by and large, through which a very few live very high off the work, invention, and creativity of very many others. It is the Grand Larceny of our particular time in history, the Grand Larceny in which a future of freedom which could have followed the collapse of feudalism was stolen from under our noses by a new bunch of bosses doing the same old

of "capitalism" – market order, business-government partnership, and rule by capitalists – helps to make clear why, like Hess, someone might be consistently committed to freedom while voicing passionate opposition to something called "capitalism." It makes sense for freed-market advocates to oppose *both* interference with market freedom by politicians and business leaders *and* the social dominance (aggressive and otherwise) of business leaders. And it makes sense for them to name what they oppose "capitalism." Doing so calls attention to the freedom movement's radical roots, emphasizes the value of understanding society as an alternative to the state, highlights the difference between freed-market ideal and present reality, underscores the fact that proponents of freedom object to non-aggressive as well as aggressive restraints on liberty, ensures that advocates of freedom aren't confused with people who use market rhetoric to prop up an unjust *status quo*, and expresses solidarity between defenders of freed markets and workers – as well as ordinary people around the world who use "capitalism" as a short-hand label for the world-system that constrains their freedom and stunts their lives. Freed-market advocates should embrace "anticapitalism" in order to encapsulate and highlight their full-blown commitment to freedom and their rejection of alternatives that use talk of liberty to conceal acquiescence in exclusion, subordination, and deprivation.[18]

---

things" (1). (Complicating the story is the fact that Hess subsequently wrote *Capitalism for Kids: Growing up to Be Your Own Boss* [Wilmington, DE: Enterprise 1987].)

18    Brian Doherty, "Ayn Rand: Radical for Something Other Than Capitalism?," *Hit and Run: Reason Magazine* (Reason Foundation, Jan, 20, 2010) <http://www.reason.com/blog/2010/01/20/ayn-rand-radical-for-something> (Jan. 21, 2010), reports: "I have been happy using capitalism in Rand's ideal sense as that which American libertarians advocate . . . , which I think is true and I don't think represents such a severe intellectual, marketing, or historical problem as Long says..." Doherty opines that Long "is far too blithe in his conclusion that the fact that Western prosperity can be attributed to the extent that it has honored property rights, free exchange, and a price system deserves only the intellectual status of that part of our culture that is 'not diseased.'" I am not clear what it means to say that "Rand's ideal sense . . . is true" (in what way are definitions or senses true?), and I am inclined to suspect that a cluster of praxeological, moral, and historical claims provides credible support for the left-libertarian critique of "capitalism" and for the diagnosis of much of the economic order that obtains in the contemporary West as diseased. (This most emphatically does not amount to a positive assessment of actually existing alternatives.)

## 10

*The Dandelion* 4.13 (Spring 1980): 24-5.

# ANARCHISM WITHOUT HYPHENS

## *KARL HESS*
## *(1980)*

THERE IS ONLY ONE KIND OF ANARCHIST. NOT TWO. JUST ONE. AN ANARCHIST, THE ONLY kind, as defined by the long tradition and literature of the position itself, is a person in opposition to authority imposed through the hierarchical power of the state. The only expansion of this that seems to me reasonable is to say that an anarchist stands in opposition to any imposed authority. An anarchist is a voluntarist.

Now, beyond that, anarchists also are people and, as such, contain the billion-faceted varieties of human reference. Some are anarchists who march, voluntarily, to the Cross of Christ. Some are anarchists who flock, voluntarily, to the communes of beloved, inspirational father figures. Some are anarchists who seek to establish the syndics of voluntary industrial production. Some are anarchists who voluntarily seek to establish the rural production of the kibbutzim. Some are anarchists who, voluntarily, seek to disestablish everything including their own association with other people; the hermits. Some are anarchists who will deal, voluntarily, only in gold, will never co-operate, and swirl their capes. Some are anarchists who, voluntarily, worship the sun and its energy, build domes, eat only vegetables, and play the dulcimer. Some are anarchists who worship the power of algorithms, play strange games, and infiltrate strange temples. Some are anarchists who see only the stars. Some are anarchists who see only the mud.

They spring from a single seed, no matter the flowering of their ideas. The seed is liberty. And that is all it is. It is not a socialist seed. It is not a capitalist seed. It is not a mystical seed. It is not a determinist seed. It is simply a statement. We can be free. After that it's all choice and chance.

Anarchism, liberty, does not tell you a thing about how free people will behave or what arrangements they will make. It simply says the people have the capacity to make the arrangements.

Anarchism is not normative. It does not say how to be free. It says only that freedom, liberty, can exist.

Recently, in a libertarian journal, I read the statement that libertarianism is an ideological movement. It may well be. In a concept of freedom it, they, you, or we, anyone, has the liberty to engage in ideology or anything else that does not coerce others denying their liberty. But anarchism is not an ideological movement. It is an ideological statement. It says that all people have a capacity for liberty. It says that all anarchists want liberty. And then it is silent. After the pause of that silence, anarchists then mount the stages of their own communities and history and proclaim their, not anarchism's, ideologies – they say how they, how they as anarchists, will make arrangements, describe events, celebrate life, work.

Anarchism is the hammer-idea, smashing the chains. Liberty is what results and, in liberty, everything else is up to people and their ideologies. It is not up to THE ideology. Anarchism says, in effect, there is no such upper case, dominating ideology. It says that people who live in liberty make their own histories and their own deals with and within it.

A person who describes a world in which everyone must or should behave in a single way, marching to a single drummer is simply not an anarchist. A person who says that they prefer this way, even wishing that all would prefer that way, but who then says that all must decide, may certainly be an anarchist. Probably is.

Liberty is liberty. Anarchism is anarchism. Neither is Swiss cheese or anything else. They are not property. They are not copyrighted. They an old, available ideas, part of human culture. They may be hyphenated but they are not in fact hyphenated. They exist on their own. People add hyphens, and supplemental ideologies.

Liberty, finally is not a box into which people are to be forced. Liberty is a space in which people may live. It does not tell you how they will live. It says, eternally, only that we can.

# 11

"Capitalism *versus* the Free Market — Part 1," *Freedom Daily* (Future of Freedom Foundation, Aug. 6, 2010) <http.//www.fff.org/freedom/fd1005b.asp> (Aug. 8, 2011); "Capitalism *versus* the Free Market — Part 2," *Freedom Daily* (Future of Freedom Foundation, Sep. 10, 2010) <http.//www.fff.org/freedom/fd1006b.asp> (Aug. 8, 2011).

# WHAT LAISSEZ FAIRE?

## SHELDON RICHMAN
## (2010)

WRITING IN THE *GUARDIAN* LAST JANUARY UNDER THE HEADLINE "CARIBBEAN COMmunism v. Capitalism," respected journalist Stephen Kinzer began his article like this:

> Visiting unhappy Cuba is especially thought-provoking for anyone familiar with its unhappy neighbours. Cubans live difficult lives and have much to complain about. So do Jamaicans, Dominicans, Haitians, Guatemalans, Hondurans, Salvadorans, and others in the Caribbean basin who live under capitalist governments. Who is worse off? Does an ordinary person live better in Cuba or in a nearby capitalist country?[1]

---

1   Stephen Kinzer, "Caribbean Communism v Capitalism," *The Guardian* (Guardian News and Media, Jan. 22, 2010) <http://www.guardian.co.uk/commentisfree/cifamerica/2010/jan/22/cuba-communism-human-rights> (March 13, 2011).

Many people would read this without pause, but presumably not libertarians. Are Jamaica, the Dominican Republic, Haiti, Guatemala, Honduras, and El Salvador capitalist countries? Kinzer's matter-of-fact statement seems to conflict with other evidence. For example, the Heritage Foundation Index of Economic Freedom (which overstates countries' degree of economic freedom) rates the Dominican Republic, Jamaica, El Salvador, and Guatemala "moderately free" (and not "free" or "mostly free), and Honduras and Haiti "mostly unfree." So how can they be "capitalist" – unless capitalism and freedom are two different things?

One may infer from Kinzer's article that he classifies any country "capitalist" as long as Marxist socialism is not its official ideology. So he states, "Comparing the two political and social systems also reminds us that for many people in the world, a truly fulfilling life is unattainable… The best hope for longtime communist Cuba and its longtime capitalist neighbours would be to learn from each other."

My purpose here is not to focus on Kinzer's curiously positive statements about Cuba and its "social safety net" but rather on his use of the word "capitalist." He apparently regards that designation so uncontroversial that he feels no need to justify it or even to define the term.

Kinzer, however, is not an anomaly. Consider Richard Posner's book about the recent financial debacle, *A Failure of Capitalism*. Posner is no left-leaning journalist. He's a federal judge with a long association with the University of Chicago and the market-oriented law-and-economics movement. Yet here he is, blaming "capitalism" for the current economic troubles and, as a result, embracing Keynesianism. He writes in his preface, "We are learning from it [the "depression"] that we need a more active and intelligent government to keep our model of a capitalist economy from running off the rails. The movement to deregulate the financial industry went too far by exaggerating the resilience – the self-healing powers – of laissez faire capitalism."

Posner is hardly a lone wolf on his side of the political spectrum. Tune in to the financial programs on the Fox News Channel and Fox Business Network any day and you'll hear Lawrence Kudlow, Ben Stein, or any number of other economic conservatives warning that Barack Obama's policies threaten to undermine "our capitalist system." That certainly implies there is today a capitalist system to undermine.

## WHAT IS CAPITALISM?

What, then, is this system called "capitalism"? It can't be the free market because we have no free market. Today the hand of government is all over the economy – from money and banking to transportation to manufacturing to agriculture to insurance to basic research to world trade. If the meaning of a concept consists in how it is used (there's no platonic form to be divined), "capitalism" can't mean "the free market." Rather it designates a system in which the means of production are de jure privately owned. Left open is the question of government intervention. Thus the phrases "free-market capitalism" and "laissez-faire capitalism" are typically not seen as redundant and the phrases "state capitalism" or "crony capitalism" are not seen as contradictions. If without controversy "capitalism" can take the qualifiers "free-market" and "state," that tells us something. (This is true regardless of what dictionaries say. From at least the time of Samuel Johnson, lexicographers have understood dictionaries to be descriptive not prescriptive. New editions routinely modify definitions in light of current usage.)

This is not just a semantic point – one wonders about the value of spending time arguing whether what we have is "really" capitalism or not – and it is more than a matter of rhetoric, or the art of persuasion – important as that is. It is a matter of historical understanding, for although Ludwig von Mises and Ayn Rand tried mightily to have "capitalism" understood as "the free market," they were swimming upstream. As historian Clarence Carson wrote in *The Freeman* in the 1980s, "'Capitalism'… does not have a commonly accepted meaning, proponents of it to the contrary notwithstanding. As matters stand, it cannot be used with precision in discourse."

Carson wondered why one would call a system in which production and exchange are carried on privately "capitalism." "So far as I can make out," he wrote, "there is no compelling reason to do so. There is nothing indicated in such arrangements that suggests why capital among the elements of production should be singled out for emphasis. Why not land? Why not labor? Or, indeed, why should any of the elements be singled out?"

There are other curious features of the word. "When an 'ism' is added to a word it denotes a system of belief, and probably what has come to be called an ideology," Carson writes. But a capitalist is not one who advocates capitalism in the way that a socialist is one who advocates socialism. He is rather one who owns capital. A capitalist can be a socialist without contradiction.

It is also useful to bear in mind that the word was not initially embraced by free-market advocates; that was apparently a 20th-century phenomenon. According to the Oxford English Dictionary, the word "capitalist" came first and was used pejoratively in the late 18th century. Of course, Marx used it and related words as condemnation. But it was not only opponents of private property who used the words that way. Most notably, Thomas Hodgskin (1787–1868), a free-market liberal and Herbert Spencer's mentor, preceded Marx in this usage. By "capitalist" he meant one who controlled capital and exploited labor *as a result of* State privilege in violation of the free market.

## A SHORT HISTORY OF CAPITALISM

As important as economic theory is to understanding history, it is no *substitute* for history. Knowing how free markets work cannot in itself tell us that the free market existed in any given historical period. Mises and Rand notwithstanding, from early on historical capitalism has been associated with government intervention in behalf of landowners and factory owners. Capitalism of course is linked to the Industrial Revolution, which began in England, but the rise of industrialism in England followed massive expropriations of yeomen from lands they had struggled to acquire de facto rights over for generations. As another Carson, Kevin Carson, wrote in *The Freeman*,

> In the Old World, especially Britain... the expropriation of the peasant majority by a politically dominant landed oligarchy took place over several centuries in the late medieval and early modern period. It began with the enclosure of the open fields in the late Middle Ages. Under the Tudors, Church fiefdoms (especially monastic lands) were expropriated by the state and distributed among the landed aristocracy. The new "owners" evicted or rack-rented the peasants.

The process continued with land "reforms" and Parliamentary Enclosures into the 19th century, turning tillers of the soil (those who mixed their labor with the land) into tenants.

Commons were "privatized" by the State (that is, given to the privileged) at the expense of people who previously had long-standing customary rights in them. Independent subsistence farmers and artisans were left no choice but to farm for someone else or to work in the new factories, with some of their income skimmed off by landlords and employers. The proletariat was born, as F.A. Hayek acknowledges. By libertarian standards, that constitutes exploitation because State power lay behind the worker's plight. The opportunity to work in the factories is often presented as a blessing, but it looks less benign when the land-theft is recognized. Further there is evidence that the new factory owners obtained some of their capital from "old money" interests, but even if that were not so, the industrialists benefited from the State's interference with the yeomen's land rights. Members of the ruling class and observers frequently expressed concern that no one would choose to work for someone else in an unpleasant factory if he could work for himself on the land or as an artisan. They shared the view of the early 19th-century British writer E.G. Wakefield: "Where land is cheap and all men are free, where every one who so pleases can obtain a piece of land for himself, not only is labour very dear, as respects the labourers' share of the product, but the difficulty is to obtain combined labour at any price."

In no way did laissez faire begin at this point. Kevin Carson writes,

> In addition, factory employers depended on harsh authoritarian measures by the government to keep labor under control and reduce its bargaining power. In England the Laws of Settlement [decried by Adam Smith] acted as a sort of internal passport system, preventing workers from traveling outside the parish of their birth without government permission. Thus workers were prevented from "voting with their feet" in search of better-paying jobs...
>
> The Combination Laws, which prevented workers from freely associating to bargain with employers, were enforced entirely by administrative law without any protections of common-law due process...

Thus the interventionist State tainted the emergence of the industrial age. (It would have emerged spontaneously otherwise.)

As Albert Jay Nock wrote,

> The horrors of England's industrial life in the last [19th] century furnish a standing brief for addicts of positive intervention. Child labour and woman labour in the mills and mines; Coketown and Mr. Bounderby; starvation wages; killing hours; vile and hazardous conditions of labour; coffin ships officered by ruffians – all these are glibly charged off by reformers and publicists to a regime of rugged individualism, unrestrained competition, and *laissez-faire*. This is an absurdity on its face, for no such regime ever existed in England. They were due to the State's primary intervention whereby the population of England was expropriated from the land; due to the State's removal of land from competition with industry for labour...

Thus, as Kevin Carson writes,

> Capitalism, arising as a new class society directly from the old
> class society of the Middle Ages, was founded on an act of
> robbery as massive as the earlier feudal conquest of the land…
> From the outset of the industrial revolution, what is nostalgi-
> cally called "laissez-faire" was in fact a system of continuing
> state intervention to subsidize accumulation, guarantee privi-
> lege, and maintain work discipline.

The taint of government intervention into economic activity carried
over to the British North American colonies. The radical nature of the
American Revolution has masked the class struggle within American
colonial society between what historian Merrill Jensen called "radicals"
and "conservatives" in his book *The Articles of Confederation: An Interpretation of the Social-Constitutional History of the American Revolution,
1774–1781*. (Class analysis was not originated by Marx, but by the earlier
laissez-faire radicals Charles Comte and Charles Dunoyer.) A privileged
politically connected elite came to dominate each colony, living off big
land grants and taxes. Power and land were handed out as royal favors,
and the wealthy recipients became entrenched. In the North, the ruling
class consisted of merchants, in the South of the big planters. Jensen
notes that in Pennsylvania, for example, "the merchants had tried by various means to overthrow the system of markets and auctions in order to
get a monopoly of the retail trade." Then as now, established business
preferred cartels to free and unpredictable competition. The elites came
to think of themselves as the wise aristocracy destined to govern, and they
were not eager to give up power when the radicals first started to push for
independence from Britain. Staying in the empire was seen as the key to
holding local political power.

The radicals and the conservatives thus had different economic and political interests and different views about independence from Great Britain.
When British usurpations made continued association with the empire intolerable even for many conservatives, those groups then disagreed over
how the new nation should be governed. The mercantile interests tended
to favor nationalist centralization, which was seen as the best way to maintain their power and restrict the radical democrats. They hoped to emulate
the British mercantilist system. In contrast, the mass of people, who felt
themselves imposed on by those interests, tended to favor decentralization
because they believed they had a better chance for justice and property
with local self-government. Thus what Jensen calls the "internal revolution"
– the effort to break the hold of the elites in the colonies – was at least as
important as the external one against the British.

# THE CONSTITUTION

Given this pre-independence picture, it should come as no surprise that independent America was no bastion of laissez-faire libertarianism. Indeed, the effort to overthrow the Articles of Confederation – with its weak central quasi government that lacked the power to tax the people directly or regulate trade – and establish a far stronger central government under the U.S. Constitution was a continuation of the internal struggle that had occurred before the Revolution. To give just one indication here, it is erroneously believed that the driving force behind the Constitution was the determination to create a free trade zone among the states. Thus, according to the standard account, the Commerce Clause was the response to widespread trade barriers between the states. But several problems present themselves. First, the United States were already a free trade zone (with the exception of rare restrictions on European goods passing from one state to another).

Second, in arguing for ratification of the Constitution in *The Federalist Papers*, Alexander Hamilton complained that tariffs were *too low*, not too high:

> It is therefore, evident, that one national government would be able, at much less expence, to extend the duties on imports, beyond comparison further, than would be practicable to the States separately, or to any partial confederacies: Hitherto I believe it may safely be asserted, that these duties have not upon an average exceeded in any State three percent... There seems to be nothing to hinder their being increased in this country, to at least *treble their present amount...* [Federalist 12; emphasis added].

In other words, competition among the states was keeping tariffs down, while uniting the states under a strong central government would curb that competition, cartel-style, and permit higher tariffs. (Indeed, the first economic act of the new Congress in 1789 – on July 4! – was a comprehensive protective tariff ranging from 5 to 10 percent. It was called "the second Declaration of Independence.")

Third, historian Calvin Johnson notes,

> In the original debates over adoption of the Constitution, "regulation of commerce" was used, *almost exclusively,* as a cover of words for specific *mercantilist* proposals related to deep-water shipping and foreign trade. The Constitution was written *before* Adam Smith, laissez faire, and free trade

came to dominate economic thinking and the Commerce Clause draws its original meaning from the preceding *mercantilist* tradition… Barriers on interstate commerce, however, were not a notable issue in the original debates. [Emphasis added.]

Thomas Jefferson's philosophy of decentralization might have been the philosophy of the people, but powerful elites throughout the new states were in Hamilton's camp. As a result, government intervention in critical parts of the economy (internal improvements and, later, subsidies to railroads) was prominent. When Jefferson and later Jeffersonians gained power, they were able to reverse some of the damage, but the nationalism and statism of Alexander Hamilton and Henry Clay were always in the wings waiting for a Lincoln to be elected.

## DISTRIBUTING LAND

A revealing story is to be found in the disposition of federal lands. As noted, political favoritism and land speculation, yielding fortunes, were scandalous in the colonial period. Things changed little after the Revolution. Despite the impression given by the Homestead Act of 1862, most land – and certainly the best land – was given or sold on sweetheart terms to influential economic interests, most prominently but not exclusively the railroad interests. Needless to say, the landless and powerless were not among the buyers.

As historian Paul Wallace Gates wrote in 1935,

[The] Homestead Law did not completely change our land system… [Its] adoption merely superimposed upon the old land system a principle out of harmony with it… [It] will appear that the Homestead Law did not end the auction system or cash sales, as is generally assumed, that speculation and land monopolization continued after its adoption as widely perhaps as before, and within as well as without the law, that actual homesteading was generally confined to the less desirable lands distant from railroad lines, and that farm tenancy developed in frontier communities in many instances as a result of the monopolization of the land.

The large land holdings produced by this policy, parts of which were kept idle, limited the opportunities of those without power and influence, increasing their dependence on employers and landlords. The situation thus bears some resemblance to that in England.

Aside from the land issue, we know from the work of Jonathan R.T. Hughes and others that from the beginning, government entwinement in the economies of the colonies and states was common. Hughes wrote in *The Governmental Habit Redux,*

> Most studies of modern nonmarket controls consider that the relevant history extends back to the New Deal. A few go back further, into the late nineteenth century. But in fact the powerful and continuous habit of nonmarket control in our economy reaches back for centuries...

Thus, during the colonial period virtually every aspect of economic life was subject to nonmarket controls. Some of this tradition would not survive, some would become even more powerful, while some would ascend to the level of federal control. The colonial background was like an institutional gene pool. Most of the colonial institutions and practices live on today in some form, and there is very little in the way of nonmarket control that does not have a colonial or English forerunner. American history did not begin in 1776.

## THE EXPANSION OF CAPITALISM

Reviewing a couple of dozen studies of state and local economic intervention in the 19th century, historian Robert Lively concluded in 1955,

> King Laissez Faire, then, was according to these reports not only dead; the hallowed report of his reign had all been a mistake. The error was one of monumental proportions, a mixture of overlooked data, interested distortion, and persistent preconception... The substantial energies of government... were employed more often for help than for hindrance to enterprise. The broad and well-documented theme reviewed here is that of public support for business development.

In the second half of the 19th century, America moved further from, not closer to, laissez faire, thanks to Lincoln's adoption of Henry Clay's statist American System, which included a national bank, internal improvements, tariffs, and, for a while, an income tax. As Joseph R. Stromberg writes, "In truth, the Gilded Age witnessed a 'great barbecue,' to use Vernon Louis

Parrington's phrase, rooted in the rampant statism of the war years, whose participants defended themselves with Spencerian rhetoric while grasping with both hands."

The 20th century only accelerated this process by shifting it further to the national level. Big business's complicity in the Progressive Era "reforms" is well documented, thanks to Gabriel Kolko and others. If you count favors for major businesses as government intervention, then there was no laissez faire in the 20th century, even during the Harding-Coolidge years. Herbert Hoover's interventionist record is well known. And it ought to be understood that big business supported Franklin Roosevelt's election in 1932 and his administration during its initial period. The corporatist National Recovery Administration was much to its liking and for some didn't go far enough. If one believes that in the throes of the Depression, America might have embraced explicit nationalization of the means of production, then one can conclude that Roosevelt did indeed "save capitalism," but not in the sense of the free market, which had already been compromised virtually beyond recognition.

The upshot is that historical capitalism was not the free market. Rather it was an anti-competitive, pro-business system of controls and subsidies in which government and mercantile interests worked together in a misguided attempt to produce economic growth and to promote the fortunes of specific well-connected interests. As in any period, there are rent-seekers and obliging rulers, with a revolving door between the two groups. But it is important to note that there was no attempt at comprehensive economic planning. Thus, there was scope for entrepreneurship, which needs little encouragement to flourish. By historical standards the burden of government was light. Grass sprouts through the cracks in the sidewalk. A little economic freedom goes a long way.

This historical account is relevant to understanding the basis from which the U.S. economy evolved and to realizing that the trajectory of development has been different from what it would have been had a real free market existed. Privilege has had long-lasting effects, which we still feel today owing to what Kevin Carson calls the "subsidy of history."

Thus those who call today's system "capitalism" cannot be said to be misusing the term. Advocates of the real free market therefore would be well advised to avoid using it to describe their preferred social system.

## 12

*Rad Geek People's Daily* (n.p., Oct.
3, 2008) <http://radgeek.com/
gt/2008/10/03/libertarianism_
through/> (Aug. 22, 2011).

# LIBERTARIANISM THROUGH THICK AND THIN

## *CHARLES W. JOHNSON*
## *(2008)*

TO WHAT EXTENT SHOULD LIBERTARIANS CONCERN THEMSELVES WITH SOCIAL COMMIT-
ments, practices, projects or movements that seek social outcomes beyond, or other than, the standard libertarian commitment to expanding the
scope of freedom from government coercion?

Clearly, a consistent and principled libertarian cannot support efforts
or beliefs that are contrary to libertarian principles – such as efforts to engineer social outcomes by means of government intervention. But if coercive laws have been taken off the table, what should libertarians say about
other religious, philosophical, social, or cultural commitments that pursue
their ends through non-coercive means, such as targeted moral agitation,
mass education, artistic or literary propaganda, charity, mutual aid, public
praise, ridicule, social ostracism, targeted boycotts, social investing, slow-
downs and strikes in a particular shop, general strikes, or other forms of
solidarity and coordinated action? Which social movements should they

oppose, which should they support, and towards which should they counsel indifference? And how do we tell the difference?

Recently, this question has often arisen in the context of debates over whether or not libertarianism should be integrated into a broader commitment to some of the social concerns traditionally associated with anti-authoritarian Left, such as feminism, anti-racism, gay liberation, counter-culturalism, labor organizing, mutual aid, and environmentalism. Chris Sciabarra has called for a "dialectical libertarianism" which recognizes that "Just as relations of power operate through ethical, psychological, cultural, political, and economic dimensions, so too the struggle for freedom and individualism depends upon a certain constellation of moral, psychological, and cultural factors,"[1] and in which the struggle for liberty is integrated into a comprehensive struggle for human liberation, incorporating (among other things) a commitment to gay liberation and opposition to racism. Kevin Carson has criticized the "vulgar libertarianism" of "apologists for capitalism" who "seem to have trouble remembering, from one moment to the next, whether they're defending actually existing capitalism or free market principles,"[2] and has argued that free market anarchists should ally themselves with those radical industrial unions, such as the IWW, that reject the interventionist methods of the state labor bureaucracy. Radical libertarians including Carol Moore, Roderick Long, and myself, have suggested that radical libertarian insights naturally complement, and should be integrated with, an anti-statist form of radical feminism.

On the other hand, Jan Narveson has argued that left libertarian concerns about the importance of cultural and social arrangements are at the most a strategic issue which libertarians should consider a separate issue from "the structure of our theory." Leonard Read, the indefatigable founder of FEE, famously promoted the argument that libertarianism is compatible with "Anything That's Peaceful." And Walter Block has criticized "left wing libertarians" for "perverting libertarianism"[3] in their effort to integrate common leftist concerns into the libertarian project. So long as cultural values are expressed without indulging in government intervention or

---

1    Chris Matthew Sciabarra, *Total Freedom: Toward a Dialectical Libertarianism* (University Park, PA: Pennsylvania State UP 2000) 383.

2    Kevin A. Carson, *Studies in Mutualist Political Economy* (Charleston, SC: BookSurge 2008) 142.

3    Walter Block, "Libertarianism is Unique; It Belongs Neither to the Right Nor the Left: A Critique of the Views of Long, Holcombe, and Baden on the Left, Hoppe, Feser and Paul on the Right," *Ludwig von Mises Institute* (Ludwig von Mises Institute, 2006) <mises.org/journals/scholar/block15.pdf> (June 16, 2010) 28.

any other form of coercion, Block argues, it should not matter to "plumb-line" libertarians whether the cultural values in question are left wing, right wing, or something else: "Give me a break; this issue has nothing to do with libertarianism... No, these are all matters of taste, and de gustibus non est disputandum."[4]

However, it is important to keep in mind that the issue at hand in these discussions goes beyond the debate over left libertarianism specifically. The debate leads to some strange bedfellows: not only left libertarians defend the claim that libertarianism should be integrated into a comprehensive critique of prevailing social relations; so do "paleolibertarians" such as Gary North or Hans-Hermann Hoppe, when they make the equal but opposite claim that efforts to build a flourishing free society should be integrated with a rock-ribbed inegalitarian cultural and religious traditionalism. As do Randian Objectivists, when they argue that political freedom can only arise from a culture of secular romantic individualism and an intellectual milieu grounded in widespread, fairly specific agreement with the tenets of Objectivist metaphysics, ethics, and epistemology. Abstracting from the numerous, often mutually exclusive details of specific cultural projects that have been recommended or condemned in the name of libertarianism, the question of general principle has to do with whether libertarianism should be seen as a "thin" commitment, which can be happily joined to absolutely any non-coercive set of values and projects, or whether it should instead be seen as one strand among others in a "thick" bundle of intertwined social commitments. These disputes are often intimately connected with other disputes concerning the specifics of libertarian rights theory, or class analysis and the mechanisms of social power. In order to better get a grip on what's at stake, it will be necessary to make the question more precise, and to tease out the distinctions between some of the different possible relationships between libertarianism and "thicker" bundles of social, cultural, religious, or philosophical commitments, which might recommend integrating the two on some level or another.

## THICKNESS IN ENTAILMENT AND CONJUNCTION

Let's start with the clearest and least interesting cases.

There are clearly cases in which certain social, cultural, religious, or philosophical commitments might just be an application of libertarian principles to some specific case, which follow from the non-aggression principle by virtue of the law of non-contradiction. An Aztec libertarian might very well say, "Of course libertarianism needs to be integrated

---

4    Block 29.

with a stance on particular religious doctrines! It means you have to give up human sacrifice to Huitzilopochtli!" Or, to take a politically current debate, it might well be argued that libertarians ought to actively oppose certain traditional cultural practices that involve the systematic use of violence against peaceful people – such as East African customs of forcing clitoridectomy on unwilling girls, or the American and European custom of excusing or justifying a man's murder of an unfaithful wife or her lover (although not allowed for by government laws, revenge murderers were until very recently often acquitted or given a lesser sentence by judges and juries). What's going on in these cases is that consistent, principled libertarianism logically entails criticism of these social and cultural practices, for the same reason that it entails criticism of government intervention: because the non-aggression principle condemns any violence against individual rights to life, liberty, and property, regardless of who commits them. Thus we might call this level of integration "thickness in entailment." Thickness in entailment does raise one important issue: it is vital for libertarians to recognize that the non-aggression principle commits them to political opposition to any form of systematic coercion, not just the forms that are officially practiced by the government. Thus principled libertarianism is politically committed not only to anti-statism, but also to opposition to "private" forms of systematic coercion, such as chattel slavery or domestic violence against women. But in the end, it is dubious how far thickness in entailment really counts as a form of "thickness" at all, since at bottom it amounts only to the claim that libertarians really ought to be committed to libertarianism all the time.

At the opposite extreme, we might consider the extent to which there are social or cultural commitments that libertarians ought to adopt because they are worth adopting for their own sakes, independent of libertarian considerations. For example, it may be worthwhile for libertarians to all be kind to their children, because (among other things) being kind to your children is a worthwhile thing to do in its own right. You might call this "thickness in conjunction," since the only relationship it asserts between libertarianism and some other social commitment (here, kindness to children), is that you ought to accept the one (for whatever reason), and also, as it happens, you ought to accept the other (for reasons that are independent of libertarianism). But again, it is unclear how far this counts as an interesting form of "thickness" for libertarianism to demand. If libertarianism is true, then we all ought to be libertarians; and besides being libertarians, we all ought to be good people, too. True, that, but it's hardly an interesting conclusion, and it's not clear who would deny it. Certainly not those who generally advocate the "thin libertarian" line.

Thickness in entailment and thickness in conjunction tell us little interesting about the relationship between libertarianism and other social commitments. But they do show the extent to which our original question needs to be asked in terms more precise than those in which it is usually asked. Considerations of entailment make clear that consistent libertarianism means not a narrow concern with government intervention only, but also opposition to all forms of coercion against peaceful people, whether carried out within or outside of the official policy of the state. And considerations of conjunction make clear that what is really of interest is not whether libertarians should also oppose social or cultural evils other than those involved in coercion (no doubt they should), but more specifically whether there are any other evils that libertarians should oppose as libertarians, that is, whether there are any further commitments that libertarians should make, beyond principled non-aggression, at least in part because of their commitment to libertarianism. In the two cases we have considered, the logical "relationship" between libertarian principles and the further commitments is either so tight (logical entailment) or else so loose (mere conjunction) that either the commitments cease to be further commitments, or else they become commitments that are completely independent of libertarianism. Thin-conception advocates like Block and Narveson often argue as if these two dubious forms of "thickness" were the only sorts of relationships that are on offer, and if they are right, then it seems unlikely that there is anything very interesting to say about thick libertarianism. But I will argue that, in between the tightest possible connection and the loosest possible connection, there are at least four other interesting connections that might exist between libertarianism and further social or cultural commitments. To the extent that they allow for connections looser than entailment but tighter than mere conjunction, they offer a number of important, but subtly distinct, avenues for thick libertarian analysis and criticism.

## THICKNESS FOR APPLICATION

One of the most important, but most easily overlooked, forms of thickness is what I will call "thickness for application." There might be some commitments that a libertarian can reject without formally contradicting the non-aggression principle, but which she cannot reject without in fact interfering with its proper application. Principles beyond libertarianism alone may be necessary for determining where my rights end and yours begin, or stripping away conceptual blinders that prevent certain violations of liberty from being recognized as such.

Consider the way in which garden-variety political collectivism prevents many non-libertarians from even recognizing taxation or legislation by a democratic government as being forms of coercion in the first place. (After all, didn't "we" consent to it?) Or, perhaps more controversially, think of the feminist criticism of the traditional division between the "private" and the "political" sphere, and of those who divide the spheres in such a way that pervasive, systemic violence and coercion within families turn out to be justified, or excused, or simply ignored, as something "private" and therefore less than a serious form of violent oppression. To the extent that feminists are right about the way in which sexist political theories protect or excuse systematic violence against women, there is an important sense in which libertarians, because they are libertarians, should also be feminists. Importantly, the commitments that libertarians need to have here aren't just applications of general libertarian principle to a special case; the argument calls in resources other than the non-aggression principle to determine just where and how the principle is properly applied. In that sense the thickness called for is thicker than entailment thickness; but the cash value of the thick commitments is still the direct contribution they make towards the full and complete application of the non-aggression principle.

## THICKNESS FROM GROUNDS

A second logical relationship that might hold between libertarianism and some further commitment is what I will call "thickness from grounds." Libertarians have many different ideas about the theoretical foundation for the non-aggression principle – that is to say, about the best reasons for being a libertarian. But whatever general foundational beliefs a given libertarian has, those beliefs may have some logical implications other than libertarianism alone. Thus, there may be cases in which certain beliefs or commitments could be rejected without contradicting the non-aggression principle per se, but could not be rejected without logically undermining or contradicting the deeper reasons that justify the non-aggression principle. Although you could consistently accept libertarianism without accepting these commitments or beliefs, you could not do so reasonably: rejecting the commitments means rejecting the proper grounds for libertarianism.

Consider the conceptual reasons that libertarians have to oppose authoritarianism, not only as enforced by governments but also as expressed in culture, business, the family, and civil society. Social systems of status and authority include not only exercises of coercive power by the government, but also a knot of ideas, practices, and institutions based on deference to traditionally constituted authority. In politics, these patterns of deference show up most clearly in the honorary titles, submissive etiquette, and unquestioning obedience traditionally expected by, and willingly extended to, heads of state, judges, police, and other visible representatives of government "law and order." Although these rituals and habits of obedience exist against the backdrop of statist coercion and intimidation, they are also often practiced voluntarily. Similar kinds of deference are often demanded from workers by bosses, or from children by parents or teachers. Submission to traditionally constituted authorities is reinforced not only through violence and threats, but also through art, humor, sermons, written history, journalism, childrearing, and so on. Although political coercion is the most distinctive expression of political inequality, you could – in principle – have a consistent authoritarian social order without any use of force. Even in a completely free society, everyone could, in principle, still voluntarily agree to bow and scrape and speak only when spoken to in the presence of the (mutually agreed-upon) town Chief, or unthinkingly agree to obey whatever restrictions and regulations he tells them to follow over their own business or personal lives, or agree to give him as much in voluntary "taxes" on their income or property as he might ask. So long as the expectation of submission and the demands for wealth to be rendered were backed up only by means of verbal harangues, cultural glorifications of the wise and virtuous authorities, social ostracism of "unruly" dissenters, and so on, these demands would violate no one's individual rights to liberty or property. But while there's nothing logically inconsistent about a libertarian envisioning – or even championing – this sort of social order, it would certainly be weird. Yes, in a free society the meek could voluntarily agree to bow and scrape, and the proud could angrily but nonviolently demand obsequious forms of address and immediate obedience to their commands. But why should they? Non-coercive authoritarianism may be consistent with libertarian principles, but it is hard to reasonably reconcile the two; whatever reasons you may have for rejecting the arrogant claims of power-hungry politicians and bureaucrats – say, for example, the Jeffersonian notion that all men and women are born equal in political authority, and that no one has a natural right to rule or dominate other people's affairs – probably serve just as well for reasons to reject other kinds of authoritarian pretension, even if they are not expressed by means of coercive government action. While no one should be forced as a matter of policy to treat her fellows with the respect due to equals, or to cultivate independent thinking and contempt for the arrogance of power, libertarians certainly can – and should – criticize those who do not, and exhort our fellows not to rely on authoritarian social institutions, for much the same reasons that we have to endorse libertarianism in the first place.

## STRATEGIC THICKNESS – THE CAUSES OF LIBERTY

There may be also cases in which certain ideas, practices, or projects are entailed by neither the non-aggression principle nor the best reasons for it, and are not logically necessary for its correct application, either, but are causal preconditions for implementing the non-aggression principle in the real world. Although rejecting these ideas, practices, or projects would be logically compatible with libertarianism, their success might be important or even causally necessary for libertarianism to get much purchase in an existing statist society, or for a future free society to emerge from statism without widespread poverty or social conflict, or for a future free society to sustain itself against aggressive statist neighbors, the threat of civil war, or an internal collapse back into statism. To the extent that other ideas, practices, or projects are causal preconditions for a flourishing free society, libertarians have strategic reasons to endorse them, even if they are conceptually independent of libertarian principles.

Thus, for example, left libertarians such as Roderick Long have argued that libertarians have genuine reasons to be concerned about large inequalities of wealth, or large numbers of people living in absolute poverty, and to support voluntary associations – such as mutual aid societies and voluntary charity – that tend to undermine inequalities and to ameliorate the effects of poverty. The reasoning for this conclusion is not that libertarians should concern themselves with voluntary anti-poverty measures because free market principles logically entail support for some particular socioeconomic outcome (clearly they do not); nor is it merely because charity and widespread material well-being are worth pursuing for their own sake (they may be, but that would reduce the argument to thickness in conjunction). Rather, the point is that there may be a significant causal relationship between economic outcomes and the material prospects for sustaining a free society. Even a totally free society in which large numbers of people are desperately poor is likely to be in great danger of collapsing into civil war. Even a totally free society in which a small class of tycoons own the overwhelming majority of the wealth, and the vast majority of the population own almost nothing is unlikely to remain free for long, if the tycoons should decide to use their wealth to purchase coercive legal privileges against the unpropertied majority – simply because they have a lot of resources to attack with, and the majority haven't got the material resources to defend themselves. Now, to the extent that persistent, severe poverty, and large-scale inequalities of wealth are almost always the result of government intervention – and thus as much a concern for thickness from consequences, as discussed below, as for strategic thickness – it's unlikely that many totally free societies would face such dire situations; over time, many if not most of these problems would likely sort themselves out spontaneously through free market processes, even without conscious anti-poverty activism. But even where problems of poverty or economic inequality would sort themselves out in a society that has already been free for some time, they are still likely to be extremely pressing for societies like ours, which are not currently free, which libertarians hope to help become free through education and activism. Certainly in our unfree market there are large-scale inequalities of wealth and widespread poverty, most of it created by the heavy hand of government intervention, in the form of direct subsidies and the creation of rigged or captive markets. Those tycoons who now enjoy the fruit of those privileges can and have and and will continue to exercise some of the tremendous advantage that they enjoy in material resources and political pull to pressure government to perpetuate or expand the interventions from which the profiteering class benefits. Since libertarians aim to abolish those interventions, it may well make good strategic sense for them to oppose, and to support voluntary, non-governmental efforts that work to undermine or bypass, the consolidated economic power that the government-privileged robber barons currently command. Otherwise we will find ourselves trying to fight with slingshots while our enemies haul out bazookas.

Or, to take a less controversial example, many if not most libertarians, throughout the history of the movement, have argued that there are good reasons for libertarians to promote a culture in which reason and independent thinking are highly valued, and blind conformism is treated with contempt. But if this is a good thing for liberty, it must be for reasons other than some kind of entailment of the non-aggression principle. Certainly everyone has a right to believe things simply because "everybody" believes it, or to do things simply because "everybody" does it, as long as their conformism respects the equal rights of independent thinkers to think independently and act independently with their own person and property. It is logically conceivable that a society could be rigidly conformist while remaining entirely free; it would just have to be the case that the individual people within that society were, by and large, psychologically and culturally inclined to be so docile, and so sensitive to social disapproval, ostracism, and verbal peer pressure, that they all voluntarily chose to go along with the crowd.

But, again, while it is logically possible for people in such a society to be convinced to respect individual liberty, it's hardly likely to happen, or, if it does happen, it's unlikely that things will stay that way for very long. If libertarians have good reasons to believe that reason and independent thinking are good for liberty, it is because, in today's unfree society, where the vast majority of people around you are statists, it takes quite a bit of critical thinking and resistance to peer pressure in order to come to libertarian conclusions. And similarly, in a free society, it's likely that a healthy respect for critical thinking and contempt for conformism would be necessary in order to successfully resist later attempts to re-institute collectivism or other forms of statist coercion.

While the non-aggression principle doesn't entail any particular attitude towards socioeconomic equality, or independent thinking, it is quite likely that any chance of implementing the non-aggression principle in the real world will be profoundly affected by whether these material or intellectual preconditions have been met, and so principled libertarians have good strategic reasons to promote them, and to adopt forms of activism that tend to support them through non-statist, voluntary means.

## THICKNESS FROM CONSEQUENCES – THE EFFECTS OF LIBERTY

Finally, there may be social practices or outcomes that libertarians should (in some sense) be committed to opposing, even though they are not themselves coercive, because (1) background acts of government coercion are a causal precondition for them to be carried out or sustained over time; and (2) there are independent reasons for regarding them as social evils. If aggression is morally illegitimate, then libertarians are entitled not only to condemn it, but also to condemn the destructive results that flow from it – even if those results are, in some important sense, external to the actual coercion. Thus, for example, left libertarians such as Kevin Carson and Matt MacKenzie have argued forcefully for libertarian criticism of certain business practices – such as low-wage sweatshop labor – as exploitative. Throughout the twentieth century, most libertarians have rushed to the defense of such practices, on the grounds that they result from market processes, that such arrangements are often the best economic options for extremely poor people in developing countries, and that the state socialist solution of expansive government regulation of wages and conditions would distort the market, violate the rights of workers and bosses to freely negotiate the terms of labor, and harm the very workers that the regulators professed to help. But the problem is that these analyses often attempt to justify or excuse prevailing business practices by appeal to free market principles, when those very practices arose in actually existing markets, which are very far from being free. In Carson's and MacKenzie's view, while the twentieth-century libertarians were right to criticize state socialist claim that existing modes of production should not be even further distorted by expanded government regimentation, but too many twentieth-century libertarians confused that genuine insight with the delusion that existing modes of production would be the natural outcome of an undistorted market. Against these confusions, they have revived an argument drawn from the tradition of nineteenth-century individualist anarchists like Benjamin Tucker, who argued that prevailing government privileges for bosses and capitalists – monopoly, regulatory cartelization of banking, manipulation of the currency, legal restrictions and military violence against union strikers, politicized distribution of land to connected speculators and developers, etc. – distorted markets in such a way as to systematically push workers into precarious and impoverishing economic arrangements, and to force them, against the backdrop of the unfree market in land and capital, to make ends meet by entering a "free" job market on the bosses' terms.

On Tucker's view, as on Carson's and MacKenzie's, this sort of systemic concentration of wealth and market power can only persist as long as the government continues to intervene in the market so as to sustain it; free market competition would free workers to better their own lives outside of traditional corporate channels, and would allow entrepreneurs to tear down top-heavy corporate behemoths through vigorous competition for land, labor, and capital. Thus, to the extent that sweatshop conditions and starvation wages are sustained, and alternative arrangements like workers' co-ops are suppressed, because of the dramatic restrictions on property rights throughout the developing world – restrictions exploited by opportunistic corporations, which often collaborate with authoritarian governments and pro-government paramilitaries in maintaining or expanding legal privilege, land grabs, and oppressive local order – libertarians, as libertarians, have good reasons to condemn the social evils that arise from these labor practices. Though they could in principle arise in a free market, the actual market they arose in is profoundly unfree, and there is every reason to believe that in a truly free market the conditions of ordinary laborers, even those who are very poor, would be quite different, and much better. Certainly this offers no reason for libertarians to support the state socialist "solution" of giving even more power to "progressive" government in an ill-conceived attempt to correct for the predations that plutocratic government already enabled. But it is a good reason for libertarians to support voluntary, state-free forms of solidarity – such as private "fair trade" certification, wildcat unionism, or mutual aid societies – that work to undermine exploitative practices and build a new society within the shell of the old.

# ONWARD

I should make it clear, if it is not yet clear, that my aim in this essay has been to raise some questions, provoke some discussion, and offer some categories for carrying on that discussion intelligently. I've not attempted to answer all the questions I've raised, or to provide a fully detailed elaboration of thick conceptions of libertarianism. And I've deliberately left a lot of questions open for further discussion. Two of them are worth mentioning in particular, in order to avoid possible confusion.

First, pointing out that conscientious libertarians may have good reasons, as libertarians, to favor other social projects in addition to libertarianism raises a related, but importantly distinct question: whether libertarians should favor a gradualist or an immediatist stance towards the abolition of statist controls while those other social projects remain incomplete or frustrated in their progress. In particular, if getting or keeping a flourishing free society depends on having a base of certain social or intellectual preconditions in place, should libertarians still make direct efforts to abolish all statist controls immediately and completely, regardless of the social or cultural situation? Or should they hold off until the groundwork is in place, and restrict themselves to calls for limited and moderated repeals in the meantime?

For much of his career, Murray Rothbard endorsed a form of thin libertarian anarchism, arguing that libertarianism "will get nowhere until we realize that there is and can be no "libertarian" culture."[5] At the same time, he endorsed ultra-immediatism, joking that if he had a magic button that immediately abolished an aspect of the state, he'd break his finger pushing it. In *Total Freedom*, Chris Sciabarra criticizes Rothbard's thin libertarianism as "unanchored utopianism;[6] Sciabarra argues that a "dialectical sensibility" recommends a more comprehensive three-level model of social transformation, incorporating not only to the political structure of the state, but the interlocking dynamics by which political structure (Level-3) affects, and is affected by, individual psychology and philosophy (Level-1) and the framework of established cultural institutions (Level-2).

Sciabarra's critique of Rothbardianism, and his later writing foreign policy, have emphasized the dangers of directly pursuing libertarian policies in contexts where libertarian individualism and anti-authoritarianism are not well-established in the local culture. All this strongly suggests that Sciabarra prefers a form of libertarian gradualism, and suspects that any form of immediatism depends on non-dialectical disregard for the cultural base neces-

---

5    Murray N. Rothbard, "Left-Opportunism: The Case of SLS," *Libertarian Vanguard*, Feb.-Mar. 1981: 11.

6    Sciabarra 202.

sary to sustain liberty. But whether Sciabarra's right about that, or wrong about that, you need to keep in mind that endorsing a form of strategic thickness does not, just by itself, commit you to gradualism; that's a separate issue that needs a separate argument. Believing in particular material or cultural preconditions for the flourishing or long-term survival of a free society, once statist interventions are repealed, does not entail any particular position on whether those invasions ought to continue until that base is established. A dialectical sensibility requires us to consider the possibility that individual attitudes and cultural institutions might adjust dynamically as the political structure changes, and that these changes might be favorable rather than hostile to the cultural base that we advocate. Or they may not: illiberal attitudes may be intransigent, and even without statism they may nevertheless find new, equally destructive expressions. They may even worsen. The point awaits further investigation, and is not settled simply by accepting a thick conception over a thin conception of libertarianism.

But even if you concede that immediate repeal of statist controls, without the preconditions in place, would eventually result in disaster, rather than cultural adaptation, that still doesn't settle the argument in favor of gradualism. To do that, you would need to add some kind of further moral argument that would show that people are entitled to continue invading the rights of other people in order to maintain a particular standard of living, or to stave off aggression that would otherwise be committed by some unrelated third party at some point in the future. I happen to think that the kind of arguments that you'd need to add to thick libertarianism in order to justify gradualism are morally indefensible. Fortunately, since they are separable from strategic thickness itself, there is no reason why advocates of strategic thickness need to adopt them. That's an important debate, and one worth having – but it's worth having elsewhere, since it's independent of the debate over thickness.

Second, it should be clear that I have not attempted to provide detailed justifications for the specific claims that I made on behalf of particular "thick" commitments – for example the claims that libertarians have strong reasons to oppose sexism or to support state-free efforts at mutual aid and labor solidarity. To explain the different forms of thickness, I drew most of my examples from the left libertarian literature, and I happen to think that there are good arguments to be made on that literature's behalf. But for the purposes of this essay, these claims are intended as particular illustrations of underlying concepts – not as proofs of a detailed left libertarian analysis. For all I have said here, it might still be true that further argument would reveal reasons of thickness in application, or from grounds, or in strategy, or from consequences, that support a form of libertarianism quite different from that which I advocate, such as orthodox Objectivism, or even support a form that is almost exactly the opposite, such as Hoppean "paleolibertarianism." Consider the reasons that Objectivists give for going beyond laissez-faire principles alone, and culturally glorifying big business specifically – it's basically thickness from grounds (Randian egoism) and strategic thickness (in the belief that vilifying big business provides grist for the altruist-statist mill). Or consider the reasons that Hoppe offers for ostracizing homosexuals and condemning large-scale migration of unskilled laborers – it's basically thickness from consequences, on the belief that without statist intervention against restrictive uses of property rights, these lifestyle choices would not be sustainable in the face of opposition from civil society. I, as a left libertarian, find these specific appeals specious (or, in Hoppe's case, grotesque). But that means only that I disagree with the specific premises, not with the general forms of argument that all thick forms of libertarianism help themselves to.

Just which actual social and cultural projects libertarians, as libertarians, should incorporate into theory and practice still needs to be hashed out in a detailed debate over specifics. But I hope that here I have at least cleared some of the ground that must be cleared for that debate to sensibly proceed.

# 13

*Liberty* 2.16 (May 17, 1884): 4.

# SOCIALISM: WHAT IT IS

## BENJAMIN R. TUCKER
## (1884)

DO YOU LIKE THE WORD *SOCIALISM?*" SAID A LADY TO ME THE OTHER DAY; "I FEAR I DO not; somehow I shrink when I hear it. It is associated with so much that is bad! Ought we to keep it?"

The lady who asked this question is an earnest Anarchist, a firm friend of Liberty, and – it is almost superfluous to add – highly intelligent. Her words voice the feeling of many. But after all it is only a feeling, and will not stand the test of thought. "Yes," I answered, "it is a glorious word, much abused, violently distorted, stupidly misunderstood, but expressing better than any other the purpose of political and economic progress, the aim of the Revolution in this century, the recognition of the great truth that Liberty and Equality, through the law of Solidarity, will cause the welfare of each to contribute to the welfare of all. So good a word cannot be spared, must not be sacrificed, shall not be stolen."

How can it be saved? Only by lifting it out of the confusion which obscures it, so that all may see it clearly and definitely, and what it fundamentally means. Some writers make Socialism inclusive of all efforts to ameliorate social conditions. Proudhon is reputed to have said something of the kind. However that may be, the definition seems to broad. Etymologically it is not unwarrantable, but derivatively the word has a more technical and definite meaning.

Today (pardon the paradox!) society is fundamentally anti-social. The whole so-called social fabric rests on privilege and power, and is disordered and strained in every direction by the inequalities that necessarily result therefrom. The welfare of each, instead of contributing to that of all, as it naturally should and would, almost invariably detracts from that of all. Wealth is made by legal privilege a hook with which to filch from labor's pockets. Every man who gets rich thereby makes his neighbor poor. The better off one is, the worse off the rest are. As Ruskin says, "every grain of calculated Increment to the rich is balanced by its mathematical equivalent of Decrement to the poor." The Laborer's Deficit is precisely equal to the Capitalist's Efficit.

Now, Socialism wants to change all this. Socialism says that what's one man's meat must no longer be another's poison; that no man shall be able to add to his riches except by labor; that in adding to his riches by labor alone no man makes another man poorer; that on the contrary every man thus adding to his riches makes every other man richer; that increase and concentration of wealth through labor tend to increase, cheapen, and vary production; that every increase of capital in the hands of the laborer tends, in the absence of legal monopoly, to put more products, better products, cheaper products, and a greater variety of products within the reach of every man who works; and that this fact means the physical, mental, and moral perfecting of mankind, and the realization of human fraternity. Is that not glorious? Shall a word that means all that be cast aside simply because some have tried to wed it with authority? By no means. The man who subscribes to that, whatever he may think himself, whatever he may call himself, however bitterly he may attack the thing which he mistakes for Socialism, is himself a Socialist; and the man who subscribes to its opposite and acts upon its opposite, however benevolent he may be, however pious he may be, whatever his station in society, whatever his standing in the Church, whatever his position in the State, is not a Socialist, but a Thief. For there are at bottom but two classes – the Socialists and the Thieves. Socialism, practically, is war upon usury in all its forms, the great Anti-Theft Movement of the nineteenth century; and Socialists are the only people to whom the preachers of morality have no right or occasion to cite the eighth commandment, "Thou shalt not steal!" That commandment is Socialism's flag. Only not as a commandment, but as a law of nature. Socialism does not order; it prophesies. It does not say: "Thou shalt not steal!" It says: "When all men have Liberty, thou wilt not steal."

Why, then, does my lady questioner shrink when she hears the word *Socialism*? I will tell her. Because a large number of people, who see the evils of usury and are desirous of destroying them, foolishly imagine they can do so by authority, and accordingly are trying to abolish privilege by centring all production and activity in the State to the destruction of competition and its blessings, to the degradation of the individual, and to the putrefaction of Society. They are well-meaning but misguided people, and their efforts are bound to prove abortive. Their influence is mischievous principally in this: that a large number of other people, who have not yet seen the evils of usury and do not know that Liberty will destroy them, but nevertheless earnestly believe in Liberty for Liberty's sake, are led to mistake this effort to make the State the be-all and end-all of society for the whole of Socialism and the only Socialism, and, rightly horrified at it, to hold it up as such to the deserved scorn of mankind. But the very reasonable and just criticisms of the individualists of this stripe upon State Socialism, when analyzed, are found to be directed, not against the Socialism, but against the State. So far Liberty is with them. But Liberty insists on Socialism, nevertheless – on true Socialism, Anarchistic Socialism: the prevalence on earth of Liberty, Equality, and Solidarity. From that my lady questioner will never shrink.

# 14

*Socialist Ends, Market Means. Five Essays*
(Tulsa, OK. Tulsa Alliance of the Libertarian Left 2011) 7-11.

# SOCIALIST ENDS, MARKET MEANS

## GARY CHARTIER
## (2009)

I BELIEVE THERE IS A WAY OF UNDERSTANDING SOCIALISM THAT RENDERS IT COMPATIBLE WITH a genuinely market-oriented anarchism. If socialism must mean either conventional state-socialism or state socialism with ownership of the means of production vested in local micro-states or some vaguely defined model of collective ownership rooted in a gift economy, then it has to be clear that socialism and market anarchism aren't compatible.

But it ought to be troubling, then, that one of the founding spirits of market anarchism, Benjamin Tucker, clearly considered his variety of market anarchism to be an alternative to state-socialism – as a form of socialism. Words (nod to Nicholas Lash) are known by the company they keep, and I think it's worth reminidng readers of the diverse company kept by "socialism." I think it makes sense, therefore, to offer a definition of "socialism" that will make clear why Tucker, at least, clearly ought to be included.

With that in mind, then, I suggest that we understand socialism negatively as any economic system marked by the abolition (*i*) of wage labor as the primary mode of economic activity and (*ii*) of the dominance of society by (*a*) the minority of people who regularly employ significant numbers of wage laborers and (*b*) a tiny minority of people owning large quantities of wealth and capital goods. We might understand socialism in positive terms as any economic system marked by (*i*) wide dispersal of control over the means of production; (*ii*) worker management as the primary mode of economic activity; together with (*iii*) the social pre-eminence of ordinary people, as those who both operate and manage the means of production.

State socialism has attempted to realize socialism through the power of the state. Not surprisingly, given everything we know about states, state socialism has proven in most respects to be a disaster. Coupled with the economic inefficiencies associated with central planning, the secret police, the barbed wire fences, and the suppression of dissent are all elements of state socialism's disastrous record.

If you want to define socialism as state socialism, be my guest. Many people do so. But the history of the term makes clear that many people have not meant state control or society-wide ownership of the means of production when they have talked about socialism.

## "SOCIALISM" AS GENUS, "STATE-SOCIALISM" AS SPECIES

There is good reason to use "socialism" to mean, at minimum, something like opposition to:

1. bossism (that is, subordinative workplace hierarchy); and
2. deprivation (that is, persistent, exclusionary poverty, whether resulting from state-capitalist depredation, private theft, disaster, accident, or other factors.

"Socialism" in this sense is the genus; "state-socialism" is the (much-to-be-lamented) species.

Indeed, using the "socialist" label provides the occasion for a clear distinction between the genus "socialism" and the species "state-socialism." Thus, it offers a convenient opportunity to expose and critique the statist assumptions many people reflexively make (assumptions that make it all-too-easy for political theory to take as given the presupposition that its subject matter is the question, 'What should the state do?').

I am more sympathetic than perhaps I seem to the claims of those who object to linguistic arguments that they fear may have no real impact on anyone's political judgment. I wouldn't dismiss as silly someone who said that no market anarchist could employ "socialist" without creating inescapable confusion.

## "CAPITALISM": SEEMINGLY IN THE SAME BOAT

So the first thing to say, I think, is that the same is true of "capitalism." It's a word with a history, and the history is, very often, rather less than pretty.

Consider people on the streets of a city in Latin America, or Africa, or Asia, or Europe, chanting their opposition to neoliberalism and, yes, capitalism. I find it difficult to imagine that hordes of protestors would turn out in the streets to assail po'-lil'-ol' private ownership. When a great many people say that "capitalism," is the enemy, that's surely because, among many people around the world, "capitalism" has come to mean something like "social dominance by the owners of capital," a state of affairs many people might find unappealing.

In accordance with the kind of libertarian class analysis it's easy to find in the work of people like Murray Rothbard, John Hagel, Butler Shaffer, and Roderick Long, Kevin Carson – author of the original C4SS article and Stephan Kinsella's target (to Kinsella's credit, he is not only blunt but also good-natured) – maintains that this social dominance is dependent on the activity of the state. Remove the props provided by the state, he argues, and "capitalism" in this sense – the sense in which the term is employed pejoratively by millions of people who have no ideological investment in statism or bureaucratic tyranny – is finished.

## SOCIALIST ENDS, MARKET MEANS

That doesn't mean that the market anarchist must somehow have forgotten her commitment to markets. As Kevin Carson, Brad Spangler, Charles Johnson, and others have observed, as a historical matter there clearly have been people who have argued for the abolition of state-supported privilege and who have enthusiastically favored freed markets who have worn the label "socialist" confidently. Tucker and Hodgskin wouldn't have agreed that socialism is synonymous with collective ownership. Rather, they would have said, various schemes for state ownership (or for collective ownership by some quasi-state entity) are ways of achieving the underlying goal of socialism – an end to bossism in the workplace, the dominance of the owners of capital in society, and to significant, widespread deprivation. But, Tucker and Hodgskin would have said, these are both unjust and ineffective means of achieving this goal – better to pursue it by freeing the market than by enhancing the power of the state.

Of course, if "socialism" means "state [or para-state] ownership of the means of production," there is no sense in characterizing Carson or any other market anarchist as defending "clearly pro-socialist positions." On the other hand, if "socialism" can have a sufficiently broad meaning – one compatible with market anarchism – that it makes sense to say that Kevin (or another market anarchist) does defend such positions, then it is unclear why talk of "socialism" should be objectionable.

## DISTINGUISHING MARKET-ORIENTED SOCIALISTS FROM STATE-SOCIALISTS

Carson, for one, clearly supports the existence of private ownership rights. And I have seen nothing to suggest that he would disagree with the claim that market interactions have to feature non-state ownership if they are to be voluntary. He's consistently clear that there could, would, should be alternate kinds of property regimes in a stateless society, but none of those he considers appropriate would be rooted in coercion. So I'm puzzled by the implication that he's an opponent of private ownership.

None of that means that one can't point to despicable regimes (Pol Pot, anyone?) who've worn the "socialist" label proudly. But surely if the idea is to point to despicable applications of a term, one can do the same with "capitalism" as with "socialism"? (Think Pinochet-era Chile.) The association of "capitalism" with mercantilism and corporatism and the dominance of entrenched elites is hardly a creation of left libertarians and other market anarchists: it's an association that's common in the minds of many people around the world and which is thoroughly warranted by the behavior of states and of many businesses and socially powerful individuals.

## BEYOND SEMANTICS

So, in short, I'm not sure that using "socialism" as the label for a particular sort of market anarchist project, or of "capitalism" for what that project opposes, has to be seen as just an exercise in semantic game-playing.

1. *Emancipatory intent.* For instance: labeling a particular sort of market anarchist project "socialist" clearly identifies its emancipatory intent: it links that project with the opposition to bossism and deprivation that provide the real moral and emotional force of socialist appeals of all sorts.

2. *Warranted opposition to "capitalism."* Thus, identifying one's project as "socialist" is a way of making clear one's opposition to "capitalism" – as that term is understood by an enormous range of ordinary people around the world. The "socialist" label signals to them that a market anarchist project like Kevin's is on their side and that it is opposed to those entities they identify as their oppressors.

3. *Forcing the state-socialist to distinguish between her attachment to ends and her attachment to means.* A final rationale: suppose a market anarchist like Kevin points out to the state-socialist – by sincerely owning the "socialist" label – that she or he shares the state-socialist's ends, while disagreeing radically with the state-socialist's judgments about appropriate means to those ends. This simultaneously sincere and rhetorically effective move allows the market anarchist to challenge the state-socialist to confront the reality that there is an inconsistency between the state-socialist's emancipatory goals and the authoritarian means she or he professes to prefer. It sets the stage for the market anarchist to highlight the fact that purported statist responses to bossism create more, and more powerful, bosses, that the state is much better at causing deprivation than curing it.

Thus, the market anarchist's use of "socialism" creates an occasion for the state-socialist to ask her- or himself, perhaps for the first time, "Am I really more attached to the means or to the end?" I realize that what I intend as a rhetorical question may not – if the state-socialist cares more about power than principle – elicit the intended answer. But it seems to me that, for many state-socialists, the recognition that the left-wing market anarchist sought socialist goals by non-statist means provides the state-socialist with good reason to rethink her attachment to the state, to conclude that it was pragmatic and unnecessary, and that her genuinely principled attachment was to the cause of human emancipation.

This means there's a meaningful opportunity for education – to highlight the existence of a credible tradition advancing a different meaning of "socialism."

## LIBERTARIANISM AND THE SOCIALIST VISION

Now, it is obviously open to a critic to maintain that she has no particular concern with workplace hierarchies or with deprivation, or that they should be of no concern to the libertarian-qua-libertarian, since objections to them do not flow from libertarian principles.

I am happy to identify as an anarchist who favors markets, as well as individual autonomy. But I do not ask myself whether my appreciation for "socialism" in this sense is something to which I am committed qua libertarian. Rather, my willingness to identify as a libertarian is licensed by a more fundamental set of moral judgments which also make "socialism" in the relevant sense attractive, and which help to ensure that the senses in which I am a libertarian and in which I am a socialist consistent.

At minimum, there seems to be some reason for using the label "capitalism," so clearly understood to be the altar of "socialism," for the kind of economic system we have now, backed up so clearly by state-granted and state-maintained privilege. But I think it's worth emphasizing that "capitalism" – both because of its history and because of its superficial content – seems to suggest more than merely state-supported privilege (though surely it implies at least this): it seems to suggest "social dominance by the owners of capital (understood to be other than the owners of labor)."

Now, it happens to be the case that I agree with Kevin, Roderick, and others that this dominance is dependent in large measure on state abuses. But I don't want simply to emphasize my objection to these abuses – though I certainly do – but also to express my opposition, per se, to the dominance of the owners of capital, thus understood. That's why I am disinclined to regard talk of "socialism" as important, as highlighting, at minimum, the trajectory toward which the market anarchist project be thought to lead, and as identifying morally important values to which my sort of market anarchist, at least, is committed, and which do not seem to me like good candidates for the status of "particular interests," if these are understood as arbitrary, even if morally licit.

I am avowedly opposed to the institutionalized use of force against persons, and against their (Aristotelian-Thomist) ownership rights, and I am quite willing to say so loudly or clearly. That makes me, by my own lights, a libertarian. But I am not prepared to dismiss my invocation of "socialism" as a label that has not lost its usefulness for the left-libertarian project, as simply an expression of individual preference with which no good libertarian ought to interfere, simply because interference would be unreasonably aggressive. Rather, "socialism" names a set of concerns, including ones regarding attractive patterns of social organization, that there is good reason for left-libertarians whole-heartedly to endorse.

# PART THREE

## Ownership

# 15

*Formulations* 5.3 (Spring 1998) <http://
freenation.org/a/f5311.html><http://
praxeology.net/libertariannation/a/
f5311.html>(Aug. 22, 2011).

# A PLEA FOR PUBLIC PROPERTY

## RODERICK T. LONG
## (1998)

### PUBLIC OR PRIVATE?

LIBERTARIANS OFTEN ASSUME THAT A FREE SOCIETY WILL BE ONE IN WHICH ALL (OR NEARLY all) property is private. I have previously expressed my dissent from this consensus, arguing that libertarian principles instead support a substantial role for public property.[1] In this article I develop this heretical position further.

Let me specify once again what sort of public property I am defending. To most people, "public property" means "government property," on the (dubious) theory that governments hold their property in trust for the public, and administer such property with an eye to the public interest. As an anarchist, I do not regard government as a legitimate institution, and so do not advocate government property of any sort. But this is not the only kind of public property. As I wrote in my earlier article:

---

1    "In Defense of Public Space," *Formulations* 3.3 (Spring 1996).

Throughout history, legal doctrine has recognized, alongside property owned by the organized public (that is, the public as organized into a state and represented by government officials), an additional category of property owned by the unorganized public. This was property that the public at large was deemed to have a right of access to, but without any presumption that government would be involved in the matter at all.

It is public property in this sense that I am defending.

I want to stress, however, that in defending public property I do not mean to be criticizing private property. I am a strong proponent of private property. But what I am maintaining is that the very features that make private property valuable are also possessed, in certain contexts, by public property, and so public property can be valuable for the same reasons.

First I shall consider three common libertarian arguments for private property, and I shall try to show that each of these arguments also supports a role for public property. Second, I shall consider several objections I have encountered to my position, and I shall attempt to meet them.

## THE NATURAL-RIGHTS ARGUMENT FOR PRIVATE PROPERTY

The standard libertarian natural-rights argument for private property goes back to John Locke's *Second Treatise of Government*, and rests on two basic claims: a normative claim about how we should treat other people, and a descriptive claim about the boundaries of the person.

The normative claim we may call the Respect Principle. This principle says that it is morally wrong to subject other people to one's own ends without their consent, except as a response to aggression by those others. (There is disagreement as to what deeper moral truths, if any, provide the grounding for this principle, but that question lies beyond my present topic.)

The descriptive claim we may call the Incorporation Principle. This principle says that once I "mix my labor" with an external object – i.e., alter it so as to make it an instrument of my ongoing projects – that object becomes part of me. The case for this principle is that it explains why the matter I'm made of is part of me. After all, I wasn't born with it; living organisms survive through constant replacement of material. The difference between an apple I eat (whose matter becomes part of my cellular composition) and a wooden branch that I carve into a spear (a detachable extension of my hand) is only one of degree.[2]

When we put the Respect Principle and the Incorporation Principle together, the result is that it is wrong to appropriate the products of other people's labor; for if your spear is a part of you, then I cannot subject your spear to my ends without thereby subjecting you to my ends. In the words of the 19th-century French libertarians Leon Wolowski and Émile Levasseur:

> The producer has left a fragment of his own person in the thing which has thus become valuable, and may hence be regarded as a prolongation of the faculties of man acting upon external nature. As a free being he belongs to himself; now the cause, that is to say, the productive force, is himself; the effect, that is to say, the wealth produced, is still himself... Property, made manifest by labor, participates in the rights of the person whose emanation it is; like him, it is inviolable so long as it does not extend so far as to come into collision with another right...[3]

The Incorporation Principle transforms the Respect Principle from a simple right to personal security into a general right to private property.

## HOW NATURAL RIGHTS SUPPORT PUBLIC PROPERTY TOO

But this Lockean argument for private property rights can be adapted to support public property rights as well. Lockeans hold that individuals have a property right to the products of their labor (so long as they trespass on no one else's rights in producing them); they also typically hold that individuals have a property right to any goods that they receive by voluntary transfer from their legitimate owners (since to deny such a right would be to interfere with the right of the givers to dispose of their property as they choose). But the public at large can acquire property rights in both these ways. To quote once more from "In Defense of Public Space":

2    For a fuller defense of this claim, see Samuel C. Wheeler III, "Natural Property Rights as Body Rights," *The Main Debate: Communism versus Capitalism*, ed. Tibor R. Machan (New York: Random 1987) 272–89.

3    Qtd. Murray N. Rothbard, *For A New Liberty: The Libertarian Manifesto*, rev. ed. (San Francisco: Fox 1994) 36–37.

Consider a village near a lake. It is common for the villagers to walk down to the lake to go fishing. In the early days
of the community it's hard to get to the lake because of all
the bushes and fallen branches in the way. But over time, the
way is cleared and a path forms – not through any centrally
coordinated effort, but simply as a result of all the individuals
walking that way day after day.

The cleared path is the product of labor – not any individual's labor, but of all of them together. If one villager decided
to take advantage of the now-created path by setting up a gate
and charging tolls, he would be violating the collective property right that the villagers together have earned.

Public property can also be the product of gift. In 19th-
century England, it was common for roads to be built privately and then donated to the public for free use. This was
done not out of altruism but because the roadbuilders owned
land and businesses alongside the site of the new road, and
they knew that having a road there would increase the value
of their land and attract more customers to their businesses.

Since collectives, like individuals, can mix their labor with unowned
resources to make those resources more useful to their purposes, collectives,
too can claim property rights by homestead. And since collectives, like individuals, can be the beneficiaries of free voluntary transfer, collectives too
can claim property rights by bequest.

I should note one important difference between the homesteading case
and the bequest case. In the homesteading case, it is presumably not the
human race at large, but only the inhabitants of the village, that acquire a
collective property right in the cleared path; since it would be difficult for
humankind as a whole, or even a substantial portion thereof, to mix its
labor with a single resource, and so the homesteading argument places an
upper limit on the size of property-owning collectives. But there seems to
be no analogous limit to the size of the collective to which one can freely
give one's property, so here the recipient might well be the human race as
a whole.

I have argued that the Lockean argument does not specify private property as the only justifiable option, but makes a place for public property as
well. It should also be noted that in at least one case, the Lockean argument
positively forbids private property: namely, the case of intellectual property.

This fact is not always recognized by Lockeans. But consider: suppose
Proprius, a defender of protectionist legislation, were to invoke Lockean

principles, saying, "Well, surely private property is a good thing, right? So the market for widgets should be my private property; no one else should be allowed to enter that market without my permission. I demand a government-granted monopoly in widget production." No Lockean would take this argument seriously, for a market consists in the freely chosen interactions of individuals – so Proprius cannot own a market without owning people, and ownership of other people is forbidden by the Respect Principle.

Suppose, however, that Proprius, our would-be monopolist, is also the inventor of the widget. Is his plea for exclusive control of the widget market now justified? Many Lockeans would think so, because we have a right to control the products of our labor, and if the product of Proprius' labor is the idea of the widget, then no one should be able to use or implement that idea without Proprius' permission.

But the Lockean view is not that we come to own whatever we mix our labor with; rather, we come to own whatever previously unowned item we mix our labor with. My plowing a field does not make it mine, if the field was yours to begin with. Likewise, the fact that my labor is the causal origin of the widget-idea in your mind may mean that in some sense I have mixed my labor with your mind; but it was your mind to begin with, so you, not I, am the legitimate owner of any improvements I make in it. (For a fuller discussion, see my "The Libertarian Case Against Intellectual Property Rights," Formulations, Vol. III, No. 1 (Autumn 1995).)

## THE AUTONOMY ARGUMENT FOR PRIVATE PROPERTY

A somewhat different libertarian argument for private property focuses on the human need for autonomy: the ability to control one's own life without interference from others. Without private property, I have no place to stand that I can call my own; I have no protected sphere within which I can make decisions unhampered by the will of others. If autonomy (in this sense) is valuable, then we need private property for its realization and protection.

## HOW AUTONOMY SUPPORTS PUBLIC PROPERTY TOO

It is true that private property provides a protected sphere of free decision-making – for the property's owners. But what is the position of those who are not property owners (specifically, those who do not own land)? A system of exclusively private property certainly does not guarantee them a "place to stand." If I am evicted from private plot A, where can I go, except adjoining private plot B, if there is no public highway or parkland connecting the various private spaces? If everywhere I can stand is a place where I have no right to stand without permission, then, it seems, I exist only by the sufferance of the "Lords of the Earth" (in Herbert Spencer's memorable phrase).

Far from providing a sphere of independence, a society in which all property is private thus renders the propertyless completely dependent on those who own property. This strikes me as a dangerous situation, given the human propensity to abuse power when power is available.[4]

It may be argued in response that a libertarian society will be so economically prosperous that those who own no land will easily acquire sufficient resources either to purchase land or to guarantee favorable treatment from existing land owners. This is true enough in the long run, if the society remains a genuinely libertarian one. But in the short run, while the landless are struggling to better their condition, the land owners might be able to exploit them in such a way as to turn the society into something other than a free nation.

## THE RIVALRY ARGUMENT FOR PRIVATE PROPERTY

For many libertarians, the most important argument for private property is what Garret Hardin has labeled "the tragedy of the commons" (though the basic idea goes back to Aristotle). Most resources are rivalrous – that is to say, the use of the resource by one person diminishes the amount, or the value, of that resource for others. If a rivalrous resource is also public property, meaning that no member of the public may be excluded from its use, there will be no incentive to conserve or improve the resource (why bother to sow what others may freely reap?); on the contrary, the resource will be overused and swiftly exhausted, since the inability to exclude other users makes it risky to defer consumption (why bother to save what others may freely spend?). Hence private property is needed in order to prevent depletion of resources.

## HOW RIVALRY SUPPORTS PUBLIC PROPERTY TOO

The rivalry argument is quite correct as far as it goes. But how far is that?

First, let's notice that the argument only applies to goods that are in fact rivalrous. So once again it doesn't apply to intellectual property; my use of

---

4    This is a reason for my reservations about the proprietary-community model for a free nation, in which all land in the nation is held by a central agency and leased to its inhabitants. See "The Return of Leviathan: Can We Prevent It?," *Formulations* 3.3 (Spring 1996).

the idea of the widget doesn't make less available for others. Nor does it make others' widgets less valuable; on the contrary, the more widgets there are, the more uses for widgets are likely to be discovered or developed, and so the value of each widget increases. Ideas are public property, in that no one may be legitimately excluded from their use.

Another example of a largely nonrivalrous good is the Internet. I say *largely* nonrivalrous, because the Internet does have a physical basis, which, though constantly expanding, is finite at any given time, and an increase in users can cause delays for everyone. But this rivalrous aspect is offset by the reverse effect: the value of the Internet to any one user increases as the volume of available information, potential correspondents, etc., increases; so additional users on balance increase the value of the good as a whole.

It might be argued that this the-more-the-merrier effect occurs only with goods that are wholly or largely nonphysical, but could never apply to more concrete resources like land. As Carol Rose and David Schmidtz have shown,[5] however, although any physical resource is finite and so inevitably has some tragedy-of-the-commons aspects, many resources have "comedy-of-the-commons" aspects as well, and in some cases the latter may outweigh the former, thus making public property more efficient than private property.

For instance (to adapt one of Carol Rose's examples), suppose that a public fair is a comedy-of-the-commons good; the more people who participate, the better (within certain limits, at any rate). Imagine two such fairs, one held on private property and the other on public. The private owner has an incentive to exclude all participants who do not pay him a certain fee; thus the fair is deprived of all the participants who cannot afford the fee. (I am assuming that the purpose of the fair is primarily social rather than commercial, so that impecunious participants would bring as much value to the fair as wealthy ones.) The fair held on public property will thus be more successful than the one held on private property.

Yet, it may be objected, so long as a comedy-of-the-commons good still has some rivalrous, tragedy-of-the-commons aspects, it will be depleted, and thus the comedy-of-the-commons benefits will be lost anyway. But this assumes that privatization is the only way to prevent overuse. In fact, however, most societies throughout history have had common areas whose users were successfully restrained by social mores, peer pressure, and the like.

---

5    Carol Rose, "The Comedy of the Commons: Custom, Commerce, and Inherently Public Property," *University of Chicago Law Review* 53.3 (Sum. 1986): 711–81; David Schmidtz, "The Institution of Property," *Social Philosophy and Policy* 11 (1994): 42–62.

## OBJECTION ONE: THE COHERENCE OF PUBLIC PROPERTY

One common libertarian objection to public property – and particularly, public ownership of land – is that the whole idea makes no sense: a resource cannot be collectively owned unless every part of the resource admits of simultaneous use by all members of the collective. This objection has been forcefully stated by Isabel Paterson:

> Two bodies cannot occupy the same place at the same time... Ten men may be legally equal owners of one field, but none of them can get any good of it unless its occupancy and use is allotted among them by measures of time and space... If all ten wished to do exactly the same thing at the same time in the same spot, it would be physically impossible... [G]roup ownership necessarily resolves into management by one person...[6]

Paterson does, however, offer the following qualification to her claim that public property is inherently impossible:

> [I]t is practicable – whether or not it is necessary or advisable – to make roads public property, because the use of a road is to traverse it. Though the user does in fact occupy a given space at a given moment, the duration is negligible, so that there is no need to take time and space into account except by negation, a prohibition: the passenger is not allowed to remain as of right indefinitely on any one spot in the road. The same rule applies to parks and public buildings. The arrangement is sufficiently practicable in those conditions to admit the fiction of 'public ownership.' To be sure, even in the use of a road, if too many members of the public try to move along it at once, the rule reverts to first come, first served (allotment in time and space), or the authorities may close the road. The public has not the essential property right of continuous and final occupancy... Public property then admits of use by the public only in transit, not for production, exchange, consumption, or for security as standing ground.[7]

---

6    Isabel Paterson, *The God of the Machine* (New Brunswick: Transaction 1993) 180–1.

7    Paterson 181-2.

Note that here Paterson actually points out three ways in which public property can be feasible. First, it may be the case that not enough people are competing for use of the same portion of the property to cause a conflict. Paterson assumes this will only happen in cases where any one user's occupancy of a given area is of minimal duration; but clearly the same result could be achieved when the total volume of users is low enough, and the resource itself is homogeneous enough, that a lengthier occupancy of any particular portion of the resource is no inconvenience to anyone else.

Second and third, in cases where use is becoming rivalrous, Paterson offers two different possible solutions. One solution is to require frequent turnover, so that no one member of the public is allowed to monopolize any portion of the resource for longer than a certain time period; the other solution is to adopt "first come, first served," meaning that those who currently occupy portions of the property may stay there and exclude newcomers. Paterson thinks that both of these options take away from the genuinely "public" nature of the property. But do they?

According to Paterson, the turnover requirement takes away from the publicness of the property because the public then lacks "the essential property right of continuous and final occupancy." But is this true? If no individual member of the public has "the essential property right of continuous and final occupancy," it hardly follows that the public as such lacks this right; in fact, the turnover requirement is precisely a means of implementing that right.

What about the first-come-first-served rule? Paterson may think that this ends the publicness of the property because it gives individuals the right to exclude others from the particular portions they have claimed. But this falls short of a full private property right. If I have private ownership of a portion of land, then that land remains mine, off limits to others, even when I am away from the land. But if I leave the particular area of a public park that I've been squatting in, I lose all rights to it; in that respect, what I have a "right" to is more like a place in line than it is like freehold property.

Which is preferable, the turnover rule or the first-come-first-served rule? Presumably it depends on the function of the resource in question. In the case of a road, it is in the interest of the owners – the public – that the turnover rule be applied, because a road loses its usefulness if it cannot be traversed. However, the autonomy argument suggests that not all public property should be subject to the turnover rule, so in some cases the first-come-first-served rule is appropriate.

Suppose a conflict arises between two users of the property, one who thinks it should be governed by the turnover rule, and another who thinks it should be governed by the first-come-first-served rule. What happens?

Well, ideally the decision should be made by the owner: the public. But only a unanimous decision could count as the will of the public, and unanimous decisions are hard to come by. (Putting the matter to a vote would reveal only the will of a majority faction of the public.) In that case, the public is in the same situation as an infant, a lunatic, a missing person, or a person in a coma: the public has the right to decide the matter, but is currently incapable of making a coherent decision, and so the decision must be made for them by a court which attempts (presumably in response to a class-action suit) to determine what is in the best interest of the rights-holder.

## OBJECTION TWO: POLICING PUBLIC PROPERTY

As Rich Hammer is fond of pointing out, shopping malls are generally safer than city streets. As Rich notes, this is so for two reasons. First, the owners of the malls have a financial incentive to police their premises so as to avoid losing customers, while government police face much weaker incentives. Second, mall owners can set higher standards for what is permissible behavior on their premises, and can exclude undesirable persons more or less at will, while the police have less power to kick people off the city streets. Does this mean that public property in a libertarian society will be under-policed?

Not necessarily. Consider the incentive issue first. Since the property is public, everyone has an equal right to police it. But some will have stronger motives for policing than others. Consider the case mentioned earlier, of the road built for and donated to the public by those who owned property alongside the road and hoped the road's proximity would raise their property values and bring increased traffic to their businesses. The same incentives that led the owners to build this road would also lead them to police it, since property values will be higher and customers will be more plentiful if the road is safe.

Moreover, the unsafeness of city streets results not only from the fact that they are public but from the fact that the police enjoy a monopoly on protection services. A competitive market in security would probably find some way to offer its customers protection while on public property. For example, public parks might be patrolled by a consortium of insurance companies, if a substantial number of their customers enjoy visiting public parks.

As for the higher-standards issue, it is true that users of public property face a somewhat greater risk from their fellow users than users of private property do. A private mall (particularly in a libertarian society where the right to control access to one's private property is legally protected) can exclude users who simply appear to pose a threat to other users, even if they have committed no overt act (or can admit them only if they post a bond, disarm themselves, show proof of insurance or a letter from their pastor, etc.). Public property, by contrast, must be open to anyone whose conduct so far is peaceful. By the same token, however, public property allows more freedom. That is why the best option is a society that makes room for both public and private property. Those who place a high value on security, and are willing to put up with some burdensome restrictions in order to get it (call them the Little Old Ladies), will be free to patronize private property, while those who seek self-expression, are averse to restrictions, and are willing to put up with more risk from others (call them the Gun-Toting Pot-Smoking Nudist Bikers), will likewise be free to patronize public property.

## OBJECTION THREE: LIABILITY AND PUBLIC PROPERTY

In a free society, people are liable for harm that they cause. Now suppose I own the road that runs past your house, and I decide to donate that road to the general public. Now it is no longer possible to exclude undesirables from the road. There used to be guards at the toll gate who checked drivers' IDs, but now they are gone, and one day some loony who in the old days would have been excluded takes the public road to your house and massacres your family. Since the loss to your security was caused by my decision, it has been suggested to me (by Rich Hammer) that I should be legally liable for the result. And if this is so, then public property would not be tolerated in a free nation, because the liability costs would simply be too high.

But surely a libertarian legal system will not hold people liable for every harm to which they merely made a causal contribution. The current statist trend of holding gun manufacturers liable for the use of guns by criminals, and so forth, flies in the face of the libertarian principle of personal responsibility. An owner is not obligated to check out the background of everyone he gives or sells property to.

## OBJECTION FOUR: REVERSION OF PUBLIC PROPERTY

Once property becomes public, how can it ever become private again? In a free-market economy, property tends to be assigned to its highest-valued use, because those who value the property more will purchase it from those who value it less. But if I value Central Park more than the public at large does, how do I go about purchasing it from the public? The dispersed, disorganized, and divided public lacks the ability to consent to the sale.

This is a difficult problem, to which I do not have a full solution. But let me try out a few possibilities.

There are two ways I can lose my claim to property. I can give or sell it, or I can abandon it. The public is not in a position to give or sell its property,[8] but perhaps it is capable of abandoning it.

What counts as the public's having abandoned a piece of property? Well, the easiest case would be if no one has used it for a very long time. (How long? Well, the length of time should presumably be the same as whatever is accepted in the case of abandoning private property.) But what if only a few people have used it? Does that count as the public's using it (given that the property has never been used by the entire public)?

Or suppose I privatize some portion of the property, claiming it for my own use, fencing it in and so forth. Perhaps it then counts as mine so long as no one protests. (How widely do I have to advertise the fact that I've done this?) But again, what if just a few people protest – does that count?

Ultimately these problems will have to be resolved by a libertarian legal system, through evolving common-law precedents. That's fine with me. What I would want to insist on, though, is that some role for public property is important for a libertarian society. An all-private system can be oppressive, just as an all-public one can be; but a system that allows networks of private spaces and public spaces to compete against each other offers the greatest scope for individual freedom.

---

8    At least I don't think so. Someone could argue that the court could act on behalf of the people's interests, authorizing the transfer of ownership from the collective to me, in exchange for the "price" of my doing something judged to be of general benefit to the public. But I am wary of heading too far down that path. For one thing, if the court acquires too much power to administer the property of the "disorganized public," we start to move back toward the "organized public" model of government property, and the whole idea of free access is replaced by access-in-the-interests-of-the-public-as-determined-by-some-official. For another, the value of public property is severely undermined if it can be unpredictably privatized on some judge's say-so.

## 16

*Human Iterations* (n.p., Nov. 13, 2009)
<http://humaniterations.wordpress.
com/2009/11/13/from-whence-do-
property-titles-arise/> (Aug. 22, 2011).

# FROM WHENCE DO PROPERTY TITLES ARISE?

## *WILLIAM GILLIS*
## *(2009)*

MANY MARKET THEORISTS TAKE PROPERTY TITLES AS AXIOMATIC AND THEN DEVELOP coercive apparatuses to enforce them – justifying such coercion by appealing to notions like implicit consent and/or the justness of contracts that sell off part of one's agency in the future. This rightfully bugs the crap out of many anarcho-communists. Left market theorists in turn tend to write off these apprehensions as a contention over differing ideal systems of property – ie differences over what constitutes abandonment and the general viability of collective property.

But this, as I've argued time and time again, is a profoundly limited understanding of the criticisms being lobbed against them.

First off, not every system of mediating between different people's desires or uses for objects is describable in terms of property titles. Property titles are claims by discrete agents to absolute veto power over the use of an object; they're a construct used for negotiating between the justness of uses by individuals with competing intentions for an object. Property titles solve the problem by determining whether A or

B then gets to personally make the decision between direction 1 or 2 for a given object.

But this clearly isn't the only way to approach such situations.

When anarcho-communists talk of societies without the concept of property they often mean a social system where decisions over how to use any specific object or resource are never limited to a discrete body of select individuals but are rather discussions open to anyone and everyone with a stake, desire or idea to contribute. There the critical economic entities are directions rather than veto-titles, concepts rather than individuals. The mediation processes possible can be incredibly complex and dynamic. So on a protozoic level you might have simple discussion or unchallenged focus (I specialize in the use of a single toothbrush and consequently, given that toothbrushes' historical context, not many people are going to have a more useful proposal for its use). While aggregate systems of more advanced mechanisms are visible in the open source development. In short where the most scarce resource is personal time and the weight of one's voice is the nearest thing to currency. At the same time there are often scarcities in space (functionally identical to material) for widely varying projects and in response entire ecosystems of discussion open up. It's worth noting that under many systems of property-titles if the legal experts cannot reach consensus on who is the legitimate owner of an object nothing is done with the object in the meantime. Those involved in contending differing uses for an object in a property-less society are directly capable of far more diverse means of negotiation, but so to, if they can't reach consensus, then nothing is done with the object. Because literally everyone in the world has the capacity to veto.

To some this might appear – while a philosophically coherent counter-proposal to property, and even briefly workable on a small level – completely batshit insane. And maybe so. But in practice such external-to-property approaches are often workable enough. The lone immature interjecting troublemaker, or any other conceivable exploit of consensus, simply doesn't exist after a few social iterations. Because everyone is dependent upon everyone else, no matter how distant a community they come from and thus its in their interest to maintain, develop and convey goodwill.

Obviously however, just because such differing economic approaches might make better software for a fraction of the energy Microsoft spends doesn't mean that it can do things like move goods between locations to satisfy demand efficiently or signal all the costs of one consumption versus another. Without the capacity to assign value to spatial/physical relationships (as with the realm of actors and objects) one can't concretely mediate between those relationships. And whatever the dominant dilemmas might be in primitive cultures of plenty or posthuman hives of nanobots, it shouldn't be particularly controversial to assert that the placement of material objects is the central calculational problem in the world today. Some form of property titles seems called for, however sticky, however collectively or individually managed.

The point is that's a debate over fitness. While it may be undesirable, it remains entirely possible to construct a society outside of property altogether.

Following the popular slogan "Everything for Everyone" the stubborn market theorist might still proclaim that such a society would still count as a system with property title expanded to everyone. While practically meaningless this wouldn't necessarily be wrong. But as a theoretical framework in such instance property titles would be missing the point. No one in that society would think in anything approaching such terms.

Which leads us to a second critique of property.

It's not hard to come to the conclusion that the very adoption of property titles in our minds leads toward a worldview of increasing compartmentalization and taxonomy. Indeed this is a popular assumption. By progressively chopping up the world around us, the notion goes, we become inclined to view the world solely as a tally sheet of ownership.

Forgive the digression to my 90s Nickelodeon childhood, but in illustration I am reminded of an episode of Angry Beavers in which the brothers suddenly discover that they each have a musk pouch capable of marking items with a colored personal stench that repels everyone but themselves. This quickly sets off a war of personal claim until the entire world is divvied up with one stench or the other, each brother more and more completely obsessed with the tally until they can think of nothing else.

This is perhaps the most classic criticism of capitalism – one of simple psychology – and yet it seems to be a critique market theorists are incapable of parsing. To many an anticapitalist the problem with the capitalist framework is its inherent bent towards materialism, ultimately to the point of treating human beings as objects. But this is incomprehensible for Libertarians because they see respect for property titles as entirely stemming from a respect for personal agency. In practical, everyday terms respect for another person's agency often comes down to a respect for the inviolability of their body. Do not shoot them, do not rape them, do not torture them. Because humans are tool-using creatures like hermit crabs there is often no clear line between our biomass and our possessions (we use clothes instead of fur, retain dead mass excreted as hair follicles, etc.), and so a respect for another's person seems to extend in some ways to a respect for things that they use. Begin to talk of Rights and these associations must be drawn more absolutely. And sure enough we already have a common sense proscription often enforced in absolutist terms that matches this intuition; do not steal.

Yet the anticapitalists are clearly on to something. Even setting aside the evolutionary cognitive biases of homo sapiens, we as individuals have limited processing. We can't think everything at the same time. If some of the thought processes necessary to succeed and flourish under in a given system run out of control and take up more and more space, others – like those behind why we adopted that system in the first place – will get pushed to the periphery.

If a certain metric is set as the alpha and omega of a society, whether it be the acquisition of a specific universal currency or simply aggregate atoms, its status as the requirement or key to any pursuit or desire can end up having an effect upon those pursuits and desires.

Anticapitalists often disingenuously blur the distinction between wealth and coercive power – wealth and/or disequilibria in wealth do not inherently have to grant any capacity for social control – but it's certainly true that direct pursuits of power and wealth share the same form. Singlemindedness is progressively rewarded, until the inertia of this approach crowds out of mind the reason we originally assigned value to wealth or power.

Consequently, rather than focus on accumulating property titles or money as a gateway to opportunity, anarcho-communists argue, we should focus on accumulating goodwill.

I don't disagree.

But once you characterize this focus on goodwill in market terms, a la something similar to Doctorow's reputation markets, the path out of all these tangles becomes apparent. It seems pretty damn clear that property titles are a tool with incredible utility in the world as it exists today and the technical challenges we face. As such it stands to reason that those within a goodwill focused anarcho-communist society stand a comparative advantage to negotiate and adopt a second-order system for developing and recognizing property titles. Regardless of precisely how their market ends up dynamically mediating this, goodwill would remain the primary good capable of being turned into, among other things, selective veto use titles to physical objects. As such we can clear the psychological hurtle: without a state coerced enforcement system underpinning property titles or centralized banks and currency, property titles are not as stable or universally applicable an investment as goodwill. And goodwill, as opposed to property titles, is directly, methodologically tied to appreciating and respecting people as agents.[1]

---

1    There is a point to be made here about the problem of manipulation, but
     I think it's a much broader point that no structural system can address di-

This suggests a way to tackle fringe conditions in ownership. Rothbard readily recognized, for instance, that a world in which one man held title to everything would clearly be indiscernible from tyranny. Expand the number of owners and you'd still have an oligarchy. Even granting a token amount of wealth to the rest of the populace wouldn't necessarily jump start the market and allow it to drift back in a more dynamic and egalitarian direction, because said wealth may simply be insufficient as capital.

However, if property is a second-order good derived from market institutions based in reputation/goodwill/credit, then if one class systematically fucked over their credit with all of another class the underclass would no longer have any incentive to respect their title claims because no individual within it would fear even marginal sanction or loss of goodwill for occupying and appropriating their wealth. Simply put, if before anyone else can do anything on a new colony I create robots to till the entire surface of the planet, that doesn't inherently create an incentive among the rest of the colonists to respect a veto-use claim on my part to the entire planet. If others admire and derive value from my mass-tilling project (or from the potential products of it) then my voice is more likely to be respected in discussion over its uses, but if I want to obtain acceptance of a veto-use claim, it would have to derive from the desire of others' desire of social conditions of respect conducive to undertaking their own projects and having their own stuff respected. One gravitates towards adopting property titles because through their exchange one can much further maximize the satiation of one's desires (agreeing to butt the hell out of other people's decisions when it comes to the use of certain objects in exchange for them butting the hell out of your decisions with other objects). Accepting my ownership of literally everything would make that impossible.

Not only does this cope with such boundary conditions, but it also addresses old marxist paranoia about the runaway accumulation of wealth through usury.

Viewed in the light of a reputation market, Jeremy Weiland's old point is even more apt: without the state the more wealth you control the more ridiculously you stand to risk having to pay through the nose to secure against theft and betrayal from those you're paying.

It's easier to steal a million dollars from the bank, or a vault, than to rob a thousand or so common people... It may be that in a free market there

---

rectly, because on such a level we can't dictate intent, we can only recognize and work around biases. So it's no more a fundamental problem than it is for anarcho-communism. That said, I think intent and psychological issues of control are rightfully at the very core of the anarchist project. It just falls outside the purview of this discussion.

will exist a natural, mean personal wealth value, beyond which diminishing returns enter quickly, and below which one is extremely disposed towards profit and enrichment.

It's a distinction between information and objects; ultimately you can't steal good credit. People's trust, goodwill and their whole panorama of intention towards you exists within them internally. It's accessible by anyone anywhere, but they're the only ones capable of changing it. There are no banks it can be kept within, only distributed collective or institutional relay points through which it can be conveyed. And trust critically underlies all material transactions.

Incidentally this renders the entire debate over proposed systematic prohibitions of wages, rent, and interest moot. Obviously all will be, in some contexts, however fringe, desirably or neutrally regarded by all parties. But even if they crop up as large phenomenon, that's not reason to panic, flip the fuck out and organize shit like armed roving 'homesteaders' with ideologically precise definitions of legitimate property. Instead the market will already be ready to grind down or impede any vast swathes of accumulated wealth because it will be the market that negotiates the acceptance of said wealth. Not necessarily through malicious crime, but through higher-level market mechanisms that ultimately give rise the extent and strength of claim.

As a market it might not look much like the idealized American myth of our simplistic contemporary 'market.' But then we knew it wouldn't.

## 17

*Two-Gun Mutualism and the Golden Rule*
(n.p., Sep. 25, 2008) <http://libertarian-
labyrinth.blogspot.com/2008/09/gift-
economy-of-property.html> (Aug. 22,
2011).

# THE GIFT ECONOMY
# OF PROPERTY

## *SHAWN WILBUR*
## *(2008)*

I THINK MOST ANARCHISTS AND LIBERTARIANS SHARE A FAITH THAT IT IS POSSIBLE FOR NEEDS to be met, goods to be distributed and some level of general prosperity achieved, in a way that is voluntary and at least approximately just. But we couldn't differ more, it seems, when we start to ask how to get the work done. Probably most of us aim, in the long run, for a society where there is sufficient prosperity that we could be much less concerned about such things, where generosity would be a logical response to plenty. But we live in the midst of a society and economic system which is very far from that ideal, and dream our dreams of the future and freedom while we deal with a very unfree present. On a day when we've just witnessed the largest US bank failure in history, in the context of a government-brokered market-move by JPMorgan, who also benefited from the Bear Stearns maneuver, talk about "genuinely free markets" seems a bit pipe-dreamy. But if it's going to be a long struggle to whatever freedom we manage to wrest from the corrupt bastards who are currently monkeying with our lives, we can probably take the time to get on something like the same page.

Recently, I've been presenting some of Proudhon's ideas about individuality and free will,[1] as well as reviewing his work on property. I have begun to suggest some of the ways in which the early critique of property as a despotic, absolutist principle, became the basis for Proudhon's later reluctant propertarianism, which he based on his analysis of the human self, the *moi*, which he found was itself naturally absolutist, and despotic when given a chance.

Like Fourier, Proudhon could not accept any with any notion of original sin, in part because, like Fourier, he associated present errors with a progressive process that led ultimately to closer and closer approximations to justice (the "pact of liberty"), through the equilibration of forces, faculties, projects, parties, federations, etc. Having had done with the divine Absolute, he could only depend on human ethical actors themselves to accomplish the march towards justice, the justification of their institutions, the perfection of their concepts, etc. But it was obvious to him that they would never do it alone. Absolutism and despotism, if allowed entirely free play, are unlikely to lead to any pact, let alone a just one. No social atomist, however, and a thinker prone to expect every force to evoke a counterforce, he wasn't content to turn that absolutist character into a secular version of innate depravity. What he did do is a bit peculiar, involving a hijacking of Leibniz in directions that anticipate folks like Gilles Deleuze. The psychological and social physics that is at the center of his mature work on liberty and justice reads like poststructuralism in places, and I will have some recourse to the vocabulary of more contemporary continental philosophy as I talk about it.

If the self is not innately depraved, neither is it simple, centered, clean and "proper." Any body or being, Proudhon says, possesses a quantity of collective force, derived from the organization of its component parts. Though these component parts may be subject to rigid determination, the resultant force exceeds the power of the parts and, to the extent that the collective force is great and the organization that it rises from is complex, it escapes any particular constituent destiny. The collective force is the "quantity of liberty" possessed by the being. Freedom is thus a product of necessity, and expresses itself, at the next level, as a new sort of necessity. And perhaps at most levels of Proudhon's analysis (and we can move up and down the scale of "beings" from the simplest levels of organization up to complex societal groupings and perhaps to organization on even larger scales) the quantity

---

1   See Shawn Wilbur, "Proudhon on Freedom and Free Will," *Two-Gun Mutualism & the Golden Rule* (n.p., Sep. 12, 2008) <libertarian-labyrinth. blogspot.com/2008/09/proudhon-on-freedom-and-free-will.html> (March 13, 2011).

of liberty introduced wouldn't look much like the "individual freedom" that we value. But the human "free absolute," distinguished by the ability to say "moi" and to reflect on her position in this scheme, has her absolutism tempered by its encounters with its fellows, also "free absolutes," also pursuing a line drawn by the play of liberty and necessity. Out of their encounters, out of mutual recognition, the "pact of liberty" arises (or fails to arise, where lack or recognition or misrecognition take place), and a "collective reason," possessed (in social organs and institutions, in "common sense," etc) by a higher-order being, which is to say a higher-order (but latent, rather than free, because it lacks that ability to say "moi") absolute.

In the system that emerges around these notions, individual human beings hold a very special place, as the chief architects and artisans of justice. Again, like Fourier, Proudhon makes a point of not stigmatizing the impulses of individuals, and, far more than Fourier, he actually makes a virtue of individual egoism and absolutism, as long as we are not so self-absorbed that we can't recognize our fellow egoists and absolutists as such. Even the "higher wisdom" that is possessed by the higher-order collective beings, like "society" and "the state" (which, in his later works, takes on a very different meaning than anarchists generally give it), is really in large part in the hands of human individuals.

Necessity gives rise to liberty, which tends to a kind of necessity. "Individualism," even "complete insolidarity," tends (as we have seen elsewhere in Proudhon's work) to centralization, to the *dangerous* "socialism" that Leroux warned against in 1834, but also, if equilibrium can be maintained, to an expanded space of social freedom ("the liberty of the social being") for the individual. It's all a little dizzying; and in the middle of it, star of the show, sits the individual self, the *moi*, which, while off the hook for original sin, still has to deal with something we might think of as "original impropriety."

What can the man who never backed down about property being robbery say about this self which is, whatever else it is, a kind of by-product of the forces of necessity, that tends, according to him, to see itself as an absolute? What can that self say about its own position? Proudhon suggests that we have put off a certain amount of soul searching by projecting our own absolutism outwards, onto gods and onto governments, but that this has kept us from dealing with some important stuff – and we're not fooling ourselves much anymore. If progress, as Proudhon believed, is "the justification of humanity by itself," one of the spurs for that progress has to be, for us "free absolutes," an internal tension, maybe even a suspicion that the absolutism of the individual is not so different from that of the proprietor, and for many of the same reasons. Property might be as "impossible" in the psychological realm as Proudhon believed it was in the economic.

We're talking about a "decentered" subject that claims more "identity" than might be precisely justified. (I have often joked that Derrida's claims about identity might be reduced to "property is theft.") But we're not talking about "lack." Instead, we're talking about the self as a kind of excess, a force or pressure. (It would be very easy to move here from Proudhon to, say, Georges Bataille, and certainly easy to compare either or both to the anarchistic ethics of Guyau.) We are not committing ourselves to some social organism theory; Proudhon is explicit about this. (And, again, we might reach without much straining for points of contact with the thoughts of Deleuze on organization, etc.)

If we switch to the language of libertarianism, we're likely to find that Proudhon's vision of overlapping beings, and of human "free absolutes" as the foam at the top of the boiling pot of necessity, at least complicates the question of "self-ownership." Some of my friends will naturally object to this claim, and I'm sympathetic to the basic assumptions associated with a presumed right of self-ownership – indeed, as Proudhon said, "My principle, which will appear astonishing to you, citizens, my principle is yours; it is property itself" – but it does seem to me that if the self is characterized by a radical, unresolvable antinomy, then "property" cannot, by itself, express the "natural right" implied by the nature of the individual.

Like Proudhon, I suspect that "property is theft," and following his thread, I suspect that "self-ownership" is an expression of our absolutism. Still, like Proudhon, in the end, I am for property, or at least the right to it. Which leaves the questions *How?* and *Why?* Aren't there alternatives?

It seems to me that the search for alternatives to property, the right to control the fruits of one's labor, is, like the general resistance to the notion of markets in anarchism, based in our quite natural frustration and disgust with so much of what passes for commerce under current conditions. We're in the middle of far-too-fine an example of how despotic property can be, when married to governmental power and shielded from any countervailing force, to have many illusions about the risks involved in embracing it. Mutualists, in particular, never quite get off this hook; our "greatest hit," Proudhon's *What is Property?* (or its most famous slogan) is a constant reminder. It is a commonplace in social anarchist circles, and mutualists are not immune, to want to distance ourselves from the details of "getting and spending" as much as possible, and we have constructed a variety of means of putting off the hard discussions of property relations that will eventually, inevitably come.

One of those means, it seems to me, has been reference to the notion of "gift economies." Like the proponents of "the right of self-ownership," the advocates of gift economies have meant quite a variety of things by the term. In general, gift economies are differentiated from exchange economies precisely by the lack of exchanges, expectation of any remuneration or quid pro quo. Some institutionalized forms of gift exchange, like the "really, really free markets," forbid even barter. While it's clear enough to me what present desires are addressed by this alternative to capitalist commerce, this seems to be one of those practices that could always only operate on the edges of another, more organized and efficient kind of economy. That economy might well be freer in some senses than the enforced "gift economy," and it is not entirely clear to me that what is involved in that economy is "gifting" anyway.

In order to give, it is necessary to be free to give. One needs to be, in some sense at least, an owner of the gift, and the recipient cannot have an equal claim to appropriating the item. Collective property cannot be gifted within the collective, at least without changing rather substantially the meaning of "giving." Philosophical and anthropological accounts of the gift set all sorts of other conditions. The recipient of a gift may be required by custom, or by the "spirit of the gift," to some giving of his own. Gifts are notorious for the "poison" elements that they often contain. Some of the "gift economies" we know from anthropology did indeed operate without recompense in goods, but transformed material capital into prestige or cultural capital, sometimes in an extremely competitive manner. The philosophical accounts of the gift suggest that the "pure gift" is almost impossibly tied up in conflicting requirements; if one acknowledges a gift, accepts thanks in exchange for a gift, perhaps even if one knows one is giving and feels some internal compensation, then the pure gift is impossible. Gifts seem, in any event, to matter. Something other than indifference is required from us, and gaining "punk points" may not be it. Disposing of our excess stuff may just not reach the bar.

The gift economy seems to presuppose individual property, as much as it would like to subvert its absolutism, its covetous, tit-for-tat mentality. Is the gift, perhaps, related to the other half of our human antinomy?

What if it was? What, much too quickly (as I've gone on much too long), if the gift was indeed the mark of our other half. As our absolutism is necessity expressing itself in us, gratuity might well be the expression of liberty, of freedom. Perhaps "property," understood, as Proudhon understood it, as a bulwark around the individual, in the face of centralizing, collectivizing forces (which, lest we forget, have their role to play in the march to justice and the expansion of liberty), starting with "self-ownership," is the right implied by our basic human predicament, our in-progress nature, our need for space in which to experiment, err, advance.

Would such a property be compatible with a gift economy? Or does Proudhon finally leave us in a place where neither property, strictly speaking, nor the gift, *ditto*, can arise?

My intuition, based in part on some language various places in Proudhon's work and in part on the connections I've been making to other continental thought, is that a "gift economy," in the sense of a system in which something, which can be rightfully given, is given, with no specific expectations of return, could only arise in fairly limited circumstances, and perhaps can only have one application within Proudhon's thought – but that one application may be a bit of a doozy. We know that there is, for Proudhon, some opening for society to emerge as a "pact of liberty" leading towards approximations of equality and finally of justice. We know that freedom rises from the interplay of necessity and liberty, and that property too has its internal contradictions. Proudhon's *moi* has very little that he can rightfully give, if even his own "property" is theft. But he can, perhaps, give property to the other, through recognition, which steals nothing, robs no one, and is perfectly gratuitous, even if, and this is the character of the gift economy, he cannot be sure of reciprocation. To the extent, however, that commerce is based in equal recognition, if not *necessarily* any other sort of equality, then this particular gift economy might be strangely (given all we have said, and some of the names we have invoked) foundational.

My social anarchist friends may object to this yoking of absolutism and gratuity in, of all things, property. My libertarian friends will doubtless wince a bit at the notion that self-ownership is a gift (as opposed to a given). But I think there is at least food for thought here.

## 18

# FAIRNESS AND POSSESSION

## *GARY CHARTIER*
## *(2011)*

J USTICE IN POSSESSION IS NOT, *PER SE,* A MATTER OF RELATIONSHIPS BETWEEN PEOPLE AND things. Rather, it's a matter of relationships among people. Like many (perhaps not all) moral requirements, it has to do with how it's reasonable for us to treat each other. The basic moral requirement of fairness means that we have good reason to take each others' interests into account when we make decisions. In tandem with a set of truisms about human behavior and the human condition, this principle entails respect for a set of rules about possession. There is good reason for a just legal system to treat these rules as exceptionless, though somewhat less reason for individual moral actors to do so.

We can fail to be reasonable in relation to each other in various ways. For instance, I can opt to attack some aspect of your well being out of spite or a desire for revenge, or as a means to accomplishing some goal of mine. And this kind of unreasonableness is extremely important – it's at the root of much injustice in war, for instance. But it's not the kind of unreasonableness that typically arises when people ignore or actively violate each other's legitimate possessory interests. Generally, the kind of unreasonable action at issue in such cases is arbitrary discrimination among those affected by an agent's choices. This kind of unreasonableness violates what I'll call the Principle of Fairness.

There are different ways to express this principle, none immune to criticism. For present purposes, I want to highlight a fairly simple aspect of the principle, which can be formulated something like this: avoid treating others in ways you wouldn't be willing to be treated in relevantly similar circumstances. This formulation is rooted in what I take to be the intuitively plausible suggestion that those affected by our acts and omissions are generally quite like ourselves, and that simple numerical difference is insufficient to warrant fundamentally different treatment.

This aspect of the Principle of Fairness can serve as the basis of a set of possessory rules.

First, the Principle establishes a presumption in favor of allowing people to retain control of the things they actually possess. Most of us aren't willing most of the time for others violently or deceptively to snatch our stuff. So it's generally not reasonable for us to take theirs.

Of course, that basic presumption can be defeated – as the notion of objectionable snatching itself suggests. Thieves don't like their possessions taken any more than do those who come by what they have honestly and peacefully, but our reactions to thieves' possessory claims tend, I think justifiably, to be rather different from our responses to the claims of those the thieves have dispossessed.

Further considerations help to clarify the reach and narrow the range of just possessory rules. Taken in tandem with the Principle of Fairness, these considerations provide considerable support for what I call the *baseline rules*: (*i*) someone establishes a just possessory claim to an unclaimed physical object or tract of land by establishment effective possession of it; (*ii*) once a person takes possession of a physical object or tract of land, it's up to her how it is used and what is done with it (to the extent that, in so doing, she doesn't attack other people's bodies or justly acquired possessions); (*iii*) this means, in particular, that someone with a just possessory claim that freely permit someone else to take possession of an object or tract of land that is hers, on any mutually agreeable terms. If I'm right about the baseline rules, then, while it will be true in some sense that possessory norms are conventions, they are tightly constrained conventions, since fairness seems to require that reasonable possessory norms incorporate the baseline rules.

A look at some relevant considerations will help to make clear how they support the baseline rules.

- *Accessibility.* All other things being equal (presuming, in particular, that costs can't be shifted onto the unwilling, as so often happens in connection with abuses ranging from slavery to pollution), everyone benefits as supplies of the goods and services people want increases and their costs decrease. If people's possessory rights are stable, so that they can bargain with others and keep what they are promised in return for goods and services they provide, they are more likely to produce those goods and services in desirable quantities at desirable prices.

- *Autonomy.* People tend to want autonomy: they want to be able to make their own decisions without, at minimum, forcible interference from others. Stable possessory claims enable people to preserve their autonomy. So it will be unreasonable for most people not to favor rules that protect such claims.
- *Coordination.* Coordinating the behavior of economic actors – setting prices and determining production levels and distribution patterns – can be a rational activity only if people have stable possessory rights.
- *Compensation.* Stable possessory rights enable people to bargain effectively with each other – such rights create a baseline for bargaining – and make people to be compensated for their past efforts.
- *Generosity.* You can't be generous if you don't have stable possessory rights and those to whom you give lack such rights.
- *Incentivization.* People are likely to be productive – in ways that benefit themselves and others alike – when they can keep what they earn. This means, in turn, that they and those with whom they bargain need stable possessory rights.
- *Peacemaking.* Stable possessory rights, acknowledged as such by everyone, reduce conflict over scarce resources.
- *Productivity.* Having stable possessory rights means that people are likely to put resources to their most productive use. (This point needs some qualifying, of course, since different people have different goals; one person's goal for a piece of land, for instance, may be precisely that it function effectively as a nature preserve.)
- *Reliability.* Reliability makes for stability and effective planning.
- *Simplicity.* Simple rules are easier to formulate, articulate, understand, and apply. The baseline rules are simpler than almost all alternatives. (They are less so, perhaps, than a set of rules allowing everyone access to everything, but the other considerations certainly suggest that such rules would be undesirable.)
- *Stability.* Some rules are likely to be rooted in self-enforcing conventions. Such rules are easier to understand and apply. And there is good reason to think that the baseline rules are, precisely, stable, self-enforcing conventions.
- *Stewardship.* Stewardship matters: everyone benefits when things are well taken care, and things are well taken care of when someone in particular is responsible for everything.

These various considerations contribute to overlapping latticeworks of justification for the baseline possessory rules. In general, all of them (concern for the productivity of individual assets is arguably the one exception) tilt in the same direction: to treat others fairly, to take their interests appropriately into account, is to act in a way that takes each of these considerations seriously.

The Principle of Fairness will require compensation for violations of interests protected by the baseline rules. After all, the rules are pretty meaningless if they can be violated with impunity. Legitimate interests deserve protection. Those considering the possibility of causing harm to others' possessions are best-situated to avoid or prevent the harms they're considering causing; further, fairness suggests that they should not shift the costs of compensating their victims to others. And a compensation requirement will obviously serve to incentivize those who might cause harm to avoid doing so.

Exceptionless rules are simpler, more reliable, and more stable than ones that allow for exceptions. So it makes sense for a just legal system to embody such rules and for people to support them. However (I maintain), this means only that people should support the provision of compensation for actual harms resulting from the violation of such rules, not that they should favor, for instance, legal principles that would allow the use of unlimited physical violence to protect the interests delineated by the rules. Also, while the Principle of Fairness gives everyone significant reason to support the maintenance of the baseline rules, this does not mean that the Principle itself will not sometimes warrant violation of the possessory interests.

That's because fairness is finally a characteristic of individual choices. When you're implementing or supporting a rule that's going to be applied across a range of cases, it makes sense to think of the rule *as* a general rule. But when you're deciding for yourself in a particular case – while you still need to think of the impact of your choice on, for instance, general confidence that just possessory interests will be respected – you have to ask what's fair for you to do in that case. So it will make sense for someone simultaneously to (*a*) support a rule that requires compensation for damage done while trespassing or breaking and entering without exceptions and (*b*) break into an abandoned mountain cabin to escape an avalanche.

Does that mean that it's consistent with the Principle of Fairness for people to violate others' just possessory interests with impunity as long as they're willing to pay compensation when they've caused actual harm? Not quite, since there will be, as I've suggested, reason for someone contemplating a possible violation to recognize that the action in which she is deciding whether to engage might be unreasonable because it would tend to undermine confidence in the reliability of just possessory claims, something everyone has reason to favor. This won't always be the case, but it certainly will on occasion.

People will also have further reasons to avoid interfering with others' possessions willy-nilly. For one thing, just compensation for interfering with someone's possessions won't just amount to the value of harm resulting from the interference; it will also include the reasonable costs of recovery — the costs of identifying the person responsible for the interference and securing compensation from her. And responsibility for those costs will certainly serve as a disincentive. In addition, people who take or damage or trespass unjustly won't be viewed very kindly by others. They're likely to be subjected to various kinds of social sanctions over and above the demand that they compensate their victims.

Together with a range of plausible generalizations about human behavior and human preferences, the Principle of Fairness can ground a set of simple, reliable rules about justice in possession — the baseline possessory rules. The Principle doesn't resolve all questions about possession, and it's compatible with multiple legal frameworks. But it does constrain quite significantly what will count as a reasonable legal rule regarding possession and also, if somewhat less severely, what will count as a reasonable choice to interfere with someone else's justly acquired possessions. Among other things, taking the rules seriously will mean avoiding the interference with others' possessions that seems to be the defining characteristic of the predatory state.

# 19

*Formulations* 3.1 (Aut. 1995) <http://
freenation.org/a/f3l11.html><http://
praxeology.net/libertariannation/a/
f3l11.html> (Aug. 22, 2011).

# THE LIBERTARIAN CASE AGAINST INTELLECTUAL PROPERTY RIGHTS

## *RODERICK T. LONG*
## *(1995)*

> It would be interesting to discover how far a seriously critical
> view of the benefits to society of the law of copyright… would
> have a chance of being publicly stated in a society in which the
> channels of expression are so largely controlled by people who
> have a vested interest in the existing situation.
> – Friedrich A. Hayek, "The Intellectuals and Socialism"

## A DISPUTE AMONG LIBERTARIANS

THE STATUS OF INTELLECTUAL PROPERTY RIGHTS (COPYRIGHTS, PATENTS, AND THE LIKE) IS
an issue that has long divided libertarians. Such libertarian luminaries
as Herbert Spencer, Lysander Spooner, and Ayn Rand have been strong

supporters of intellectual property rights. Thomas Jefferson, on the other hand, was ambivalent on the issue, while radical libertarians like Benjamin Tucker in the last century and Tom Palmer in the present one have rejected intellectual property rights altogether.

When libertarians of the first sort come across a purported intellectual property right, they see one more instance of an individual's rightful claim to the product of his labor. When libertarians of the second sort come across a purported intellectual property right, they see one more instance of undeserved monopoly privilege granted by government.

I used to be in the first group. Now I am in the second. I'd like to explain why I think intellectual property rights are unjustified, and how the legitimate ends currently sought through the expedient of intellectual property rights might be secured by other, voluntary means.

## THE HISTORICAL ARGUMENT

Intellectual property rights have a tainted past. Originally, both patents and copyrights were grants of monopoly privilege pure and simple. A printing house might be assigned a "copyright" by royal mandate, meaning that only it was allowed to print books or newspapers in a certain district; there was no presumption that copyright originated with the author. Likewise, those with political pull might be assigned a "patent," i.e., an exclusive monopoly, over some commodity, regardless of whether they had had anything to do with inventing it. Intellectual property rights had their origin in governmental privilege and governmental protectionism, not in any zeal to protect the rights of creators to the fruits of their efforts. And the abolition of patents was one of the rallying cries of the 17th-century Levellers (arguably the first libertarians).

Now this by itself does not prove that there is anything wrong with intellectual property rights as we know them today. An unsavory past is not a decisive argument against any phenomenon; many worthwhile and valuable things arose from suspect beginnings. (Nietzsche once remarked that there is nothing so marvelous that its past will bear much looking into.) But the fact that intellectual property rights originated in state oppression should at least make us pause and be very cautious before embracing them.

## THE ETHICAL ARGUMENT

Ethically, property rights of any kind have to be justified as extensions of the right of individuals to control their own lives. Thus any alleged property rights that conflict with this moral basis – like the "right" to own slaves

– are invalidated. In my judgment, intellectual property rights also fail to pass this test. To enforce copyright laws and the like is to prevent people from making peaceful use of the information they possess. If you have acquired the information legitimately (say, by buying a book), then on what grounds can you be prevented from using it, reproducing it, trading it? Is this not a violation of the freedom of speech and press?

It may be objected that the person who originated the information deserves ownership rights over it. But information is not a concrete thing an individual can control; it is a universal, existing in other people's minds and other people's property, and over these the originator has no legitimate sovereignty. You cannot own information without owning other people.

Suppose I write a poem, and you read it and memorize it. By memorizing it, you have in effect created a "software" duplicate of the poem to be stored in your brain. But clearly I can claim no rights over that copy so long as you remain a free and autonomous individual. That copy in your head is yours and no one else's.

But now suppose you proceed to transcribe my poem, to make a "hard copy" of the information stored in your brain. The materials you use – pen and ink – are your own property. The information template which you used – that is, the stored memory of the poem – is also your own property. So how can the hard copy you produce from these materials be anything but yours to publish, sell, adapt, or otherwise treat as you please?

An item of intellectual property is a universal. Unless we are to believe in Platonic Forms, universals as such do not exist, except insofar as they are realized in their many particular instances. Accordingly, I do not see how anyone can claim to own, say, the text of *Atlas Shrugged* unless that amounts to a claim to own every single physical copy of *Atlas Shrugged*. But the copy of *Atlas Shrugged* on my bookshelf does not belong to Ayn Rand or to her estate. It belongs to me. I bought it. I paid for it. (Rand presumably got royalties from the sale, and I'm sure it wasn't sold without her permission!)

The moral case against patents is even clearer. A patent is, in effect, a claim of ownership over a law of nature. What if Newton had claimed to own calculus, or the law of gravity? Would we have to pay a fee to his estate every time we used one of the principles he discovered?

> … the patent monopoly… consists in protecting inventors…
> against competition for a period long enough to extort from
> the people a reward enormously in excess of the labor measure
> of their services – in other words, in giving certain people a
> right of property for a term of years in laws and facts of Na-

ture, and the power to exact tribute from others for the use of this natural wealth, which should be open to all.[1]

Defenders of patents claim that patent laws protect ownership only of inventions, not of discoveries. (Likewise, defenders of copyright claim that copyright laws protect only implementations of ideas, not the ideas themselves.) But this distinction is an artificial one. Laws of nature come in varying degrees of generality and specificity; if it is a law of nature that copper conducts electricity, it is no less a law of nature that this much copper, arranged in this configuration, with these other materials arranged so, makes a workable battery. And so on.

Suppose you are trapped at the bottom of a ravine. Sabre-tooth tigers are approaching hungrily. Your only hope is to quickly construct a levitation device I've recently invented. You know how it works, because you attended a public lecture I gave on the topic. And it's easy to construct, quite rapidly, out of materials you see lying around in the ravine.

But there's a problem. I've patented my levitation device. I own it – not just the individual model I built, but the universal. Thus, you can't construct your means of escape without using my property. And I, mean old skinflint that I am, refuse to give my permission. And so the tigers dine well.

This highlights the moral problem with the notion of intellectual property. By claiming a patent on my levitation device, I'm saying that you are not permitted to use your own knowledge to further your ends. By what right?

Another problem with patents is that, when it comes to laws of nature, even fairly specific ones, the odds are quite good that two people, working independently but drawing on the same background of research, may come up with the same invention (discovery) independently. Yet patent law will arbitrarily grant exclusive rights to the inventor who reaches the patent office first; the second inventor, despite having developed the idea on his own, will be forbidden to market his invention.

Ayn Rand attempts to rebut this objection:

> As an objection to the patent laws, some people cite the fact that two inventors may work independently for years on the same invention, but one will beat the other to the patent office by an hour or a day and will acquire an exclusive monopoly, while the loser's work will then be totally wasted. This type of

---

1    Benjamin Tucker, *Instead of a Book, By a Man Too Busy to Write One: A Fragmentary Exposition of Philosophical Anarchism* (New York: Tucker 1893) 13.

objection is based on the error of equating the potential with the actual. The fact that a man might have been first, does not alter the fact that he wasn't. Since the issue is one of commercial rights, the loser in a case of that kind has to accept the fact that in seeking to trade with others he must face the possibility of a competitor winning the race, which is true of all types of competition.[2]

But this reply will not do. Rand is suggesting that the competition to get to the patent office first is like any other kind of commercial competition. For example, suppose you and I are competing for the same job, and you happen to get hired simply because you got to the employer before I did. In that case, the fact that I might have gotten there first does not give me any rightful claim to the job. But that is because I have no right to the job in the first place. And once you get the job, your rightful claim to that job depends solely on the fact that your employer chose to hire you.

In the case of patents, however, the story is supposed to be different. The basis of an inventor's claim to a patent on X is supposedly the fact that he has invented X. (Otherwise, why not offer patent rights over X to anyone who stumbles into the patent office, regardless of whether they've ever even heard of X?) Registering one's invention with the patent office is supposed to record one's right, not to create it. Hence it follows that the person who arrives at the patent office second has just as much right as the one who arrives first – and this is surely a reductio ad absurdum of the whole notion of patents.

## THE ECONOMIC ARGUMENT

The economic case for ordinary property rights depends on scarcity. But information is not, technically speaking, a scarce resource in the requisite sense. If A uses some material resource, that makes less of the resource for B, so we need some legal mechanism for determining who gets to use what when. But information is not like that; when A acquires information, that does not decrease B's share, so property rights are not needed.

Some will say that such rights are needed in order to give artists and inventors the financial incentive to create. But most of the great innovators in history operated without benefit of copyright laws. Indeed, sufficiently stringent copyright laws would have made their achievements impossible: Great playwrights like Euripides and Shakespeare never wrote an original plot in their lives; their masterpieces are all adaptations and improvements

---

2    Ayn Rand, *Capitalism: The Unknown Ideal* (New York: NAL 1967) 133.

of stories written by others. Many of our greatest composers, like Bach, Tchaikovsky, and Ives, incorporated into their work the compositions of others. Such appropriation has long been an integral part of legitimate artistic freedom.

Is it credible that authors will not be motivated to write unless they are given copyright protection? Not very. Consider the hundreds of thousands of articles uploaded onto the Internet by their authors everyday, available to anyone in the world for free.

Is it credible that publishers will not bother to publish uncopyrighted works, for fear that a rival publisher will break in and ruin their monopoly? Not very. Nearly all works written before 1900 are in the public domain, yet pre-1900 works are still published, and still sell.

Is it credible that authors, in a world without copyrights, will be deprived of remuneration for their work? Again, not likely. In the 19th century, British authors had no copyright protection under American law, yet they received royalties from American publishers nonetheless.

In his autobiography, Herbert Spencer tells a story that is supposed to illustrate the need for intellectual property rights. Spencer had invented a new kind of hospital bed. Out of philanthropic motives, he decided to make his invention a gift to mankind rather than claiming a patent on it. To his dismay, this generous plan backfired: no company was willing to manufacture the bed, because in the absence of a guaranteed monopoly they found it too risky to invest money in any product that might be undercut by competition. Doesn't this show the need for patent laws?

I don't think so. To begin with, Spencer's case seems overstated. After all, companies are constantly producing items (beds, chairs, etc.) to which no one holds any exclusive patent. But never mind; let's grant Spencer's story without quibbling. What does it prove?

Recall that the companies who rejected Spencer's bed in favor of other uses for their capital were choosing between producing a commodity in which they would have a monopoly and producing a commodity in which they would not have a monopoly. Faced with that choice, they went for the patented commodity as the less risky option (especially in light of the fact that they had to compete with other companies likewise holding monopolies). So the existence of patent laws, like any other form of protectionist legislation, gave the patented commodity an unfair competitive advantage against its unpatented rival. The situation Spencer describes, then, is simply an artifact of the patent laws themselves! In a society without patent laws, Spencer's philanthropic bed would have been at no disadvantage in comparison with other products.

## THE INFORMATION-BASED ARGUMENT

Though never justified, copyright laws have probably not done too much damage to society so far. But in the Computer Age, they are now becoming increasingly costly shackles on human progress.

Consider, for instance, Project Gutenberg, a marvelous non-profit volunteer effort to transfer as many books as possible to electronic format and make them available over the Internet for free. Unfortunately, most of the works done to date have been pre-20th-century – to avoid the hassles of copyright law. Thus, copyright laws today are working to restrict the availability of information, not to promote it. (And Congress, at the behest of the publishing and recording industries, is currently acting to extend copyright protection to last nearly a century after the creator's death, thus ensuring that only a tiny fraction of the information in existence will be publicly available.)

More importantly, modern electronic communications are simply beginning to make copyright laws unenforceable; or at least, unenforceable by any means short of a government takeover of the Internet – and such a chilling threat to the future of humankind would clearly be a cure far worse than the disease. Copyright laws, in a world where any individual can instantaneously make thousands of copies of a document and send them out all over the planet, are as obsolete as laws against voyeurs and peeping toms would be in a world where everyone had x-ray vision.

## FIRST TOLKIEN STORY

Here's a story that illustrates some of the needless irritation that intellectual property laws can cause.

Several years ago the avant-garde film animator Ralph Bakshi decided to make a movie of J. R. R. Tolkien's classic fantasy trilogy *The Lord of the Rings*. Or rather, he decided to split the trilogy into two movies, since the work is really too long to fit easily into a single film.

So Bakshi started off with *Lord of the Rings (Part One)*. This movie covered the first volume of the trilogy, and part of the second volume. The second movie was to have covered the rest of the second volume, and then the whole of the third volume. To make the first movie, then, Bakshi needed to buy the rights to the first two volumes, and this is what he (or, presumably, his studio) did.

But Bakshi never got around to making the second movie (probably because the first movie turned out to be less successful financially than had been anticipated). Enter Rankin-Bass, another studio. Rankin-Bass had made an animated TV-movie of Tolkien's earlier novel *The Hobbit*, and they were interested in doing the same for the second part of *Lord of the Rings*, left unfilmed by Bakshi.

But there was a problem. Bakshi's studio had the rights to the first two volumes of the trilogy. Only the rights to the third volume were available. So Rankin-Bass' sequel (released as *The Return of the King*) ended up, of necessity, covering only the third volume. Those events from the second volume that Bakshi had left unfilmed were simply lost. (Not even flashbacks to events in the first two volumes were permitted – although flashbacks to *The Hobbit* were okay, because Rankin-Bass had the rights to that.)

Video catalogues now sell *The Hobbit*, *The Lord of the Rings*, and *The Return of the King* as a unified package. But viewers unfamiliar with the books will be a bit puzzled. In the Bakshi film, the evil wizard Saruman is a looming force to be reckoned with; in the Rankin-Bass sequel, he is not even mentioned. Likewise, at the end of the Bakshi film, Frodo, Sam, and Gollum are traveling together; at the beginning of the Rankin-Bass sequel we find them split up, without explanation. The answers lie in the unfilmed portion of the second volume, which deals with Saruman's defeat, Gollum's betrayal of Frodo, Sam's battle with Shelob, and Frodo's capture by the Orcs. Not unimportant events, these. But thanks to intellectual property laws, the viewer is not allowed to know about them.

Is this a catastrophe? I suppose not. The aesthetic unity and continuity of a work of art was mangled, pursuant to the requirements of law. But it was just an animated TV-movie. So what?

So what, perhaps. But my story does serve to cast doubt on the idea that copyright is a bulwark of artistic expression. When a work of art involves reworking material created by others (as most art historically has), copyright laws can place it in a straitjacket.

## ALTERNATIVES TO INTELLECTUAL PROPERTY RIGHTS: SOME FORMULATIONS

I may have given the impression, thus far, that intellectual property rights serve no useful function whatever. That is not my position. I think some of the ends to which copyrights and patents have been offered as the means are perfectly legitimate. I believe, however, that those ends would be better served by other means.

Suppose I pirate your work, put my name on it, and market it as mine. Or suppose I revise your work without your permission, and market it as yours. Have I done nothing wrong?

On the contrary, I have definitely committed a rights-violation. The rights I have violated, however, are not yours, but those of my customers. By selling one person's work as though it were the work of another, I am defrauding those who purchase the work, as surely as I would be if I sold soy steaks as beef steaks or vice versa. All you need to do is buy a copy (so you can claim to be a customer) and then bring a class-action suit against me.

There are other legal options available to the creators of intellectual products. For example, many software manufacturers can and do place copy-protection safeguards on their programs, or require purchasers to sign contracts agreeing not to resell the software. Likewise, pay-TV satellite broadcasters scramble their signal, and then sell descramblers.

None of these techniques is foolproof, of course. A sufficiently ingenious pirater can usually figure out how to get around copy protections or descramble a signal. And conditional-sale contracts place no restriction on third-party users who come by the software in some other way. Still, by making it more difficult to pirate their intellectual products, such companies do manage to decrease the total amount of piracy, and they do stay in business and make profits.

But what if I do go ahead and market your work without your permission, and without offering you any share of the profits? Is there nothing wrong with this? Can nothing be done about this?

In the case described, I don't think what I've done is unjust. That is, it's not a violation of anyone's rights. But it's tacky. Violating someone's rights is not the only way one can do something wrong; justice is not the only virtue.

But justice is the only virtue that can be legitimately enforced. If I profit from pirating your work, you have a legitimate moral claim against me, but that claim is not a right. Thus, it cannot legitimately use coercion to secure compliance. But that doesn't mean it can't be enforced through other, voluntary methods.

A good deal of protection for the creators of intellectual products may be achieved through voluntary compliance alone. Consider the phenomenon of shareware, in which creators of software provide their products free to all comers, but with the request that those who find the program useful send along a nominal fee to the author. Presumably, only a small percentage of shareware users ever pay up; still, that percentage must be large enough to keep the shareware phenomenon going.

There are more organized and effective ways of securing voluntary compliance, however. I have in mind the strategy of boycotting those who fail to respect the legitimate claims of the producers. Research conducted by libertarian scholar Tom Palmer has turned up numerous successful instances of such organized boycotts. In the 1930's, for example, the Guild of Fashion Originators managed to protect dress styles and the like from piracy by other designers, without any help from the coercive power of government.

A voluntary boycott is actually a much safer tool than government for protecting the claims of intellectual producers, because, in the course of trying to strike a pragmatic balance between the economic power of producers and the economic power of consumers, a private effort is more likely than a government monopoly freed from market incentives to strike an analogous balance between the legitimate moral claims of the two groups – the producers' moral claim to remuneration, and the consumers' moral claim to easily accessible information.

Something more formal can easily be imagined. In the late Middle Ages a voluntary court system was created by merchants frustrated with the inadequacies of governmentally-provided commercial law. This system, known as the Law Merchant ("law" being the noun and "merchant" the adjective), enforced its decisions solely by means of boycott, and yet it was enormously effective. Suppose producers of intellectual products – authors, artists, inventors, software designers, etc. – were to set up an analogous court system for protecting copyrights and patent rights – or rather, copyclaims and patent claims (since the moral claims in question, though often legitimate, are not rights in the libertarian sense). Individuals and organizations accused of piracy would have a chance to plead their case at a voluntary court, but if found guilty they would be required to cease and desist, and to compensate the victims of their piracy, on pain of boycott.

What if this system went too far, and began restricting the free flow of information in the same undesirable ways that, I've argued, intellectual property laws do?

This is certainly a possibility. But I think the danger is much greater with coercive enforcement than with voluntary enforcement. As Rich Hammer likes to point out: ostracism gets its power from reality, and its power is limited by reality. As a boycotting effort increases in scope, the number and intensity of frustrated desires on the part of those who are being deprived by the boycott of something they want will become greater. As this happens, there will also be a corresponding increase in the number of people who judge that the benefits of meeting those desires (and charging a hefty fee to do so) outweigh the costs of violating the boycott. Too strenuous and restrictive a defense of copyclaims will founder on the rock of consumer preferences; too lax a defense will founder on the rock of producer preferences.

## SECOND TOLKIEN STORY

Let me close with a second story about Tolkien and his famous trilogy. The first edition of *The Lord of the Rings* to be published in the United States was a pirated edition from Ace Books. For reasons which I now forget, Tolkien could not take legal action against Ace. But when Ballantine came out with its own official author-approved American edition of *The Lord of the Rings*, Tolkien started a campaign against the Ace edition. The Ballantine edition was released with a notice from Tolkien in a green box on the back cover stating that this was the only authorized edition, and urging any reader with respect for living authors to purchase no other. Moreover, every time he answered a fan letter from an American reader, Tolkien appended a footnote explaining the situation and requesting that the recipient spread the word among Tolkien fans that the Ace edition should be boycotted.

Although the Ace edition was cheaper than the Ballantine, it quickly lost readers and went out of print. The boycott was successful.

It might be objected that Tolkien devotees tend to be more fanatical than the average readers, and so such a strategy of boycott could not be expected to succeed in ensuring such loyalty generally. True enough. But on the other hand, Tolkien's boycott was entirely unorganized; it simply consisted of a then-obscure British professor of medieval language and literature scribbling hand-written responses to fan letters. Think how effective an organized boycott might have been!

# PART FOUR

## Corporate Power and Labor Solidarity

# 20

Cato Unbound (Cato Institute, Nov. 10,
2008) <http://www.cato-unbound.
org/2008/11/10/roderick-long/
corporations-versus-the-market-or-whip-
conflation-now/> (Aug. 11, 2011).

# CORPORATIONS VERSUS THE MARKET, OR WHIP CONFLATION NOW

### RODERICK T. LONG
### (2008)

DEFENDERS OF THE FREE MARKET ARE OFTEN ACCUSED OF BEING APOLOGISTS FOR BIG business and shills for the corporate elite. Is this a fair charge?

No and yes. Emphatically no – because corporate power and the free market are actually antithetical; genuine competition is big business's worst nightmare. But also, in all too many cases, yes – because although liberty and plutocracy cannot coexist, simultaneous advocacy of both is all too possible.

First, the no. Corporations tend to fear competition, because competition exerts downward pressure on prices and upward pressure on salaries; moreover, success on the market comes with no guarantee of permanency, depending as it does on outdoing other firms at correctly figuring out how best to satisfy forever-changing consumer preferences, and that kind of vulnerability to loss is no picnic. It is no surprise, then, that throughout U.S. history corporations have been overwhelmingly hostile to the free market. Indeed, most of the existing regulatory apparatus – including those regulations widely misperceived as restraints on corporate power – were vigorously supported, lobbied for, and in some cases even drafted by the corporate elite.[1]

Corporate power depends crucially on government intervention in the marketplace.[2] This is obvious enough in the case of the more overt forms of government favoritism such as subsidies, bailouts,[3] and other forms of corporate welfare; protectionist tariffs; explicit grants of monopoly privilege; and the seizing of private property for corporate use via eminent domain (as in *Kelo v. New London*). But these direct forms of pro-business intervention are supplemented by a swarm of indirect forms whose impact is arguably greater still.

---

1    For documentation and analysis see James Weinstein, *The Corporate Ideal in the Liberal State, 1900-1918* (New York: Farrar 1976); Gabriel Kolko, *The Triumph of Conservativm: A Reinterpretation of American History, 1900-1916* (New York: Free 1963); Gabriel Kolko, *Railroads and Regulation, 1877-1916* (Princeton: Princeton University Press 1965); Paul Weaver, *The Suicidal Corporation: How Big Business Fails America* (New York: Touchtose-Simon 1988); Butler D. Shaffer, *In Restraint of Trade: The Business Campaign Against Competition, 1918-1938* (Lewisburg PA: Bucknell University Press 1997). For briefer accounts see Roy A. Childs, "Big Business and the Rise of American Statism," ch. 23 (223-240), in this volume; Joseph R. Stromberg, "The Political Economy of Liberal Corporatism," *Individualist*, May 1972: 2-11 <http://anarchyisordergovernmentiscivilwar.blogspot.com/2010/08/political-economy-of-liberal.html> (March 13, 2011).

2    This is especially true if, as some libertarians argue, the corporate form itself (involving legal personality and limited liability) is inconsistent with free-market principles. For this position, see Frank Van Dun, "Is the Corporation a Free-Market Institution?," *The Freeman: Ideas on Liberty* 53.3 (March 2003): 29-33 (Foundation for Economic Education, 2003) <http://www.thefreemanonline.org/featured/is-the-corporation-a-free-market-institution> (March 13, 2011); for the other side see Norman Barry, "The Theory of the Corporation," *The Freeman: Ideas on Liberty* 53.3 (March 2003): 22-6 (Foundation for Economic Education, 2003) <http://www.thefreemanonline.org/featured/the-theory-of-the-corporation> (March 13, 2011). For the purposes of the present discussion, however, let us assume the legitimacy of the corporation.

3    Roderick T. Long, "Regulation: The Cause, Not the Cure, of the Financial Crisis," ch. 24 (241-246), in this volume.

As I have written elsewhere:

> One especially useful service that the state can render the corporate elite is cartel enforcement. Price-fixing agreements are unstable on a free market, since while all parties to the agreement have a collective interest in seeing the agreement generally hold, each has an individual interest in breaking the agreement by underselling the other parties in order to win away their customers; and even if the cartel manages to maintain discipline over its own membership, the oligopolistic prices tend to attract new competitors into the market. Hence the advantage to business of state-enforced cartelisation. Often this is done directly, but there are indirect ways too, such as imposing uniform quality standards that relieve firms from having to compete in quality. (And when the quality standards are high, lower-quality but cheaper competitors are priced out of the market.)
>
> The ability of colossal firms to exploit economies of scale is also limited in a free market, since beyond a certain point the benefits of size (e.g., reduced transaction costs) get outweighed by diseconomies of scale (e.g., calculational chaos stemming from absence of price feedback) – unless the state enables them to socialise these costs by immunising them from competition – e.g., by imposing fees, licensure requirements, capitalisation requirements, and other regulatory burdens that disproportionately impact newer, poorer entrants as opposed to richer, more established firms.[4]

Nor does the list end there. Tax breaks to favored corporations represent yet another non-obvious form of government intervention. There is of

---

4    Roderick T. Long, "Those Who Control the Past Control the Future," *Art of the Possible Essays* (n.p., Sep. 18, 2008) <http://praxeology.net/aotp.htm#4>; cf. Roderick T. Long, "History of an Idea; or, How an Argument Against the Workability of Authoritarian Socialism Became an Argument Against the Workability of Authoritarian Capitalism," *Art of the Possible Essays* (n.p., Oct. 2, 2008) <http://praxeology.net/aotp.htm#5> (March 13, 2011); Kevin A. Carson, "Economic Calculation in the Corporate Commonwealth," ch. 22 (213-222) in this volume. For a more detailed case see Kevin A. Carson, *Studies in Mutualist Political Economy* (Charleston, SC: BookSurge 2007) (Mutualist.org, 200) <http://mutualist.org/id47.html> (March 13, 2011); Kevin A. Carson, *Organization Theory: A Libertarian Perspective* (Charleston, SC: BookSurge 2008).

course nothing anti-market about tax breaks per se; quite the contrary. But when a firm is exempted from taxes to which its competitors are subject, it becomes the beneficiary of state coercion directed against others, and to that extent owes its success to government intervention rather than market forces.

Intellectual property laws also function to bolster the power of big business. Even those who accept the intellectual property as a legitimate form of private property[5] can agree that the ever-expanding temporal horizon of copyright protection, along with disproportionately steep fines for violations (measures for which publishers, recording firms, software companies, and film studios have lobbied so effectively), are excessive from an incentival point of view, stand in tension with the express intent of the Constitution's patents-and-copyrights clause, and have more to do with maximizing corporate profits than with securing a fair return to the original creators.

Government favoritism also underwrites environmental irresponsibility on the part of big business. Polluters often enjoy protection against lawsuits, for example, despite the pollution's status as a violation of private property rights.[6] When timber companies engage in logging on public lands, the access roads are generally tax-funded, thus reducing the cost of logging below its market rate; moreover, since the loggers do not own the forests they have little incentive to log sustainably.[7]

In addition, inflationary monetary policies on the part of central banks also tend to benefit those businesses that receive the inflated money first in the form of loans and investments, when they are still facing the old, lower prices, while those to whom the new money trickles down later, only after they have already begun facing higher prices, systematically lose out.

And of course corporations have been frequent beneficiaries of U.S. military interventions abroad, from the United Fruit Company in 1950s Guatemala to Halliburton in Iraq today.

Vast corporate empires like Wal-Mart are often either hailed or condemned (depending on the speaker's perspective) as products of the free market. But not only is Wal-Mart a direct beneficiary of (usually local) government in-

---

5    Another disputed issue among libertarians; see, e.g., Cato Unbound's symposium, *The Future of Copyright* (Cato Institute, June 2008) <http://www.cato-unbound.org/archives/june-2008-the-future-of-copyright> (March 13, 2011).

6    Murray N. Rothbard, "Law, Property Rights, and Air Pollution," *Cato Journal* 2.1 (Spring 1982): 55-99 (Cato Institute, 1982) <http://www.cato.org/pubs/journal/cj2n1/cj2n1-2.pdf> (March 13, 2011).

7    Mary J. Ruwart, *Healing Our World in an Age of Aggression* (Kalamazoo: Sun-Star 2003) 117-9.

tervention in the form of such measures as eminent domain and tax breaks, but it also reaps less obvious benefits from policies of wider application. The funding of public highways through tax revenues, for example, constitutes a de facto transportation subsidy, allowing Wal-Mart and similar chains to socialize the costs of shipping and so enabling them to compete more successfully against local businesses; the low prices we enjoy at Wal-Mart in our capacity as consumers are thus made possible in part by our having already indirectly subsidized Wal-Mart's operating costs in our capacity as taxpayers.

Wal-Mart also keeps its costs low by paying low salaries; but what makes those low salaries possible is the absence of more lucrative alternatives for its employees – and that fact in turn owes much to government intervention. The existence of regulations, fees, licensure requirements, et cetera does not affect all market participants equally; it's much easier for wealthy, well-established companies to jump through these hoops than it is for new firms just starting up. Hence such regulations both decrease the number of employers bidding for employees' services (thus keeping salaries low) and make it harder for the less affluent to start enterprises of their own.[8] Legal restrictions on labor organizing also make it harder for such workers to organize collectively on their own behalf.[9]

I don't mean to suggest that Wal-Mart and similar firms owe their success solely to governmental privilege; genuine entrepreneurial talent has doubtless been involved as well. But given the enormous governmental contribution to that success, it's doubtful that in the absence of government intervention such firms would be in anything like the position they are today.

In a free market, firms would be smaller and less hierarchical, more local and more numerous (and many would probably be employee-owned); prices would be lower and wages higher; and corporate power would be in shambles. Small wonder that big business, despite often paying lip service to free market ideals, tends to systematically oppose them in practice.

So where does this idea come from that advocates of free-market libertarianism must be carrying water for big business interests? Whence the pervasive conflation of corporatist plutocracy with libertarian laissez-faire? Who is responsible for promoting this confusion?

There are three different groups that must shoulder their share of the blame. (Note: in speaking of "blame" I am not necessarily saying that the

---

8    On this latter point see Charles W. Johnson, "Scratching By: How Government Creates Poverty as We Know It," ch. 41 (377-384), this volume.

9    For some of the ways in which purportedly pro-labor legislation turns out to be anti-labor in practice, see Charles W. Johnson, "Free the Unions (and All Political Prisoners)," *RadGeek People's Daily* (n.p., May 1, 2004) <http://radgeek.com/gt/2004/05/01/free_the> (March 13, 2011).

"culprits" have deliberately promulgated what they knew to be a confusion; in most cases the failing is rather one of negligence, of inadequate attention to inconsistencies in their worldview. And as we'll see, these three groups have systematically reinforced one another's confusions.)

Culprit #1: the left. Across the spectrum from the squishiest mainstream liberal to the bomb-throwingest radical leftist, there is widespread (though not, it should be noted, universal)[10] agreement that laissez-faire and corporate plutocracy are virtually synonymous. David Korten, for example, describes advocates of unrestricted markets, private property, and individual rights as "corporate libertarians" who champion a "globalized free market that leaves resource allocation decisions in the hands of giant corporations"[11] – as though these giant corporations were creatures of the free market rather than of the state – while Noam Chomsky, though savvy enough to recognize that the corporate elite are terrified of genuine free markets, yet in the same breath will turn around and say that we must at all costs avoid free markets lest we unduly empower the corporate elite.[12]

Culprit #2: the right. If libertarians' left-wing opponents have conflated free markets with pro-business intervention, libertarians' right wing opponents have done all they can to foster precisely this confusion; for there is a widespread (though again not universal) tendency for conservatives to cloak corporatist policies in free-market rhetoric. This is how conservative politicians in their presumptuous Adam Smith neckties have managed to get themselves perceived – perhaps have even managed to perceive themselves – as proponents of tax cuts, spending cuts, and unhampered competition despite endlessly raising taxes, raising spending, and promoting "government-business partnerships."

Consider the conservative virtue-term "privatization," which has two distinct, indeed opposed, meanings. On the one hand, it can mean returning some service or industry from the monopolistic government sector to the competitive private sector – getting government out of it; this would be the libertarian meaning. On the other hand, it can mean "contracting out," i.e., granting to some private firm a monopoly privilege in the provision some

---

10   Especially given that many anti-corporate libertarians identify themselves as part of the left, e.g., the Alliance of the Libertarian Left; see *Alliance of the Libertarian Left* (Alliance of the Libertarian Left, n.d.) <http://all-left.net>) (March 13, 2011).

11   David C. Korten, *When Corporations Rule the World*, 2d ed. (San Francisco: Berrett-Koehler 2001) 77.

12   Roderick T. Long, "Chomsky's Augustinian Anarchism," *Center for a Stateless Society* (Molinari Institute, Jan. 7, 2010) <http://c4ss.org/content/1659> (March 13, 2011).

service previously provided by government directly. There is nothing free-market about privatization in this latter sense, since the monopoly power is merely transferred from one set of hands to another; this is corporatism, or pro-business intervention, not laissez-faire. (To be sure, there may be competition in the bidding for such monopoly contracts, but competition to establish a legal monopoly is no more genuine market competition than voting – one last time – to establish a dictator is genuine democracy.)

Of these two meanings, the corporatist meaning may actually be older, dating back to fascist economic policies in Nazi Germany;[13] but it was the libertarian meaning that was primarily intended when the term (coined independently, as the reverse of "nationalization") first achieved widespread usage in recent decades. Yet conservatives have largely co-opted the term, turning it once again toward the corporatist sense.

Similar concerns apply to that other conservative virtue-term, "deregulation." From a libertarian standpoint, deregulating should mean the removal of governmental directives and interventions from the sphere of voluntary exchange. But when a private entity is granted special governmental privileges, "deregulating" it amounts instead to an increase, not a decrease, in governmental intrusion into the economy. To take an example not exactly at random, if assurances of a tax-funded bailout lead banks to make riskier loans than they otherwise would, then the banks are being made freer to take risks with the money of unconsenting taxpayers. When conservatives advocate this kind of deregulation they are wrapping redistribution and privilege in the language of economic freedom. When conservatives market their plutocratic schemes as free-market policies, can we really blame liberals and leftists for conflating the two? (Well, okay, yes we can. Still, it is a mitigating factor.)

Culprit #3: libertarians themselves. Alas, libertarians are not innocent here – which is why the answer to my opening question (as to whether it's fair to charge libertarians with being apologists for big business) was no and yes rather than a simple no. If libertarians are accused of carrying water for corporate interests, that may be at least in part because, well, they so often sound like that's just what they're doing (though here, as above, there are plenty of honorable exceptions to this tendency). Consider libertarian icon Ayn Rand's description of big business as a "persecuted minority,"[14] or the

13 Germà Bel, "Retrospectives: The Coining of 'Privatization' and Germany's National Socialist Party," Journal of Economic Perspectives 20.3 (Sum. 2006): 187-194. Bel's article unfortunately shows little sensitivity to the distinction between libertarian and corporatist senses of "privatization."

14 Ayn Rand, "America's Persecuted Minority: Big Business," Capitalism: The Unknown Ideal (New York: Signet-NAL 1967) 44-62. In fairness to Rand, she was not entirely blind to the phenomenon of corporatism; in her article

way libertarians defend "our free-market health-care system" against the alternative of socialized medicine, as though the health care system that prevails in the United States were the product of free competition rather than of systematic government intervention on behalf of insurance companies and the medical establishment at the expense of ordinary people.[15] Or again, note the alacrity with which so many libertarians rush to defend Wal-Mart and the like as heroic exemplars of the free market. Among such libertarians, criticisms of corporate power are routinely dismissed as anti-market ideology. (Of course such dismissiveness gets reinforced by the fact that many critics of corporate power are in the grip of anti-market ideology.) Thus when left wing analysts complain about "corporate libertarians" they are not merely confused; they're responding to a genuine tendency even if they've to some extent misunderstood it.

Kevin Carson has coined the term "vulgar libertarianism" for the tendency to treat the case for the free market as though it justified various unlovely features of actually existing corporatist society.[16] (I find it preferable to talk of vulgar libertarianism rather than of vulgar libertarians, because very few libertarians are consistently vulgar; vulgar libertarianism is a tendency that can show up to varying degrees in thinkers who have many strong anti-corporatist tendencies also.) Likewise, "vulgar liberalism" is Carson's term for the

---

"The Roots of War" (*Capitalism* 35-44), for example, she condemns "men with political pull" who seek "special advantages by government action in their own countries" and "special markets by government action abroad," and so "acquire fortunes by government favor... which they could not have acquired on a free market." Moreover, while readers often come away from her novel *Atlas Shrugged* (New York: Penguin 1999) with the vague memory that the heroine, Dagny Taggart, was fighting against evil bureaucrats who wanted to impose unfair regulations on her railroad company, in fact Taggart's struggle is against evil bureaucrats (in league with her power-hungry brother/employer) who want to give her company special favors and privileges at its competitors' expense. For an analysis of what Rand got right and wrong about corporatism, see Roderick T. Long, "Toward a Libertarian Theory of Class," *Social Philosophy and Policy* 15.1 (1998): 321-5 (Social Philosophy and Policy Center, 1998) <http://praxeology.net/libclass-theory-part-1.pdf>, <http://praxeology.net/libclass-theory-part-2.pdf> (March 13, 2011).

15   See Roderick T. Long, "Poison As Food, Poison As Antidote," *Art of the Possible Essays* (n.p., Aug. 28, 2008) <http://praxeology.net/aotp.htm#13>.

16   Kevin A. Carson, "Vulgar Libertarianism Watch, Part 1," *Mutualist Blog: Free Market Anticapitalism* (n.p., Jan. 11, 2005) <http://mutualist.blogspot.com/2005/01/vulgar-libertarianism-watch-part-1.html> (March 13, 2011).

corresponding tendency to treat the undesirability of those features of actually existing corporatist society as though they constituted an objection to the free market.[17] Both tendencies conflate free markets with corporatism, but draw opposite morals; as Murray Rothbard notes, "Both left and right have been persistently misled by the notion that intervention by the government is ipso facto leftish and antibusiness."[18] And if many leftists tend to see dubious corporate advocacy in libertarian pronouncements even when it's not there, so likewise many libertarians tend not to see dubious corporate advocacy in libertarian pronouncements even when it is there.

There is an obvious tendency for vulgar libertarianism and vulgar liberalism to reinforce each other, as each takes at face value the conflation of plutocracy with free markets assumed by the other. This conflation in turn tends to bolster the power of the political establishment by rendering genuine libertarianism invisible: Those who are attracted to free markets are lured into supporting plutocracy, thus helping to prop up statism's right or corporatist wing; those who are repelled by plutocracy are lured into opposing free markets, thus helping to prop up statism's left or social-democratic wing. But as these two wings have more in common than not, the political establishment wins either way.[19] The perception that libertarians are shills for big business thus has two bad effects: First, it tends to make it harder to attract converts to libertarianism, and so hinders its success; second, those converts its does attract may end up reinforcing corporate power through their advocacy of a muddled version of the doctrine.

In the nineteenth century, it was far more common than it is today for libertarians to see themselves as opponents of big business.[20] The long

---

17   Kevin A. Carson, "Vulgar Liberalism Watch (Yeah, You Read It Right)," *Mutualist Blog: Free Market Anticapitalism* (n.p., Dec. 21, 2005) <online: http:// mutualist.blogspot.com/2005/12/vulgar-liberalism-watch-yeah-you-read. html> (March 13, 2011).

18   Murray N. Rothbard, "Left and Right: The Prospects for Liberty," *Left and Right* 1.1 (Spring 1965): 4-22 <http://mises.org/journals/lar/ pdfs/1_1/1_1_2.pdf> (March 13, 2011).

19   The relationship between big business and big government is like the relation between church and state in the Middle Ages; it's not an entirely harmonious cooperation, since each would like to be the dominant partner (and whether the result looks more like socialism or more like fascism depends on which side is in the ascendant at the moment), but the two sides share an interest in subordinating society to the partnership. See Long, "Poison."

20   See Roderick T. Long, "They Saw it Coming: The 19th-Century Libertarian Critique of Fascism," *Ludwig von Mises Institute Conference on the Economics of Fascism* (Nov. 2, 2005) <http://lewrockwell.com/long/long15.html>

20th-century alliance of libertarians with conservatives against the common enemy of state-socialism probably had much to do with reorienting libertarian thought toward the right; and the brief rapprochement between libertarians and the left during the 1960s foundered when the New Left imploded.[21] As a result, libertarians have been ill-placed to combat left wing and right wing conflation of markets with privilege, because they have not been entirely free of the conflation themselves.

Happily, the left/libertarian coalition is now beginning to re-emerge;[22] and with it is emerging a new emphasis on the distinction between free markets and prevailing corporatism. In addition, many libertarians are beginning to rethink the way they present their views, and in particular their use of terminology. Take, for example, the word "capitalism," which libertarians during the past century have tended to apply to the system they favor. As I've argued elsewhere, this term is somewhat problematic; some use it to mean free markets, others to mean corporate privilege, and still others (perhaps the majority) to mean some confused amalgamation of the two:

By "capitalism" most people mean neither the free market simpliciter nor the prevailing neomercantilist system simpliciter. Rather, what most people mean by "capitalism" is this free-market system that currently prevails in the western world. In short, the term "capitalism" as generally used conceals an assumption that the prevailing system is a free market. And since the prevailing system is in fact one of government favoritism toward business, the ordinary use of the term carries with it the assumption that the free market is government favoritism toward business.[23]

Hence clinging to the term "capitalism" may be one of the factors reinforcing the conflation of libertarianism with corporatist advocacy.[24] In any case, if libertarianism advocacy is not to be misperceived – or worse yet, correctly perceived! – as pro-corporate apologetics, the antithetical relationship between free markets and corporate power must be continually highlighted.

---

(March 13, 2011).

21 John Payne, "Rothbard's Time on the Left," *Journal of Libertarian Studies* 19.1 (Winter 2005): 7-24 (Ludwig von Mises Institute, 2005) <http://mises.org/journals/jls/19_1/19_1_2.pdf> (March 13, 2011).

22 See, for example, *LeftLibertarian.org* (n.p., n.d.) <http://leftlibertarian.org> (March 13, 2011).

23 Roderick T. Long, "Rothbard's 'Left and Right': Forty Years Later," Rothbard Memorial Lecture 2006 (Ludwig von Mises Institute, April 8, 2006) <http://mises.org/story/2099> (March 13, 2011).

24 William Gillis has likewise suggested abandoning "free market" in favor of "freed market"; see William Gills, "The Freed Market," ch. 1 (19-20), this volume.

# DOES COMPETITION MEAN WAR?

## BENJAMIN R. TUCKER
## (1888)

"Your thought-provoking controversy with Herr Most suggests this question: Whether is Individualism or Communism more consistent with a society resting upon credit and mutual confidence, or, to put it another way, whether is competition or cooperation the truest expression of that mutual trust and fraternal goodwill which alone can replace present forms of authority, usages and customs as the social bond of union?

"The answer seems obvious enough. Competition, if it means anything at all, means war, and, so far from tending to enhance the growth of mutual confidence, must generate division and hostility among men. If egoistic liberty demands competition as its necessary corollary, every man becomes a social Ishmael. The state of veiled warfare thus implied where underhand cunning takes the place of open force is doubtless not without its attractions to many minds, but to propose mutual confidence as its regulative principle has all the appearance of making a declaration of war in terms of peace. No, surely credit and mutual confidence, with everything thereby implied, rightly belong to an order of things where unity and good-fellowship characterize all human relations, and would flourish best where cooperation finds its complete expression – viz., in Communism."

W. T. Horn.

THE SUPPOSITION THAT COMPETITION MEANS WAR RESTS UPON OLD NOTIONS AND FALSE phrases that have been long current, but are rapidly passing into the limbo of exploded fallacies. Competition means war only when it is in some way restricted, either in scope or intensity – that is, when it is not perfectly free competition; for then its benefits are won by one class at the expense of another, instead of by all at the expense of nature's forces. When universal and unrestricted, competition means the most perfect peace and the truest cooperation; for then it becomes simply a test of forces resulting in their most advantageous utilization. As soon as the demand for labor begins to exceed the supply, making it an easy matter for every one to get work at wages equal to his product, it is for the interest of all (including his immediate competitors) that the best man should win; which is another way of saying that, where freedom prevails, competition and cooperation are identical. For further proof and elaboration of this proposition I refer Mr. Horn to Andrews's Science of Society and Fowler's pamphlets on Cooperation. The real problem, then, is to make the demand for labor greater than the supply, and this can only be done through competition in the supply of money or use of credit. This is abundantly shown in Greene's Mutual Banking and the financial writings of Proudhon and Spooner. My correspondent seems filled with the sentiment of good-fellowship, but ignorant of the science thereof, and even of the fact that there is such a science. He will find this science expounded in the works already named. If, after studying and mastering these, he still should have any doubts, Liberty will then try to set them at rest.

# 22

*The Freeman. Ideas on Liberty* 57.5 (June
2007): 13-8.

# ECONOMIC CALCULATION IN THE CORPORATE COMMONWEALTH

## KEVIN CARSON
## (2007)

THE GENERAL LINES OF LUDWIG VON MISES'S RATIONAL-CALCULATION ARGUMENT ARE well known. A market in factors of production is necessary for pricing production inputs so that a planner may allocate them rationally. The problem has nothing to do either with the volume of data or with agency problems. The question, rather, as Peter Klein put it, is "[h]ow does the principal know what to tell the agent to do?"

This calculation argument can be applied not only to a state-planned economy, but also to the internal planning of the large corporation under interventionism, or state capitalism. (By state capitalism, I refer to the means by which, as Murray Rothbard said, "our corporate state uses the coercive taxing power either to accumulate corporate capital or to lower corporate costs," in addition to cartelizing markets through regulations, enforcing artificial property rights like "intellectual property," and otherwise protecting privilege against competition.)

Rothbard developed the economic calculation argument in just this way. He argued that the further removed the internal transfer pricing of a corporation became from real market prices, the more internal allocation of resources was characterized by calculational chaos.

Mises's calculation argument can be applied to the large corporation – both under state capitalism and to some extent in the free market – in another way not considered by Rothbard. The basic cause of calculational chaos, as Mises understood it, was the separation of entrepreneurial from technical knowledge and the attempt to make production decisions based on technical considerations alone, without regard to such entrepreneurial considerations as factor pricing. But the principle also works the other way: production decisions based solely on input and product prices, without regard to the details of production (the typical MBA practice of considering only finance and marketing, while treating the production process as a black box), also result in calculational chaos.

The chief focus of this article, however, is Mises's calculation argument in the light of distributed information. F. A. Hayek, in "The Uses of Knowledge in Society," raised a new problem: not the generation or source of data, but the sheer volume of data to be processed. In so doing, he is commonly understood to have opened a second front in Mises's war against state planning. But in fact his argument was almost as damaging to Mises as to the collectivists.

Mises minimized the importance of distributed information in his own criticisms of state planning. He denied any correlation between bureaucratization and large size in themselves. Bureaucracy as such was a particular rules-based approach to policy-making, in contrast to the profit-driven behavior of the entrepreneur. The private firm, therefore, was by definition exempt from the problem of bureaucracy.

In so arguing, he ignored the information and coordination problems inherent in large size. The large corporation necessarily distributes the knowledge relevant to informed entrepreneurial decisions among many departments and sub-departments until the cost of aggregating that knowledge outweighs the benefits of doing so.

Try as he might, Mises could not exempt the capitalist corporation from the problem of bureaucracy. One cannot define bureaucracy out of existence, or overcome the problem of distributed knowledge, simply by using the word "entrepreneur." Mises tried to make the bureaucratic or non-bureaucratic character of an organization a simple matter of its organizational goals rather than its functioning. The motivation of the corporate employee, from the CEO down to the production worker, by definition, will be profit-seeking; his will is in harmony with that of the stockholder because he belongs to the stockholder's organization.

By defining organizational goals as "profit-seeking," Mises – like the neoclassicals – treated the internal workings of the organization as a black box. In treating the internal policies of the capitalist corporation as inherently profit-driven, Mises simultaneously treated the entrepreneur as an indivisible actor whose will and perception permeate the entire organization. Mises's entrepreneur was a brooding omnipresence, guiding the actions of every employee from CEO to janitor.

He viewed the separation of ownership from control, and the knowledge and agency problems resulting from it, as largely nonexistent. The invention of double-entry bookkeeping, which made possible the separate calculation of profit and loss in each division of an enterprise, has "reliev[ed] the entrepreneur of involvement in too much detail," Mises writes in *Human Action*. The only thing necessary to transform every single employee of a corporation, from CEO on down, into a perfect instrument of his will was the ability to monitor the balance sheet of any division or office and fire the functionary responsible for red ink. Mises continues:

> It is the system of double-entry bookkeeping that makes the functioning of the managerial system possible. Thanks to it, the entrepreneur is in a position to separate the calculation of each part of his total enterprise in such a way that he can determine the role it plays within his whole enterprise... Within this system of business calculation each section of a firm represents an integral entity, a hypothetical independent business, as it were. It is assumed that this section "owns" a definite part of the whole capital employed in the enterprise, that it buys from other sections and sells to them, that it has its own expenses and its own revenues, that its dealings result either in a profit or in a loss which is imputed to its own conduct of affairs as distinguished from the result of the other sections. Thus the entrepreneur can assign to each section's management a great deal of independence. The only directive he gives to a man whom he entrusts with the management of a circumscribed job is to make as much profit as possible. An examination of the accounts shows how successful or unsuccessful the managers were in executing this directive. Every manager and submanager is responsible for the working of his section or subsection... His own interests impel him toward the utmost care and exertion in the conduct of his section's affairs. If he incurs losses, he will be replaced by a man whom

the entrepreneur expects to be more successful, or the whole section will be discontinued.

## CAPITAL MARKETS AS CONTROL MECHANISM

Mises also identified outside capital markets as a control mechanism limiting managerial discretion. Of the popular conception of stockholders as passive rentiers in the face of managerial control, he wrote:

> This doctrine disregards entirely the role that the capital and money market, the stock and bond exchange, which a pertinent idiom simply calls the "market," plays in the direction of corporate business… In fact, the changes in the prices of… stock and of corporate bonds are the means applied by the capitalists for the supreme control of the flow of capital. The price structure as determined by the speculations on the capital and money markets and on the big commodity exchanges not only decides how much capital is available for the conduct of each corporation's business; it creates a state of affairs to which the managers must adjust their operations in detail.

One can hardly imagine the most hubristic of state socialist central planners taking a more optimistic view of the utopian potential of numbers-crunching.

Peter Klein argued that this foreshadowed Henry Manne's treatment of the mechanism by which entrepreneurs maintain control of corporate management. So long as there is a market for control of corporations, the discretion of management will be limited by the threat of hostile takeover. Although management possesses a fair degree of administrative autonomy, any significant deviation from profit-maximization will lower stock prices and bring the corporation into danger of outside takeover.

The question, though, is whether those making investment decisions – whether senior management allocating capital among divisions of a corporation or outside finance capitalists – even possess the information needed to assess the internal workings of firms and make appropriate decisions.

How far the real-world, state capitalist allocation of finance differs from Mises's picture is suggested by Robert Jackall's account in *Moral Mazes* of the internal workings of a corporation (especially the notorious practices of "starving," or "milking," an organization in order to inflate its apparent short-term profit). Whether an apparent profit is sustainable, or an illusory side effect of eating the seed corn, is often a judgment best made by those directly involved in production. The purely money calculations of those at the top do not suffice for a valid assessment of such questions.

One big problem with Mises's model of entrepreneurial central planning by double-entry bookkeeping is this: it is often the irrational constraints imposed from above that result in red ink at lower levels. But those at the top of the hierarchy refuse to acknowledge the double bind they put their subordinates in. "Plausible deniability," the downward flow of responsibility and upward flow of credit, and the practice of shooting the messenger for bad news, are what lubricate the wheels of any large organization.

As for outside investors, participants in the capital markets are even further removed than management from the data needed to evaluate the efficiency of factor use within the "black box." In practice, hostile takeovers tend to gravitate toward firms with low debt loads and apparently low short-term profit margins. The corporate raiders are more likely to smell blood when there is the possibility of loading up an acquisition with new debt and stripping it of assets for short-term returns. The best way to avoid a hostile takeover, on the other hand, is to load an organization with debt and inflate the short-term returns by milking.

Another problem, from the perspective of those at the top, is determining the significance of red or black ink. How does the large-scale investor distinguish losses caused by senior management's gaming of the system in its own interest at the expense of the productivity of the organization from losses occurring as normal effects of the business cycle? Mises of all people, who rejected the neoclassicals' econometric approach precisely because the variables were too complex to control for, should have anticipated such difficulties.

Management's "gaming" might well be a purely defensive response to structural incentives, a way of deflecting pressure from those above whose only concern is to maximize apparent profits without regard to how short-term savings might result in long-term loss. The practices of "starving" and "milking" organizations that Jackall made so much of – deferring needed maintenance costs, letting plant and equipment run down, and the like, in order to inflate the quarterly balance sheet – resulted from just such pressure, as irrational as the pressures Soviet enterprise managers faced from Gosplan.

## SHARED CULTURE

The problem is complicated when the same organizational culture – determined by the needs of the managerial system itself – is shared by all the corporations in a state-induced oligopoly industry, so that the same pattern of red ink appears industry-wide. It's complicated still further when the general atmosphere of state capitalism enables the corporations in a cartelized industry to operate in the black despite excessive size and dysfunctional internal culture. It becomes impossible to make a valid assessment of why the corporation is profitable at all: does the black ink result from efficiency or from some degree of protection against the competitive penalty for inefficiency? If the decisions of MBA types to engage in asset-stripping and milking, in the interest of short-term profitability, result in long-term harm to the health of the enterprise, they are more apt to be reinforced than censured by investors and higher-ups. After all, they acted according to the conventional wisdom in the Big MBA Handbook, so it couldn't have been that that caused them to go in the tank. Must've been sunspots or something.

In fact, the financial community sometimes censures transgressions against the norms of corporate culture even when they are quite successful by conventional measures. Costco's stock fell in value, despite the company's having outperformed Wal-Mart in profit, in response to adverse publicity in the business community about its above-average wages. Deutsche Bank analyst Bill Dreher snidely remarked, "At Costco, it's better to be an employee or a customer than a shareholder." Nevertheless, in the world of faith-based investment, Wal-Mart "remains the darling of the Street, which, like Wal-Mart and many other companies, believes that shareholders are best served if employers do all they can to hold down costs, including the cost of labor."[1]

On the other hand, management may be handsomely rewarded for running a corporation into the ground, so long as it is perceived to be doing everything right according to the norms of corporate culture. In a *New York Times* story that Digg aptly titled "Home Depot CEO Gets $210M Severance for Sucking at Job," it was reported that departing Home Depot CEO Robert Nardelli received an enormous severance package despite abysmal performance. It's a good thing he didn't raise employee wages too high, though, or he'd be eating in a soup kitchen.

As you might expect, the usual suspects stepped in to defend Nardelli's honor. An Allan Murray article at the *Wall Street Journal* noted that he had "more than doubled… earnings."

But Tom Blumer of BizzyBlog, whose sources for obvious reasons prefer to remain anonymous, pointed out some inconvenient facts about how Nardelli achieved those increased earnings:

1   Stanley Holmes and Wendy Zellner, "The Costco Way: Higher Wages Mean Higher Profits. But Try Telling Wall Street," *Bloomberg Businessweek* (Bloomberg LLP, April 12, 2004) <http://www.businessweek.com/magazine/content/04_15/b3878084_mz021.htm> (March 13, 2011).

- His consolidation of purchasing and many other functions to Atlanta from several regions caused buyers to lose touch with their vendors...

- Firing knowledgeable and experienced people in favor of uninformed newbies and part-timers greatly reduced payroll and benefits costs, but has eventually driven customers away, and given the company a richly-deserved reputation for mediocre service...

- Nardelli and his minions played every accounting, acquisition, and quick-fix angle they could to keep the numbers looking good, while letting the business deteriorate.

In a follow-up comment directed to me personally, Blumer provided this additional bit of information:

> I have since learned that Nardelli, in the last months before he walked, took the entire purchasing function out of Atlanta and moved it to... India – of all the things to pick for foreign outsourcing.
>
> I am told that "out of touch" doesn't even begin to describe how bad it is now between HD stores and Purchasing, and between HD Purchasing and suppliers.
>
> Not only is there a language dialect barrier, but the purchasing people in India don't know the "language" of American hardware – or even what half the stuff the stores and suppliers are describing even is.
>
> I am told that an incredible amount of time, money, and energy is being wasted – all in the name of what was in all likelihood a bonus-driven goal for cutting headcount and making G&A [general and administrative] expenses look low ("look" low because the expenses have been pushed down to the stores and suppliers).

More than one observer has remarked on the similarity, in their distorting effects, of the incentives within the Soviet state-planning system and the Western corporate economy. We already noted the systemic pressure to create the illusion of short-term profit by undermining long-term productivity.

Consider Hayek's prediction of the uneven development, irrationality, and misallocation of resources within a planned economy:

> There is no reason to expect that production would stop, or that the authorities would find difficulty in using all the avail-

able resources somehow, or even that output would be permanently lower than it had been before planning started… [We
should expect] the excessive development of some lines of production at the expense of others and the use of methods which
are inappropriate under the circumstances. We should expect
to find overdevelopment of some industries at a cost which
was not justified by the importance of their increased output
and see unchecked the ambition of the engineer to apply the
latest development elsewhere, without considering whether
they were economically suited in the situation. In many cases
the use of the latest methods of production, which could not
have been applied without central planning, would then be a
symptom of a misuse of resources rather than a proof of success.[2]

As an example he cited "the excellence, from a technological point of
view, of some parts of the Russian industrial equipment, which often strikes
the casual observer and which is commonly regarded as evidence of success."

To anyone observing the uneven development of the corporate economy
under state capitalism, this should inspire a sense of déjà vu. Entire categories of goods and production methods have been developed at enormous
expense, either within military industry or by state-subsidized R&D in the
civilian economy, without regard to cost. Subsidies to capital accumulation, R&D, and technical education radically distort the forms taken by
production. (On these points see David Noble's works, *Forces of Production*
and *America by Design*.) Blockbuster factories and economic centralization
become artificially profitable, thanks to the Interstate Highway system and
other means of externalizing distribution costs.

## PERVASIVE IRRATIONALITY

It also describes quite well the environment of pervasive irrationality
within the large corporation: management featherbedding and self-dealing;
"cost-cutting" measures that decimate productive resources while leaving
management's petty empires intact; and the tendency to extend bureaucratic domain while cutting maintenance and support for existing obligations. Management's allocation of resources no doubt creates use value of

2    "Socialist Calculation II: The State of the Debate," *Individualism and Economic Order* (Chicago: University of Chicago Press 1949) 150 <http://mises.
org/books/individualismandeconomicorder.pdf> (March 13, 2011).

a sort – but with no reliable way to assess opportunity cost or determine whether the benefit was worth it.

A good example is a hospital, part of a corporate chain, that I've had occasion to observe first-hand. Management justifies repeated downsizings of nurses and technicians as "cost-cutting" measures despite increased costs from errors, falls, and MRSA (Methicillin-resistant Staphylococcus aureus) infections that exceed the alleged savings. Of course the "cost-cutting" justification for downsizing direct caregivers doesn't extend to the patronage network of staff RNs attached to the Nursing Office. Meanwhile, management pours money into ill-considered capital projects (like remodeling jobs that actually make wards less functional, or the extremely expensive new ACE unit that never opened because it was so badly designed); an expensive surgical robot, purchased mainly for prestige value, does nothing that couldn't be accomplished by scrubbing in an extra nurse. But the management team is hardly likely to face any negative consequences, when the region's three other large hospitals are run exactly the same way.

Such pathologies, obviously, are not the result of the free market. That is not to say, of course, that bigness as such would not produce inefficiency costs in some firms that might exist under laissez faire. The calculation problem (in the broad sense that includes Hayekian information problems) may or may not exist to some extent in the private corporation in a free market. But the boundary between market and hierarchy would be set by the point at which the benefits of size cease to outweigh the costs of such calculation problems. The inefficiencies of large size and hierarchy may be a matter of degree, but, as Ronald Coase said, the market would determine whether the inefficiencies are worth it.

The problem is that the state, by artificially reducing the costs of large size and restraining the competitive ill effects of calculation problems, promotes larger size than would be the case in a free market – and with it calculation problems to a pathological extent. The state promotes inefficiencies of large size and hierarchy past the point at which they cease to be worth it, from a standpoint of net social efficiency, because those receiving the benefits of large size are not the same parties who pay the costs of inefficiency.

The solution is to eliminate the state policies that have created the situation, and allow the market to punish inefficiency. To get there, though, some libertarians need to reexamine their unquestioned sympathies for big business as an "oppressed minority" and remember that they're supposed to be defending free markets – not the winners under the current statist economy.

# 23

"Big Business and the Rise of American
Statism — Part 1," *Reason* 2.11 (Feb.
1971): 12-8; "Big Business and the Rise of
American Statism — Part 2," *Reason* 2.12
(Mar. 1971): 9-12.

# BIG BUSINESS AND THE RISE OF AMERICAN STATISM

### ROY A. CHILDS, JR.
### (1971)

THE PURPOSE OF THIS PARTICULAR ESSAY IS SIMPLY TO APPLY SOME OF THE PRINCIPLES OF libertarianism to an interpretation of events in a very special and important period of human history. I have attempted to give a straightforward summary of New Left revisionist findings in one area of domestic history: the antitrust movement and Progressive Era. But I have done so not as a New Leftist, not as a historian proper, but as a libertarian, that is, a social philosopher of a specific school.

In doing this summary, I have two interrelated purposes: first, to show Objectivists and libertarians that certain of their beliefs in history are wrong and need to be revised under the impact of new evidence, and simultaneously to illustrate to them a specific means of approaching historical problems, to identify one cause of the growth of American statism and to indicate a new way of looking at history. Secondly, my purpose is to show New

Left radicals that far from undermining the position of laissez-faire capital-ism (as opposed to what they call state capitalism, a system of government controls which is not yet socialism in the classic sense), their historical dis-coveries actually support the case for a totally free market. Then, too, I wish to illustrate how a libertarian would respond to the problems raised by New Left historians. Finally, I wish implicitly to apply Occam's razor by showing that there is a simpler explanation of events than that so often colored with Marxist theory. Without exception, Marxist postulates are not necessary to explain the facts of reality.

## CONFLICTING SCHOOLS OF THOUGHT

In historiography different schools of thought exist in much the same way and for the same reason as in many other fields. And in history, as in those other fields, different interpretations, no matter how far removed from real-ity, tend to go on forever, oblivious to new evidence and theories. In his book, *The Structure of Scientific Revolutions*, Thomas Kuhn shows in the physical sciences how an existing paradigm of scientific explanation tends to ignore new evidence and theories, being overthrown only when: (a) the puzzles and problems generated by a false paradigm pile up to an increasingly obvious extent, so that an ever-wider range of material cannot be integrated into the paradigm, and an ever-growing number of problems cannot be solved, and (b) there arises on the scene a new paradigm to replace the old.

In history, perhaps more than in most other fields, the criteria of truth have not been sufficiently developed, resulting in a great number of schools of thought that tend to rise and fall in influence more because of political and cultural factors than because of epistemological factors. The result also has been that in history there are a number of competing paradigms to explain different sets of events, all connected to specific political views. In this essay, I shall consider three of them: the Marxist view, the conservative view and the liberal view. I shall examine how these paradigms function with reference to one major area of American history – the Progressive Era – and with respect to one major issue: the roots of government regulation of the economy, particularly through the antitrust laws and the Federal Reserve System. Other incidents will also be mentioned, but this issue will be the focus.

Among these various schools, nearly everyone agrees on the putative facts of American history; disagreements arise over frameworks of interpre-tation and over evaluation.

The Marxists, liberals, and conservatives all agree that in the economic history of America in the nineteenth century, the facts were roughly as follows. After midcentury, industrialization proceeded apace in America, as a consequence of the laissez-faire policies pursued by the United States government, resulting in increasing centralization and concentration of economic power.

According to the liberal, in the nineteenth century there was an individualistic social system in the United States, which, when left unchecked, led inevitably to the "strong" using the forces of a free market to smash and subdue the "weak," by building gigantic, monopolistic industrial enterprises which dominated and controlled the life of the nation. Then, as this centralization proceeded to snowball, the "public" awoke to its impeding subjugation at the hands of these monopolistic businessmen. The public was stirred by the injustice of it all and demanded reform, whereupon altruistic and far-seeing politicians moved quickly to mash the monopolists with antitrust laws and other regulation of the economy, on behalf of the ever-suffering "little man" who was saved thereby from certain doom. Thus did the American government squash the greedy monopolists and restore competition, equality of opportunity and the like, which was perishing in the unregulated laissez-faire free market economy. Thus did the American state act to save both freedom and capitalism.

The Marxists also hold that there was in fact a trend toward centralization of the economy at the end of the last century, and that this was inherent in the nature of capitalism as an economic system. (Some modern, more sophisticated Marxists maintain, on the contrary, that historically the state was always involved in the so-called capitalistic economy.) Different Marxists see the movement towards state regulation of the economy in different ways. One group basically sees state regulation as a means of prolonging the collapse of the capitalistic system, a means which they see as inherently unstable. They see regulation as an attempt by the ruling class to deal with the "inner contradictions" of capitalism. Another group, more sophisticated, sees the movement towards state regulation as a means of hastening the cartelization and monopolization of the economy under the hands of the ruling class.

The conservative holds, like the liberal, that there was indeed such a golden age of individualism, when the economy was almost completely free of government controls. But far from being evil, such a society was near-utopian in their eyes. But the government intervened and threw things out of kilter. The consequence was that the public began to clamor for regulation in order to rectify things that were either not injustices at all, or were injustices imposed by initial state actions. The antitrust laws and other acts of state interference, by this view, were the result. But far from seeing the key large industrialists and bankers as monopolistic monsters, the conservatives defend them as heroic innovators who were the victims of misguided or power-lusting progressives who used big businessmen as scapegoats and sacrifices on the altar of the "public good."

All three of the major schools of interpretation of this crucial era in American history hold two premises in common: (a) that the trend in economic organization at the end of the nineteenth century was in fact towards growing centralization of economic power, and (b) that this trend was an outcome of the processes of the free market. Only the Marxists, and then only a portion of them, take issue with the additional premise that the actions of state regulation were anti-big business in motivation, purpose and results. And both the conservatives and the liberals see a sharp break between the ideas and men involved in the Progressive Movement and those of key big business and financial leaders. Marxists disagree with many of these views, but hold the premise that the regulatory movement itself was an outgrowth of the capitalistic economy.

The Marxists, of course, smuggle in specifically nonhistorical conclusions and premises, based on their wider ideological frame of reference, the most prominent being the idea of necessity applied to historical events.

Although there are many arguments and disputes between adherents of the various schools, none of the schools has disputed the fundamental historical premise that the dominant trend at the end of the last century was toward increasing centralization of the economy, or the fundamental economic premise that this alleged increase was the result of the operations of a laissez-faire free market system.

Yet there are certain flaws in all three interpretations, flaws that are both historical and theoretical, flaws that make any of the interpretations inadequate, necessitating a new explanation. Although it is not possible here to argue in depth against the three interpretations, brief reasons for their inadequacy can be given.

Aside from the enormous disputes in economics over questions such as whether or not the "capitalistic system" inherently leads toward concentration and centralization of economic power in the hands of a few, we can respond to the Marxists, as well as to others, by directing our attention to the premise that there was in fact economic centralization at the turn of the century. In confronting the liberals, once more we can begin by pointing to the fact that there has been much more centralization since the Progressive Era than before, and that the function, if not the alleged purpose, of the antitrust and other regulatory laws has been to increase, rather than decrease, such centralization. Since the conservatives already question, on grounds of economic theory, the premise that the concentration of economic power results inevitably from a free market system, we must question them as to why they believe that (a) a free market actually existed during the period in question, and (b) how, then, such centralization of economic power resulted from this supposed free market.

Aside from all the economic arguments, let us look at the period in question to see if any of the schools presented hold up, in any measure or degree.

## THE ROOTS OF REGULATION

In fact and in history, the entire thesis of all three schools is botched, from beginning to end. The interpretations of the Marxists, the liberals and the conservatives are a tissue of lies.

As Gabriel Kolko demonstrates in his masterly *The Triumph of Conservatism* and in *Railroads and Regulation*, the dominant trend in the last three decades of the nineteenth century and the first two of the twentieth was not towards increasing centralization, but rather, despite the growing number of mergers and the growth in the overall size of many corporations,

> toward growing competition. Competition was unacceptable to many key business and financial leaders, and the merger movement was to a large extent a reflection of voluntary, unsuccessful business efforts to bring irresistible trends under control... As new competitors sprang up, and as economic power was diffused throughout an expanding nation, it became apparent to many important businessmen that only the national government could [control and stabilize] the economy... Ironically, contrary to the consensus of historians, it was not the existence of monopoly which caused the federal government to intervene in the economy, but the lack of it.[1]

While Kolko does not consider the causes and context of the economic crises which faced businessmen from the 1870s on, we can at least summarize some of the more relevant aspects here. The enormous role played by the state in American history has not yet been fully investigated by anyone. Those focusing on the role of the federal government in regulating the economy often neglect to mention the fact that America's ostensive federalist system means that the historian concerned with the issue of regulation must look to the various state governments as well. What he will find already has been suggested by a growing number of historians: that nearly

---

1    Gabriel Kolko, *The Triumph of Conservatism: A Reinterpretation of American History, 1900-1916* (Chicago: Quadrangle 1967) 4-5.

every federal program was pioneered by a number of state governments, including subsidies, land grants and regulations of the antitrust variety. Furthermore, often neglected in these accounts is the fact that the real process of centralization of the economy came not during the Progressive Era, but rather (initially) during the Civil War, with its immense alliance between the state and business (at least in the more industrialized North). Indeed, such key figures in the progressive Era as J. P. Morgan got their starts in alliances with the government of the North in the Civil War. The Civil War also saw the greatest inflationary expansion of the monetary supply and greatest land grants to the railroads in American history. These and other related facts mean that an enormous amount of economic malinvestment occurred during and immediately after the Civil War, and the result was that a process of liquidation of malinvestment took place: a depression in the 1870s.

It was this process of inflationary book caused by the banking and credit system spurred by the government and followed by depressions, that led the businessmen and financial leaders to seek stabilizing elements from the 1870s on. One of the basic results of this process of liquidation, of course, was a growth in competition. The thesis of the Kolko books is that the trend was towards growing competition in the United States before the federal government intervened, and that various big businessmen in different fields found themselves unable to cope with this trend by private, economic means. Facing falling profits and diffusion of economic power, these businessmen then turned to the state to regulate the economy on their behalf. What Kolko and his fellow revisionist James Weinstein (*The Corporate Ideal in the Liberal State, 1900-1918*) maintain is that business and financial leaders did not merely react to these situations with concrete proposals for regulations, but with the ever more sophisticated development of a comprehensive ideology which embraced both foreign and domestic policy. Weinstein in particular links up the process of businessmen turning to the state for favors in response to problems which they faced and the modern "corporate liberal" system. he maintains that the ideology now dominant in the U.S. had been worked out for the most part by the end of the First World War, not during the New Deal, as is commonly held, and that the "ideal of a liberal corporate social order" was developed consciously and purposefully by those who then, as now, enjoyed supremacy in the United States: "the more sophisticated leaders of America's largest corporations and financial institutions."[2] In examining this thesis, I shall focus predominantly on the activities of the national Civics Federation (NCF),

---

2    James Weinstein, *The Corporate Ideal in the Liberal State, 1900-1918* (Boston: Beacon 1968) ix.

a group of big businessmen that was the primary ideological force behind many "reforms."

Since the basic pattern of regulation was first established in the case of the railroads, a glance at this industry will set the basis for an examination of the others.

American industry as a whole was intensely competitive in the period from 1875 on. Many industries, including the railroads, had overexpanded and were facing a squeeze on profits. American history contains the myth that the railroads faced practically no competition at all during this period, that freight rates constantly rose, pinching every last penny out of the shippers, especially the farmers, and bleeding them to death. Historian Kolko shows that:

> Contrary to the common view, railroad freight rates, taken as a whole, declined almost contiuously over the period [from 1877 to 1916] and although consolidation of railroads proceeded apace, this phenomenon never affected the long-term decline of rates or the ultimately competitive nature of much of the industry. In their desire to establish stability and control over rates and competition, the railroads often resorted to voluntary, cooperative efforts.
>
> When these efforts failed, as they inevitably did, the railroad men turned to political solutions to [stabilize] their increasingly chaotic industry. They advocated measures designed to bring under control those railroads within their own ranks that refused to conform to voluntary compacts... [F]rom the beginning of the 20th century until at least the initiation of World War I, the railroad industry resorted primarily to political alternatives and gave up the abortive efforts to put its own house in order by relying on voluntary cooperation... Insofar as the railroad men did think about the larger theoretical implications of centralized federal regulation, they rejected... the entire notion of laissez-faire [and] most railroad leaders increasingly relied on a Hamiltonian conception of the national government.[3]

The two major means used by competitors to cut into each other's markets were rate wars (price cutting) and rebates; the aim of business leaders was to stop these. Their major, unsuccessful, tool was the "pool" which was

---

3    Gabriel Kolko, *Railroads and Regulation* (Princeton: Princeton UP 1965) 3-5.

continuously broken up by competitive factors.[4] The first serious pooling effort in the East, sponsored by the New York Central, had been tried as early as 1874 by Vanderbilt; the pool lasted for six months. In September 1876, a Southwestern Railroad Association was formed by seven major companies in an attempt to voluntarily enforce a pool; it didn't work and collapsed in early 1878. Soon it became obvious to most industrial leaders that the pooling system was ineffective.

In 1876 the first significant federal regulatory bill was introduced into the House by J. R. Hopkins of Pittsburgh. Drawn up by the attorney for the Philadelphia and Reading Railroad, it died in committee.

By 1879, there was "a general unanimity among pool executives… that without government sanctions, the railroads would never maintain or stabilize rates."[5] By 1880, the railroads were in serious trouble; the main threat was identified as "cutthroat competition."

Far from pushing the economy toward greater centralization, economic forces indicated that centralization was inefficient and unstable. The push was towards decentralization, and smaller railroads often found themselves much less threatened by economic turns of events than the older, more established and larger business concerns.

Thus the Marxist model finds itself seriously in jeopardy in this instance, for the smaller forms and railroads, throughout the crises of the 1870s and 1880s often were found to be making larger profits on capital invested than the giant businesses. Furthermore, much of the concentration of economic power which was apparent during the 1870s and on, was the result of massive state aid immediately before, during, and after the Civil War, not the result of free market forces. Much of the capital accumulation – particularly in the cases of the railroads and banks – was accomplished by means of government regulation and aid, not by free trade on a free market.

Also, the liberal and conservative models which stress the supposed fact that there was growing centralization in the economy and that competition either lessened or became less intense, are both shaken by historical facts. And we already have seen that it was the railroad leaders, faced with seemingly insurmountable problems, who initiated the drive for federal government regulation of their industry.

---

4   See both Kolko books for factual proof of this. Weinstein does not take this fact into account in his book, and thus underestimates this as a motivating force in the actions and beliefs of businessmen. For a theoretical explanation, see Murray N. Rothbard, *Man, Economy and State with Power and Market* (Auburn, AL: Mises 2009) 636-61 (ch. 10, Sect. 2: Cartels and Their Consequences).

5   Kolko, *Railroads* 26.

Rate wars during 1881 pushed freight rates down 50 percent between July and October alone; between 1882 and 1886, freight rates declined for the nation as a whole by 20 percent. Railroads were increasingly talking about regulation with a certain spark of interest. Chauncey Depew, attorney for the New York Central, had become convinced "of the [regulatory commission's] necessity… for the protection of both the public and the railroads.[6] He soon converted William H. Vanderbilt to his position.[7]

Agitation for regulation to ease competitive pains increased, and in 1887, the Interstate Commerce Act was passed. According to the Railway Review, an organ of the railroad, it was only a first step.

The Act was not enough, and it did not stop either the rate wars or rebates. So, early in 1889 during a prolonged rate war, J. P. Morgan summoned presidents of major railroads to New York to find ways to maintain rates and enforce the act, but this, too, was a failure. The larger railroads were harmed most by this competition; the smaller railroads were in many cases more prosperous than in the early 1880s. "Morgan weakened rather than strengthened many of his roads… [and on them] services and safety often declined. Many of Morgan's lines were overexpanded into areas where competition was already too great."[8] Competition again increased. The larger roads then led the fight for further regulation, seeking more power for the Interstate Commerce Commission (ICC).

In 1891, the president of a midwestern railroad advocated that the entire matter of setting rates be turned over to the ICC. An ICC poll taken in 1892 of fifteen railroads showed that fourteen of them favored legalized pooling under Commission control.

Another important businessman, A. A. Walker, who zipped back and forth betwene business and govenrment agencies, said that "railroad men had had enough of competition. The phrase 'free competition' sounds well enough as a universal regulator," he said, "but it regulates by the knife."[9]

In 1906, the Hepburn Act was passed, also with business backing. The railroad magnate Cassatt spoke out as a major proponent of the act and said that he had long endorsed federal rate regulation. Andrew Carnegie, too, popped up to endorse the act. George W. Perkins, an important Morgan associate, wrote his boss that the act "is going to work out for the ultimate

---

6  Kolko, *Railroads* 17.

7  The twin facts here that Vanderbilt needed "converting" and that he had other options open to him should by themselves put to rest the more simplistic Marxist theories of "class consciousness," awareness of interests and relationships to the means of production.

8  Kolko, *Railroads* 65-6.

9  Kolko, *Railroads* 74.

and great good of the railroad." But such controls were not enough for some big businessmen. Thus E. P. Ripley, the president of the Santa Fe, suggested what amounted to a Federal Reserve System for the railroads, cheerfully declaring that such a system "would do away with the enormous wastes of the competitive system, and permit business to follow the line of least resistance" – a chant later taken up by Mussolini.

In any case, we have seen that (a) the trend was not towards centralization at the close of the nineteenth century – rather, the liquidation of previous malinvestment fostered by state action and bank-led inflation worked against the bigger businesses in favor of the smaller, less overextended businesses; (b) there was, in the case of the railroads anyway, no sharp dichotomy or antagonism between big businessmen and the progressive Movement's thrust for regulation; and (c) the purpose of the regulations, as seen by key business leaders, was not to fight the growth of "monopoly" and centralization, but to foster it.

The culmination of this big-business-sponsored "reform" of the economic system is actually today's system. The new system took effect immediately during World War I when railroads gleefully handed over control to the government in exchange for guaranteed rate increases and guaranteed profits, something continued under the Transportation Act of 1920. The consequences, of course, are still making themselves felt, as in 1971, when the Pennsylvania Railroad, having cut itself off from the market and from market calculation nearly entirely, was found to be in a state of economic chaos. It declared bankruptcy and later was rescued, in part, by the state.

## REGULATION COMES TO THE REST OF THE ECONOMY

Having illustrated my basic thesis through a case study of the origins of regulation in the railroad industry, I shall now look at the rest of the American economy in this period and examine, however briefly, the role that big business had in pushing through acts of state regulation.

I should also mention, at least in passing, big businessmen not only had a particularly important effect in pushing through domestic regulation, but they fostered interventionism in foreign policy as well. What was common to both spheres was the fact that the acts of state intervention and monetary expansion by the state-manipulated banking system had precipitated depressions and recessions from the 1870s though the 1890s. The common response of businessmen, particularly big businessmen – the leaders in various fields – was to promote further state regulation and aid as a solution to the problems caused by the depressions. In particular vogue at the time – in vogue today, as a matter of fact – was the notion that continued American prosperity required (as a necessary condition) expanded markets for American goods and manufactured items. This led businessmen to seek markets in foreign lands though various routes, having fulfilled their "manifest destiny" at home.

Domestically, however, the immediate result was much more obvious. From about 1875 on, many corporations, wishing to be large and dominant in their field, overexpanded and overcapitalized. Mediocre entrepreneurship, administrative difficulties and increasing competition cut deeply into the markets and profits of many giants. Mergers often were tried, as in the railroad industry, but the larger mergers brought neither greater profits nor less competition. As Kolko states: "Quite the opposite occurred. There was more competition, and profits, if anything, declined." A survey of ten mergers showed, for instance, that the companies earned an average of 65 percent of their preconsolidation profits after consolidation. Overcentralization inhibited their flexibility of action, and hence their ability to respond to changing market conditions. In short, things were not as bad for other industries as for the railroads – they were often worse.

In the steel industry, the price of most steel goods declined more or less regularly until 1895, and even though prices rose somewhat thereafter, there was considerable insecurity about what other competitors might choose to do next. A merger of many corporations in 1901, based on collaboration between Morgan and Carnegie, resulted in the formation of U. S. Steel. Yet U. S. Steel's profit margin declined over 50 percent between 1902 and 1904. In its first two decades of existence, U. S. Steel held a continually shrinking share of the market. Due to technological conservatism and inflexible leadership, the company became increasingly costly and inefficient. Voluntary efforts at control failed. U. S. Steel turned to politics.

In the oil industry, where Standard Oil was dominant, the same situation existed. In 1899 there were 67 petroleum refiners in the U.S.; within ten years, the number had grown to 147 refiners.

In the telephone industry, things were in a similar shape. From its foundation in 1877 until 1894, Bell Telephone (AT&T) had a virtual monopoly in the industry based on its control of almost all patents.[10] In 1894 many of the patents expired. "Bell immediately adopted a policy of harassing the host of aspiring competitors by suing them (27 suits were instituted in

---

10    It is instructive to note that most of these patents were illegitimate according to libertarian ownership theories, since many other men had independently discovered the telephone and subsequent items besides Bell and the AT&T group, yet they were coercively restrained from enjoying the product of such creativity. On the illegitimacy of such patent restriction, see Rothbard 745-54 [Chapter 10, Section 7: Patents and Copyrights]

234 | Roy A. Childs, Jr.

1894-95 alone) for allegedly infringing Bell patents."[11] But such efforts to stifle competition failed; by 1902, there were 9,100 independent telephone systems; by 1907, there were 22,000. Most had rates lower than AT&T.

In the meat packing industry too, the large packers felt threatened by increasing competition. Their efforts at control failed. Similar diffusion of economic power was the case in other fields, such as banking, where the power of the eastern financiers was being seriously eroded by midwestern competitors.

This, then, was the basic context of big business; these were the problems that it faced. How did it react? Almost unanimously, it turned to the power of the state to get what it could not get by voluntary means. Big business acted not only through concrete political pressure, but by engaging in large-scale, long-run ideological propaganda or "education" aimed at getting different sections of the American society united behind statism, in principle and practice.

Let us look at some of the activities of the major organizational tool of big business, the National Civics Federation. The NCF was actually a reincarnation of Hamiltonian views on the relation of the state to business. Primarily an organization of big businessmen, it pushed for the tactical and theoretical alliance of business and government, a primitive version of the modern business-government partnership. Contrary to the consensus of many conservatives, it was not ideological innocence that led them to create a statist economic order – they knew what they were doing and constantly said so.

The working partnership of business and government was the result of the conscious activities of organizations such as the NCF created in 1900 (coincided with the birth of what is called the "Progressive Movement") to fight with increasing and sustained vigor against what it considered to be its twin enemies: "the socialists and radicals among workers and middle class reformers, and the 'anarchists' among the businessmen" (as the NCF characterized the National Association of Manufacturers). The smaller businessmen, who constituted the NAM, formed an opposition to the new liberalism that developed through cooperation between political leaders such as Theodore Roosevelt, William H. Taft and Woodrow Wilson, and the financial and corporate leaders in the NCF and other similar organizations. The NCF before World War I was "the most important single organization of the socially conscious big businessmen and their academic and political theorists." The NCF "took the lead in educating the businessmen to the changing needs in political economy which accompanied the changing nature of America's business system."[12]

---

11    Kolko, *Triumph* 30-9.
12    Weinstein 82.

The early leaders of the NCF were such big business leaders as Marcus A. Hanna, utilities magnate Samuel B. Insull, Chicago banker Franklin MacVeagh (later Secretary of the treasury), Charles Francis Adams and several partners in J. P. Morgan & Co. The largest contributor to the group was Andrew Carnegie; other important members of the executive committee included George W. Perkins, Elbert H. Gary (a Morgan associate and a head of U. S. Steel after Carnegie), Cyrus McCormick, Theodore N. Vail (president of AT&T) and George Cortelyou (head of Consolidated Gas).

The NCF sponsored legislation to promote the formation of "public utilities," a special privilege monopoly granted by the state, reserving an area of production to one company. Issuing a report on "Public Ownership of Public Utilities," the NCF established a general framework for regulatory laws, stating that utilities should be conducted by legalized independent commissions. Of such regulation one businessman wrote another: "Twenty-five years ago we would have regarded it as a species of socialism"; but seeing that the railroads were both submitting to and apparently profiting from regulation, the NCF's self-appointed job of "educating" municipal utilities corporations became much easier.

Regulation in general, far from coming against the wishes of the regulated interests, was openly welcomed by them in nearly every case. As Upton Siclair said of the meat industry, which he is given credit for having tamed, "the federal inspection of meat was historically established at the packers' request... It is maintained and paid for by the people of the United States for the benefit of the packers."[13]

However, one interesting fact comes in here to refute the Marxist theory further. For the Marxists hold that there are fundamentally two opposing "interests" which clash in history: the capitalists and the workers. But what we have seen, essentially, is that the interests (using the word in a journalistic sense) of neither the capitalists nor the workers, so-called, were uniform or clear-cut. The interests of the larger capitalists seemed to coincide, as they saw it, and were clearly opposed to the interests of the smaller capitalists. (However, there were conflicts among the big capitalists, such as between the Morgan and Rockefeller interests during the 1900s, as illustrated in the regimes of Roosevelt and Taft.) The larger capitalists saw regulation as being in their interest, and competition as opposed to it; with the smaller businessmen, the situation was reversed. The workers for the larger businesses also may have temporarily gained at the expense of others through slight wage increases caused by restrictions on production. (The situation is made even more complicated when we remember that the Marxist belief is that one's relationship to the means of production determines one's

---

13    Kolko, *Triumph* 103.

interests and hence, apparently, one's ideas. Yet people with basically the same relationship often had different "interests" and ideas. If this in turn is explained by a Marxist in terms of "mystification," an illuminating explanation in a libertarian context, then mystification itself is left to be explained. For if one's ideas and interests are an automatic function of the economic system and one's relationship to the means of production, how can "mystification" arise at all?)

In any case, congressional hearings during the administration of Theodore Roosevelt revealed that "the big Chicago packers wanted more meat inspection both to bring the small packers under control and to aid them in their position in the export trade." Formally representing the large Chicago packers, Thomas E. Wilson publicly announced: "We are now and have always been in favor of the extension of the inspection."[14]

In both word and deed American businessmen sought to replace the last remnants of laissez-faire in the United States with government regulation – for their own benefit. Speaking at Columbia University in February 1908, George W. Perkins, a Morgan associate, said that the corporation "must welcome federal supervision administered by practical businessmen."[15]

As early as 1908, Andrew Carnegie and Ingalls had suggested to the NCF that it push for an American version of the British Board of Trade, which would have the power to judge mergers and other industrial actions. As Carnegie put it, this had "been found sufficient in other countries and will be so with us. We must have our industrial as we have a Judicial Supreme Court."[16] Carnegie also endorsed government actions to end ruinous competition.

> It always comes back to me that government control, and that alone, will properly solve the problem... There is nothing alarming in this; capital is perfectly safe in the gas company, although it is under court control. So will all capital be, although under government control.[17]

AT&T, controlled by J. P. Morgan as of 1907, also sought regulation. The company got what it wanted in 1910, when telephones were placed under the jurisdiction of the ICC, and rate wars became a thing of the past. President T. N. Vail of AT&T said, "we believe in and were the first to advocate... governmental control and regulation of public utilities."

---

14   Kolko, *Triumph* 103.
15   Kolko, *Triumph* 129.
16   Weinstein 180.
17   Kolko, *Triumph* 180.

By June of 1911, Elbert H. Gary of U. S. Steel appeared before a congressional committee and announced to astonished members, "I believe we must come to enforced publicity and governmental control even as to prices." He virtually offered to turn price control over to the government. Kolko states that

> the reason Gary and Carnegie were offering the powers of price control to the federal government was not known to the congressmen, who were quite unaware of the existing price anarchy in steel. The proposals of Gary and Carnegie, the Democratic majority on the committee reported, were really 'semisocialistic' and hardly worth endorsing.[18]

Gary also proposed that a commission similar to the ICC be set up to grant, suspend and revoke licenses for trade and to regulate prices.

In the fall of 1911, the NCF moved in two fronts: it sent a questionnaire to 30,000 businessmen to seek out their positions on a number of issues. Businessmen favored regulation of trade by three to one.

In November of 1911, Theodore Roosevelt proposed a national commission to control organization and capitalization of all inter-state businesses. The proposal won an immediate and enthusiastic response from Wall Street.

In 1912, Arthur Eddy, an eminent corporation lawyer, working much of the time with Standard Oil, and one of the architects of the FTC, stated boldly in his magnum opus, *The New Competition*, what had been implicit in the doctrines of businessmen all along: Eddy trumpeted that "competition was inhuman and war, and that war was hell."

Thus did big businessmen believe and act.

Meanwhile, back at the bank, J. P. Morgan was not to be left out. For Morgan, because of his ownership or control of many major corporations, was in the fight for regulation from the earliest days onward. Morgan's financial power and reputation were largely the result of his operations with the American and European governments; his many dealings in currency manipulations and loans to oppressive European states earned him the reputation of a "rescuer of governments." One crucial aspect of the banking system at the beginning of the 1900s was the relative decrease in New York's financial dominance and the rise of competitors. Morgan was fully aware of the diffusion of banking power that was taking place, and it disturbed him.

Hence, bankers too turned to regulation. From very early days, Morgan had championed the cause of a central bank, of gaining control over the na-

---

18    Kolko, *Triumph* 173-4.

tion's credit through a board of leading bankers under government supervision. By 1907, the NCF had taken up the call for a more elastic currency and for greater centralization of banking.

Nelson Aldrich proposed a reform bank act and called a conference of twenty-two bankers from twelve cities to discuss it. The purpose of the conference was to "discuss winning the banking community over to government control directed by the bankers for their own ends." A leading banker, Paul Warburg, stated that "it would be a blessing to get these small banks out of the way."[19]

Most of his associates agreed. In 1913, two years after the conference, and after any squabbles over specifics, the Federal Reserve Act was passed. The big bankers were pleased.

These were not the only areas in which businessmen and their political henchmen were active. Indeed, ideologically speaking, they were behind innumerable "progressive" actions, and even financed such magazines as *The New Republic*. Teddy Roosevelt made a passing reference to the desirability of an income tax in his 1906 message to Congress, and the principle received support from such businessmen as George W. Perkins and Carnegie, who often referred to the unequal distribution of wealth as "one of the crying evils of our day." Many businessmen opposed it, but the *Wall Street Journal* said that it was certainly in favor of it.

The passage of the Clayton Antitrust Act and the creation of the Federal Trade Commission occurred in 1914. Once established, the FTC began its attempt to secure the "confidence" of "well-intentioned" businessmen. In a speech before the NCF, one of the pro-regulation powerhouses, J. W. Jenks, "affirmed the general feeling of relief among the leaders of large corporations and their understanding that the FTC was helpful to the corporations in every way."[20]

In this crucially important era, I have focused on one point: big business was a major source of American statism. Further researches would show, I am convinced, that big business and financial leaders were also the dominant force behind America's increasingly interventionist foreign policy, and behind the ideology of modern liberalism. In fact, by this analysis sustained research might show American liberal intellectuals to be the "running dogs" of big businessmen, to twist a Marxist phrase a bit.

Consider the fact that the *New Republic* has virtually always taken the role of defender of the corporate state which big businessmen carefully constructed over decades. Consider the fact that such businessmen as Carnegie not only supported all the groups mentioned and the programs referred to,

---

19    Kolko, *Triumph* 183.
20    Weinstein 91.

but also supported such things as the Big Navy movement at the turn of the century. He sold steel to the United States government that went into the building of the ships and he saw in the Venezuela boundary dispute the possibility of a large order for armor from the United States Navy.[21] Carnegie, along with Rockefeller and, later, Ford, was responsible for sustained support of American liberalism through the foundations set up in his name.

J. P. Morgan, the key financial leader, was also a prime mover of American statism. His foreign financial dealings led him to become deeply involved with Britain during World War I, and this involvement in turn led him to help persuade Wilson to enter the war on Britain's behalf, to help save billions of dollars of loans which would be lost in the event of a German victory.

In a more interesting light, consider the statements made in 1914 by S. Thruston Ballard, owner of the largest wheat refinery in the world. Ballard not only supported vocational schools as a part of the public schools (which would transfer training costs to taxpayers), restrictions on immigration, and a national minimum wage, he saw and proposed a way to "cure" unemployment. He advocated a federal employment service, public works, and if these wee insufficient, "government concentration camps where work with a small wage would be provided, supplemented by agricultural and industrial training."[22]

Consider the role of big businessmen in pushing through public education in many states after World War I. Senator Wadsworth spoke before a NCF group in 1916, pointing out that compulsory government education was needed "to protect the nation against destruction from within. It is to train the boy and girl to be good citizens, to protect against ignorance and dissipation." This meant that the reason to force children to go to school, at gunpoint if necessary, was so that they could be brainwashed into accepting the status quo, almost explicitly so that their capacity for dissent (i.e., their capacity for independent thinking) could be destroyed. Thus did Wadsworth also advocate compulsory and universal military training: "Our people shall be prepared mentally as well as in a purely military sense. We must let our young men know that they owe some responsibility to this country."

Indeed, we find V. E. Macy, president of the NCF at the close of the war, stating that it was not "beside the mark to call attention to the nearly

---

21    Walter LeFeber, *The New Empire: An Interpretation of American Expansion, 1860-1890* (Ithaca: Cornell UP 1963) 239, 273n. The note on Carnegie's linking of the Venezuela boundary dispute with obtaining large orders of steel from the Navy was taken from Carnegie's correspondence.

22    Weinstein 91.

thirty million minors marching steadily toward full citizenship," and ask "at what stage of their journey we should lend assistance to the work of quickening... the sense of responsibility and partnership in the business of maintaining and perfecting the splendid social, industrial, and commercial structure which has been reared under the American flag." The need, Macy noted, was most urgent. Among American youths there was a widespread "indifference toward, and aloofness from, individual responsibility for the successful maintenance and upbuilding of the industrial and commercial structure which is the indispensable shelter of us all."[23]

Big business, then, was behind the existence and curriculum of the public educational system, explicitly to teach young minds to submit and obey, to pay homage to the "corporate liberal" system which the politicians, a multitude of intellectuals and many big businessmen created.

My intention here simply has been to present an alternative model of historical interpretation of key events in this one crucial era of American history, an interpretation which is neither Marxist, liberal nor conservative, but which may have some elements in common with each.

From a more ideological perspective, my purpose has been to present an accurate portrait of one aspect of "how we got here," and indicate a new way of looking at the present system in America.

To a large degree it has been and remains big businessmen who are the fountainheads of American statism. If libertarians are seeking allies in their struggle for liberty, then I suggest that they look elsewhere. Conservatives, too, should benefit from this essay, and begin to see big business as a destroyer, not as a unit, of the free market. Liberals should also benefit, and reexamine their own premises about the market and regulation. Specifically, they might reconsider the nature of a free market, and ponder on the question of why big business has been opposed to precisely that. Isn't it odd that the interests of liberals and key big businessmen have always coincided? The Marxists, too, might rethink their economics, and reconsider whether or not capitalism leads to monopoly. Since it can be shown scientifically that economic calculation is impossible in a purely socialistic economy, and that pure statism is not good for man, perhaps the Marxists might also look at the real nature of a complete free market, undiluted by state control.

Libertarians themselves should take heart. Our hope lies, as strange as it may seem, not with any remnants from an illusory "golden age" of individualism, which never existed, but with tomorrow. Our day has not come and gone. It has never existed at all. It is our task to see that it will exist in the future. The choice and the battle are ours.

---

23   Weinstein 133-5.

# 24

*Praxeology.Net* (n.p., Oct. 9, 2008)
<http://praxeology.net/aotp.htm#6>
(Aug. 22, 2011).

# REGULATION: THE CAUSE, NOT THE CURE, OF THE FINANCIAL CRISIS

## RODERICK T. LONG
### (2008)

PEOPLE WHO BLAME THE CRISIS ON THE FREE MARKET HAVE THINGS PRECISELY BACKWARD. Market prices are the mechanism that allows consumer rankings of consumption goods to determine choices among production goods; if consumers rank goods made from steel higher than goods made from rubber, steel prices will rise relative to those of rubber, thus encouraging economising of existing steel and increased production of new steel. (This is incidentally why anti-gouging laws are such a bad idea; they prolong the very shortages whose effects they're trying to mitigate, by suppressing the price signals that function to end the shortage. When prices are legally prevented from rising during a shortage, that's like sending out a signal into the market saying "hey everybody, no shortage here, no reason to economise on this item, no reason to increase production of this item, feel free to focus your investment elsewhere" – which is obviously the worst possible message to send.)

Interest rates are a kind of price also; they signal the extent to which consumers are willing and able to defer present satisfactions for the sake of greater future satisfactions. To take the standard example, if Crusoe makes a net he'll be able to catch far more fish than he can with his hands, but time making the net takes away from time catching fish; if Crusoe can afford to defer some present fish-catching in order to make the net, then it's rational for him to make it, but if instead he's on the edge of starvation and might not be able to survive on reduced rations long enough to finish the net, he'd better stick to catching fish with his hands for the moment and save the net project for another day. Whether it makes sense for him to divert time and effort from fish catching to net making thus depends on how urgently he needs fish now – in short, on his time-preference.

In a free market, low interest rates signal low time-preference and high interest rates, high time-preference. If your time-preference (i.e. the urgency of your preference for present over future satisfactions) is low, then I would only have to offer you slightly more than X a year from now in order to induce you to part with X today; if it is high, then I would have to offer you a lot more than X a year from now in exchange for X today. The prevailing interest rate thus guides investors in their choice between short-term, less productive projects and those that are more productive but whose benefits will take longer to achieve.

But when central banks, through their manipulation of the money supply, artificially lower the interest rate, then the signals get distorted; investors are led to act as though consumers have a lower time-preference than they actually do. Thus investors are led to invest in longer-term projects that are unsustainable, since the deferred consumption on which such projects depend is not actually going to get deferred, so that the goods that the investors are counting on in order to complete their long-term projects are not all going to be there when the investors need them. Such unsustainable investment is the boom or bubble; the bust comes when the unsustainability is recognised and a costly process of liquidation ensues.

The Austrian theory of the business cycle is sometimes called an "over-investment" theory, but that's misleading. The problem is not that investors over-invest across the board, but that they over-invest in higher-yield longer-term projects and under-invest in lower-yield shorter-term. That's why Austrians talk about "malinvestment" rather than over-investment. The prevailing mainstream tendency to treat capital as homogeneous ignores the difference between higher and lower levels of production goods and thus fails to appreciate the costs of having to switch from the high to the low when the bubble bursts.

In additional to the general misallocation of investment between lower-order and higher-order inputs, monetary inflation produces further imbalances. When the central bank creates money, the new money doesn't propagate throughout the economy instantaneously; some sectors get the new money first, while they're still facing the old, lower prices, while other sectors get the new money last, after they've already begun facing the higher prices. The result of such "Cantillon effects" is not only a systematic redistribution of wealth from those less to those more favoured by the banking-government complex, but an artificial stimulation of certain sectors of the economy, making them look more inherently profitable than they are and so directing economically unjustified levels of investment toward them.

Does the Austrian account, as is often claimed, underestimate the ability of investors and entrepreneurs to recognise the effects of government policies and compensate for them? No. Even if you know that a given price represents some mix of genuine market signals and governmental distortion, you may not know how much of the price represents which factor, so how can you compensate for the distorting factor? (Likewise, if you know there are magnetic anomalies in the area that are throwing off your compass, that's not terribly helpful information unless you know exactly where the anomalies are and how strong they are compared with earth's magnetic field; otherwise you have no way to correct for them. And given that the direction of your compass's needle is at least partly responsive to true north, you're better off trusting it, despite its distortions, than simply abandoning your compass and proceeding by coin-flip.)

On the Austrian understanding, governmental inflation of the money supply, thereby artificially lowering interest rates, was the chief cause of the Great Depression. (Mainstream economists dispute this, holding that the Fed's policy could not have been genuinely inflationary, since prices were relatively stable during the period leading up to the crash. But for Austrians the crucial question is not whether prices were higher than they had previously been, but whether they were higher than they would have been in the absence of monetary inflation.) Likewise, for Austrians the housing bubble that precipitated the current crisis was the product of the Federal Reserve's low-interest policies of recent years. (An aside to address a frequent misunderstanding: on the Austrian view there is nothing wrong with low interest rates per se; indeed, low interest rates are a symptom of a healthy economy, since the more prosperous people are, the likelier they are to be willing to defer present consumption. But one cannot make an economy healthy by artificially inducing symptoms of health in the absence of their underlying cause. By the same principle, absence of scabbing on one's skin is a sign of physical health, but if there is scabbing, one does not promote health by ripping the scabs away; advocates of minimum wage laws, take note.)

In the 1920s, while mainstream economists were claiming that stock prices had reached a "permanently high plateau," Mises and Hayek were predicting a crash (as incidentally was my grandfather Charles Roderick McKay, who as Deputy Governor of the Federal Reserve Bank of Chicago protested against the Fed's policy of artificially lowered interest rates, kept the Chicago branch out of the easy-money policy until centrally overridden, foresaw the likely results, and got the hell out of the stock market well before the crash); likewise, in recent years Austrians kept warning of a housing bubble while folks like Greenspan and Bernanke blithely insisted that the housing market was sound.

Now everyone these days is saying, quite sensibly, that in the present crisis we need to avoid the mistakes that lengthened the Great Depression; the problem is that this advice is useless without an accurate understanding of what those mistakes were. By Austrian standards, the current plan to inject more "liquidity" into the economy is simply treating the disease with more of the poison that originally caused it. Attempting to cure an illness by artificially simulating symptoms of health is, literally, voodoo economics.

Of course the Federal Reserve is not solely to blame; there are still further government policies that encouraged riskier loans. There's been some media attention paid to Clinton-era changes in the Community Reinvestment Act, for example, that encouraged laxer lending standards in order to attract minority borrowers. The claim that this explanation is "racist" is confusing the reason why a given loan is risky with the reason why the loan, despite its riskiness, gets made; all the same, focusing on this narrow example misses the wider picture, which is that when the federal government sponsors massive credit corporations like Freddie Mac and Fannie Mae, it creates an expectation (whether codified in law or not) that the government is guaranteeing their solvency. Just as with the S&L crisis of the 80s, the expectation of reimbursement in the case of failure encourages riskier loans because the risk is socialised. (And beyond this are the still deeper factors that stifle affluence for the vast majority and so make it necessary for them to borrow money to buy a home in the first place; taking that necessity for granted requires justification.)

Even George Bush, in his speech on the crisis, recognised (or read words written by people who recognised) that the expectation that a bailout would be forthcoming if needed had helped to encourage riskier loans – though he seemed to miss the further implication that by going on to urge a bailout he was confirming and reinforcing the very expectations that had helped fuel the crisis – thus setting the economy up for a repeat of the crisis in the future.

The grain of truth in the otherwise ludicrous statist mantra that the financial crisis was caused by "lack of regulation" is that when you pass regulation A granting a private or semi-private firm the right to play with other people's money, but then repeal or fail to enact regulation B restricting the firm's ability to take excessive risks with that money, the ensuing crisis is in a sense to be attributed in part to the absence of regulation B. But the fatal factor is not the absence of regulation B per se but the absence of B when combined with the presence of A; the absence of B would cause no problem if A were absent as well. So, sure, there was insufficient regulation, if by "insufficient regulation" you mean a failure on government's part to rein in, via further regulations, the problems created by its initial regulations.

So if the problem is caused by A without B, it might be objected, why must we adopt the libertarian solution of getting rid of A? Can't we solve the problem just as well by keeping A but adding regulation B alongside it? The answer is no, because central planning doesn't work; when one responds to bad regulations by adding new regs to counteract the old ones, rather than simply repealing the old ones, one adds more and more layers between decisions and the market, increasingly muffling price-system feedback and courting calculational chaos.

But, the objector may continue, what if we're in a situation where we have regulation A but no regulation B, and where, further, repealing A is not politically possible but adding regulation B is – in that case, shouldn't we push to add B? In some circumstances, depending on the details, maybe so; but the more important question, to my mind, is to which should we devote more of our time and energy – tweaking the details of a fundamentally unsound system within the parameters of what is currently considered politically possible, or working to shift those parameters themselves? In Hayek's words: "Those who have concerned themselves exclusively with what seemed practicable in the existing state of opinion have constantly found that even this had rapidly become politically impossible as the result of changes in a public opinion which they have done nothing to guide."

Okay, some will say, maybe it was government, not laissez-faire, that got us into the mess; but now that we're in it, don't we need government to get us out? My answer is that government doesn't have the ability to get us out. There's just not much the government can do that will help (apart from repealing the laws, regulations, and subsidies that first created and then perpetuate the mess – but that would be less a doing than a ceasing-to-do, and anyway given the incentives acting on government decision-makers there's no realistic chance of that happening). The bailout is just diverting resources from the productive poor and middle-class to the failed rich, which doesn't seem like a very good idea on either ethical or economic grounds. The only good effect such a bailout could possibly have (at least if you prefer costly boondoggles without piles of dead bodies to costly boondoggles with them) is if it convinced the warmongers that they just can't afford a global war on terror right now – but there's no sign that they're being convinced of anything of the sort.

If the price system were allowed to function fully, the crisis would right itself – not instantly or painlessly, to be sure, but far more quickly and with less dislocation than any government could manage. What the government should do is, in the final analysis, nothing.

But such a response would be politically impossible? Quite true; but what makes it politically impossible? Is it some corporatist bias on the part of the American people? Did Congress pass the bailout because the voters were clamouring for it? On the contrary, most of the voters seem to have been decidedly against it. The bailout passed because Congress is primarily accountable, not to the electorate, but to big business. And that's a source of political impossibility that stems not from shiftable ideology but from the inherent nature of representative government. A government that was genuinely responsible to the people would hardly be a paradise (since the people are hardly free from ignorance and bias, and majority rule is all too often simply a mechanism for externalising the costs of majority prefer-ences onto minorities) – but debating the merits of a government genuinely responsible to the people is purely academic, because such a government, whatever its merits or demerits, is impossible; you cannot make a monopo-ly responsive to the people. Other than the market itself, no political system has ever been devised or discovered that will subordinate the influence of concentrated interests to that of dispersed interests. Monopoly cannot be "reformed"; it has to be abolished.

Now that is of course not to say that some governments can't be less un-responsive than others, just as some forms of slavery can be less awful than others. One of the striking features of slavery in the antebellum Ameri-can south, for example, is how much worse it was, on average, than most other historical forms of slavery; and if the abolitionists, despairing of the prospects of actually freeing the slaves, had focused their efforts on reform-ing American slavery to make it more like ancient Greco-Roman slavery or medieval Scandinavian slavery, I'm not going to say that wouldn't have been worth doing or wouldn't have made a lot of people's lives significantly better – but isn't it setting on one's political sights a tad low?

# 25

The Economics of Anarchy: A Study of the Industrial Type (New York: Twentieth Century 1890).

# INDUSTRIAL ECONOMICS

## DYER D. LUM
## (1890)

I DESIRE TO GROUP CERTAIN DEDUCTIONS, BOTH CRITICAL AND CONSTRUCTIVE, THAT WE MAY better see the paramount importance of freedom in industrial economics.

**1. DIVISION OF LABOR** is an outgrowth of social progress, essential to the augmentation of wealth, the evils incidental to it being the result of extraneous causes; and Economists, in speaking of limitations and disadvantages of this social law, have shown their incompetence to clearly analyze the essential factors of the industrial problem. It is not in division, but in the subordination of division to privilege that the Economists make the error of ascribing disadvantages to a law evolved in social growth. The element of freedom lacking in exchange, division consequently falls under the control of prerogative, hence the limitations and disadvantages of which Economists learnedly prate.

**2. MACHINERY** socializes where division isolates. Machinery is to the industrial toiler what the musket is to the militant supporter, a tool by which their respective lines of activity are rendered effective. In the cheapening of products, in the annihilation of time by the telegraph and of space by the railway, and the countless facilities to comfort with which we are surrounded, we see the social results of machinery. Economists never weary of dwelling on the benefits of labor saved by the use of machinery, but gloss over the actual fact that a rapid increase of mechanical appliances tends to render the artisan a superfluous quantity and a marketless tool. Under natural relations whatever tends to lessen the exhaustiveness of toil and cheapen products, should also redound to the direct, no less than the indirect, benefit of the individual laborer. Here, again, we find freedom lacking in distribution and are forced to look elsewhere for the source of the restrictions to ascertain whether they arise from natural causes or artificial interference.

**3. MONOPOLY** has been fostered under the delusive pretext of protecting industry by hedging in a portion of human activity at the expense of the rest; and at the same time, as zealously protecting the very restrictions of which labor complains. The opposite school, having a partial view of the truth that the law of supply and demand can only have full course under liberty, and that all interference but hampers their natural adaptation to each other, still believed that they were contending under that standard while limiting their demands for freedom of trade to the manufactured product, an error which even Herbert Spencer has not escaped. In asserting theoretical liberty for labor and capital, they are blind to the fact that labor was handicapped, inasmuch as the capital employed was the offspring of monopoly. Thus their freedom only enters in after monopolized production has thrown the product on the market, and is never conceived as entering into relations prior to production. Consequently, in the present "strained relations between capital and labor" we find the "freedom of contract" a meaningless phrase, and professed apostles of liberty, like Amasa Walker, delivering themselves as follows:

> [I]n relation to capital and labor,... there must be a just proportion of each to the most efficient production – sufficient labor for the capital, and capital for the labor: so there must be sufficient enterprise, business talent and tact to use both; and the several parties must be left to act voluntarily; under the instincts of human nature and the laws of value.[1]

---

1  [Amasa Walker, *The Science of Wealth: A Manual of Political Economy Embracing the Laws of Trade, Currency, and Finance* (Boston: Little 1866) 281 <http://tinyurl.com/4lyn8tm> (March 13, 2011). The text of the quotation has been slightly corrected from Lum's original text to ensure that it matches Walker's.]

Whether legalization of the lower instincts and the speculative laws now dominant tend to the higher evolution of free action, our apostle of liberty sayeth not.

**4. COMPETITION** is the exact opposite, not parent of monopoly. Freedom is essential to true competition, and wherever restriction exists on one side, it implies privilege on the other, and in so far competition ceases: monopoly rather than competition now exists. In the abrogation of privilege competition becomes not only free, but acts, as the governor on an engine, self-regulative and bringing cost as the mean of price. "Our friends, the enemy," the Socialists, in flying into a passion at the mention of competition but thereby betray their own logical adherence to the militant camp, for liberty includes and implies freedom to compete.

But that cannot in justice be called a competitive system where wages are constantly depressed as with an iron hand as a definite residual dividend; and the divorce between labor and capital justified as calling in an "indispensable" go-between whose earnings, or profits, "constitute a special or fourth branch of the national income, co-ordinate with rent, wages, and interest on capital" – and hailed as an extension of freedom.[2]

**5. THE REAL PROBLEM** is a far deeper one than enters into the arguments of the advocates of protection and restriction, or of a post-production liberty. It is the same as has for centuries past underlain all struggles in social progress and which, looking back over the centuries, we find recorded as ever won for the sovereignty of the individual, the widening of the sphere of personal initiative, the conflict between militant authority and personal liberty. The renaissance of mind from scholastic tyranny; the revolt of Luther and his followers against mental dictation; the temporary compromise in religious toleration; the insurrection against kingcraft leading in its triumph to the toleration of political opinions; have now logically led to an insurrection against economic subjection to the privileges usurped and hotly defended by capital in its alliance with labor, and calling from thinkers of all schools – even from economic Hessian allies – the prediction that unless an equitable adjustment be found, civilization must again go through the parturition pangs of revolutionary strife and bloodshed. By one or other of these antagonistic principles must every proposed solution be tested, and reposing confidently on the historical development of progress, wherein even the man of genius is but "the secretary of his age," we assert that no answer can be given to the eternal conflict that is not based upon full freedom to human activity: for freedom destroys strife by removing its cause – denial of freedom.

2    [Wilhelm Roscher, *Principles of Political Economy*, trans. John J. Lalor, 2 vols. (New York: Holt 1878) 2: 146 <http://tinyurl.com/4bymw33> (March 13, 2011).]

With these deductions for our guide we began the search for economic laws based upon justice, enlightened by wisdom, supported by truth, in which alone industry can find its goal in equitable cooperation. Taking these, therefore, as the basis of industrial economics, rather than laws describing modes of action under inequitable conditions, we have been led to demand for labor:

**6. FREE LAND,** that labor in its struggle shall not forever find the source of production the ward of monopoly, and thus left upon as unequal a footing to compete in production as existed between the slave and his master. That as land is the source of production its real, or natural, value lies in its use, not what it will bring where privilege exists to give it a fictitious value. One of the effects of this would be the elimination of rent as a necessary prelude to occupancy, or a factor in the distribution of the shares of production. That under freedom of access to vacant land, and the spring it would give to production, labor would determine a juster proportionality of values between products, wherein alone real value exists.

We see in nationalization of land but a recurrence to militancy in its methods, and its application beset with many fatal compromises... To one who accepts authority, rather than liberty, as a guiding principle, the conclusion may be natural; but to one who endeavors to square his principles by the test of liberty, whether land be called private property or not, after it has ceased to be a factor in economic exploitation, is immaterial. Liberty cannot deny the calling of one's possession of anything his own. It is in the power given by legalization to hold for speculative purposes, not particular possession for occupancy, that the danger to civilization lies. We also submit that making it "common property" involves invasion of individual freedom to use, for it can be neither so made nor so maintained except by militant methods, whether under George's or Most's attempted organization of liberty...

**7. FREE EXCHANGE...** would break the monopoly now possessed by currency, the instrument of exchange, and also could open full use of the possession of land. To day the small retail dealer cannot compete with the merchant prince in the purchase of goods, any more than the mechanic who buys his coal by the bushel enters into competition with one who buys his year's supply by the cargo. Has the workman equal freedom to compete with the employer of labor? Can "hands" enter the market on equal term with the wealthy contractor? But why not? Because behind the capitalist, as we now find him, privilege lends support which transforms the result of honest industry into a hideous Moloch standing with outstretched arms to receive as sacrificial victims the toilers who have made that capital possible. The legalized power given to money determines the difference; it makes it more than the mere instrument of exchange; it becomes an implement of exploitation, having a fictitious value and culling from industry to increase by payment for use. Thus claiming that "yesterday's labor" is more than wealth acquired, and through interest entitled to prerogatives not granted to today's labor, but even taken from it. We thus see that it is not capital *per se* that liberty assails, but the artificial power it usurps; that under equal freedom, where no privilege exists to entail exploitation, it is as harmless as we have seen private property would be. Capital itself is man's best friend, the true social savior that opens the march of progress and that has transformed society from warlike to peaceful pursuits. But under the crucifying hands of legalization, where prerogative mocks at penury, its mission is thwarted and it becomes a ravenous beast. As Satan is said to have once been an angel of light, so, in the denial of equal freedom to the capitalization of the fruits of labor, capital has become a demon of hell, and beyond the power of redemption by single-tax sanctification.

**8. Mutual Banking** we have seen would open the door for relief. In the absence of artificial restraint upon individual activity, that every one in possession of returns for labor applied, indorsed by business capacity or not, whether individually or by association, could command credit to the extent of their honestly acquired wealth, or confidence in their pledge of labor force, and use their own labor as a basis for increased production. Whether production would then be individualistic or associative – on which point the author has strong convictions – would not in the least alter the case. Freedom to normal growth secured, its natural course is a detail which would regulate itself. The fact remains that under release from compulsory rent, and cessation of usury, energy and capacity would be more assiduously cultivated and command greater confidence than a State certificate for honesty, and thereby create an ample medium for exchange based on labor products. To doubt it is to assert that capacity and energy, together with inventive talent, can only germinate where exhaustive mental or manual labor most exist, and where rest and recreation are least known.

Credit would be a matter of confidence in both security and character, and character would be as essential an element then as shrewdness and cunning are now. "Business" emancipated from inequitable conditions would continue as uninterruptedly as under the present system of a mortgage security on the source of production where labor toils for another's benefit, and the benumbing effect of a Frankenstein-State no longer repress individuality nor inspire the superstitious with awe.

## INSURANCE OR SECURITY

… Under equal freedom wherever demand exists supply necessarily will be forthcoming, and guarantees for security will arise as easy as guarantees for politeness in the ballroom or parlor.

Under equal opportunities wherever mankind are thrown upon their own resources, when being fed from a spoon by government pap shall have become a traditionary tale of a past superstition, what is there in the power of activity that co-operative enterprise cannot undertake? We now see on every hand a thousand instances of voluntary association to attain certain objects. Many such deemed impracticable a few centuries since are commonplaces today. Who will say the limit has been reached? Even in functions government assumes as necessary we find voluntary militia and homeguards; fire departments in many places in which all members risk their lives and turn out in all weather to render the lives and property of their neighbors secure; associations of private watchmen who find support even though their patrons pay taxes for municipal police protection; a fire patrol in the interests of insurance companies to protect property from destruction. These are instances of cooperation applied to guaranteeing security, of supply seeking demand without difficulty or friction, a demand by no means dependent upon legalization, but supplementing its deficiencies.

All relations under equal freedom will tend to become associative when and where it is seen to be most effective. Freedom for the individual cannot be construed into compulsory isolation…

What is even now done by wealthy mill-owners may be done by all when equal opportunities to exploit nature shall have removed special privileges to exploit fellow men, when cooperation in all needed relations lies open before us and labor enjoys its full, just share of the wealth, or values, it creates. With its resultant release from rent, interest, profits, and taxation as enforced tribute, the causes for vice and crime would rapidly diminish, for free access to nature would open to all more than a competence, and in ease give greater scope to the purely human sympathies for the unfortunate… And so far as protection from the still vicious and idle is concerned, an extension of the scope of insurance can meet all requirements. An organization for protection to person and labor product, or property if you will, composed of those who felt the need for the exercise of such functions, in which loss by depredation would involve no greater difficulty than loss by fire, would naturally arise where such demand existed. The difference between the watchmen of such an organization, whose functions consist in mutual protection and defence of the equal limits of personal freedom, for commercial needs, and a political-policy system wherein personal liberty is subordinated to inanimate things as of a greater importance than their creators, is so apparent to the candid reader that I need not pause to dwell upon it… Progress and order is the true expression of social evolution, rather than the reverse, for law is ever fixity and its resulting order but uniformity wherein progress finds its grave. Order based upon progress, on the contrary, ever retains the plasticity essential to the latter, and this can only be realized in the further evolution of "the law of equal freedom" required by the Industrial Type…

Such is Anarchy!

## 26

*Thumb Jig* (n.p., Nov. 1, 2008) <http://thumbjig.blogspot.com/2008/11/labor-struggle-in-free-market.html> (Aug. 22, 2011)

# LABOR STRUGGLE IN A FREE MARKET

*KEVIN A. CARSON*
*(2008)*

ONE OF THE MOST COMMON QUESTIONS RAISED ABOUT A HYPOTHETICAL FREE MARKET society concerns worker protection laws of various kinds. As Roderick Long puts it,

> In a free nation, will employees be at the mercy of employers?… Under current law, employers are often forbidden to pay wages lower than a certain amount; to demand that employees work in hazardous conditions (or sleep with the boss); or to fire without cause or notice. What would be the fate of employees without these protections?

Long argues that, despite the absence of many of today's formal legal protections, the shift of bargaining power toward workers in a free labor market will result in "a reduction in the petty tyrannies of the job world."

> Employers will be legally free to demand anything they want of their employees. They will be permitted to sexually harass

them, to make them perform hazardous work under risky conditions, to fire them without notice, and so forth. But bargaining power will have shifted to favor the employee. Since prosperous economies generally see an increase in the number of new ventures but a decrease in the birth rate, jobs will be chasing workers rather than vice versa. Employees will not feel coerced into accepting mistreatment because it will be so much easier to find a new job. And workers will have more clout, when initially hired, to demand a contract which rules out certain treatment, mandates reasonable notice for layoffs, stipulates parental leave, or whatever. And the kind of horizontal coordination made possible by telecommunications networking opens up the prospect that unions could become effective at collective bargaining without having to surrender authority to a union boss.

This last is especially important. Present day labor law limits the bargaining power of labor at least as much as it reinforces it. That's especially true of reactionary legislation like Taft-Hartley and state right-to-work laws. Both are clearly abhorrent to free market principles.

Taft-Hartley, for example, prohibited many of the most successful labor strategies during the CIO organizing strikes of the early '30s. The CIO planned strikes like a general staff plans a campaign, with strikes in a plant supported by sympathy and boycott strikes up and down the production chain, from suppliers to outlets, and supported by transport workers refusing to haul scab cargo. At their best, the CIO's strikes turned into regional general strikes.

Right wing libertarians of the vulgar sort like to argue that unions depend primarily on the threat of force, backed by the state, to exclude non-union workers. Without forcible exclusion of scabs, they say, strikes would almost always turn into lockouts and union defeats. Although this has acquired the status of dogma at Mises.Org, it's nonsense on stilts. The primary reason for the effectiveness of a strike is not the exclusion of scabs, but the transaction costs involved in hiring and training replacement workers, and the steep loss of productivity entailed in the disruption of human capital, institutional memory, and tacit knowledge.

With the strike is organized in depth, with multiple lines of defense – those sympathy and boycott strikes at every stage of production – the cost and disruption have a multiplier effect far beyond that of a strike in a single plant. Under such conditions, even a large minority of workers walking off the job at each stage of production can be quite effective.

Taft-Hartley greatly reduced the effectiveness of strikes at individual plants by prohibiting such coordination of actions across multiple plants or industries. Taft-Hartley's cooling off periods also gave employers advance warning time to prepare for such disruptions, and greatly reduced the informational rents embodied in the training of the existing workforce. Were such restrictions on sympathy and boycott strikes in suppliers [not] in place, today's "just-in-time" economy would likely be far more vulnerable to disruption than that of the 1930s.

But long before Taft-Hartley, the labor law regime of the New Deal had already created a fundamental shift in the form of labor struggle.

Before Wagner and the NLRB-enforced collective bargaining process, labor struggle was less focused on strikes, and more focused on what workers did in the workplace itself to exert leverage against management. They focused, in other words, on what the Wobblies call "direct action on the job"; or in the colorful phrase of a British radical workers' daily at the turn of the century, "staying in on strike." The reasoning was explained in the Wobbly Pamphlet *How to Fire Your Boss: A Worker's Guide to Direct Action*:

> The bosses, with their large financial reserves, are better able to withstand a long drawn-out strike than the workers. In many cases, court injunctions will freeze or confiscate the union's strike funds. And worst of all, a long walkout only gives the boss a chance to replace striking workers with a scab (replacement) workforce.
>
> Workers are far more effective when they take direct action while still on the job. By deliberately reducing the boss' profits while continuing to collect wages, you can cripple the boss without giving some scab the opportunity to take your job.

Such tactics included slowdowns, sick-ins, random one-day walkouts at unannounced intervals, working to rule, "good work" strikes, and "open mouth sabotage." Labor followed, in other words, a classic asymmetric warfare model. Instead of playing by the enemy's rules and suffering one honorable defeat after another, they played by their own rules and mercilessly exploited the enemy's weak points.

The whole purpose of the Wagner regime was to put an end to this asymmetric warfare model. As Thomas Ferguson and G. William Domhoff have both argued, corporate backing for the New Deal labor accord came mainly from capital-intensive industry – the heart of the New Deal coalition in general. Because of the complicated technical nature of their production processes and their long planning horizons, their management required long-term stability and predictability. At the same time, because they were extremely capital-intensive, labor costs were a relatively modest part of total costs. Management, therefore, was willing to trade significant wage increases and job security for social peace on the job. Wagner came about, not because the workers were begging for it, but because the bosses were begging for a regime of enforceable labor contracts.

The purpose of the Wagner regime was to divert labor away from the asymmetric warfare model to a new one, in which union bureaucrats enforced the terms of contracts on their own membership. The primary function of union bureaucracies, under the new order, was to suppress wildcat action by their rank and file, to suppress direct action on the job, and to limit labor action to declared strikes under NLRB rules.

The New Deal labor agenda had the same practical effect as telling the militiamen at Lexington and Concord to come out from behind the rocks, put on bright red uniforms, and march in parade ground formation, in return for a system of arbitration to guarantee they didn't lose all the time.

The problem is that the bosses decided, long ago, that labor was still winning too much of the time even under the Wagner regime. Their first response was Taft-Hartley and the right-to-work laws. From that point on, union membership stopped growing and then began a slow and inexorable process of decline that continues to the present day. The process picked up momentum around 1970, when management decided that the New Deal labor accord had outlived its usefulness altogether, and embraced the full union-busting potential under Taft-Hartley in earnest. But the official labor movement still foregoes the weapons it lay down in the 1930s. It sticks to wearing its bright red uniforms and marching in parade-ground formation, and gets massacred every time.

Labor needs to reconsider its strategy, and in particular to take a new look at the asymmetric warfare techniques it has abandoned for so long.

The effectiveness of these techniques is a logical result of the incomplete nature of the labor contract. According to Michael Reich and James Devine,

> Conflict is inherent in the employment relation because the employer does not purchase a specified quantity of performed labor, but rather control over the worker's capacity to work over a given time period, and because the workers' goals differ from those of the employer. The amount of labor actually done is determined by a struggle between workers and capitalists.

Conflict is inherent in the employment relation because the employer does not purchase a specified quantity of performed labor, but rather control over the worker's capacity to work over a given time period, and because the workers' goals differ from those of the employer. The amount of labor actually done is determined by a struggle between workers and capitalists.

The labor contract is incomplete because it is impossible for a contract to specify, ahead of time, the exact levels of effort and standards of performance expected of workers. The specific terms of the contract can only be worked out in the contested terrain of the workplace.

The problem is compounded by the fact that management's authority in the workplace isn't exogenous: that is, it isn't enforced by the external legal system, at zero cost to the employer. Rather, it's endogenous: management's authority is enforced entirely with the resources and at the expense of the company. And workers' compliance with directives is frequently costly – and sometimes impossible – to enforce. Employers are forced to resort to endogenous enforcement

> when there is no relevant third party... when the contested attribute can be measured only imperfectly or at considerable cost (work effort, for example, or the degree of risk assumed by a firm's management), when the relevant evidence is not admissible in a court of law... when there is no possible means of redress... or when the nature of the contingencies concerning future states of the world relevant to the exchange precludes writing a fully specified contract.
>
> In such cases the ex post terms of exchange are determined by the structure of the interaction between A and B, and in particular on the strategies A is able to adopt to induce B to provide the desired level of the contested attribute, and the counter strategies available to B...
>
> An employment relationship is established when, in return for a wage, the worker B agrees to submit to the authority of the employer A for a specified period of time in return for a wage w. While the employer's promise to pay the wage is legally enforceable, the worker's promise to bestow an adequate level of effort and care upon the tasks assigned, even if offered, is not. Work is subjectively costly for the worker to provide, valuable to the employer, and costly to measure. The manager-worker relationship is thus a contested exchange.[1]

---

1   Samuel Bowles and Herbert Gintis, "Is the Demand for Workplace Democracy Redundant in a Liberal Economy?," *Democracy and Efficiency in the Economic Enterprise*, ed. Ugo Pagano and Robert Rowthorn (London: Routledge 1996) 64-81.

Since it is impossible to define the terms of the contract exhaustively up front, "bargaining" – as Oliver Williamson puts it – "is pervasive."

The classic illustration of the contested nature of the workplace under incomplete labor contracting, and the pervasiveness of bargaining, is the struggle over the pace and intensity of work, reflected in both the slow-down and working to rule.

At its most basic, the struggle over the pace of work is displayed in what Oliver Williamson calls "perfunctory cooperation" (as opposed to consummate cooperation):

> Consummate cooperation is an affirmative job attitude–to include the use of judgment, filling gaps, and taking initiative in an instrumental way. Perfunctory cooperation, by contrast, involves job performance of a minimally acceptable sort... The upshot is that workers, by shifting to a perfunctory performance mode, are in a position to "destroy" idiosyncratic efficiency gains.

He quotes Peter Blau and Richard Scott's observation to the same effect:

> ... [T]he contract obligates employees to perform only a set of duties in accordance with minimum standards and does not assure their striving to achieve optimum performance... [L]egal authority does not and cannot command the employee's willingness to devote his ingenuity and energy to performing his tasks to the best of his ability... It promotes compliance with directives and discipline, but does not encourage employees to exert effort, to accept responsibilities, or to exercise initiative.

Legal authority, likewise, "does not and cannot" proscribe working to rule, which is nothing but obeying management's directives literally and without question. If they're the brains behind the operation, and we get paid to shut up and do what we're told, then by God that's just what we'll do.

Disgruntled workers, Williamson suggests, will respond to intrusive or authoritarian attempts at surveillance and monitoring with a passive-aggressive strategy of compliance in areas where effective metering is possible – while shifting their perfunctory compliance (or worse) into areas where it is impossible. True to the asymmetric warfare model, the costs of management measures for verifying compliance are generally far greater than the costs of circumventing those measures.

As frequent commenter Jeremy Weiland says, "You are the monkey wrench":

Their need for us to behave in an orderly, predictable manner is a vulnerability of theirs; it can be exploited. You have the ability to transform from a replaceable part into a monkey wrench.

At this point, some libertarians are probably stopping up their ears and going "La la la la, I can't hear you, la la la la!" Under the values most of us have been encultured into, values which are reinforced by the decidely pro-employer and anti-worker libertarian mainstream, such deliberate sabotage of productivity and witholding of effort are tantamount to lèse majesté.

But there's no rational basis for this emotional reaction. The fact that we take such a viscerally asymmetrical view of the respective rights and obligations of employers and employees is, itself, evidence that cultural hangovers from master-servant relationships have contaminated our understanding of the employment relation in a free market.

The employer and employee, under free market principles, are equal parties to the employment contract. As things normally work now, and as mainstream libertarianism unfortunately take for granted, the employer is expected as a normal matter of course to take advantage of the incomplete nature of the employment contract. One can hardly go to Cato or Mises. Org on any given day without stumbling across an article lionizing the employer's right to extract maximum effort in return for minimum pay, if he can get away with it. His rights to change the terms of the employment relation, to speed up the work process, to maximize work per dollar of wages, are his by the grace of God.

Well, if the worker and employer really are equal parties to a voluntary contract, as free market theory says they are, then it works both ways. The worker's attempts to maximize his own utility, under the contested terms of an incomplete contract, are every bit as morally legitimate as those of the boss. The worker has every bit as much of a right to attempt to minimize his effort per dollar of wages as the boss has to attempt to maximize it. What constitutes a fair level of effort is entirely a subjective cultural norm, that can only be determined by the real-world bargaining strength of bosses and workers in a particular workplace.

And as Kevin Depew argues, the continued barrage of downsizing, speedups, and stress will likely result in a drastic shift in workers' subjective perceptions of a fair level of effort and of the legitimate ways to slow down.

Productivity, like most "financial virtues," is the product of positive social mood trends.

As social mood transitions to negative, we can expect to see less and less "virtue" in hard work.

Think about it: real wages are virtually stagnant, so it's not as if people have experienced real reward for their work.

What has been experienced is an unconscious and shared herding impulse trending upward; a shared optimistic mood finding "joy" and "happiness" in work and denigrating the sole pursuit of leisure, idleness.

If social mood has, in fact, peaked, we can expect to see a different attitude toward work and productivity emerge.

The problem is that, to date, bosses have fully capitalized on the potential of the incomplete contract, whereas workers have not. And the only thing preventing workers from doing so is the little boss inside their heads, the cultural holdover from master-servant days, that tells them it's wrong to do so. I aim to kill that little guy. And I believe that when workers fully realize the potential of the incomplete labor contract, and become as willing to exploit it as the bosses have all these years, we'll mop the floor with their asses. And we can do it in a free market, without any "help" from the NLRB. Let the bosses beg for help.

One aspect of direct action that especially interests me is so-called "open-mouth sabotage," which (like most forms of networked resistance) has seen its potential increased by several orders of magnitude by the Internet.

Labor struggle, at least the kind conducted on asymmetric warfare principles, is just one subset of the general category of networked resistance. In the military realm, networked resistance is commonly discussed under the general heading of Fourth Generation Warfare.

In the field of radical political activism, networked organization represents a quantum increase in the "crisis of governability" that Samuel Huntington complained of in the early '70s. The coupling of networked political organization with the Internet in the '90s was the subject of a rather panic-stricken genre of literature at the Rand Corporation, most of it written by David Ronfeldt and John Arquilla. The first major Rand study on the subject concerned the Zapatistas' global political support network, and was written before the Seattle demos. Loosely networked coalitions of affinity groups, organizing through the Internet, could throw together large demonstrations with little notice, and swarm government and mainstream media with phone calls, letters, and emails far beyond their capacity to absorb. Given this elite reaction to what turned out to be a mere foreshadowing, the Seattle demonstrations of December 1999 and the anti-globalization demonstrations that followed must have been especially dramatic. There is strong evidence that the "counter-terrorism" powers sought by Clinton, and by the Bush administration after 9/11, were desired by federal law enforcement mainly to go after the anti-globalization movement.

Let's review just what was entailed in the traditional technique of "open mouth sabotage." From the same Wobbly pamphlet quoted above:

> Sometimes simply telling people the truth about what goes on at work can put a lot of pressure on the boss. Consumer industries like restaurants and packing plants are the most vulnerable. And again, as in the case of the Good Work Strike, you'll be gaining the support of the public, whose patronage can make or break a business.
>
> Whistle Blowing can be as simple as a face-to-face conversation with a customer, or it can be as dramatic as the P.G.&E. engineer who revealed that the blueprints to the Diablo Canyon nuclear reactor had been reversed. Upton Sinclair's novel *The Jungle* blew the lid off the scandalous health standards and working conditions of the meatpacking industry when it was published earlier this century.
>
> Waiters can tell their restaurant clients about the various shortcuts and substitutions that go into creating the faux-haute cuisine being served to them. Just as Work to Rule puts an end to the usual relaxation of standards, Whistle Blowing reveals it for all to know.

The Internet has increased the potential for "open mouth sabotage" by several orders of magnitude.

The first really prominent example of the open mouth, in the networked age, was the so-called McLibel case, in which McDonalds used a SLAPP lawsuit to suppress pamphleteers highly critical of their company. Even in the early days of the Internet, bad publicity over the trial and the defendants' savvy use of the trial as a platform, drew far, far more negative attention to McDonalds than the pamphleteers could have done without the company's help.

In 2004, the Sinclair Media and Diebold cases showed that, in a world of bittorrent and mirror sites, it was literally impossible to suppress information once it had been made public. As recounted by Yochai Benkler, Sinclair Media resorted to a SLAPP lawsuit to stop a boycott campaign against their company, aimed at both shareholders and advertisers, over their airing of an anti-Kerry documentary by the SwiftBoaters. Sinclair found the movement impossible to suppress, as the original campaign websites were mirrored faster than they could be shut down, and the value of their stock imploded. As also reported by Benkler, Diebold resorted to tactics much like those the RIAA uses against file-sharers, to shut down sites which published internal company documents about their voting machines. The memos were quickly distributed, by bittorrent, to more hard drives than anybody could count, and Diebold found itself playing whack-a-mole as the mirror sites displaying the information proliferated exponentially.

One of the most entertaining cases involved the MPAA's attempt to suppress DeCSS, Jon Johansen's CSS descrambler for DVDs. The code was posted all over the blogosphere, in a deliberate act of defiance, and even printed on T-shirts.

In the Alisher Usmanov case, the blogosphere lined up in defense of Craig Murray, who exposed the corruption of post-Soviet Uzbek oligarch Usmanov, against the latter's attempt to suppress Murray's site.

Finally, in the recent Wikileaks case, a judge's order to disable the site

> didn't have any real impact on the availability of the Baer documents. Because Wikileaks operates sites like Wikileaks.cx in other countries, the documents remained widely available, both in the United States and abroad, and the effort to suppress access to them caused them to rocket across the Internet, drawing millions of hits on other web sites.

This is what's known as the "Streisand Effect": attempts to suppress embarrassing information result in more negative publicity than the original information itself.

The Streisand Effect is displayed every time an employer fires a blogger (the phenomenon known as "Doocing," after the first prominent example of it) over embarrassing comments about the workplace. The phenomenon has attracted considerable attention in the mainstream media. In most cases, employers who attempt to suppress embarrassing comments by disgruntled workers are blindsided by the much, much worse publicity resulting from the suppression attempt itself. Instead of a regular blog readership of a few hundred reading that "Employer X Sucks," the blogosphere or a wire service picks up the story, and tens of millions of people read "Blogger Fired for Revealing Employer X Sucks." It may take a while, but the bosses will eventually learn that, for the first time since the rise of the large corporation and the broadcast culture, we can talk back — and not only is it absolutely impossible to shut us up, but we'll keep making more and more noise the more they try to do so.

To grasp just how breathtaking the potential is for open mouth sabotage, and for networked anti-corporate resistance by consumers and workers, just consider the proliferation of anonymous employernamesucks.com sites. The potential results from the anonymity of the writeable web, the comparative ease of setting up anonymous sites (through third country proxy servers, if necessary), and the possibility of simply emailing large volumes of embarrassing information to everyone you can think of whose knowledge might be embarrassing to an employer.

Regarding this last, it's pretty easy to compile a devastating email distribution list with a little Internet legwork. You might include the management of your company's suppliers, outlets, and other business clients, reporters who specialize in your industry, mainstream media outlets, alternative news outlets, worker and consumer advocacy groups, corporate watchdog organizations specializing in your industry, and the major bloggers who specialize in such news. If your problem is with the management of a local branch of a corporate chain, you might add to the distribution list all the community service organizations your bosses belong to, and CC it to corporate headquarters to let them know just how much embarrassment your bosses have caused them. The next step is to set up a dedicated, web-based email account accessed from someplace secure. Then it's pretty easy to compile a textfile of all the dirt on their corruption and mismanagement, and the poor quality of customer service (with management contact info, of course). The only thing left is to click "Attach," and then click "Send." The barrage of emails, phone calls and faxes should hit the management suite like an A-bomb.

So what model will labor need to follow, in the vacuum left by the near total collapse of the Wagner regime and the near-total defeat of the establishment unions? Part of the answer lies with the Wobbly "direct action on the job" model discussed above. A great deal of it, in particular, lies with the application of "open mouth sabotage" on a society-wide scale as exemplified by cases like McLibel, Sinclair, Diebold, and Wikileaks, described above.

Another piece of the puzzle has been suggested by the I.W.W.'s Alexis Buss, in her writing on "minority unionism":

> If unionism is to become a movement again, we need to break out of the current model, one that has come to rely on a recipe increasingly difficult to prepare: a majority of workers vote a union in, a contract is bargained. We need to return to the sort of rank-and-file on-the-job agitating that won the 8-hour day and built unions as a vital force...

Minority unionism happens on our own terms, regardless of legal recognition…

U.S. & Canadian labor relations regimes are set up on the premise that you need a majority of workers to have a union, generally government-certified in a worldwide context[;] this is a relatively rare set-up. And even in North America, the notion that a union needs official recognition or majority status to have the right to represent its members is of relatively recent origin, thanks mostly to the choice of business unions to trade rank-and-file strength for legal maintenance of membership guarantees.

The labor movement was not built through majority unionism-it couldn't have been.

How are we going to get off of this road? We must stop making gaining legal recognition and a contract the point of our organizing…

We have to bring about a situation where the bosses, not the union, want the contract. We need to create situations where bosses will offer us concessions to get our cooperation. Make them beg for it.

But more than anything, the future is being worked out in the current practice of labor struggle itself. We're already seeing a series of prominent labor victories resulting from the networked resistance model.

The Wal-Mart Workers' Association, although it doesn't have an NLRB-certified local in a single Wal-Mart store, is a de facto labor union. And it has achieved victories through "associates" picketing and pamphleting stories on their own time, through swarming via the strategic use of press releases and networking, and through the same sort of support network that Ronfeldt and Arquilla remarked on in the case of the pro-Zapatista campaign. By using negative publicity to embarrass the company, the Association has repeatedly obtained concessions from Wal-Mart. Even a conventional liberal like Ezra Klein understands the importance of such unconventional action.

The Coalition of Imolakee Workers, a movement of Indian agricultural laborers who supply many of the tomatoes used by the fast food industry, has used a similar support network, with the coordinated use of leaflets and picketing, petition drives, and boycotts, to obtain major concessions from Taco Bell, McDonalds, Burger King, and KFC. Blogger Charles Johnson provides inspiring details.

In another example of open mouth sabotage, the IWW-affiliated Starbucks union publicly embarrassed Starbucks Chairman Howard Schultz. It organized a mass email campaign, notifying the board of a co-op apartment he was seeking to buy into of his union-busting activities.

Such networked labor resistance is making inroads even in China, the capitalist motherland of sweatshop employers. Michel Bauwens, at P2P Blog, quotes a story from the Taiwanese press:

> The factory closure last November was a scenario that has been repeated across southern China, where more than 1,000 shoe factories – about a fifth of the total – have closed down in the past year. The majority were in Houjie, a concrete sprawl on the outskirts of Dongguan known as China's "Shoe Town."
>
> "In the past, workers would just swallow all the insults and humiliation. Now they resist," said Jenny Chan, chief coordinator of the Hong Kong-based pressure group Students and Scholars against Corporate Misbehavior, which investigates factory conditions in southern China.
>
> "They collect money and they gather signatures. They use the shop floors and the dormitories to gather the collective forces to put themselves in better negotiating positions with factory owners and managers," she said.
>
> Technology has made this possible.
>
> "They use their mobile phones to receive news and send messages," Chan said "Internet cafes are very important, too. They exchange news about which cities or which factories are recruiting and what they are offering, and that news spreads very quickly."
>
> As a result, she says, factories are seeing huge turnover rates. In Houjie, some factories have tripled workers' salaries, but there are still more than 100,000 vacancies.

The AFL-CIO's Lane Kirkland once suggested, half-heartedly, that things would be easier if Congress repealed all labor laws, and let labor and management go at it "mano a mano." It's time to take this proposal seriously. So here it is – a free market proposal to employers:

We give you the repeal of Wagner, of the anti-yellow dog provisions of Norris-LaGuardia, of legal protections against punitive firing of union organizers, and of all the workplace safety, overtime, and fair practices legislation. You give us the repeal of Taft-Hartley, of the Railway Labor Relations

Act and its counterparts in other industries, of all state right-to-work laws, and of SLAPP lawsuits. All we'll leave in place, out of the whole labor law regime, is the provisions of Norris-LaGuardia taking intrusion by federal troops and court injunctions out of the equation.

And we'll mop the floor with your asses.

## 27

*Liberty* 5.19 (April 28, 1888): 4.

# SHOULD LABOR BE PAID OR NOT?

### BENJAMIN R. TUCKER
### (1888)

IN No. 121 OF *LIBERTY*, CRITICISING AN ATTEMPT OF KROPOTKIN TO IDENTIFY COMMUnism and Individualism, I charged him with ignoring the real question whether Communism will permit the individual to labor independently, own tools, sell his labor or his products, and buy the labor or products of others. In Herr Most's eyes this is so outrageous that, in reprinting it, he puts the words the labor of others in large black type. Most being a Communist, he must, to be consistent, object to the purchase and sale of anything whatever; but why he should particularly object to the purchase and sale of labor is more than I can understand. Really, in the last analysis, labor is the only thing that has any title to be bought or sold. Is there any just basis of price except cost? And is there anything that costs except labor or suffering (another name for labor)? Labor should be paid! Horrible, isn't it? Why, I thought that the fact that it is not paid was the whole grievance. Unpaid labor has been the chief complaint of all Socialists, and that labor should get its reward has been their chief contention. Suppose I had said to Kropotkin that the real question is whether Communism will permit individuals to exchange their labor or products on their own terms. Would Herr Most have been so shocked? Would he have printed that in black type? Yet in another form I said precisely that.

If the men who oppose wages – that is, the purchase and sale of labor – were capable of analyzing their thought and feelings, they would see that what really excites their anger is not the fact that labor is bought and sold, but the fact that one class of men are dependent for their living upon the sale of their labor, while another class of men are relieved of the necessity of labor by being legally privileged to sell something that is not labor, and that, but for the privilege, would be enjoyed by all gratuitously. And to such a state of things I am as much opposed as any one. But the minute you remove privilege, the class that now enjoy it will be forced to sell their labor, and then, when there will be nothing but labor with which to buy labor, the distinction between wage-payers and wage-receivers will be wiped out, and every man will be a laborer exchanging with fellow-laborers. Not to abolish wages, but to make every man dependent upon wages and to secure to every man his whole wages is the aim of Anarchistic Socialism. What Anarchistic Socialism aims to abolish is usury. It does not want to deprive labor of its reward; it wants to deprive capital of its reward. It does not hold that labor should not be sold; it holds that capital should not be hired at usury.

But, says Herr Most, this idea of a free labor market from which privilege is eliminated is nothing but consistent Manchesterism. Well, what better can a man who professes Anarchism want than that? For the principle of Manchesterism is liberty, and consistent Manchesterism is consistent adherence to liberty. The only inconsistency of the Manchester men lies in their infidelity to liberty in some of its phases. And this infidelity to liberty in some of its phases is precisely the fatal inconsistency of the Freiheit school – the only difference between its adherents and the Manchester men being that in many of the phases in which the latter are infidel the former are faithful, while in many of those in which the latter are faithful the former are infidel. Yes, genuine Anarchism is consistent Manchesterism, and Communistic or pseudo-Anarchism is inconsistent Manchesterism.

# PART FIVE

## Neoliberalism, Privatization, and Redistribution

## 28

The Freeman: Ideas on Liberty 58.7 (Sep.
2008): 28-31 <http://www.thefree-
manonline.org/featured/free-market-
reforms-and-the-reduction-of-statism/>
(Aug. 22, 2011).

# FREE MARKET REFORMS AND THE REDUCTION OF STATISM

## KEVIN A. CARSON
## (2008)

OBJECTIVIST SCHOLAR CHRIS SCIABARRA, IN HIS BRILLIANT BOOK *TOTAL FREEDOM*, called for a "dialectical libertarianism." By dialectical analysis, Sciabarra means to "grasp the nature of a part by viewing it systemically – that is, as an extension of the system within which it is embedded." Individual parts receive their character from the whole of which they are a part, and from their function within that whole.

This means it is a mistake to consider any particular form of state intervention in isolation, without regard to the role it plays in the overall system.[1]

Another libertarian, blogger Arthur Silber, contrasts dialectical libertarianism with what he calls "atomistic libertarianism," whose approach is to

---

1   Chris Matthew Sciabarra, "Dialectics and Liberty," *The Freeman: Ideas on Liberty* 55.7 (Sep. 2005): 34-8.

"focus on the basic principles involved, but with scant (or no) attention paid to the overall context in which the principles are being analyzed. In this manner, this approach treats principles like Plato's Forms…" Atomistic libertarians argue "as if the society in which one lives is completely irrelevant to an analysis of any problem at all."

To determine the function a particular form of state intervention serves in the structure of state power, we must first ask what has been the historical objective of the state. This is where libertarian class analysis comes in.

The single greatest work I'm aware of on libertarian class theory is Roderick Long's article, "Toward a Libertarian Theory of Class."[2] Long categorizes ruling-class theories as either "statocratic" or "plutocratic," based on the respective emphasis they place on the state apparatus and the plutocracy (the wealthy "private-sector" beneficiaries of government intervention) as components of the ruling class.

The default tendency in mainstream libertarianism is a high degree of statocracy, to the point not only of (quite properly) emphasizing the necessary role of state coercion in enabling "legal plunder" (Frédéric Bastiat's term) by the plutocracy, but of downplaying the significance of the plutocracy even as beneficiaries of statism. This means treating the class interests associated with the state as ad hoc and fortuitous. Although statocratic theory treats the state (in Franz Oppenheimer's phrase) as the organized political means to wealth, it still tends to view government as merely serving the exploitative interests of whatever assortment of political factions happens to control it at any given time. This picture of how the state works does not require any organic relation between the various interest groups controlling it at any time, or between them and the state. It might be controlled by a disparate array of interest groups, including licensed professionals, rent-seeking corporations, farmers, regulated utilities, and big labor; the only thing they have in common is that they happen to be currently the best at latching onto the state.

Murray Rothbard's position was far different. Rothbard, Long argues, saw the state as controlled by "a primary group that has achieved a position of structural hegemony, a group central to class consolidation and crisis in contemporary political economy. Rothbard's approach to this problem is, in fact, highly dialectical in its comprehension of the historical, political, economic, and social dynamics of class."

I have argued in the past that the corporate economy is so closely bound up with the power of the state, that it makes more sense to think of the corporate ruling class as a component of the state, in the same way that

---

2    Roderick T. Long, "Toward a Libertarian Theory of Class," *Social Philosophy and Policy* 15.2 (Sum. 1998): 303-49.

landlords were a component of the state under the Old Regime. Blogger Brad Spangler used the analogy of a gunman and bagman to illustrate the relationship:

> Let's postulate two sorts of robbery scenarios.
>
> In one, a lone robber points a gun at you and takes your cash. All libertarians would recognize this as a micro-example of any kind of government at work, resembling most closely State Socialism.
>
> In the second, depicting State Capitalism, one robber (the literal apparatus of government) keeps you covered with a pistol while the second (representing State allied corporations) just holds the bag that you have to drop your wristwatch, wallet and car keys in. To say that your interaction with the bagman was a "voluntary transaction" is an absurdity. Such nonsense should be condemned by all libertarians. Both gunman and bagman together are the true State.

Given this perspective, it doesn't make much sense to consider particular proposals for deregulating or cutting taxes without regard to the role the taxes and regulations play in the overall structure of state capitalism. That's especially true considering that most mainstream proposals for "free market reform" are generated by the very class interests that benefit from the corporate state.

No politico-economic system has ever approximated total statism, in the sense that "everything not forbidden is compulsory." In every system there is a mixture of compulsory and discretionary behavior. The ruling class allows some amount of voluntary market exchange within the interstices of a system whose overall structure is defined by coercive state intervention. The choice of what areas to leave to voluntary exchange, just as much as of what to subject to compulsory regulation, reflects the overall strategic picture of the ruling class. The total mixture of statism and market activity will be chosen as most likely, in the estimation of the ruling class, to maximize net exploitation by the political means.

## PRIMARY AND SECONDARY INTERVENTIONS

Some forms of state intervention are primary. They involve the privileges, subsidies, and other structural bases of economic exploitation through the political system. This has been the primary purpose of the state: the organized political means to wealth, exercised by and for a particular class of people. Some forms of intervention, however, are secondary. Their purpose is stabilizing, or ameliorative. They include welfare-state measures, Keynesian demand management, and the like, whose purpose is to limit the most destabilizing side effects of privilege and to secure the long-term survival of the system.

Unfortunately, the typical "free market reform" issuing from corporate interests involves eliminating only the ameliorative or regulatory forms of intervention, while leaving intact the primary structure of privilege and exploitation.

The strategic priorities of principled libertarians should be just the opposite: first to dismantle the fundamental, structural forms of state intervention, whose primary effect is to enable exploitation, and only then to dismantle the secondary, ameliorative forms of intervention that serve to make life bearable for the average person living under a system of state-enabled exploitation. As blogger Jim Henley put it, remove the shackles before the crutches.

To welcome the typical "free market" proposals as "steps in the right direction," without regard to their effect on the overall functioning of the system, is comparable to the Romans welcoming the withdrawal of the Punic center at Cannae as "a step in the right direction." Hannibal's battle formation was not the first step in a general Carthaginian withdrawal from Italy, and you can be sure the piecemeal "privatizations," "deregulations," and "tax cuts" proposed are not intended to reduce the amount of wealth extracted by the political means.

## REGULATIONS AND INCREASING STATISM

Moreover, regulations that limit and constrain the exercise of privilege do not involve, properly speaking, a net increase in statism at all. They are simply the corporate state's stabilizing restrictions on its own more fundamental forms of intervention.

Silber illustrated the dialectical nature of such restrictions with reference to the question of whether pharmacists ought to be able to refuse to sell items (such as "morning after" pills) that violate their conscience. The atomistic-libertarian response is, "Of course. The right to sell, or not sell, is a fundamental free-market liberty." The implicit assumption here, as Silber pointed out, is "that this dispute arises in a society which is essentially free." But pharmacists are in fact direct beneficiaries of compulsory occupational licensing, a statist racket whose central purpose is to restrict competition and enable them to charge a monopoly price for their services. Silber wrote:

The major point is a very simple one: the pharmacy profession is a state-enforced monopoly. In other words: the consumer and the pharmacist are not equal competitors on the playing field. The state has placed its thumb firmly on the scales – and on one side only. That is the crucial point, from which all further analysis must flow…

… [T]he state has created a government-enforced monopoly for licensed pharmacists. Given that central fact, the least the state can do is ensure that everyone has access to the drugs they require – and whether a particular pill is of life and death importance is for the individual who wants it to decide, not the pharmacist and most certainly not the government.

When the state confers a special privilege on an occupation, a business firm, or an industry, and then sets regulatory limits on the use of that privilege, the regulation is not a new intrusion of statism into a free market. It is, rather, the state's limitation and qualification of its own underlying statism. The secondary regulation is not a net increase, but a net reduction in statism.

On the other hand, repeal of the secondary regulation, without an accompanying repeal of the primary privilege, would be a net increase in statism. Since the beneficiaries of privilege are a de facto branch of the state, the elimination of regulatory constraints on their abuse of privilege has the same practical effect as repealing a constitutional restriction on the state's exercise of its own powers.

To expand Spangler's bagman analogy, a great deal of alleged statism amounts to the gunman telling the bagman, after the victim has handed his wallet over at gunpoint, to give the victim back enough money for cab fare so he can get safely back home and keep on earning money to be robbed of.

When the state is controlled by "legal plunderers" and every decision for or against state intervention in a particular circumstance reflects their strategic assessment of the ideal mixture of intervention and non-intervention, it's a mistake for a genuine anti-state movement to allow the priorities for "free market reform" to be set by the plunderers' estimation of what forms of intervention no longer serve their purpose. If the corporate representatives in government are proposing a particular "free market reform," you can bet your bottom dollar it's because they believe it will increase the net political extraction of wealth.

The corporate ruling class's approach to "free market reform" is a sort of mirror-image of "lemon socialism." Under lemon socialism, the political capitalists (acting through the state) choose to nationalize those industries that corporate capital will most benefit from having taken off its hands, and to socialize those functions the cost of which capital would most prefer the state to bear. They shift functions from the private to the state sector when they are perceived as necessary for the functioning of the system, but not sufficiently profitable to justify the bother of running them under "private sector" auspices. Under "lemon market reform," on the other hand, the political capitalists liquidate interventionist policies after they have squeezed all the benefit out of state action.

A good example: British industrialists felt it was safe to adopt "free trade" in the mid-nineteenth century, after mercantilism had served its purpose. Half the world had been hammered into a unified market by British force of arms and was held together by a British merchant fleet. Britain had stamped out competing industry in the colonial world. It had reenacted the Enclosures on a global scale, stealing enormous amounts of land from native populations and converting it to cash crops for the imperial market. The commanding position of British capital was the direct result of past mercantilism; having established this commanding position, it could afford "free trade."

The so-called "free trade" movement in the contemporary United States follows the same pattern. A century ago, high tariff barriers served the interests of American political capitalists. Today, when the dominant corporate interests in America are transnational, tariffs are no longer useful to them. They actually impede the transfer of goods and partially finished products between the national subdivisions of a single global corporation.

On the other hand, so-called "intellectual property" today serves exactly the same protectionist function for transnational corporations that tariffs used to serve for the old national corporations a century ago. So the political capitalists promote a version of "free trade" that involves doing away with outmoded tariff barriers while greatly strengthening the new protectionism of "intellectual property" law.

We must remember that the measure of statism inheres in the functioning of the overall system, not in the formal statism of its separate parts. A reduction in the formal statism of some separate parts, chosen in accordance with the strategic priorities of the statists, may actually result in a net increase in the overall level of statism. Our strategic agenda as libertarians, in dismantling the state, must reflect our understanding of the overall nature of the system.

## 29

*Contemporary Individualist Anarchism: The Broadsides of the Boston Anarchist Drinking Brigade, 1988-2000*, Political Notes 184, by Joe Peacott, Jim Baker, *et al.* (London: Libertarian Alliance 2003) 21-2 <http://www.libertarian.co.uk/lapubs/polin/po-lin184.pdf> (Aug. 22, 2011).

# FREE TRADE IS FAIR TRADE
## An Anarchist Looks at World Trade

*JOE PEACOTT*
*(2000)*

MANY OF THOSE WHO OPPOSE THE WORLD TRADE ORGANIZATION (WTO) advocate something they call "fair trade," in contrast to the "free trade" the WTO advocates. In fact, the kind of commerce promoted by the WTO is anything but free, while the alternatives defended by its opponents are in no way fair. Both the WTO and most of its critics, who range from old-fashioned right wing nationalists to labor activists, environmentalists, and leftists of various kinds, favor continued government intervention in economic activities, whether domestic or international. And any such state-regulated trade will never be either free or fair.

All governments around the world interfere in the economies of the countries they rule and intervene in cross-border trade on a regular basis. They subsidize some businesses, like agriculture in the united states and europe, pay for international advertising for wealthy corporations, and institute tariffs and customs rules that ban or complicate the free flow of goods between people on opposite sides of political borders. Such rules and regulations favor powerful domestic businesses at the expense of producers in other countries.

"Free" trade agreements and organizations like NAFTA and WTO may alter some of the details of this intervention, but do not challenge the principle that governments are entitled to tell their subjects what they may and may not buy and whom they may trade with. Under NAFTA, for instance, it is illegal to buy lower-priced therapeutic drugs in Canada and resell them in the United States. WTO does not propose to free up trade between individuals, either. It sets rules which the bureaucrats who run the organization feel best serve the interests of corporations favored by the various governments that make it up. It does not even take into consideration private, voluntary arrangements among individuals and groups, unsupervised by regulatory bodies, customs officials, border guards, "public health" functionaries, coast guards, etc. It just promotes continued government oversight of people trying to engage in commerce with each other.

Most critics of WTO also advocate government supervision of economic matters. Unions urge governments to bar imports of goods which sell more cheaply than those produced by their members. Environmentalists want governments to implement regulations that protect wildlife and limit pollution. Human rights activists want governments to force businesses to allow their employees to organize to improve their working conditions. The goals of these people are admirable: protecting well-paid jobs, defending plants and animals against exploitation and death, and enabling low-wage workers to improve their economic status. However, the means advocated to achieve these goals are the same sort WTO promotes: government force. No one seems to be proposing an alternate means of achieving a better world for working people in all countries, as well as the beings with whom we share this planet.

Many have expressed concerns about the WTO weakening national sovereignty, implying that the United States government is a force for good that should be defended. They seem to forget that the federal government robs workers in this country while dispensing corporate welfare. Such critics fail to understand that the United States and other national governments routinely limit individual sovereignty, the only kind that is really important. Different levels of government may be more or less oppressive or just, depending on the specific situation and the specific interests of the individual concerned, but none have any moral justification for any of their actions. They all steal money from workers in the form of taxes, enforce laws perpetuating unfair land ownership, maintain a monopoly on the means of exchange, and defend the unjustly-gained wealth of the rich, thus impoverishing working people. And they should all be opposed.

Protestors against WTO have pointed out that it is not democratic, unlike at least some of the national governments to which it is contrasted. Granted, the governments of the United States, the European Union, Canada, India, Japan and elsewhere are elected, democratic ones, but this does not mean they are legitimate, benign, or represent the interests of individual residents of the countries they rule. The democratic government of the United States, for instance, makes war on people in Kosovo and Iraq, supports the Chinese police state, subsidizes the growing of tobacco and other favored crops in the united states, and bans the domestic use of therapeutic drugs available in other countries. And this is the same government some critics of WTO seem to feel can be an advocate for the interests of the world's workers and natural environment. We need to get the various national democratic governments, as well as the WTO, off the backs of the people they push around and brutalize. If democracy, like voting, really changed anything, it would be prohibited.

Abolishing WTO and NAFTA will not benefit working people here or abroad. Abolishing government would. Stemming crossborder trade will not raise the wages of Mexican workers, improve conditions in Malaysian factories, or lighten the load of chinese farmers and laborers. International trade has not hurt these people: international governments have, by restricting their freedoms in such a way that they have little choice but to slave away at unjust wages for wealthy others. Governments all over the world deny their working subjects economic freedom and favor the interests of the wealthy owners of land and industry, thus impoverishing the many and enriching the few, who in turn enrich the politicians.

Real free trade would look nothing like what exists now or would exist with WTO in charge. Without governments to prohibit people from living their lives as they see fit, free people could set up their own forms of money and banks to increase the availability of credit to regular people. Their money would not be stolen from them by predatory governments. They would not de disarmed by their democratic representatives and rendered unable to defend their land and property from voracious multinational corporations favored by politicians. They would not be forced by governments to pay rent to landowners who can claim title to land and property only because governments support ownership of land neither used nor occupied by the owners. And workers would be free to take possession of the factories and other means of production which they currently use, since there would be no government to enforce the demand of the current "owners" for a portion of the labor of others. Without having to sacrifice any portion of the wealth generated by their own labor, free workers would be affluent workers. Such people would be free to exchange goods and services with others, regardless of geographic location or ethnicity, as long as the interaction was voluntary. If trade were really free, the only exchanges that people would agree to would be fair ones. And true, unhindered competition between various worker-owners all over the world would prevent some from accumulating vast amounts of wealth at the expense of others.

Real free trade would be risky in ways that a government supervised economy would not be. There would be no state-run welfare system, no labor laws, no laws against pollution and the wanton slaughter of wildlife. But that does not mean individuals and the natural environment would be set adrift to fend for themselves. People are more than capable of forming voluntary organizations to provide for hard times, assist each other with creating jobs, facilitate direct commerce between producers, and campaign for a more humane treatment of nonhuman beings. People free to trade with each other would also be free to look at the ways they live and work and come up with ways to do both that are more humane and ecologically sound than those that currently exist. They have done this all through history and do it now, alongside the institutions of the warfare/welfare state.

Anarchy and free trade would not solve all problems or lead to utopia. They simply would free up people to interact with others as they choose, to the benefit of both, or all, parties. Individuals and voluntary associations would then be free to trade fairly with each other, band together as they see fit to promote their common interests, and protect their shared environment, all without being pushed around by politicians and the economic elites they empower and defend.

## 30

*Rad Geek People's Daily* (n.p., Nov.
8, 2007) <http://radgeek.com/
gt/2007/11/08/sprachkritik_privatiza-
tion/> (Aug. 22, 2011).

# TWO WORDS ON "PRIVATIZATION"

## CHARLES W. JOHNSON
## (2007)

LEFT LIBERTARIANS, LIKE ALL LIBERTARIANS, BELIEVE THAT ALL STATE CONTROL OF INDUSTRY and all State ownership of natural resources should be abolished. In that sense, libertarian Leftists advocate complete and absolute privatization of, well, everything. Governments, or quasi-governmental "public" monopolies, have no business building or running roads, bridges, railroads, airports, parks, housing, libraries, post offices, television stations, electric lines, power plants, water works, oil rigs, gas pipelines, or anything else of the sort. (Those of us who are anarchists add that governments have no business building or running fire departments, police stations, courts, armies, or anything else of the sort, because governments – which are necessarily coercive and necessarily elitist – have no business existing or doing anything at all.)

It's hard enough to sell this idea to our fellow Leftists, just on the merits. State Leftists have a long-standing and healthy skepticism towards the more utopian claims that are sometimes made about how businesses might act on the free market; meanwhile, they have a long-standing and very unhealthy naïveté towards the utopian claims that are often made on behalf of government bureaucracies under an electoral form of government.[1] But setting the substantive issues aside, there's another major roadblock for us to confront, just from the use of language.

There is something called "privatization" which has been a hot topic for the past 15-20 years. It has been a big deal in Eastern Europe, in third world countries under the influence of the IMF, and in some cases in the United States, too. Naomi Klein has a new book[2] on the topic, which focuses on the role that natural and artificial crises play in establishing the conditions for what she calls "privatization." But "privatization," as understood by the IMF, the neoliberal governments, and the robber baron corporations, is a very different beast from "privatization" as understood by free market radicals. What consistent libertarians advocate is the devolution of all wealth to the people who created it, and the reconstruction of all industry on the principle of free association and voluntary mutual exchange. But the IMF and Naomi Klein both seem to agree on the idea that "privatization" includes "reforms" like the following:

- Tax-funded government contracts to corporations like Blackwater or DynCorp for private mercenaries to fight government wars. This has become increasingly popular as a way for the U.S. to wage small and large wars over the past 15 years; I think it was largely pioneered through the U.S. government's efforts to suppress international free trade in unauthorized drugs, and is currently heavily used by the U.S. in Colombia, the Balkans, and Iraq.
- Tax-funded government contracts to corporations like Wackenhut for government-funded but privately managed prisons, police forces, firefighters, etc. This has also become increasingly popular in the U.S. over the past 15 years; in the case of prisons, at least, it was largely inspired by the increasing number of people imprisoned by the U.S. government for using unauthorized drugs or selling them to willing customers.
- Government auctions or sweetheart contracts in which nationalized monopoly firms – oil companies, water works, power companies, and the like – are sold off to corporations, with the profits going into the State treasury, and usually with some form of legally-enforced monopoly left intact after "privatization." One of the most notori-

---

1    See Charles Johnson, "State of Grace," *Rad Geek People's Daily* (n.p., Oct. 9, 2005) <http://www.radgeek.com/gt/2005/10/09/state_of> (March 13, 2011).

2    Naomi Klein, *The Shock Doctrine: The Rise of Disaster Capitalism* (New York: Metropolitan 2007).

ous cases is the cannibalistic bonanza that Boris Yeltsin and a select class of politically-connected "Oligarchs" helped themselves to after the implosion of Soviet Communism. Throughout the third world, similar auction or contract schemes are suggested or demanded as a condition for the national government to receive a line of tax-funded credit from the member states of the International Monetary Fund.

- Yet Another Damn Account schemes for converting government pension systems from a welfare model to a forced savings model, in which workers are forced to put part of their paycheck into a special, government-created retirement account, where it can be invested according to government-crafted formulas in one of a limited number of government-approved investment vehicles offered by a tightly regulated cartel of government-approved uncompetitive investment brokers. This kind of government retirement plan is supposedly the centerpiece of "privatization" in Pinochet's Chile, and has repeatedly been advocated by George W. Bush and other Republican politicians in the United States.

Klein and other state Leftists very often claim that these government "privatization" schemes are closely associated with Right wing authoritarian repression, up to and including secret police, death squads, and beating, torturing, or "disappearing" innocent people for exercising their rights of free speech or free association in labor unions or dissident groups.

And they are right. Those police state tactics aren't compatible with any kind of free market, but then, neither are any of the government auctions, government contracting, government loans, and government regulatory schemes that Klein and her comrades present as examples of "privatization." They are examples of government-backed corporate kleptocracy. The problem is that the oligarchs, the robber barons, and their hirelings dishonestly present these schemes – one and all of them involving massive government intervention and government plunder from ordinary working people – as if they were "free market" reforms. And Klein and her comrades usually believe them; the worst sorts of robber baron state capitalism are routinely presented as if they were arguments against the free market, even though pervasive government monopoly, government regulation, government confiscation, government contracting, and government finance have nothing even remotely to do with free markets.

I'd like to suggest that this confusion needs to be exposed, and combated. In order to combat it, we may very well need to mint some new language. As far as I know, "privatization" was coined by analogy with "nationalization;" if "nationalization" was the seizure of industry or resources by government, then "privatization" was the reversal of that process, devolving the industry or the resources into private hands. It is clear that the kind of government outsourcing and kleptocratic monopolies that Klein et al condemn don't match up very well with the term. On the other hand, the term has been abused and perverted so long that it may not be very useful to us anymore, either.

So here's my proposal for linguistic reform. What we advocate is the devolution of state-confiscated wealth and state-confiscated industries back to *civil society*. In some cases, that might mean transferring an industry or a resource to private proprietorship (if, for example, you can find the person or the people from whom a nationalized factory was originally seized, the just thing to do would be to turn the factory back over to them). But in most cases, it could just as easily mean any number of other ways to devolve property back to the people:

1. Some resources should be ceded to the joint ownership of those who habitually use them. For example, who should own your neighborhood streets? Answer: you and your neighbors should own the streets that you live on. For the government to seize your tax money and your land and use it to build neighborhood roads, and then to sell them out from under you to some unrelated third party who doesn't live on them, doesn't habitually use them, etc., would be theft.

2. Government industries and lands where an original private owner cannot be found could, and probably should, be devolved to the co-operative ownership of the people who work in them or on them. The factories to the workers; the soil to those who till it.

3. Some universally-used utilities (water works, regional power companies, perhaps highways) which were created by tax money might be ceded to the joint ownership of all the citizens of the area they serve. (This is somewhat similar to the Czechoslovakian model of privatization, in which government industries were converted into joint-stock companies, and every citizen was given so many shares.)

4. Some resources (many parks, perhaps) might be ceded to *the unorganized public* – that is, they would become real public property, in Roderick's sense,[3] rather than in the sense of government control.

Now, given the diversity of cases, and all of the different ways in which government might justly devolve property from State control to civil society, "privatization" is really too limiting a term. So instead let's call what we want the *"socialization of the means of production."*

As for the IMF/Blackwater model of "privatization," again, the word doesn't fit the situation very well, and we need something new in order to

---

3  See Roderick Long, "A Plea for Public Property." ch. 15 (157-168), in this volume.

help mark the distinction. Whereas what we want could rightly be called "socialization," I think that the government outsourcing, government-backed monopoly capitalism, and government goon squads, might more accurately be described as *"privateering."*

I'm just sayin'.

# 31

*Libertarian Forum* 1.6 (June 15, 1969): 2.

# WHERE ARE THE SPECIFICS?

## KARL HESS
## (1969)

LIBERTARIANISM IS CLEARLY THE MOST, PERHAPS THE ONLY TRULY RADICAL MOVEMENT IN America. It grasps the problems of society by the roots. It is not reformist in any sense. It is revolutionary in every sense.

Because so many of its people, however, have come from the right there remains about it at least an aura or, perhaps, miasma of defensiveness, as though its interests really center in, for instance, defending private property. The truth, of course, is that libertarianism wants to advance principles of property but that it in no way wishes to defend, willy nilly, all property which now is called private.

Much of that property is stolen. Much is of dubious title. All of it is deeply intertwined with an immoral, coercive state system which has condoned, built on, and profited from slavery; has expanded through and exploited a brutal and aggressive imperial and colonial foreign policy, and continues to hold the people in a roughly serf-master relationship to political-economic power concentrations.

Libertarians are concerned, first and foremost, with that most valuable of properties, the life of each individual. That is the property most brutally and constantly abused by state systems whether they are of the right or left. Property rights pertaining to material objects are seen by libertarians as stemming from and as importantly secondary to the right to own, direct, and enjoy one's own life and those appurtenances thereto which may be acquired without coercion.

Libertarians, in short, simply do not believe that theft is proper whether it is committed in the name of a state, a class, a crisis, a credo, or a cliche.

This is a far cry from sharing common ground with those who want to create a society in which super capitalists are free to amass vast holdings and who say that that is ultimately the most important purpose of freedom. This is proto-heroic nonsense.

Libertarianism is a people's movement and a liberation movement. It seeks the sort of open, non-coercive society in which the people, the living, free, distinct people may voluntarily associate, dis-associate, and, as they see fit, participate in the decisions affecting their lives. This means a truly free market in everything from ideas to idiosyncrasies. It means people free collectively to organize the resources of their immediate community or individualistically to organize them; it means the freedom to have a community-based and supported judiciary where wanted, none where not, or private arbitration services where that is seen as most desirable. The same with police. The same with schools, hospitals, factories, farms, laboratories, parks, and pensions. Liberty means the right to shape your own institutions. It opposes the right of those institutions to shape you simply because of accreted power or gerontological status.

For many, however, these root principles of radical libertarianism will remain mere abstractions, and even suspect, until they are developed into aggressive, specific proposals.

There is scarcely anything radical about, for instance, those who say that the poor should have a larger share of the Federal budget. That is reactionary, asking that the institution of state theft be made merely more palatable by distributing its loot to more sympathetic persons. Perhaps no one of sound mind could object more to giving Federal funds to poor people than to spending the money on the slaughter of Vietnamese peasant fighters. But to argue such relative merits must end being simply reformist and not revolutionary.

Libertarians could and should propose specific revolutionary tactics and goals which would have specific meaning to poor people and to all people; to analyze in depth and to demonstrate in example the meaning of liberty, revolutionary liberty to them.

I, for one, earnestly beseech such thinking from my comrades.

The proposals should take into account the revolutionary treatment of stolen 'private' and 'public' property in libertarian, radical, and revolutionary terms; the factors which have oppressed people so far, and so forth.

Murray Rothbard and others have done much theoretical work along these lines but it can never be enough for just a few to shoulder so much of the burden.

Let me propose just a few examples of the sort of specific, revolutionary and radical questions to which members of our Movement might well address themselves.

– Land ownership and/or usage in a situation of declining state power. The Tijerina situation suggests one approach. There must be many others. And what about (realistically, not romantically) water and air pollution liability and prevention?

– Worker, share-owner, community roles or rights in productive facilities in terms of libertarian analysis and as specific proposals in a radical and revolutionary context. What, for instance, might or should happen to General Motors in a liberated society?

Of particular interest, to me at any rate, is focusing libertarian analysis and ingenuity on finishing the great unfinished business of the abolition of slavery. Simply setting slaves free, in a world still owned by their masters, obviously was an historic inequity. (Libertarians hold that the South should have been permitted to secede so that the slaves themselves, along with their Northern friends, could have built a revolutionary liberation movement, overthrown the masters, and thus shaped the reparations of revolution.) Thoughts of reparations today are clouded by concern that it would be taken out against innocent persons who in no way could be connected to former oppression. There is an area where that could be avoided: in the use of government-'owned' lands and facilities as items of exchange in compensating the descendants of slaves and making it possible for them to participate in the communities of the land, finally, as equals and not wards.

Somewhere, I must assume, there is a libertarian who, sharing the idea, might work out a good and consistent proposal for justice in that area.

Obviously the list is endless. But the point is finite and finely focused.

With libertarianism now developing as a Movement, it earnestly and urgently requires innovative proposals, radical and specific goals, and a revolutionary agenda which can translate its great and enduring principles into timely and commanding courses of possible and even practical action.

# 32

*Libertarian Forum* 1.6 (June 15, 1969):
3-4.

# CONFISCATION AND THE HOMESTEAD PRINCIPLE

## MURRAY N. ROTHBARD
## (1969)

Karl Hess's brilliant and challenging article in this issue[1] raises a problem of specifics that ranges further than the libertarian movement. For example, there must be hundreds of thousands of "professional" anti-Communists in this country. Yet not one of these gentry, in the course of their fulminations, has come up with a specific plan for de-Communization. Suppose, for example, that Messers. Brezhnev and Co. become converted to the principles of a free society; they then ask our anti-Communists, all right, how do we go about de-socializing? What could our anti-Communists offer them?

This question has been essentially answered by the exciting developments of Tito's Yugoslavia. Beginning in 1952, Yugoslavia has been de-socializing at a remarkable rate. The principle the Yugoslavs have used is the libertarian "homesteading" one: the state-owned factories to the workers that work in them! The nationalized plants in the "public" sector

---

1    Karl Hess (1969), "Where Are the Specifics?," ch. 31 (289-292), in this volume.

have all been transferred in virtual ownership to the specific workers who work in the particular plants, thus making them producers' coops, and moving rapidly in the direction of individual shares of virtual ownership to the individual worker. What other practicable route toward destatization could there be? The principle in the Communist countries should be: land to the peasants and the factories to the workers, thereby getting the property out of the hands of the State and into private, homesteading hands.

The homesteading principle means that the way that unowned property gets into private ownership is by the principle that this property justly belongs to the person who finds, occupies, and transforms it by his labor. This is clear in the case of the pioneer and virgin land. But what of the case of stolen property?

Suppose, for example, that A steals B's horse. Then C comes along and takes the horse from A. Can C be called a thief? Certainly not, for we cannot call a man a criminal for stealing goods from a thief. On the contrary, C is performing a virtuous act of confiscation, for he is depriving thief A of the fruits of his crime of aggression, and he is at least returning the horse to the innocent "private" sector and out of the "criminal" sector. C has done a noble act and should be applauded. Of course, it would be still better if he returned the horse to B, the original victim. But even if he does not, the horse is far more justly in C's hands than it is in the hands of A, the thief and criminal.

Let us now apply our libertarian theory of property to the case of property in the hands of, or derived from, the State apparatus. The libertarian sees the State as a giant gang of organized criminals, who live off the theft called "taxation" and use the proceeds to kill, enslave, and generally push people around. Therefore, any property in the hands of the State is in the hands of thieves, and should be liberated as quickly as possible. Any person or group who liberates such property, who confiscates or appropriates it from the State, is performing a virtuous act and a signal service to the cause of liberty. In the case of the State, furthermore, the victim is not readily identifiable as B, the horse-owner. All taxpayers, all draftees, all victims of the State have been mulcted. How to go about returning all this property to the taxpayers? What proportions should be used in this terrific tangle of robbery and injustice that we have all suffered at the hands of the State? Often, the most practical method of de-statizing is simply to grant the moral right of ownership on the person or group who seizes the property from the State. Of this group, the most morally deserving are the ones who are already using the property but who have no moral complicity in the State's act of aggression. These people then become the "homesteaders" of the stolen property and hence the rightful owners.

Take, for example, the State universities. This is property built on funds stolen from the taxpayers. Since the State has not found or put into effect a way of returning ownership of this property to the taxpaying public, the proper owners of this university are the "homesteaders," those who have already been using and therefore "mixing their labor" with the facilities. The prime consideration is to deprive the thief, in this case the State, as quickly as possible of the ownership and control of its ill-gotten gains, to return the property to the innocent, private sector. This means student and/or faculty ownership of the universities.

As between the two groups, the students have a prior claim, for the students have been paying at least some amount to support the university whereas the faculty suffer from the moral taint of living off State funds and thereby becoming to some extent a part of the State apparatus.

The same principle applies to nominally "private" property which really comes from the State as a result of zealous lobbying on behalf of the recipient. Columbia University, for example, which receives nearly two-thirds of its income from government, is only a "private" college in the most ironic sense. It deserves a similar fate of virtuous homesteading confiscation.

But if Columbia University, what of General Dynamics? What of the myriad of corporations which are integral parts of the military-industrial complex, which not only get over half or sometimes virtually all their revenue from the government but also participate in mass murder? What are their credentials to "private" property? Surely less than zero. As eager lobbyists for these contracts and subsidies, as co-founders of the garrison state, they deserve confiscation and reversion of their property to the genuine private sector as rapidly as possible. To say that their "private" property must be respected is to say that the property stolen by the horsethief and the murdered [sic] must be "respected."

But how then do we go about destatizing the entire mass of government property, as well as the "private property" of General Dynamics? All this needs detailed thought and inquiry on the part of libertarians. One method would be to turn over ownership to the homesteading workers in the particular plants; another to turn over pro-rata ownership to the individual taxpayers. But we must face the fact that it might prove the most practical route to first nationalize the property as a prelude to redistribution. Thus, how could the ownership of General Dynamics be transferred to the deserving taxpayers without first being nationalized enroute? And, further more, even if the government should decide to nationalize General Dynamics – without compensation, of course – per se and not as a prelude to redistribution to the taxpayers, this is not immoral or something to be combatted. For it would only mean that one gang of thieves – the government – would be confiscating property from another previously cooperating gang, the corporation that has lived off the government. I do not often agree with John Kenneth Galbraith, but his recent suggestion to nationalize businesses which get more than 75% of their revenue from government, or from the military, has considerable merit. Certainly it does not mean aggression against private property, and, furthermore, we could expect a considerable diminution of zeal from the military-industrial complex if much of the profits were taken out of war and plunder. And besides, it would make the American military machine less efficient, being governmental, and that is surely all to the good. But why stop at 75%? Fifty percent seems to be a reasonable cutoff point on whether an organization is largely public or largely private.

And there is another consideration. Dow Chemical, for example, has been heavily criticized for making napalm for the U.S. military machine. The percentage of its sales coming from napalm is undoubtedly small, so that on a percentage basis the company may not seem very guilty; but napalm is and can only be an instrument of mass murder, and therefore Dow Chemical is heavily up to its neck in being an accessory and hence a co-partner in the mass murder in Vietnam. No percentage of sales, however small, can absolve its guilt.

This brings us to Karl's point about slaves. One of the tragic aspects of the emancipation of the serfs in Russia in 1861 was that while the serfs gained their personal freedom, the land – their means of production and of life, their land was retained under the ownership of their feudal masters. The land should have gone to the serfs themselves, for under the homestead principle they had tilled the land and deserved its title. Furthermore, the serfs were entitled to a host of reparations from their masters for the centuries of oppression and exploitation. The fact that the land remained in the hands of the lords paved the way inexorably for the Bolshevik Revolution, since the revolution that had freed the serfs remained unfinished.

The same is true of the abolition of slavery in the United States. The slaves gained their freedom, it is true, but the land, the plantations that they had tilled and therefore deserved to own under the homestead principle, remained in the hands of their former masters. Furthermore, no reparations were granted the slaves for their oppression out of the hides of their masters. Hence the abolition of slavery remained unfinished, and the seeds of a new revolt have remained to intensify to the present day. Hence, the great importance of the shift in Negro demands from greater welfare handouts to "reparations," reparations for the years of slavery and exploitation and for the failure to grant the Negroes their land, the failure to heed the

Radical abolitionist's call for "40 acres and a mule" to the former slaves. In many cases, moreover, the old plantations and the heirs and descendants of the former slaves can be identified, and the reparations can become highly specific indeed.

Alan Milchman, in the days when he was a brilliant young libertarian activist, first pointed out that libertarians had misled themselves by making their main dichotomy "government" vs. "private" with the former bad and the latter good. Government, he pointed out, is after all not a mystical entity but a group of individuals, "private" individuals if you will, acting in the manner of an organized criminal gang. But this means that there may also be "private" criminals as well as people directly affiliated with the government. What we libertarians object to, then, is not government per se but crime, what we object to is unjust or criminal property titles; what we are for is not "private" property per se but just, innocent, non-criminal private property. It is justice vs. injustice, innocence vs. criminality that must be our major libertarian focus.

# PART SIX

----------

## Inequality and Social Safety Nets

# 33

*Anarchy without Bombs* (n.p., March 13, 2010) <http://anarchywithoutbombs. com/2010/03/13/let-the-free-market- eat-the-rich/> (Aug. 22, 2011).

# LET THE FREE MARKET EAT THE RICH!
## Economic Entropy as Revolutionary Redistribution

*JEREMY WEILAND*
*(2011)*

## ANARCHY AND DISTRIBUTION

CIVIL SOCIETY HAS BECOME SO CONFUSED WITH THE INSTITUTION OF THE STATE THAT anarchists often find it difficult to extricate one from the other when positing a voluntary society. The effects of privilege permeate our culture, our infrastructure, our economic relationships, and our thinking. There-fore, the ability to describe a coherent and distinctive picture of a post-state, post-privilege world is crucial in that it throws contemporary con-structs of privilege into stark relief. While disputes about proper means towards a stateless society abound in the anarchist milieu, the most striking distinctions can be discovered by examining the varied predictions of the likely ends of anarchism. Perhaps nothing sets these approaches apart and divides efforts more than competing visions of just property distribution.

A long running debate among anarchists, especially between the individualist and collectivist schools, centers around the justice of wealth disparities. Certainly the existence of the State serves to enrich particular interests at the expense of others, but in anarchy would the rich dominate society – just as they do with the State? Should private property be abolished altogether to force an egalitarian society into existence? Or will private property be the basis for a new, voluntary order where the wealth gap will no longer matter? Even if we could immediately switch off the institutions that forcibly manipulate society, many fear that the legacy of privilege and accumulated wealth could persist for some time, distorting markets and continuing the frustrate the balance of power between individuals.

Individualist anarchists have had a variety of responses to the problems of historical property and wealth maldistribution. Even anarcho-capitalists who see large scale social coordination as the natural direction of society have different views, such as Hans Hermann Hoppe's theory of a natural elite and Murray Rothbard's support of syndicalist takeover of State-supported corporations. On the other side of the coin, left-leaning individualists also entertain a variety of approaches: from agorist advocacy of revolutionary entrepreneurship as a leveling force to mutualists such as Benjamin Tucker and Kevin Carson speculating about the possible need for short term State sponsored redistribution and reform.

At the root of all these competing theories, the key question for anarchists remains: what does a stateless society look like? What exactly are we working towards? It is this difference of vision that divides the efforts of anarchists much more than purely strategic differences. Is a more ecumenical anarchism possible – one that can bring the schools together, at least for activist purposes, not by fighting over predictions and visions but by agreeing on the means by which a voluntary society is achieved?

In the midst of all this theorizing, it is easy to forget that anarchy is – anarchy becomes defined by – however humans naturally interact, not how we wish they would interact. In other words, true anarchy is an empirical reality, and we have only to discover it by removing privilege. Arguing over what it shall be and shall not be presumes we can dictate how humans interact, a positively authoritarian concept. Whatever human nature might be, any anarchism worth pursuing starts there, and the kernel of proportionality and balance that could inform this matter may be sought there as well. Given this approach to anarchism, what can human nature tell us about distributive justice?

In any statist society, those who benefit from the status quo rely first and foremost on the stability and security of the social order. How they achieve this defines politics as we experience it. The purpose of this essay is to demonstrate how large scale aggregations of wealth require an outside stabilizing force and defensive agency to maintain, and how in a free, dynamic market there are entropies that move imbalances back to equilibrium. There is also a proposed basis for a relative equilibrium among people once privileges are abolished. This investigation will identify two main institutions that arise from state intervention in capitalist society: corporations and personal estates.

## THE MODERN CORPORATION

The modern corporation is a legal entity chartered by the State. Corporations benefit from an arsenal of privileges, such as fiat entity status, personhood and limited liability, which serve to set the rules of the market on terms favorable to corporate investors and managers. The trend has always been to correct any perceived problems with big business by large, top-down regulation, rather than to reexamine the legal constructs that give these institutions such outsized power in our society.

For instance, it is conceivable that a firm could argue effectively in front of a judge for certain of the rights of being a human citizen on a case by case basis, but current established law mandates a clumsy legal equivalence between living human beings and abstract organizations of people and assets (which is historically dubious). The benefit to big business, of course, is to regularize and simplify business legal proceedings, setting aside the legal advantages this gives corporations over individual humans. In the United States, for instance, the ability to exercise first and fourth amendment rights as if the firm were a human being results in corporate campaign contributions and protection from random inspections. It is interesting to see the framers' document limiting government prerogative used to defend not merely the rights of human beings but those of the government's own abstract inventions.

Yet while human rights are invoked, privileges granted by the State to corporations that no human can claim, such as limited liability, represent a fiat subsidy. Imagine the cost of privately insuring the value of the total market capitalization of the world's corporations! But the utility of the subsidy goes even further, because it allows investors to hire managers who have a legal mandate to pursue profits while maintaining a distance from the way the profits are pursued. Highly capitalized firms, who by their sheer size wield far more potential for harm than any single individual, essentially obfuscate the way decisions are made so that if third parties to the stockholder-manager relationship are harmed, stockholders cannot lose more than their investment.

The imbalance of responsibility this enables cannot be underestimated, for it goes to the very heart of corporate economic behavior. What would be different about business, socioeconomics, and politics if stockholders knew that their managers' activities would leave them fully liable for the actions of the corporation and could lose their savings, their car, their house? Limited liability and corporate personhood make possible a way of doing business in a far riskier way than normal people would. How do we know this? Because few people, anarchist or not, would limit the liability of regular human beings, knowing that it is the consequences of undesirable behavior such as violence or theft that helps prevent it.

In a free market, corporations would not be able to rely on the State for their very existence. Any ability to do business as an entity would come from the consent and cooperation of the market – customers, suppliers, contractors, service providers, banks, but most importantly management. Without a Securities and Exchange Commission and intrusive reporting requirements, oversight, and regulatory enforcement, it would be very hard to protect the shareholders at firms of any appreciable size and organizational complexity from outright fraud in a variety of ways. The well-understood legal relationships that govern so much capital finance and business activity would become much more ad hoc and peculiar. Shares in corporations would become even less uniform constructs from business to business, since their terms could vary wildly and they couldn't simply be traded as almost fungible commodities. Unpredictability and risk would skyrocket, which is a much more favorable environment for the small-time entrepreneur than the big, clumsy, bureaucratic corporation.

Think about the huge stabilizing effect of the federal government for making big business anything less than a total ripoff for investors right from the start. Think about the ways government regulation rationalizes markets to make them safe for large industries to exploit and oligopolize. Think about how much leeway the modern CEO is afforded to run the business in pursuit of short term gain, with stockholders often supporting them even as they engage in questionable activities. Enron's reckless destruction of shareholder value is hardly remarkable, when you think about the level of complexity in which they schemed and strategized – the fact that it doesn't happen more often is (until you check your tax bill and realize you're subsidizing the stability and security of others' investments!).

## THE PERSONAL ESTATE

Obviously the most direct way in which people benefit from the institutional character of our statist society is through direct ownership. While there are few (if any) rich people who aren't heavily and diversely invested in corporate capitalism and share in its redistribution of wealth and special favors from the government, there are additional State provisions to benefit individuals. Unlike corporate privileges, those which govern the stability of personal estates arguably serve the interests of more modest individuals, especially the middle class. However, I intend to show that the rich benefit far more from fiat stability and socialized security than the rest of us.

The biggest subsidy enjoyed by the wealthy lies in government regulation of finance. By regulating banking through inspections, audits, and the centralized monetary maintenance practiced by the Federal Reserve System, depositors enjoy a level of stability in the system that is quite unrivaled in history. Of course, regular joes like you and I prefer our current experience to frequent crashes and bank runs, but there's a catch: we don't pay for this "service" in proportion to our deposits (or the interest we earn!). Instead, we help subsidize the regulation and maintenance of the financial system from which the elite depositors benefit disproportionately.

Rich depositors are more likely to invest in instruments and accounts which yield higher interests rates. Plus, they're more likely to earn a greater amount of their income directly from the interest on their deposits. The barriers to entry in banking prevent individuals from forming their own mutual banks and force them to rely on the aggregated wealth of big depositors at some level of the hierarchical financial establishment. And because the rich can afford to pay for maintenance of their wealth by managers, accountants, and brokers, they are more likely to anticipate and capitalize upon market shifts than us.

Keep in mind that central regulation and maintenance of markets, groomed and rationalized by the Federal Reserve System, the Federal Deposit Insurance Corporation, and other departments encourages the sort of investment patterns that count on steady profits and interest – phenomena much more likely to benefit the wealthy than those of us investing in 401-Ks and IRAs. By lowering risks, any entrepreneurial profit opportunities for the little guy that regulation kills translate into the stability of markets and the steadiness of investment income. Of course, that benefits those who've already accumulated capital much more than those of us who've yet to achieve our fortune.

However, the extent of State intervention to benefit the rich extends beyond finance into the very real area of asset security. The rich depend on the stability and predictability of systems that ensure and protect their title to their property, but again their benefit from these phenomena dwarfs ours. For example, they count on the government keeping a central repository of property titles to justify excluding others. This takes property off the market and thus raises the value of their property. While it is true that middle class homeowners benefit from these systems, it does not benefit them to nearly the degree it does the rich. Socializing the costs of kicking people off one's land necessarily favors those who have more land to guard.

Police patrols of moneyed neighborhoods provide an example of socialized security, where defense and sentry costs are not paid directly by the beneficiaries. Sure, many wealthy types hire security guards, but they would have to hire many more – and pay much higher insurance premiums – if it were not for public law enforcement at least helping to defend their property, nor the extensive, expensive system of socialized criminal investigation that makes it less likely property will stay stolen and criminals remain at large.

## THE ENTROPY OF AGGREGATED WEALTH

As I stated earlier, we may find the answer to the problem of persistent wealth imbalances in human nature. Two aspects of that nature are greed and envy. In a market without socialized regulation, stockholders are in constant danger of management and employees siphoning off profits and imperiling the long term viability of the business. Rich individuals face similar uncertainties of theft and fraud by those they employ to maintain and protect their assets. Because the lack of a State would force these costs to be internalized within the entity rather than externalized onto the public, it is highly likely that the costs of maintaining these outsized aggregations of wealth would begin to deplete it.

The balance of power between the rich and non-rich is key here. Direct plundering of wealth, though fraud or theft, threatens the rich in a crippling way. It raises their costs directly in proportion to their wealth, either through insurance costs, defense costs, or losses. They have to worry not just about outside threats, but also the threats posed by their servants, employees, and even their family members. Because the wealth is centralized around one individual or one management team, it is near impossible to find any fair way to distribute the responsibilities of stewardship without distributing the wealth itself. Having a lot of stuff becomes more trouble than it's worth.

Meanwhile, less rich people economize on these costs by banding together with other modest individuals to either hire outside defense (socializing protection on their own, voluntary terms) or by personally organizing to defend property (via institutions such as militias). Because the ratio of person to wealth is relatively greater, there are more interested individuals wiling to play a role in defense and maintenance of property. The distribution of the wealth over more people necessarily eases its protection. And since everybody has basically the same amount of stuff, nobody has an interest in taking advantage of, nor stealing from, others.

In fact, normal human greed suggests that there will always be an element of society that wishes to steal and cheat others. In anarchy, the wealth offer themselves as easy targets to such criminals, because big estates are harder to defend and so invite more opportunities for plunder. Additionally, it is far more likely that wealthy estates will be targeted because, for instance, it is easier to steal a million dollars worth of cash or property from one location such as a bank or mansion than it is to rob a thousand or so common people. The larger the disparity in wealth, the more intensively the wealthy will be targeted by criminals.

On the other hand, normal people would necessarily be less likely to be targeted by the criminal, for a few reasons. First, since the ratio of human bodies to wealth in a modest community would be much greater, the deterrent effect would be insurmountable to all but the most stupid crooks. Second, once statist regulations and privileges stop making an honest living less of a bad deal, the criminal elements in a modest community are more likely to share in the legitimate wealth of the economy, easing their need to prey on their neighbors. Markets freed from dehumanizing, deracinated centralization imposed for corporate convenience would be fathomable, with plenty of opportunities for entrepreneurship. While by no means a utopia, a genuinely free market would ease the pressures on the lower and middle classes.

## THE FREE MARKET AS EGALITARIAN EQUALIZER

This phenomenon of disadvantaged rich and advantaged poor, brought about by the costs of estate and business management, suggests an interesting dynamic. It may be that in a free market there will exist a natural, mean personal wealth value, beyond which diminishing returns enter quickly, and below which one is extremely disposed towards enrichment. If this is true, then that means that normal, productive, and non-privileged people will tend to have similar estate values. This wide distribution of wealth will tend to reinforce bottom-up society and a balance of power unrivaled in history (except maybe in frontier experiences).

In a stateless society, institutions for business and personal organization must derive their permanence from their usefulness not just to an elite few, but from the respect of the entire community – customers, suppliers, neighbors, etc. An entity that can operate efficiently and deliver a steady stream of income, whether an estate or a corporate business, becomes less viable the larger it grows because internal transaction and maintenance costs start to skyrocket. This is a function not of wealth itself, but rather of the inherent difficulty in convincing those with less to honor and defend the property of those with more. The more people benefit from a body of wealth, the more people will support it.

Indeed, the State can be seen as a mechanism for acquiring the consent of the governed to sign onto a program of stabilization that is inherently artificial, precisely due to its disproportionate dividends to established elites. The State co-opts authentic community support or opposition and channels it into modes that are predictable and stable, establishing its institutional identity as indispensable mediator between the very interests in which it promotes opposition. But authentic community stability is no harder to realize in a genuine, stateless society where people participate only in voluntary organizations. Similarly, inauthentic, imposed stability usually benefits those who cannot maintain their position without outside help. Wealthy interests use the State as a way to marshal public support without yielding control or spreading the wealth, as it were.

A truly free market without subsidized security, regulation, and arbitration imposes costs on large scale aggregations of assets that quickly deplete them. I do not think they would be able to survive for very long without the State, even if "natural elites" exist or some form of social darwinism is proven correct, because natural hierarchies such as those would not need State intervention to maintain their cohesion. One can chalk this up to the fickle and often dark side of human nature, but it's a phenomenon that we cannot just wish away – indeed, we should see a place for these dynamics in the legitimate, bottom-up society.

This theory is not an ironclad prescription of how anarchy must emerge. It is merely a demonstration of how individualist and collectivist visions can both be served without compromising either's interests. Markets and egalitarian distribution of property and wealth are not necessarily mutually exclusive. Perhaps authentic libertarian means of genuinely free markets, taken to their logical conclusion, can effect far more egalitarian and redistributionist ends than we ever dreamed – not as a function of any central State, but rather as a result of its absence.

# 34

*Bad Press Articles* (Bad Press, n.d.)
<http://www.bad-press.net/Bad_Press/
articles_files/Individualism%20and%20
Inequality.htm> (Aug. 22, 2011).

# INDIVIDUALISM AND INEQUALITY

### JOE PEACOTT
### (2007)

## ECONOMICS: A MEANS OR AN END FOR ANARCHISTS?

ALL ANARCHISTS SEEK A WORLD FREE OF GOVERNMENT AND EVERY OTHER COERCIVE institution. This is what makes them libertarians. But this is often the only thing on which they can agree among themselves.

Different anarchists have all sorts of priorities and visions for the future society. Their ideas about what goals are most important to achieve in an anarchist world influence their thoughts about how economic exchanges, decision-making, and social relations would take place in a libertarian setting. For instance, many anarchists seem to consider economic equality as their primary aim, and a libertarian social order organized on some sort of collective or communal basis as the way to achieve it. They seek anarchy because they believe it is the best method of attaining economic parity.

Individualists, on the other hand, believe that individual freedom of action, as long as it does not impinge on the equal freedom of others, is the most important goal of anarchists. According to this view, libertarian economic and social interactions should serve to promote and protect the autonomy of the participants. And individualists believe that an anarchist society based on private property, free exchange, and use and occupancy land tenure would be best suited to this purpose.

## PRIVATE PROPERTY AND CAPITALISM

Anarchist individualists advocate private ownership (or in the case of land, tenure) of property and free exchange of goods and services both now and in any future anarchist society. We believe that individuals should retain the full value of whatever they produce and should be free to occupy and use only that land which they can put to use without employing the labor of others. Of course, being anarchists, we also maintain that individuals would be free to pool their labor, property, and/or land in order to increase their economic efficiency, better provide for others in need, or simply enjoy the company of their fellows. But these would still be voluntary, private arrangements, wherein the individuals concerned would share the products of their labor and contribute to the joint project as long as they see fit, while retaining their freedom to leave the enterprise if and when they so desire.

Although individualists envision a society based on private property, we oppose the economic relationships of capitalism, whose supporters misuse words like private enterprise and free markets to justify a system of monopoly ownership in land and the means of production which allows some to skim off part or even most of the wealth produced by the labor of others. Such a system exists only because it is protected by the armed power of government, which secures title to unjustly acquired and held land, monopolizes the supply of credit and money, and criminalizes attempts by workers to take full ownership of the means of production they use to create wealth. This state intervention in economic transactions makes it impossible for most workers to become truly independent of the predation of capitalists, banks, and landlords. Individualists argue that without the state to enforce the rules of the capitalist economy, workers would not allow themselves to be exploited by these thieves and capitalism would not be able to exist.

## INEQUALITY IN AN INDIVIDUALIST SOCIETY

One of the criticisms of individualist economic proposals raised by other anarchists is that a system based on private ownership would result in some level of difference among people in regard to the quality or quantity of possessions they have. In a society where people are able to realize the full value of their labor, one who works harder or better than another will possess or have the ability to acquire more things than someone who works less or is less skilled at a particular occupation. But economic inequality would not have the same significance in a non-capitalist anarchist society that it does in today's societies.

The differences in wealth that arise in an individualist community would likely be relatively small. Without the ability to profit from the labor of others, generate interest from providing credit, or extort rent from letting out land or property, individuals would not be capable of generating the huge quantities of assets that people can in a capitalist system. Furthermore, the anarchist with more things does not have them at the expense of another, since they are the result of the owner's own effort. If someone with less wealth wishes to have more, they can work more, harder, or better. There is no injustice in one person working 12 hours a day and six days a week in order to buy a boat, while another chooses to work three eight hour days a week and is content with a less extravagant lifestyle. If one can generate income only by hard work, there is an upper limit to the number and kind of things one can buy and own.

More important, though, than the actual amount of economic inequality between individuals is whether the person who has more wealth thereby acquires more power or advantage over others. In a statist world, one can buy political favors with one's money and influence government action affecting oneself and others. This would not be an option in an anarchist society since there would be no government or other political structure through which individuals or groups could coerce others and use their greater wealth to further aggrandize themselves through political means, as happens in a society of rulers and subjects.

But even if money could not buy power in a libertarian community, some might object to a private property system and its inevitable inequality on another basis. They may believe that economic differences are necessarily unjust, or that people unable to work much or at all because of physical limitations would be unable to obtain the resources to make a life for themselves. Individualists would argue that economic inequality of some sort is inevitable in any truly free society. People have varied needs, wants, and mental and physical abilities and are therefore unequal in many ways. Some produce more, some produce less, and there is no injustice in the fact that this would result in different amounts of wealth. A society or community that prohibited those who so desired from retaining the full value of what they produce in order to create an artificial economic leveling would infringe on the freedom of individuals and thus violate a basic anarchist principle.

As for those who produce little or nothing because of some disability, there are other means of providing for the less fortunate than communal economic arrangements. There is a long tradition of groups of individuals taking care of sick, injured, and otherwise incapacitated people through voluntary organizations from friendly societies to cooperatives of various sorts to trade unions. People who value private property are no less benevolent than those who favor free collectives, and would figure out any number of ways to care for those in need of assistance from others.

## INEQUALITY IN THE COMMUNE AND COLLECTIVE

While individualists concede that there would be some economic inequality in the society they promote, their critics among other anarchists often presume that the kind of societies they envision would be completely egalitarian and free of inequity. But, although the collectives proposed by anarchist syndicalists, communist anarchists, and libertarian socialists might well be free of economic differences, this would likely take place only at the expense of the liberty of some of the members of such communities, creating an inequality in individual freedom.

It is unlikely that people in any future world would all be of one mind about everything, any more than they are today. Some will wish to live and work alone, interacting with others only when necessary. Others will wish to work in groups and share everything. And others, perhaps most, will prefer one of these models to another at different times and for different purposes, or even some combination of the two. And any anarchist society worthy of the name must allow for this.

As noted above, individualists believe that pooling of resources, land, or anything else by autonomous individuals can be fully compatible with individual freedom. Unfortunately, however, there are some anarchists who advocate the outright abolition of private property, not allowing any opportunity for those who prefer a different economic arrangement. If such an economic model was imposed on the world, those who wished to live otherwise would not have the freedom to do so. Allowing people no alternative to joining the local commune or syndicate would simply replace the tyranny of state capitalism with the oppression of an involuntary "community." There would consequently be an inequality between the society, or more likely, the committee or other "delegates" who presume to represent it, and the individual. The group will make decisions and the dissenting individual must comply. Thus, in many a collective or commune no one will be poorer than another, but some will certainly be less free.

This is not to imply that all communist or collectivist anarchists believe in imposing their economic views on those who view the world differently. Many who advocate some form of communal society are as committed to personal liberty as are private property advocates. But there is a tendency on the part of many anarchists to present a "one size fits everyone" economic model for the future, not realizing the possible implications of such an all-encompassing ideal.

## FOR ECONOMIC AND SOCIAL FREEDOM

Individualists see the economic system they propose as simply the means to an end. And that end is a free society of free individuals. We believe that only free economic exchange, based on private property, can produce and protect every individual's autonomy, their freedom to live as they see fit, which we believe is the essential goal of the anarchist project. Moreover, while such an arrangement would encourage and reward individual initiative, more collectively-oriented people would be free to construct whatever group enterprises they wish by coming together and sharing production, consumption, or both.

People in a society based on individual ownership of property and tenure of land would be able to choose whatever economic or social system best suits their interests, personal relationships, geographic location, and temperaments, without sacrificing the option of changing their minds and making other arrangements whenever they decide to do so. While some amount of economic inequality would be unavoidable in such a world, schemes which seek to bring about absolute parity in wealth and possessions would simply produce another kind of inequality, where individual wants and desires would be subservient to those of the group, and limits would be placed on the freedom of those who wish to live their lives in their own way. Such social inequality between and among individuals and groups and the limits on liberty which it would produce are precisely what individualists, and, one would hope, all other genuine anarchists, seek to eliminate from the world.

## 35

*Formulations* (Winter 1993-4) <http://
freenation.org/a/f1213.html> <http://
praxeology.net/libertariannation/a/
f1213.html> (Aug. 22, 2011).

# HOW GOVERNMENT SOLVED THE HEALTH CARE CRISIS

## *RODERICK T. LONG*
## *(1993)*

TODAY, WE ARE CONSTANTLY BEING TOLD, THE UNITED STATES FACES A HEALTH CARE crisis. Medical costs are too high, and health insurance is out of reach of the poor. The cause of this crisis is never made very clear, but the cure is obvious to nearly everybody: government must step in to solve the problem.

Eighty years ago, Americans were also told that their nation was facing a health care crisis. Then, however, the complaint was that medical costs were too low, and that health insurance was too accessible. But in that era, too, government stepped forward to solve the problem. And boy, did it solve it!

In the late 19th and early 20th centuries, one of the primary sources of health care and health insurance for the working poor in Britain, Australia, and the United States was the fraternal society. Fraternal societies (called "friendly societies" in Britain and Australia) were voluntary mutual-aid associations. Their descendants survive among us today in the form of the Shriners, Elks, Masons, and similar organizations, but these no longer play the central role in American life they formerly did. As recently as 1920, over one-quarter of all adult Americans were members of fraternal societies. (The figure was still higher in Britain and Australia.) Fraternal societies were particularly popular among blacks and immigrants. (Indeed, Teddy Roosevelt's famous attack on "hyphenated Americans" was motivated in part by hostility to the immigrants' fraternal societies; he and other Progressives sought to "Americanize" immigrants by making them dependent for support on the democratic state, rather than on their own independent ethnic communities.)

The principle behind the fraternal societies was simple. A group of working-class people would form an association (or join a local branch, or "lodge," of an existing association) and pay monthly fees into the association's treasury; individual members would then be able to draw on the pooled resources in time of need. The fraternal societies thus operated as a form of self-help insurance company.

Turn-of-the-century America offered a dizzying array of fraternal societies to choose from. Some catered to a particular ethnic or religious group; others did not. Many offered entertainment and social life to their members, or engaged in community service. Some "fraternal" societies were run entirely by and for women. The kinds of services from which members could choose often varied as well, though the most commonly offered were life insurance, disability insurance, and "lodge practice."

"Lodge practice" refers to an arrangement, reminiscent of today's HMOs, whereby a particular society or lodge would contract with a doctor to provide medical care to its members. The doctor received a regular salary on a retainer basis, rather than charging per item; members would pay a yearly fee and then call on the doctor's services as needed. If medical services were found unsatisfactory, the doctor would be penalized, and the contract might not be renewed. Lodge members reportedly enjoyed the degree of customer control this system afforded them. And the tendency to overuse the physician's services was kept in check by the fraternal society's own "self-policing"; lodge members who wanted to avoid future increases in premiums were motivated to make sure that their fellow members were not abusing the system.

Most remarkable was the low cost at which these medical services were provided. At the turn of the century, the average cost of "lodge practice" to an individual member was between one and two dollars a year. A day's wage would pay for a year's worth of medical care. By contrast, the average cost of medical service on the regular market was between one and two dollars per visit. Yet licensed physicians, particularly those who did not come from "big name" medical schools, competed vigorously for lodge contracts, perhaps because of the security they offered; and this competition continued to keep costs low.

The response of the medical establishment, both in America and in Britain, was one of outrage; the institution of lodge practice was denounced in harsh language and apocalyptic tones. Such low fees, many doctors charged, were bankrupting the medical profession. Moreover, many saw it as a blow to the dignity of the profession that trained physicians should be eagerly bidding for the chance to serve as the hirelings of lower-class tradesmen. It was particularly detestable that such uneducated and socially inferior people should be permitted to set fees for the physicians' services, or to sit in judgment on professionals to determine whether their services had been satisfactory. The government, they demanded, must do something.

And so it did. In Britain, the state put an end to the "evil" of lodge practice by bringing health care under political control. Physicians' fees would now be determined by panels of trained professionals (i.e., the physicians themselves) rather than by ignorant patients. State-financed medical care edged out lodge practice; those who were being forced to pay taxes for "free" health care whether they wanted it or not had little incentive to pay extra for health care through the fraternal societies, rather than using the government care they had already paid for.

In America, it took longer for the nation's health care system to be socialized, so the medical establishment had to achieve its ends more indirectly; but the essential result was the same. Medical societies like the AMA imposed sanctions on doctors who dared to sign lodge practice contracts. This might have been less effective if such medical societies had not had access to government power; but in fact, thanks to governmental grants of privilege, they controlled the medical licensure procedure, thus ensuring that those in their disfavor would be denied the right to practice medicine.

Such licensure laws also offered the medical establishment a less overt way of combating lodge practice. It was during this period that the AMA made the requirements for medical licensure far stricter than they had previously been. Their reason, they claimed, was to raise the quality of medical care. But the result was that the number of physicians fell, competition dwindled, and medical fees rose; the vast pool of physicians bidding for lodge practice contracts had been abolished. As with any market good, artificial restrictions on supply created higher prices – a particular hardship for the working-class members of fraternal societies.

The final death blow to lodge practice was struck by the fraternal societies themselves. The National Fraternal Congress – attempting, like the AMA, to reap the benefits of cartelization – lobbied for laws decreeing a legal minimum on the rates fraternal societies could charge. Unfortunately for the lobbyists, the lobbying effort was successful; the unintended consequence was that the minimum rates laws made the services of fraternal societies no longer competitive. Thus the National Fraternal Congress' lobbying efforts, rather than creating a formidable mutual-aid cartel, simply destroyed the fraternal societies' market niche – and with it the opportunity for low-cost health care for the working poor.

Why do we have a crisis in health care costs today? Because government "solved" the last one.

# 36

Contemporary Individualist Anarchism: The
Broadsides of the Boston Anarchist Drinking
Brigade, 1988-2000, Political Notes 184,
by Joe Peacott, Jim Baker, et al. (London:
Libertarian Alliance 2003) 18-9 <http://
www.libertarian.co.uk/lapubs/polin/po-
lin184.pdf> (Aug. 22, 2011).

# THE POVERTY OF THE
# WELFARE STATE

## JOE PEACOTT
## (1998)

As the government, at various levels, attempts to cut back on welfare and other entitlement payments to poor people and/or require people to work in exchange for their welfare benefits, anarchists in the United States have been talking and writing about what the appropriate anarchist response should be. Some have come to the position that anarchists should support state welfare for poor people and actively oppose cutbacks, arguing that poor people deserve state assistance since they are the victims of capitalist economic relations, that capitalist corporations are a greater threat to poor and working people than the state, and that forcing people to work will cause even worse working conditions for many than already exist, further impoverishing people. In addition, the argument that, since the state provides welfare to corporations and the rich, it is only fair that the poor should get some, is also made by some anarchists. While these arguments are made in good faith, and with the intent of helping poor people, anarchists should be looking into the matter more deeply and coming up with critiques of state welfare and solutions to poverty more consistent with libertarian thinking, instead of falling in line behind the modern nanny state.

It certainly makes sense to make the best of the existence of a welfare state and take advantage of the programs that have been instituted in response to the demands and movements of radical or progressive statists, but it is quite another thing to look to these programs as the preferred way to solve social problems. Calling for the dismantling of the welfare system for poor people may not be the best place for anarchists to start in the fight against the very existence of the state, but arguing for its continued maintenance – or even its expansion – as if this were the only way to help people in need, is not the right course of action either. As we do in regard to other social problems, anarchists should be advocating nonstatist solutions to the problems of poverty. While doing away entirely with government is the ultimate remedy for poverty, other measures which could be proposed and implemented under the state, such as decreased taxation to increase the wealth of the working poor, deregulation of health care to decrease health care costs, and a return to mutual aid societies in place of extortionate insurance companies, are much more in line with anarchist principles than cheerleading for AFDC.

Anarchists historically have tried to lessen the influence of government in the lives of poor and working people. When faced with poverty, anarchists have advocated self-organization of and direct action by workers to secure at least a greater portion of the fruit of their labor. When fighting battles against corporations, anarchists did not call for the government to enact labor laws, but criticized the state for using its police and military to defend corporate interests. They demanded the state get out of the way, not that it rescue the poor. And anarchists have foreseen a future where competent, independent individuals and/or groups, freed from the restraints of statist society, take care of themselves and their associates in whatever ways make sense to them. This historical anarchist vision would appear to have been lost on some in modern times.

A number of anarchists seem to have bought the idea that since government can sometimes be more responsive to the demands of poor people than private capitalists, the state can be seen as a guardian against their depredations. This is inconsistent both with the anarchist analysis that the state props up capitalism, and with the reality that in some cases private companies provide better for their employees and customers than state enterprises care for their clients and workers. At least part of the reason it is, at times, easier to squeeze concessions out of the state, is that it costs the individuals in government nothing: they will simply force working people to foot the bill for any increase in welfare benefits by increasing taxes. In the case of a private capitalist enterprises, the owners of the business are not always able to pass on the costs of better employees benefits to the consumer, and consequently may lose some of their profits if they give in to workers' demands for higher pay or other improved working conditions. But the only time either the state or capitalist businesses provide any benefits to anyone but themselves and their allies, is when they are pressured to do so. Welfare, social security, and other government benefit schemes were created in response to social movements, not out of governmental beneficence, just as good benefits in many private corporations are the result of strong labor movements which forced the owners to reimburse the workers for a greater portion of their labor than was the case previously. Governments and capitalist enterprises have largely the same interests, and both can be forced to make concessions by vigorous opposition from their subjects or employees.

While workers pressuring their employees for a better deal is simply a case of people demanding part of what is rightfully theirs anyway, recipients of welfare payments and other benefits are asking the government to take someone else's money and give it to them. Many advocates of maintaining the current welfare system, however, correctly state that it doesn't cost very much in the greater scheme of things. State spending on weapons of mass destruction and payments to corporations are each much more costly than welfare programs for poor individuals and families. Additionally, many working people, not commonly thought of as welfare recipients do, in fact, receive such benefits, as when middle class people get medicaid to pay for their nursing home expenses, or working people obtain free care from hospitals, the costs of which are covered by the government. While this is all true, this does not justify government theft of working people's money to give to someone else. The money raised from taxation to fund corporate welfare, AFDC, and medicaid is stolen property, as is the money from compulsory fees on insurance companies to fund free care programs, which the insurers pass on to their customers. The rich don't pay taxes, and the very poor don't pay taxes. It is the huge number of working people in the middle who do, and who support the other two groups. And, while many in the middle get some of their extorted money back in the form of benefits, most of them pay out more than they receive, otherwise there wouldn't be any left for the rich and the poor.

The rich and their corporations are wealthy because they or their ancestors were able unjustly to acquire some of the wealth produced by others. They were able to do this only because the state and its police and military support the institutions of profit, interest, and rent which transfer money from working people to those who "own" businesses, banks and dwellings.

Rich people don't deserve the wealth they already possess and certainly should not receive any of the money that is stolen directly from workers by the government, or any of the other advantages they receive at the expense of taxpayers. Among the poor people who receive money or other benefits from the state, on the other hand, there are those who are in genuine need. Some are truly the victims of circumstances largely beyond their control, and others have made bad choices and expect or hope that others will bail them out. But there are also welfare recipients who are simply parasites who feel that others should work to support them in the lifestyle to which they've become accustomed (just like the rich). Being poor does not make one virtuous or deserving. However, since at least some poor people are deserving of assistance it is preferable that tax money fund AFDC, medicaid, and food stamps, rather than corporate welfare and the military, but none of the recipients, rich or poor, are entitled to the money extracted by force from working people.

Since such forcible transfers of money are not acceptable, we need to seek other, non-coercive means, to enable people to better fend for themselves. As mentioned earlier, tax cuts, health care deregulation, and voluntary mutual aid societies would all mitigate poverty, even if implemented in a statist society. Getting rid of the state and its protection of capitalist economic relations entirely will produce even more options for people to make their own way, resulting in higher incomes; cheaper goods including health care, food, and housing; and, consequently, many fewer needy people. The end of government will mean the end of involuntary poverty, and therefore the end of the need for much of what now constitutes welfare. The small number of people unable to work who need assistance from the community can easily be helped by one form or another of mutual aid, depending on the economic structure of the community in which they live.

Anarchy is based, at least in part, on the idea that simply getting government out of the way would allow people to look at and solve their problems all by themselves. This also applies to poor people. They are generally not helpless incompetents who have no options other than having the state look out for them. In fact, poor people are victimized by corporations not because the state has failed to protect them, but because the state has prevented them from protecting themselves. Laws and other government action preserve capitalism with its profit, interest, and rent, all of which are theft from working people of all classes. Without the state and its armed thugs in the police and military, capitalism would not survive for long, since people would simply keep what was rightfully theirs and stop paying rent, do away with the banking monopoly, and work their factories and businesses for themselves. We don't need state welfare, we need state abolition.

# PART SEVEN

---

## Barriers to Entry and Fixed Costs of Living

# 37

The Freeman. Ideas on Liberty 59.8 (Oct.
2009): 17-21.

# HOW "INTELLECTUAL PROPERTY" IMPEDES COMPETITION

## KEVIN A. CARSON
## (2009)

A NY CONSIDERATION OF "INTELLECTUAL PROPERTY RIGHTS" MUST START FROM THE UN-derstanding that such "rights" undermine genuine property rights and hence are illegitimate in terms of libertarian principle. Real, tangible property rights result from natural scarcity and follow as a matter of course from the attempt to maintain occupancy of physical property that cannot be possessed by more than one person at a time.

"Intellectual property," on the other hand, creates artificial scarcity where it does not naturally exist and can only be enforced by invading real, tangible property and preventing the owner from using it in ways that violate the supposed intellectual property rights of others. As Stephan Kinsella points out, had a particularly gifted Cro-Magnon man been able to patent the building of log cabins, his heirs today would be entitled to prevent us from building cabins on our own land, with our own logs, until we paid whatever tribute they demanded.

The business model required by proprietary digital information is even more invasive of genuine property rights than was traditional copyright law. The digital copyright regime in force under the terms of the Digital Millennium Copyright Act, the WIPO Copyright Treaty, and the TRIPS provisions of the Uruguay Round of GATT, is focused entirely on preventing one from using his own hard drive and other property as he sees fit. It is actually illegal, thanks to such legislation, to sell hardware capable of circumventing DRM, or to publicize the codes enabling someone to circumvent it. As Cory Doctorow points out,

> It's funny that in the name of protecting "intellectual property," big media companies are willing to do such violence to the idea of real property – arguing that since everything we own, from our t-shirts to our cars to our ebooks, embody someone's copyright, patent and trademark, that we're basically just tenant farmers, living on the land of our gracious masters who've seen fit to give us a lease on our homes.

DRM prevents the easy transfer of content between platforms, even when it's simply a matter of the person who purchased a CD or DVD wanting to play it somewhere more convenient. And the DMCA legally prohibits circumventing such DRM, even when – again – the purchaser of the content simply wants to facilitate his own use on a wider and more convenient variety of platforms.

The levels of invasiveness required by "intellectual property," in the digital age, cannot be exaggerated. The intrusive DRM embedded in proprietary media, and the draconian legislation criminalizing technical means of circumvention, should make that clear. The logical tendency of the digital copyright regime was portrayed quite convincingly by Richard Stallman in a dystopian short story, "The Right to Read" (just Google it – it's well worth your time).

Corporations rely on increasingly authoritarian legislation to capture value from proprietary information. Johann Soderberg compares the way photocopiers were monitored in the old USSR, to protect the power of elites in that country from the free flow of information, to the way the means of digital reproduction are monitored in this country to protect corporate power.

Privileged, state-connected economic interests are becoming increasingly dependent on such controls. But unfortunately for them, such controls are becoming increasingly unenforceable thanks to Bittorrent, strong encryption, and proxy servers. The "DeCSS uprising," in which court injunctions against a code to hack DVD encryption met with the defiant publishing of the code on blogs, mirror sites and even T-shirts, is a case in point.

The unenforceability of "intellectual property" rights undermines the business model prevalent among a major share of privileged, state-connected firms.

## OBSOLETE BUSINESS MODEL

In the old days, the immense value of physical assets was the primary structural support for corporate boundaries, and in particular for the control of corporate hierarchies over human capital and other intangible assets.

The declining importance of physical assets relative to human capital has changed this. As human capital becomes the primary source of corporate equity, the old rationale for corporate institutional control is evaporating.

In the information and entertainment industries, before the digital and Internet revolutions, the initial outlay for entering the market was in the hundreds of thousands of dollars or more. The old electronic mass media, as Yochai Benkler put it, were "typified by high-cost hubs and cheap, ubiquitous, reception-only systems at the end. This led to a limited range of organizational models for production: those that could collect sufficient funds to set up a hub." The same was true of print periodicals, with the increasing cost of printing equipment from the mid-nineteenth century on serving as the main entry barrier for organizing the hubs. Between 1835 and 1850, the typical startup cost of a newspaper increased from $500 to $100,000 – or from roughly $10,000 to $2.38 million in 2005 dollars.

The networked economy, in contrast, is distinguished by "network architecture and the [low] cost of becoming a speaker." The central change that makes this possible is that "the basic physical capital necessary to express and communicate human meaning is the connected personal computer."

The desktop revolution and the Internet mean that the minimum capital outlay for entering most of the entertainment and information industry has fallen to a few thousand dollars, and the marginal cost of reproduction is zero. The networked environment, combined with endless varieties of cheap software for creating and editing content, makes it possible for the amateur to produce output of a quality once associated with giant publishing houses and recording companies. That is true of the software industry, the music industry (thanks to cheap equipment and software for high quality recording and sound editing), desktop publishing, and to a certain extent even to film (as witnessed by affordable editing technology and the success of *Sky Captain*). Podcasting technology makes it possible to distribute "radio" and "television" programming, at virtually no cost, to anyone with a broadband connection. A network of amateur contributors have peer-produced an encyclopedia, Wikipedia, which Britannica sees as a rival. As Tom Coates put it, "the gap between what can be accomplished at home and what can be accomplished in a work environment has narrowed dramatically over the last ten to fifteen years."

It's also true of news, with ever-expanding networks of amateurs in venues like Indymedia, alternative new operations like Robert Parry's and Greg Palast's, and natives and American troops blogging news firsthand from Iraq, at the very same time the traditional broadcasting networks are shutting down.

## AGENCY PROBLEMS, BREAKAWAY FIRMS

This has profoundly weakened corporate hierarchies in the information and entertainment industries, and created enormous agency problems as well. As human capital eclipses physical capital as the main source of corporate equity, it becomes increasingly feasible for the human capital assets to vote with their feet and take their skills elsewhere, forming "breakaway firms" and leaving their former employers as hollowed out firms that own little more than the company name. Maurice Saatchi's walkout from the Saatchi and Saatchi advertising agency, and the walkout of Salomon Brothers' traders responsible for 87% of the bond trading firm's profits, are two good examples. As organization theory writer Luigi Zingales put it,

> if we take the standpoint that the boundary of the firm is the point up to which top management has the ability to exercise power… the group was not an integral part of Salomon. It merely rented space, Salomon's name, and capital, and turned over some share of its profits as rent.

David Prychitko remarked on breakaway firms in the tech industry, back in the 1990s when it was barely underway:

> Old firms act as embryos for new firms. If a worker or group of workers is not satisfied with the existing firm, each has a skill which he or she controls, and can leave the firm with those skills and establish a new one. In the information age it is becoming more evident that a boss cannot control the workers as one did in the days when the assembly line was dominant. People cannot be treated as workhorses any longer, for the value of the production process is becoming increasingly embodied in the intellectual skills of the worker. This poses a new threat to the traditional firm if it denies participatory organization.

The appearance of breakaway computer firms leads one to question the extent to which our existing system of property rights in ideas and information actually protects bosses in other industries against the countervailing power of workers. Perhaps our current system of patents, copyrights, and other intellectual property rights not only impedes competition and fosters monopoly, as some Austrians argue. Intellectual property rights may also reduce the likelihood of breakaway firms in general, and discourage the shift to more participatory, cooperative formats.

In this environment, the only thing standing between the old information and media dinosaurs and their total collapse is their so-called "intellectual property" rights – at least to the extent they're still enforceable. Ownership of "intellectual property" becomes the new basis for the power of institutional hierarchies, and the primary buttress for corporate boundaries.

The increasing prevalence and imploding cost of small-scale, distributed production machinery, and the rise of "crowdsourced," distributed means of aggregating capital from small donors, mean that physical production is governed by the same phenomenon to a considerable extent.

Without "intellectual property," in any industry where the basic production equipment is widely affordable, and bottom-up networking renders management obsolete, it is likely that self-managed, cooperative production will replace the old managerial hierarchies. The network revolution, if its full potential is realized (as James Bennett put it in the appropriately titled article "The End of Capitalism and the Triumph of the Market Economy"),

> will lead to substantial redistribution of power and money from the twentieth century industrial producers of information, culture, and communications – like Hollywood, the recording industry, and perhaps the broadcasters and some of the telecommunications giants – to a combination of widely diffuse populations around the globe, and the market actors that will build the tools that make this population better able to produce its own information environment rather than buying it ready-made.

## PAYING FOR THE NAME

Another effect of the shift in importance from tangible to intangible assets is that a growing portion of product prices consists of embedded rents

330 | Kevin A. Carson

on "intellectual property" and other artificial property rights, rather than
the material costs of production. Tom Peters, in *The Tom Peters Seminar*,
was fond of gushing about the increasing portion of product "value" made
up of "ephemera" and "intellect" (i.e., the amount of final price consisting
of tribute to the owners of "intellectual property"), rather than labor and
material costs. To quote Michael Perelman,

> the so-called weightless economy has more to do with the leg-
> islated powers of intellectual property that the government
> granted to powerful corporations. For example, companies
> such as Nike, Microsoft, and Pfizer sell stuff that has high val-
> ue relative to its weight only because their intellectual property
> rights insulate them from competition.

But "intellectual property," as we have already seen, is becoming increasingly unenforceable. As a result, the ownership of proprietary content
is becoming increasingly untenable as a basis for corporate institutional
power. And we can expect the portion of commodity price resulting from
embedded rents on artificial property rights to implode.

"Intellectual property" also serves as a bulwark for planned obsolescence
and high-overhead production.

A major component of the business model that prevails under existing corporate capitalism is the offer of platforms below-cost, coupled with the sale of
patented or copyrighted spare parts, accessories, etc., at an enormous markup.
So one buys a cell phone for little or nothing, with the contractual obligation
to use only a specified service package for so many years; one buys a fairly cheap
printer, which uses enormously expensive ink cartridges; one buys a cheap glu-
cometer, with glucose testing strips that cost $100 a box. And to hack one's
phone to use a different service plan, or to manufacture generic ink cartridges
or glucose testing strips in competition with the proprietary version, is illegal.
To manufacture generic replacement parts for a car or appliance, in competition with the approved corporate suppliers, is likewise illegal.

As it is now, appliances are generally designed to thwart repair. When
the repairman tells you it would cost more that it's worth to repair your
washing machine, he's telling the truth. But that state of affairs reflects a deliberate design: the machine *could* have been designed on a modular basis,
so that the defective part might have been cheaply and easily replaced. And
if the manufacturer were subject to unfettered competition, the normal
market incentive would be to do so.

Absent legal constraints, it would be profitable to offer competing generic replacements and accessories for other firms' platforms. And in the

face of such competition, there would be strong pressure toward modular product designs that were amenable to repair, and interoperable with the modular components and accessories of other companies' platforms. Absent the legal constraints of patents, an appliance designed to thwart ease of repair through incompatibility with other companies' platforms would suffer a competitive disadvantage.

Patents, historically, promoted the stable control of markets by oligopoly firms through the control, exchange and pooling of patents.

According to David Noble, two essentially new science-based industries (those that "grew out of the soil of scientific rather than traditional craft knowledge") emerged in the late nineteenth century: the electrical and chemical industries.

> In the electric industry, General Electric had its origins first in a merger between Edison Electric (which controlled all of Edison's electrical patents) and the Sprague Electric Railway and Motor Company, and then in an 1892 merger between Edison General Electric and Thomas-Houston – both of them motivated primarily by patent considerations… From the 1890s on, the electrical industry was dominated by two large firms: GE and Westinghouse, both of which owed their market shares largely to patent control… By 1896 the litigation cost from some three hundred pending patent suits was enormous, and the two companies agreed to form a joint Board of Patent Control. General Electric and Westinghouse pooled their patents, with GE handling 62.5% of the combined business.

The structure of the telephone industry had similar origins, with the Bell Patent Association forming "the nucleus of the first Bell industrial organization" (and eventually of AT&T). The National Bell Telephone Company, from the 1880s on, fought vigorously to "occupy the field" (in the words of general manager Theodore N. Vail) through patent control. AT&T, anticipating the expiration of its original patents, had "surrounded the business with all the auxiliary protection that was possible…" By the time the FCC was formed in 1935, the Bell System had acquired patents to "some of the most important inventions in telephony and radio," and "through various radio-patent pool agreements in the 1920s… had effectively consolidated its position relative to the other giants in the industry."

The American chemical industry, in its modern form, was made possible by the Justice Department's seizure of German chemical patents in WWI.

More generally, "intellectual property" is an effective tool for cartelizing markets in industry at large. They were used in the automobile and steel industries among others, according to Noble. In a 1906 article, mechanical engineer and patent lawyer Edwin Prindle described patents as "the best and most effective means of controlling competition…" And unlike purely private cartels, which tend toward defection and instability, patent control cartels – being based on a state-granted privilege – carry a credible and effective punishment for defection.

At the global level, "intellectual property" plays the same protectionist role for transnational corporations that tariffs performed in the old national economies. It's hardly coincidental that the dominant industrial sectors in the global corporate economy are all heavily dependent on "intellectual property": software, entertainment, biotech, pharmaceuticals, and electronics. And the central focus of the neoliberal system, which has been falsely identified with "free trade" and "free markets," is on strengthening the legal "intellectual property" regime as the primary source of profits.

Trademarks and other forms of "intellectual property" are central to what Naomi Klein calls the "Nike model," by which TNCs outsource actual production to independently owned job shops while retaining control of finance, marketing and IP. Absent strong IP law, independent job shops could treat corporate headquarters and produce knockoffs of identical quality without the enormous brand name markup.

Patents are also used on a global scale to lock transnational manufacturing corporations into a permanent monopoly on productive technology. The central motivation in the GATT intellectual property regime is to permanently lock in the collective monopoly of advanced production technology by transnational corporations, and relegate Third World countries to supplying raw materials and sweatshop labor. It would, as the Third World Network's Martin Khor Kok Peng writes, "effectively prevent the diffusion of technology to the Third World…"

"Intellectual property" is central to the so-called "cognitive capitalism" model. Under that model, corporations rely on increasingly authoritarian government legislation to capture value from proprietary information. Johann Soderberg compares the way photocopiers were monitored in the old USSR, to protect the power of elites in that country, to the way the means of digital reproduction are monitored in this country to protect corporate power.

Today, "intellectual property" serves as a structural support for corporate boundaries, at a time when the imploding cost of production technology has undermined control of physical capital as their primary justification.

In this environment, the only thing standing between the old information and media dinosaurs and their total collapse is their so-called "intellectual property" rights – at least to the extent they're still enforceable. Ownership of "intellectual property" becomes the new basis for the power of institutional hierarchies, and the primary structural bulwark for corporate boundaries.

## DRAWING TO A CLOSE

But to repeat, the good news is that, in both the domestic and global economies, this business model is doomed. The shift from physical to human capital as the primary source of productive capacity in so many industries, along with the imploding price and widespread dispersion of ownership of capital equipment, means that corporate employers are increasingly hollowed out and only maintain control over the physical production process through legal fictions. When so much of actual physical production is outsourced to the independent small shop (whether it be a Chinese sweatshop, a flexible manufacturing firm in Emilia-Romagna, or a member of GM's supplier network), the corporation becomes a redundant "node" that can be bypassed. As blogger David Pollard described it, from the perspective of a future historian in 2015,

> The expensive outsourcers quickly found themselves unnecessary middlemen… The large corporations, having shed everything they thought was non 'core competency,' learned to their chagrin that in the connected, information economy, the value of their core competency was much less than the inflated value of their stock, and they have lost much of their market share to new federations of small entrepreneurial businesses.

For all the harm it does, "intellectual property" is not really even necessary as an incentive for innovation. Industrial analyst F. M. Scherer argued in the 1990s, based on a survey of 91 companies, that some 86% of all process and product innovations would have been developed from "the necessity of remaining competitive, the desire for efficient production, and the desire to expand and diversify their sales."

And copyright is no more necessary for artistic creation than patents are necessary for invention. There are many businesses, in the open-source world, that manage to make money from auxiliary services even though their content itself is not proprietary. For example, Red Hat makes money off open-source Linux software by customizing the software and offering specialized customer support. Phish has actively encouraged fans to share its music free of charge, while making money off of live performances and concessions.

Since IP is not necessary to encourage innovation, this means its main practical effect is to cause economic inefficiency by levying a monopoly charge on the use of existing technology.

In any case, whether or not "intellectual property" is necessary to profit from certain forms of economic activity should be beside the point for principled libertarians. That's the same argument used by protectionists: certain businesses would be unprofitable if they weren't protected by tariffs. But no one has a *right* to profit at someone else's expense, through the use of force. In particular, no one has the right to make a profit by using the state to prevent others from doing as they please with *their own* pen and paper, hard drives, or CDs. A business model that isn't profitable without government intervention *should* fail.

# 38

*The Freeman. Ideas on Liberty* 59.6 (2009):
33-8.

# THE AMERICAN LAND
# QUESTION

## JOSEPH R. STROMBERG
## (2009)

IN 1934 IN THE DEPTHS OF THE GREAT DEPRESSION, SOUTHERN AGRARIAN (AND HISTO-rian) Frank Owsley called for an American land reform. He suggested that "unemployed or underemployed families be staked to a homestead, even subsidized, to remain on the land and produce."[1]

This proposal was not really all that shocking: Such a program would have been consistent enough with the advertised purpose of certain phases of American land policy from 1776 on. American governments handed out land (however acquired) for over a century to veterans, settlers, land specu-lators, railroads, timber corporations, mining companies, and other parties. (I'll give you three guesses which groups made out the best). Governments did so as a source of revenue, for geostrategic reasons, to win favor with vot-ers, or to reward a small class of typically American operators who flat-out deserved to be rich.

In a new, revolutionary, and republican society, there was of course much talk about widespread property as the bulwark of republican free-

---

1    Owsley as paraphrased by Clyde N. Wilson in *Defending Dixie: Essays in Southern History and Culture* (Columbia, SC: Foundation for American Edu-cation 2006) 337.

dom. But the talk was so general that Federalists and Republicans could share it, while leaving themselves plenty of room in which to create a small class of owners of a disproportionate amount of the public domain. Overall – from the founding land speculators down to 1893, when the frontier allegedly ran out – American land policy resembled in both theory and practice the kind of "privatization" we see under mercantilist Republican administrations. One landmark in the process was *Johnson and Graham's Lessee v. William M'Intosh* (1823). Here, Chief Justice John Marshall undertook to write a long essay on the received theory of how property previously stolen by European kings or their agents is best conveyed. As was his wont, Marshall proved entirely too much, in as clear a case of Albert Jay Nock's "copper riveting" of narrowly focused property rights as we could want.[2]

Southern agrarian Andrew Lytle noted that from the settler's point of view the whole frontier process represented an attempt to get away from would-be aristocrats and other aspiring land monopolists. Consistent republican ideologists like Thomas Skidmore and George H. Evans agitated from the 1820s into the 1840s in favor of giving homesteaders first claim on the territories. Generally speaking, other claimants prevailed, while the politics of slavery and antislavery further complicated the matter. In the bigger picture, the Homestead Act of 1862 was the exception rather than the rule, as Paul W. Gates showed in a noteworthy 1936 paper.[3]

I cannot discuss here what an ideal policy based on "mixing one's labor" with resources might have looked like. Suffice it to say that sales of thou-

---

2   For international law and property stolen overseas, see Antony Anghie, "Finding the Peripheries: Sovereignty and Colonialism in Nineteenth-Century International Law," *Harvard International Law Journal* 40 (Winter 1999): 1-71. On Indian title, see Carl Watner, "Libertarians and Indians: Proprietary Justice and Aboriginal Land Rights," *Journal of Libertarian Studies* 7 (Spring 1983): 147-56; Ronald Takaki, *Iron Cages: Race and Culture in 19th Century America* (New York: OUP 1990 [ 1979]) ch. 4 ("Beyond Primitive Accumulation"); Joseph R. Stromberg, "Albert Jay Nock and Alternative History," *The Freeman: Ideas on Liberty* 58.9 (Nov. 2008): 32-8.

3   Andrew Lytle, "The Backwoods Progression," *From Eden to Babylon: The Social and Political Essays of Andrew Nelson Lytle*, ed. M. E. Bradford (Washington, DC: Gateway-Regnery 1990) 77-94. On Skidmore and Evans, see William Appleman Williams, *The Roots of the Modern American Empire* (New York: Random 1969) 75; Paul W. Gates, "The Homestead Law in an Incongruous Land System," *American Historical Review* 41 (July 1936): 652-81; Roy M. Robbins, *Our Landed Heritage* (Lincoln:Universityof NebraskaPress1942); Arthur A. Ekirch Jr., *The Decline of American Liberalism* (New York: Atheneum 1969) ch. 10, ("Pre-emption, Exploitation, Progress").

sands and tens of thousands of acres to individuals, land companies, and corporations were not especially consistent with any genuine republican ideal. The disappearance of most of the best land in California into the hands of a half-dozen individuals in a few decades comes to mind.[4] But large-scale buyers had mixed their money with federal land officers, and that no doubt counts for something.

Meanwhile, the judiciary — state and federal — busily remodeled the common law and shifted the burdens of industrialization onto third parties, extensively modifying the older law of nuisance. Harry Scheiber finds that "law was often, if not to say usually, mobilized to provide effective subsidies and immunities to heavily-capitalized special interests [under] either 'instrumentalist' or 'formalist' doctrine." Even existing doctrines of "public rights" and eminent domain came to serve business interests. Finally, federal judges' discovery in the 1880s of corporate "personhood" in the Fourteenth Amendment perfected the Federalist Party's original mercantilist program.[5] All these changes importantly influenced just who would benefit from the American State-system of land tenure (to use Nock's phrase) and its attendant modes of preemption and exploitation.

## LAND AND INDEPENDENCE

Many writers have seen a special relationship between landownership and personal independence. And here we hit on what is perhaps the truest insight of republican theory — one taken up by many classical liberals. Briefly, this holds that a broad "middle class" of property owners is essential to the maintenance of free societies. The point is as old as Aristotle. On the negative side, in decrying the social effects of England's fabled land monopoly, radical liberals like Percy Bysshe Shelley, Thomas Paine, Thomas Hodgskin, and John Bright implicitly affirmed the republican axiom.

A typical nineteenth-century American "self-help" book aimed at young men did not say, "Get a job working for wages within an increasingly intricate division of labor so as to enjoy a greater variety of consumer goods." Instead, it said, "Get yourself a competency" — a vision fraught with republican implications suitably modernized. Working for wages, if one did it at

---

4      Stewart H. Holbrook, *The Age of the Moguls* (Garden City, NY: Doubleday 1954) 118-28.

5      Harry N. Scheiber, "Regulation, Property Rights, and Definition of 'The Market': Law and the American Economy," *Journal of Economic History*, 41 (March 1981) 103-9. On corporate personhood, see Walter Prescott Webb, *Divided We Stand: The Crisis of a Frontierless Democracy* (Westport, CT: Hyperion 1985 [ 1944]) 32-48.

all, was a temporary stage – to be endured while learning a skill or trade and abandoned later in favor of real or potential independence. This independence, derided in our time as "illusory," left one free (within limits) not just from state interference but also from nineteenth-century employers. And if independence is illusory in our time, it is at least partly because the political activities of well-connected elites long since removed the preconditions of independence deliberately and systematically.

One key (but not the only one) to this much-sought-after independence was access to land, a theme taken up by Catholic writers Hilaire Belloc and G. K. Chesterton in early twentieth-century England. Sociologist Robert Nisbet commented that never, after reading Belloc, did he "imagine that there could be genuine individual liberty apart from individual ownership of property." In any case, as historian Christopher Lasch put it, "Americans took it as axiomatic that freedom had to rest on the broad distribution of property ownership."[6] Perhaps Americans were wrong to believe such a thing. But let us examine the matter a bit more.

This American axiom receives support from those political economists who believed that the land/labor ratio importantly determines social structure. Edward Gibbon Wakefield somewhat gave the game away in the 1830s by opposing easy access to land in Australia, lest potential wage-earners try for self-sufficiency before spending "enough" years working for others. Marx chided Wakefield for letting this "bourgeois secret" out and was in turn chided by Franz Oppenheimer, Achille Loria, and Nock for not learning the right lesson from Wakefield's recommendations on rigging the market.[7]

H. J. Nieboer argued (1900) that where resources are "open," few will work for big enterprises, and the latter will (if they can) institute some form of slavery. Evsey Domar writes (1970) that one never finds "free land, free peasants, and non-working owners" together. Why? Because where political leverage allows, aspiring lords and (literal) rent-seekers will eliminate the free land, the free peasants, or both.[8]

6  Robert Nisbet, "Introduction" *The Servile State*, by Hilaire Belloc (Indianapolis: Liberty Fund 1977) 14; Christopher Lasch, *The True and Only Heaven* (New York: Norton 1991) 204.

7  Karl Marx, *Capital* (New York: International 1967 [1887]) 1: ch. 33 ("The Modern Theory of Colonisation"); Franz Oppenheimer, "A Post-Morten on Cambrige Economics," *American Journal of Economics and Sociology* 3 (Oct. 1943): 121-2; Franz Oppenheimer, "The Gospel of Freedom," *American Journal of Economics and Sociology* 7 (April 1948): 363.

8  H. J. Nieboer, *Slavery as an Industrial System* (The Hague: Nijhoff 1900) 387-391; Evsey D. Domar, "The Causes of Slavery and Serfdom: A Hypoth-

## COLONIAL POLICIES

With this theorem in view, let us survey some colonial evidence. Enterprisers in colonies have always wanted regular supplies of cheap labor for their projects. Although there is no evidence in favor of a "right" to such a thing, these prospective employers were never discouraged. Aided by colonial administrators with the same assumptions, they gradually overcame native economic independence. Land was the key, and neither the colonizers nor the natives doubted it. No matter how hard natives worked on their holdings, colonialists decried their "idleness" – and their uncivilized failure to work for wages.

We may therefore give the overworked English Enclosures time off (for now) and look at some other cases.[9] Consider the Japanese colonial administrator in Okinawa who complained in 1899 that the typical Okinawan held land and therefore had low expenses and few wants. For these reasons, the native saw "no need to undertake any other business, nor to save money." Since native lands were held informally, they could not be capitalized. Such people and properties did little for the great cause of development and, shortly, the Japanese government (!) denounced Okinawans' customary arrangements as "feudal" and set out to modernize the island. American occupation later perfected this anti-agrarian revolution.[10] Doubtless, however, much "employment" was created in the post-World War II Okinawan service economy dominated by the U.S. military.

Turning to English colonies in the Caribbean and Africa, we find comparable phenomena. England abolished slavery in the colonies in the 1830s. (Never mind that, as historian Eric Foner comments, "Through a regressive tax system, the British working classes paid the bill for abolition.") By this time, English policymakers had embraced Adam Smith's view that positive incentives motivated labor better than fear of starvation or draconian punishments did. But an ocean made all the difference, Foner observes, and new peasantries made up of former slaves were "seen in London, as in the Caribbean, as a threat not simply to the economic well-being of the islands, but to civilization itself." John Stuart Mill's famous defense of peasant proprietors "did not extend to the blacks of the Caribbean; their desire to escape plantation labor and acquire land was perceived as incorrigible idleness."[11]

esis," *Journal of Economic History* 30 (March 1970): 18-32.

9    But see William Lazonick, "Karl Marx and Enclosures in England," *Review of Radical Political Economics* 6 (1974): 1-59.

10    Mark Selden, "Okinawa and American Security Imperialism," *Remaking Asia: Essays on the American Uses of Power*, ed. Selden (New York: Pantheon 1974) 279-302.

11    Eric Foner, *Nothing But Freedom: Emancipation and Its Legacy* (Baton Rouge,

(This last point has been misunderstood. It is quite separate from Mill's well-documented defense of the rights of black Jamaicans *as subjects of the Crown* after the colonial governor Edward Eyre visited savage reprisal on alleged rebels in 1865. Mill did not, however, defend the rights of Blacks in the colonies as a class of free *peasant farmers*. He expected them to work for wages or, at best, set themselves up as petty shopkeepers.[12])

And so Britain's former slave colonies put vagrancy and other laws to work and crafted taxes aimed at restricting "the freedmen's access to land." As Foner puts it, "Taxation has always been the state's weapon of last resort in the effort to promote market relations within peasant societies" – that is, to force people into markets in which they were not eager to participate. In Kenya the problem was one of "dispossessing a peasantry with a preexisting stake in the soil," but colonial legislation proved up to the task. Foner concludes that in Britain's Caribbean and African colonies "the free market [was] conspicuous by its absence" – its workings restricted "as far as possible" in the interest of the well-off and powerful.[13]

Historian Colin Bundy has studied the economic rise and political-economic fall of a class of independent African farmers in the Eastern Cape Colony and other parts of South Africa. Various Cape Location Acts (1869, 1876, and 1884) sought to lessen "the numbers of 'idle squatters' (i.e., rent-paying tenants economically active on their own behalf) on white-owned lands." Such peasant farming "conferred... a degree of economic 'independence': an ability to withhold, if he so preferred, his labour from white landowners or other employers." Further: "Both the farmer and the mine-owner perceived... the need to apply extra-economic pressures... to break down the peasant's 'independence,' increase his wants, and to induce him to part more abundantly with his labour, but at no increased price." In their view, "Africans had no right to continue as self-sufficient and independent farmers if this conflicted with white interests."[14]

---

LA: Louisiana State UP 1983) 14, 28, 30.

12   See Bart Schultz, "Mill and Sidgwick, Imperialism and Racism," *Utilitas* 19 (2007): 127-8, as well as the sources cited by Foner on the point: H. J. Perkin, "Land Reform and Class Conflict in Victorian Britain," *The Victorians and Social Protest*, ed. J. Butt & I. F. Clark (Hamden, CT: Archon 1973) 177-217, and Clive J. Dewey, "The Rehabilitation of the Peasant Proprietor in 19th-Century Economic Thought," *History of Political Economy* 6 (1974): 17-47. On Mill's defense of Black Jamaicans' *legal rights*, see Bernard Semmel, *Democracy versus Empire: The Jamaica Riots of 1865 and the Governor Eyre Controversy* (Garden City, NY: Anchor 1969).

13   Foner 25, 31-2, 37.

14   Colin Bundy, *The Rise and Fall of the South African Peasantry* (London:

Bundy observes that "Social engineering on this scale took time and effort, but the incentives were powerful." By way of a "one man one lot" rule under the Glenn Grey Act of 1894, legislators sought to keep African farming within "certain acceptable bounds." (Here, finally, was a use for John Locke's famous "proviso" about leaving enough resources for others!) Evictions increased after the Anglo-Boer War (1899-1903). Rents rose (Enclosure defenders, take note), and former tenants stayed on as laborers. Tax pressure on African farmers increased. This "employers' offensive" from 1890 to 1913 ended successfully in the South African Natives Land Act of 1913, which effectively outlawed the practices under which a particular African peasantry had shown much success.[15]

One supposes, in standard libertarian fashion, that agricultural employment increased thereafter along with land values. But that was the whole point: to proletarianize independent peasants by leaving them no option but to work for wages for Boers and Brits on farms, in mines, and elsewhere. Whether more "employment" was good in itself seems unclear. We can, at least, impute the outcome back to specific political intentions and levers. So much for the colonies, then – and all this without even mentioning the two greatest monuments to England's defense of free markets: Ireland and India.

## TELESCOPIC LAND REFORM

Colonial bureaucrats and employers saw a definite connection between small-scale landownership and independence, and resolved to cut that independence short. By now we begin to see that "the subsidy of history" – to use Kevin Carson's useful term – has been very large indeed.[16] A number of libertarians have understood the problem at hand in pretty much these terms. They have tended, however, to dwell on instances far away from our own shores, writing about land reform in Latin America, South Africa, Asia, and other places. In the mid-1970s Murray Rothbard, Roy Childs, and others addressed the matter.

Rothbard wrote that "free-market economists... go to Asia and Latin America and urge the people to adopt the free market and private property rights" while ignoring "the suppression of the genuine private property of the peasants by the exactions of quasi-feudal landlords..." In this vacuum, only the local communists appeared to support "the peasants' struggle for

Heinemann 1979) 78, 91, 115.

15   Bundy 134-135, 137.

16   Kevin Carson, "The Subsidy of History," *The Freeman: Ideas on Liberty* 58.5 (June 2008: 33-8.

their property…" And so libertarians "allowed themselves to become supporters of feudal landlords and land monopolists in the name of 'private property.'"[17]

Decades earlier, that very conservative German liberal economist Wilhelm Röpke wrote that German history would have gone better had Prussia undergone "a radical agrarian reform breaking up the great estates and putting peasant farms in their place." He adds: "Influential Social Democratic leaders opposed the transformation of the great estates in Prussia into peasant holdings… as a 'retrograde step.'" Röpke called for freeing Germany from "agrarian and industrial feudalism" and the ills "of proletarization, of concentration and overorganization, of the agglomeration of industrial power and the destruction of the individuality of labor…" In his view, the typical proletarianized worker or clerk wanted "a small house of his own with a garden and a goat shed, an undisturbed family life without training courses, mass meetings, processions, and political flag days; dignity and pleasure in his work, an independent if modest existence…"[18]

## WHY GO ABROAD?

For Enclosure-like pressures on small-holders closer to home, we need look no farther than states like Kentucky, where courts vigorously enforced the full feudal rigor of the "broad form deed," thereby ensuring the strip mining of many a mountaineer out of productive existence down to the early 1990s.[19] With the system so long stacked in favor of big landholders and bankers, well subsidized by history, one begins to understand the popularity of those New Deal programs that promoted individual home ownership.

Economist Michael Perelman has confirmed a direct relationship between rural labor without independent means of support and the applied politics of English classical economists.[20] The latter preached a great gospel of "work," mainly for others, who ought to be doing this work. Except for a narrow class of Dissenting Protestant factory owners, those most vigorously

---

17  Murray Rothbard, "Justice and Property Right," *Innovator*, Jan. 1965: 10-1.

18  Wilhelm Röpke, *The Solution of the German Problem* (New York: Putnams 1946) 184, 186, 203-4.

19  James Branscome, "Paradise Lost," *Southern Exposure*, Sum.-Fall 1973: 29-41; and John Gaventa, "In Appalachia: Property Is Theft," *Southern Exposure*, Sum.-Fall 1973: 42-52.

20  Michael Perelman, *The Invention of Capitalism: Classical Political Economy and the Secret History of Primitive Accumulation* (Duke, NC: Duke University Press 2000) 1-12 ("Introduction: Dark Designs").

espousing this gospel were not themselves noted for doing a lot of work. Together, however, owners and economists said in effect, "Work for us, join the armed forces, or emigrate, ye doughty Angles, Saxons, Jutes, and Scots." And emigrate they did, leaving us with an American folk wisdom in which old times in England, Scotland, and Ireland were not that great. (This folk memory may have at least as much heuristic value as latter-day econometric claims that everyone became better off in the new division of labor.)

And so we return to Henry George's problem: How did Americans manage as a society to seize so much land, incur whatever moral guilt goes with the seizures, and then not bloody have any of it? The chief mechanism was precisely the political means to wealth that Oppenheimer and Nock analyzed.[21] The reason the phrase "Robber Barons" struck the right note is that there were such individuals. California was a laboratory case, as George well knew, of the successful primitive accumulation of land by a microscopically small class of state-made men. As with ontogeny and phylogeny, Western accumulation recapitulated Eastern accumulation. From such causes arose the famous "end" of the frontier circa 1893. But open land did not so much disappear naturally as succumb to preemption. And then, with perfect timing, the conservation movement put enormous quantities of land beyond the reach of actual settlers.

As for those Americans who currently own property, they typically own it after 20 or more years of bank payments. Is land so genuinely scarce that a bank must always be in the middle? This remains our central question. Certainly, nineteenth-century allocations played a lasting role, and later political interventions added to concentrated property ownership.

And what of the promotion of "easy" home ownership in recent years? It is a product of 1) the widespread delusion, in the wake of Lyndon Johnson's and Richard Nixon's inflationary financing of the Vietnam War, that real estate constitutes the ultimate inflation hedge, and 2) the specific dynamics of the expansionist fractional-reserve banking under new rules ("deregulation") increasing moral hazards for bankers.

There is also the unhappy fact of property taxes – our chief surviving feudal due. Fail to pay those, and the state enrolls a new owner on your former property. This reduces somewhat the fact of private property in land.

## INDEPENDENCE, REPUBLICANISM, AND LIBERTY

Some classical liberals and libertarians downgrade personal independence. Better to participate in the going order and enjoy a wider array of comforts, they say. But socialists and corporate liberals can play the same

21    See Stromberg, "Nock."

game – and have for over a century. It seems to me that those libertarians who join in this refrain rather willfully misconstrue a very simple point: They hail the joys of the division of labor, the higher degree of civilization (that is, more stuff) to be gained from dependence, interdependence, and sundry trickles of income and utility down and up. But already in 1936, Southern agrarian John Crowe Ransom noticed a flaw in this reasoning, writing, "[I]ncome is not enough, and the distribution of income is not enough. If those blessings sufficed, we might as well come to collectivism at once; for that is probably the quickest way to get them."[22] If greater choice among consumer goods makes up for lost independence, then the case for socialism (or X) would be clinched, provided socialism (or X) could deliver the economic goods (where "X" stands for any political ideology offering us the same stuff/independence tradeoff.)

I doubt we are necessarily "better off" merely because of employment. We need to know more, including why particular sets of choices exist in the first place. Back in the '60s, Selective Service used to "channel" us into the "right" occupations by threatening to draft us. Given the parameters, our choices were "free." If it's that easy, then we are always free, no matter the historical and institutional constraints. Similarly, "To Hell or Connaught" was a choice, and never mind that Oliver Cromwell and his army arbitrarily created this particular prisoner's dilemma. But perhaps I have leapt from choices among goods to choices between ways of life. Why? Let us look into this.

What if proletarianization is not the ideal form of human life? What if a complex division of labor is merely useful or convenient, but not a moral imperative? What if most of us are hirelings, well paid or otherwise, and then we learn what that status amounts to? The post-Marxist socialist André Gorz writes, "Capitalism owes its political stability to the fact that, in return for the dispossession and growing constraints experienced at work, individuals enjoy the possibility of building an *apparently* growing sphere of individual autonomy outside of work."[23] Our interest here is the "autonomy" mentioned, which sounds like a near cousin of "independence." The sentiment seems sound enough, and the partial convergence of Röpke and Gorz is eye-opening.

Now in the view of Quentin Skinner (a modern republican theorist of note), unfreedom arises both from direct, forcible coercion and from institutional arrangements that make people dependent, since the latter always contain the possibility (realized or not) of arbitrary interference and

22   John Crowe Ransom, "The South Is a Bulwark" (1936) in Jack Salzman and Barry Wallenstein, eds., *Years of Protest* (New York: Pegasus 1967) 268.

23   André Gorz, *Farewell to the Working Class* (Boston: South End 1982) 80.

coercion. Such discussions usually center on the form of state. Utilitarian liberals like Henry Sidgwick did not care about forms. If the Sublime Porte, Tsar, or King of England leaves us substantially alone, we are "free," and that is that. In Skinner's view, if those worthies can on their own motion change their policy of leaving us alone, we are not free, no matter what they are doing right now. Freedom requires that we not be menaced by latent unknown powers.[24]

Freedom in this sense is liberty – a shared civic or public good. Like many real public goods it is not provided by the state, indeed the state may be its chief enemy. Law and settled custom may provide this public good, and consumer goods – the people's pottage – do not compensate for abandoning such an order, where it exists. Today, people often work long hours to buy some independence. In another time, they began with some independence, and then chose how hard to work. Now we see, perhaps, the difference between choices among economic goods and past choices between systems structuring our choices.

Widespread landownership long supported a kind of liberal-republican independence. Perhaps we should reexamine the nexus and ask ourselves how, in Donald Davidson's words, we "let the freehold pass," and whether that was really for the best.

---

24   Quentin Skinner, *Liberty Before Liberalism* (Cambridge, UK: CUP 1998) 68-72, 96-9.

## 39

*Agorist Quarterly* 1.1 (Fall 1995): 31-45.

# ENGLISH ENCLOSURES AND SOVIET COLLECTIVIZATION
## Two Instances of an Anti-Peasant Mode of Development

*JOSEPH R. STROMBERG*
*(1995)*

## I. INTRODUCTION: LAND MONOPOLY AS AN HISTORICAL PERENNIAL

THE CONTROL OF MAJOR MATERIAL AND HUMAN FACTORS OF PRODUCTION BY SMALL articulated minorities has been characteristic of civilized (state) societies. Of the four factors of production – land, labor, capital, and entrepreneurial ability, it is probably the control of land that has been of the greatest historical consequence, especially for pre-industrial societies. In the West, land monopoly has been intimately associated with "feudalism" in a political-economic sense.[1] Critics as far apart ideologically as Karl Marx and the

---

1    In Europe, Germanic conquest of the Roman Empire's western provinces set
     the stage for "feudalism" in both the political-military and economic mean-

liberal Austrian economist Ludwig von Mises have stressed the role of force, politics and extra-economic coercion in the creation of large landed estates. In Marx's words, "In actual history it is notorious that conquest, enslavement, robbery, murder, briefly force, play the great part."[2] And Mises:

> Nowhere and at no time has the large scale ownership of land come into being through the workings of economic forces in the market. It is the result of military and political effort. Founded by violence, it has been upheld by violence and that alone. As soon as the latifundia are drawn into the sphere of market transactions they begin to crumble, until at last they disappear completely.[3]

With the growth of urban economies in western Europe, the revival of Mediterranean trade during the Renaissance, and the development of modern banking and credit mechanisms (despite the inherited religious doctrine condemning "usury"), market relations penetrated the countryside, gradually undermining and transforming the senescent order of feudalism. This process, whose eloquent heralds include Marx, Max Weber, Barrington Moore, Jr., and Immanuel Wallerstein, made for a hybrid transitional society in which "pre-capitalist" and "capitalist" attitudes and institutions uneasily coexisted.[4] (Lost in the historical shuffle was Small Commodity Production, a possible mode of production in its own right and an alternative to both "feudalism" and capitalism. Only recently have Marxist scholars paid serious attention to this topic.[5])

---

ings of the term. Certain features of this original feudalism persisted into succeeding social formations; see Alexander Rüstow, *Freedom and Domination* (Princeton, NJ: Princeton UP 1980) and Arno Mayer, *The Persistence of the Old Regime* (New York: Pantheon 1981).

2   Karl Marx, *Capital* (New York: International 1967) 1: 714. Marx was referring of course to "primitive accumulation of capital," but his words have application to other forms of property.

3   Ludwig von Mises, *Socialism: An Economic and Sociological Analysis* (London: Jonathan Cape 1951) 375.

4   See Max Weber, "Capitalism and Rural Society in Germany," *From Max Weber: Essays in Sociology*, ed. Hans Gerth and C. Wright Mills (New York: OUP 1958) 363-85; Barrington Moore, Jr., *Social Origins of Dictatorship and Democracy* (Boston: Beacon 1966); Immanuel Wallerstein, *The Modern World-System* (New York: Academic 1974).

5   See Robert Brenner, "The Origins of Capitalist Development: A Critique of Neo-Smithian Marxism," *New Left Review*, July-August 1977, esp. 88-90;

In these circumstances, the land question loomed large; its resolution – one way or another – threatened some sections of society as much as it boded well for others. Some writers – not as sanguine as Mises concerning the tendency of market relations to dissolve large holdings of land – emphasize the persistence of political forces and economic positions stemming from the feudal past into modern times. For Franz Oppenheimer, Alexander Rüstow, Wilhelm Röpke, J. S. Mill, Joseph Schumpeter, Arno Mayer and others, remnants of the past significantly conditioned early capitalism, bringing about political economies in the West that fell rather short of the ideal market economy of classical liberal theory and aspirations.[6] A few quotations must suffice. The near-anarchist liberal poet Shelley wrote that large-scale property "has its foundation in usurpation, or imposture, or violence, without which, by the nature of things, immense possessions of gold or land could never have been accumulated. Of this nature is the principal part of the property enjoyed by the aristocracy and the great fundholders, the great majority of whose ancestors never deserved it by their skill and talents or acquired or created it by their personal labor."[7]

Despite the relatively early rise of commercial relations in England, John Stuart Mill could write that "[t]he principle of private property has never yet had a fair trial in any country; and less so, perhaps, in this country than in some others"; and "notwithstanding what industry has been doing for many centuries to modify the work of force, the system still retains many and large traces of its origin."[8] More recently, writing of the "primal distribution" of property – rather than Marx's primitive accumulation – Franz Oppenheimer said

> Rising capitalism inherited it from its predecessor, feudal absolutism. Capitalism took over all of feudalism's basic insti-

---

Claudio Katz, "Karl Marx on the transition from feudalism to capitalism," *Theory and Society* 22 (June 1993): 363-89; Arthur DiQuattro, "The Labor Theory of Value and Simple Commodity Production," *Science and Society* 71 (October 2007): 455-83.

6   See Franz Oppenheimer, *The State* (New York: Free Life 1975 [1914]); Wilhelm Röpke, *The Social Crisis of Our Time* (Chicago: University of Chicago Press1950); Joseph Schumpeter, *Imperialism and Social Classes* (New York: Meridian 1955); Rüstow; Mayer.

7   Percy Bysshe Shelley, *Political Writings*, ed. Roland Duerksen (New York: Appleton 1970) 140.

8   John Stuart Mill, *Principles of Political Economy* (London: Longmans 1909, 1891) 208.

tutions, especially two, the privileges of State-administration, and the monopoly of land.[9]

In a world increasingly unified by merchant capital, Western imperialism, and a bit more tardily, industry, the land question had persisted – right up to the present.[10] Whether or not they have followed the liberal-democratic road, the Prussian road of revolution from above, or the road of mass-based peasant revolutions led (and typically betrayed) by Marxist revolutionaries, countries the world over have had to address the problem of modernizing agrarian relations.[11] In case after case, the access of ordinary people to land and markets has been controlled ultimately by the constellation of political forces. It seems safe to say that the issue has seldom been settled in the interest of peasantries. The level of popular discontent and land-hunger is perhaps summarized best in the vast emigrations from the British Isles and Western Europe to various parts of what Walter Prescott Webb called the "great frontier." Just as the moving land frontier functioned in some sense as a "safety valve" for discontent in the eastern states of the United States, so North America, Australia, New Zealand, and South Africa functioned on a grander scale as a safety valve for European society generally.[12]

The English enclosures, standing as they do as a centerpiece in the ongoing Optimist/Pessimist debate over the industrial revolution, will be the first instance of agrarian "collectivization" or consolidation discussed in these pages. A brief aside on Latin American latifundismo will precede the treatment of another significant model of agrarian change: Soviet collectivization as a bureaucratic enclosure movement. The comparison of the English enclosures with Soviet collectivization should yield interesting insights into how – or how not – to reform an agrarian sector. To anticipate a bit, it may be that neither collectivization for a commercially active minority (the English example) nor enclosures directed by bureaucracy (the Soviet example), with its disturbing resemblances to something like an "Asiatic

---

9    Franz Oppenheimer, "A Critique of Political Economy II: A Post-Mortem on Cambridge Economics," *American Journal of Economics and Sociology* 2 (July 1943): 535.

10   Land is at the center of the problems in the Middle East. See Stephen Holbrook, "The Alienation of a Homeland: How Palestine Became Israel," *Journal of Libertarian Studies* 5 (Fall 1981): 357-74.

11   The "three roads to modernization" come from Moore, *Social Origins*.

12   Walter Prescott Webb, *The Great Frontier* (Boston: Houghton 1952). On emigration from Britain spurred by Enclosure, especially from Scotland and northern England, see Bernard Bailyn, *Voyagers to the West* (New York: Knopf 1987) 43-9, 291, 375-6, 606-8.

mode of production,"[13] provide an ideal path to modernization, at least if peasant interests and aspirations are given any weight as against competing goals such as rate-of-growth or the retention of power by political elites.

## II. THE ENGLISH ENCLOSURES AND A RURAL RESERVE ARMY

The debate among historians over the enclosures resolves itself into approximately the same optimist and pessimist camps that continue to argue the costs and benefits of industrialization in late 18th and early 19th century England. In rough summary, the optimists tend to see enclosure (as it actually took place) as essential to the introduction of technical improvements, new crop rotations, and more effective economic organization of the English countryside. This made it possible more effectively to feed England's growing population, a part of which would subsequently be available as wage labourers in incipient industries. The optimists tend to accept the "fairness" of the commissions on enclosure and would minimize the dislocations occurring as marginal peasants were moved off the land over the course of several centuries.[14] The very slowness and complexity of the enclosure movement suggest that the optimist case can be proven, on its own terms, in some narrow selection of cases; but since those terms tend to rule out the most interesting problems, the jury is still out. And a whole new literature challenging the optimists has arisen in the decades since the latter declared victory.[15]

For T. S. Ashton, the essential point about enclosure "is that it brought about an increase in the productivity of the soil." For Jonathan Chambers and Gordon Mingay, enclosure shows how "large gains in economic efficiency and output could be achieved by reorganization of existing resources." David Landes merely remarks that "the improving landlords were a powerful leaven." Sir John Clapham remains content to describe the details of enclosure, making no judgement at all.[16] And the optimist

---

13    An analysis of Communist states as atavistic phenomena is presented in Karl
      A. Wittfogel, *Oriental Despotism* (New York: Vintage 1981 [1957]). But see
      Perry Anderson, *Lineages of the Absolute State* (London: Verso 1979) 462-549
      ("The 'Asiatic Mode of Production,'").

14    Jonathan D. Chambers and Gordon E. Mingay, "Enclosures not guilty" in
      Phillip A. M. Taylor, ed., *The Industrial Revolution in Britain: Triumph or
      Disaster?* (Lexington, MA: Heath 1970) 53.

15    See n64, *infra*.

16    T. S. Ashton, *The Industrial Revolution 1760-1830* (London: OUP 1948)

viewpoint is strongly advanced by the writings of Robert Hartwell.[17] The South German free-market economist Wilhelm Röpke (whose economic views reflected a strain of conservative Protestantism) has remarked that the debate over industrialization has been between "anticapitalist intellectuals" and "anti-intellectual capitalists." For Röpke, the collection of essays edited by F. A. von Hayek, *Capitalism and the Historians*, has done little to improve the discussion.[18] The pessimist view originated with Karl Marx, Friedrich Engels, and other contemporary critics of early industrialization, and continues in the work of J. L. and Barbara Hammond, Maurice Dobb, Eric Hobsbawm and E. P. Thompson. For the pessimists – whose overlap with Marxist economic historians is evident from this partial list – enclosure represents outright expropriation of the main body of English peasants by those who possessed the political power to engross the land. While they conceded – too soon, it now appears – the long-range increase in food supply and strictly economic efficiency, the pessimists stress that enclosure was an unmitigated social and economic disaster for the immediate generations of peasants dispossessed. The difference between economic improvement qua system, and social disaster for the small and middling peasants, is particularly well put by Pauline Gregg.[19] The nature and course of the enclosures are complex matters, indeed; some of the best accounts of the process are found in the writings of those whom we might call "semi-pessimists," such as Paul Mantoux, Barrington Moore, Jr., Theda Skocpol, and Pauline Gregg (reaching back, perhaps, to Thorold Rogers).[20] To begin with, one must distinguish between the areas under cultivation as open fields, or nar-

---

26; Chambers and Mingay, "Enclosures" 63, David S. Landes, *The Unbound Prometheus: Technological Change and Industrial Development in Western Europe from 1750 to the Present* (Cambridge, UK: CUP 1969) 69; and John Clapham, *A Concise Economic History of Britain* (Cambridge, UK: CUP 1949) 194-207, 222-4.

17    See R. M. Hartwell, "History and Ideology," *Studies in History and Philosophy* 3 (Menlo Park, CA: IHS n.d.).

18    Wilhelm Röpke, *A Humane Economy: The Social Framework of the Free Market* (Indianapolis, IN: Liberty Fund 1971) 227-78; Friedrich Hayek, ed., *Capitalism and the Historians* (Chicago: University of Chicago Press 1954).

19    Pauline Gregg, *Modern Britain: A Social and Economic History Since 1760* (New York: Pegasus 1965) ch. 1.

20    See Paul Mantoux, *The Industrial Revolution in the Eighteenth Century* (New York: Harper 1961 [1928]) ch. 3 ("The Redistribution of Land"); Moore ch. 1 ("England and the Contribution of Violence to Gradualism"); Theda Skocpol, *States and Social Revolutions* (New York: CUP 1979) 140-4; and Gregg 19-35.

row strips of land randomly interspersed (such that strips 1, 5, and 9 might belong to one peasant, 2, 6, and 13 to another, and so on), and the wastes, areas on the margin of cultivation where customary rights to pasture, collection of firewood, and other benefits had developed over time. In addition to the open fields and the wastes, large areas of land were given over to commercial agriculture and stock-raising by landlords or their large-scale tenant farmers, especially in south and central England. (The situation in the north and in Scotland[21] was somewhat different, but far too complex to deal with here.)

Besides the complexities of everyday cultivation, the system was crisscrossed by several different degrees of ownership and tenancy, ranging from fee simple ownership and long-term leases through copyhold down to merely customary tenancies at the will of the landlord. In the course of enclosure, it was precisely those cultivators with modest claims and the weakest legal rights to land who fell by the wayside, becoming part of a rural proletariat. Since the term enclosure applies to any consolidation of open fields or waste into larger, more "rational" units of production (another point we will return to), and since such consolidations date from Tudor times to the late 18th and early 19th centuries (an especially brisk period), the notion is stretched almost to the breaking point. A great many authorities had to spend a great deal of time and effort to bring order and coherence to the history of the enclosures.[22]

Whatever the merits of the argument that bigger units of production are ipso facto more efficient and productive, the political dominance of large landowners determined the course of enclosure. While "improving landlords" may have believed the arguments put forward by agricultural reformers and enthusiasts like Jethro Tull and Arthur Young, it was their power in Parliament and as local Justices of the Peace that enabled them to redistribute the land in their own favor.

A typical round of enclosure began when several, or even a single, prominent landholder initiated it. In the great spurt of enclosures in the late 18th and early 19th centuries, this was done by petition to Parliament. A Parliamentary commission would be set up to work out the details and engineer the appearance of local consensus. Since, as Mantoux

---

21  For Scottish developments, see Eric J. Hobsbawm, "Scottish Reformers of the Eighteenth Century and Capitalist Agriculture," *Peasants in History*, ed Hobsbawm *et al.* (Delhi: OUP 1980) 3-29; Tom Devine, "The Highland Clearances," *Refresh* 4 (Spring 1987): 5-8; and Neil Davidson, "The Scottish Path to Capitalist Agriculture 2: The Capitalist Offensive (1747-1815)," *Journal of Agrarian Change* 4 (Oct. 2004): 411-60.

22  Two of the clearest short accounts are by Clapham and Gregg.

points out, the commissioners were invariably of the same class and out-look as the major landholders who had petitioned in the first place, it was not surprising that the great landholders awarded themselves the best land and the most of it, thereby making England a classic land of great, well-kept estates with a small marginal peasantry and a large class of rural wage labourers. Those with only customary claim to use the land fell by the wayside, as did those marginal cottagers and squatters who had de-pended on use of the wastes for their bare survival as partly independent peasants. In addition, better situated men often succumbed to the legal costs built into the enclosure process. The result was – in the words of J. L. and Barbara Hammond – that

> "The enclosures created a new organization of classes. The peasant with rights and a status, with a share in the fortunes and government of his village, standing in rags, but stand-ing on his feet, makes way for the labourer with no corporate rights to defend, no corporate power to invoke, no property to cherish, no ambition to pursue, bent beneath the fear of his masters, and the weight of a future without hope. No class in the world has so beaten and crouching a history."[23]

So a Parliament of large landowners set up commissions of large land-owners to reform the agrarian sector of English society. Mantoux com-ments that "[t]he abuse was so plain that the most determined supporters of the enclosures denounced it emphatically"[24] – Arthur Young among them. District by district, squatters, cottagers and small farmers were driv-en out as self-supporting husbandmen, becoming a free-floating pool of rural labor or emigrating to America.

Karl Marx and his successors have stressed the direct connection be-tween the enclosures and the development of an industrial proletariat.[25] Some writers, anxious to rebut the Marxist reading of the matter, have stressed the incremental nature of enclosure and the "fairness under the circumstances" of the commissioners who oversaw the process.[26] To an

---

23  J. L. and Barbara Hammond, *The Village Labourer, 1760-1832* (New York: Harper 1970 [1911]) 81.

24  Mantoux 169.

25  Marx 1: 717-49.

26  See J. D. Chambers, "Enclosure and Labour Supply in the Industrial Revolu-tion," *Economic History Review*, 2d ser., 5 (1953): 319-43; H. J. Habakkuk, "English Landownership, 1680-1740," *Economic History Review* 10 (Febru-ary 1940) 2-17; W. E. Tate, "Members of Parliament and Proceedings upon

American outsider, this necessarily seems like another exercise in convenient Whig history (without conceding the precise point the Marxists wish to make). When one of these writers, W. E. Tate, denies that the enclosures were unjust "except insofar as injustice must necessarily occur" when one class legislates concerning the property and opportunities of another class, Barrington Moore, Jr., comments that "the reader may conclude that he has destroyed his own case."[27] While enclosures did not instantly call into being an industrial reserve army, most authorities would agree that they did create a rural reserve army, many of whose descendants did ultimately become industrial workers or emigrants to the New World.

Given the role of political power in the process of enclosure, it does not seem unfair to view enclosure as collectivization of agriculture for the benefit of a narrow class. Whether or not it was the only way to increase agricultural efficiency or whether it did increase it to the degree often supposed are probably open questions. Folke Dovring writes that the enclosures "depended primarily on the de facto power of the landlord class." This naturally raises the question of whether or not England did not – at least in the agrarian sphere – follow a path closer to the "Prussian road" to capitalism than is usually believed.[28]

## III. LAND MONOPOLY AND *LATIFUNDISMO*

According to numerous authorities,[29] Latin American poverty, unemployment, and productivity so low that agricultural countries actually import food are all rooted in latifundismo or "feudal" land monopoly dating from the Spanish (and Portuguese) conquest and settlement. In most of these countries, the landed elites dominate the political structure; with its help, they exploit the peasants and maintain an agrarian reserve army of cheap and docile labor by quasifeudal labor dues, fraud, inflation (which devours small savings), and ultimately armed violence by landlord-spon-

---

Enclosure Bills," *Economic History Review* 12 (1942): 68-75.

27    Moore 22n.

28    Folke Dovring, "The Transformation of European Agriculture," *The Cambridge Economic History*, ed. M. Posten and H. J. Habakkuk (London: CUP 1966) 6.2: 628.

29    See Charles Gibson, *Spain in America* (New York: Harper 1966); Ernst Feder, *The Rape of the Peasantry: Latin America's Landholding System* (Garden City, NY: Anchor 1971); Stanislav Andreski, *Parasitism and Subversion: The Case of Latin America* (London: Weidenfeld 1969); and Irving Louis Horowitz, Josué de Castro, and John Gerassi, eds., *Latin American Radicalism* (New York: Vintage 1969).

sored vigilantes or national armies.[30]

According to Ernst Feder, the concentration of good land in the hands of a very small minority creates gross inefficiency, waste, mismanagement, and low productivity on Latin America's latifundia. "[F]orcefully shut off from the market mechanism,"[31] the peasants respond by displaying self-hatred and un-ambitious behavior which is then taken to prove their inherent stupidity. Built-in disincentives discourage the peasants, who gain nothing from harder work. Far from reflecting economies of scale arrived at in free markets, the politically based latifundia are so over-expanded that often as much as one third of the work force is required to boss the other demoralized two thirds. Hence, the great estates resemble nothing so much as islands of socialist "calculational chaos" unable to operate at optimum economic rationality.[32] In contrast, Feder argues that poor people are actually capable of great economic rationality and capital accumulation. To the extent that a small sector of family farms exists in Latin America, it is here that one finds land-intensive and productive farming as opposed to the better capitalized estate sector. Given the economic irrationality of the quasifeudal sector and the destitution of peasants who could be productive, Feder supports land reform both on the grounds of simple justice and economic progress. Like Feder, the sociologist Stanislav Andreski takes a critical view of the chief structural realities of Latin American society. He believes that most of the problems in those coun-

30   Feder 3-45. André Gunder Frank makes a strong case that Latin American economies were capitalist from the very beginning: *Capitalism and Underdevelopment in Latin America* (New York: Monthly Review 1969) 20-5. For a comparable reading of North American history, see Andrew Lytle, "The Backwoods Progression," *From Eden to Babylon: The Social and Political Essays of Andrew Nelson Lytle*, ed. M. E. Bradford (Washington, DC: Gateway-Regnery 1990) 77-94; Michael Merrill, "Putting 'Capitalism' in Its Place: A Review of Recent Literature," *William and Mary Quarterly* 52 (April 1995): 317-26.

31   Feder 148. On forceful exclusion from markets, see for example, Carol A. Smith, "Local History in Global Context: Social and Economic Transitions in Western Guatemala," *Comparative Studies in Society and History* 26 (1984): 193-228; John Lie, "The Concept of Mode of Exchange," *American Sociological Review* 57 (Aug. 1992): 508-23.

32   On the problem of rational calculation, see Murray N. Rothbard, *Man, Economy, and State with Power and Market* (2d scholars ed; Auburn, AL: Mises 2009) 614-6, 659-61. On Rothbard's analysis, any forcibly maintained monopoly represents a step in the direction of socialism, with the calculational difficulties pointed out in the 1920s by Ludwig von Mises and Max Weber.

tries stem from an inherited pattern of political parasitism. Interestingly, Andreski derives his conception of parasitism from the *Traité de Législation* (1826), the major work of the French sociologist Charles Comte, whose importance as a classical liberal theorist is only now coming to be appreciated.[33] Parasitism, by severing work from reward, is a necessarily strong barrier to social progress.

An important form of parasitism is land monopoly, which restricts production and impoverishes the masses. On this matter, Andreski differs little from Feder. Direct political appropriations of wealth by Latin American police, customs inspectors and the like is "enormous" according to Andreski. Although conditions vary from country to country, high tariffs, state loans, the licensing-and-bribery syndrome, government contracts, and even tax-farming (in Peru) contribute to the popular view that all governments are "merely bands of thieves." In Mexico, where state intervention is most extensive, pay-offs are naturally highest. Everywhere, taxation falls mainly on the poorer classes. Militarism likewise wastes needed resources. Conscription exists in Latin America mainly to justify the bloated officer corps. Since Latin American armies are too large for internal policing and too small for serious foreign adventures, they are really huge bureaucracies which often intervene directly in politics. Their normal care, plus what they rake off while running a country, make their upkeep "the most important from of parasitism in Latin America."[34]

Latin America is cursed with a "parasitic involution of capitalism," which Andreski defines as "the tendency to seek profits and alter market conditions by political means in the widest sense." As a result, the continent suffers from "hypertrophy of bureaucracy." Parasitic appropriation of wealth, constricted markets (the result of land monopoly and peasant poverty), uneconomic welfare legislation to buy off the urban poor, and rapid inflation make for permanent economic stagnation. This in turn fosters a permanent political instability. Andreski's general conclusion is that in Latin America the superimposition of liberal constitutions in seigneurial, "feudal" economies has led to "constitutional oligarchy" or outright repression.[35] In Latin America, as in other parts of the world, the underlying importance of the land question and its increasing urgency make its resolution perhaps one of

33  On Charles Comte and his colleague Charles Dunoyer, see Leonard Liggio, "Charles Dunoyer and French Classical Liberalism," *Journal of Libertarian Studies* 1 (Sum. 1977): 153-78.

34  Andreski 1-22.

35  Andreski 77, 90, 138. For the human cost of keeping entrenched elites in power in Latin America, see Penny Lernoux, *Cry of the People* (Garden City, NY: Doubleday 1980).

the more important items in the world agenda.[36]

## IV. SOVIET COLLECTIVIZATION:
## A BUREAUCRATIC ENCLOSURE MOVEMENT

In Preindustrial Eastern Europe, the role of politics in the economic life of nations had always been apparent. There the politically powerful landed elites created enormous latifundia "in recent times," as David Mitrany put it.[37] To capitalize on new markets for cereals in the West, the lords dispossessed the peasants, retaining them as cheap labor. When World War I broke the political power of the landed ruling class, the peasant masses rose up everywhere (with the exception of Hungary) and divided the great estates. Unable to do much else, the "liberal" semiparliamentary successor regimes in these countries conceded the land seized by the peasants in the postwar period. This revolutionary breakthrough continued the process begun in the French Revolution.

The situation in Russia was more complex. There the serfs had been legally emancipated in the 1860s in a reform-from-above reminiscent of the Prussian experience in the Napoleonic era. Legally free, Russian peasants found themselves with inadequate amounts of land (the bulk of the land having been retained by the lords) and stiff commutation payments against their land.[38] This unsatisfactory situation somewhat paralleled emancipation in the United States where, in the absence of land reform, the ex-slaves fell into the semi-slavery of sharecropping and peonage in the former Confederate States.[39] Thus when the strains of World War I broke the power and prestige of Russia's Tsarist regime, discontented peasants supplied a

---

36  Folke Dovring, "Land Reform: A Key to Change in Agriculture," *Agricultural Policy in Developing Countries*, ed. Nurul Islam (New York: Wiley 1974) 509-21.

37  David Mitrany, *Marx Against the Peasant: A Study in Social Dogmatism* (New York: Collier 1961) 77.

38  See A. Gerschenkron, "Agrarian Policies and Industrialization: Russia 1861-1917," in Postan and Habakkuk 706-800. Gerschenkron notes that the smallness of plots plus the commutation fees imposed on the peasants kept them from becoming a significant internal market for Russian manufactures (743).

39  See Eric Foner, *Nothing But Freedom: Emancipation and Its Legacy* (Baton Rouge, LA: Louisiana State UP 1983) and, on the persistence of the problem, Leo McGee and Robert Boone, eds., *The Black Rural Landowner—Endangered Species* (Westport, CT: Greenwood 1979).

mass base for radical revolution. In what would become a common pattern in the 20th century, land-hungry peasants provided the backbone of a revolution whose leaders, as Marxist and Leninists, had a somewhat different agenda than did the peasantry. Certainly, the Bolshevik leaders of the Russian Revolution were not inclined to let the goals of the struggle be set by the peasants. For decades, socialists had regarded peasants as retrograde individualists and natural enemies of the kinds of centralized direction that socialism demanded.[40] Like the petit bourgeoisie and the lumpen-proletariat, the peasants were the likely source of renewed private accumulation of capital and therefore – in the rather oversimplified model of base/super-structure – the likely source of "reactionary," antisocialist political activity.

The first socialist revolution had taken place in a country with an undeveloped proletariat. Having placed themselves at the head of a largely peasant-based revolution, Lenin and his vanguardists faced the very serious problem of how to hold onto power in a country where they and their supposed natural constituency, the industrial working class, were in a decided minority.[41] War Communism, the attempt in the midst of civil war, to leap into socialism by abolishing money and markets, had necessarily proved disastrous. To bring the Russian economy back to life as well as to conciliate a peasantry restive under forced levies and pro-urban exchange ratios, Lenin announced his strategic retreat from socialism – the New Economic Policy (NEP). Soon Lenin himself was writing of the need for freedom of trade and small-scale enterprise and cooperatives as intermediate steps in the path to socialism. He began to worry about dragging Russians out of "Asiatic" inefficiency and preventing the revival of stifling Tsarist bureaucracies.[42]

Of the three major contenders to Party leadership after Lenin's death – Trotsky, Stalin, and Bukharin – it was Bukharin who emerged as the strongest proponent of continuing and extending the NEP free market and pursuing what he called the worker-peasant alliance. Trostky clung fiercely

---

40    This is the theme of Mitrany 19-104.

41    Cp. V. I. Lenin, "Can the Bolsheviks Retain State Power?" *Selected Works* (New York: International 1971) 362-400; Lenin characteristically masks his genuine unease with his usual rhetorical overkill.

42    E.g., V. I. Lenin, "On Co-Operation," *Works* 690-9. For differing views of Lenin and Lenin's NEP, see Stephen Halbrook, "Lenin's Bakuninism," *International Review of History and Political Science* 8 (Feb. 1971): 89-111; Alec Nove, "Lenin and the New Economic Policy," *Lenin and Leninism: State, Law and Society*, ed. Bernard W. Eissenstadt (London: Lexington 1971) 155-71; and V. N. Bandera, "The New Economic Policy (NEP) as an Economic System," *Journal of Political Economy* 71 (1963): 265-79.

to the rigid Marxist program of creating heavy industry overnight on the backs of the peasants. Stalin held the middle ground and waited to seize power. In this fluid period before Stalin's consolidation of power, significant debates took place over economic policy which had radical implications for the fate of the peasant majority.[43]

On the "right" (as we are apparently obliged to call it) Bukharin, Rykov, Tomsky, the Institute of Red Professors and the economists at Narkomfin (the state financial ministry) proposed to continue the NEP. Some at Narkomfin even toyed with bringing back some kind of gold standard. The Bukharinists found themselves advocating a program that in other contexts might have been called "peasantist" or even "Jeffersonian."[44] They saw peasant demand as the key to Soviet economic development. In the context of the NEP free market, the rebuilding of the rural economy would go hand in hand with the development of light industries and consumer goods, with heavy industry developing as needed by the first two sectors.

Like Lenin, Bukharin had come to fear the rise of a bureaucratic "new class" of former workers which would arrogate total control over society to itself; as far back as 1916, he had written of the danger of the state in general.[45] Now he was calling for allowing the peasants to enrich themselves as the starting point of Soviet development. His whole program was intended to avoid the level of bureaucratism implied in the program of the "left" (especially Trostky and Preobrazhensky). Isaac Deutscher calls Bukharin "[a] Bolshevik Bastiat" who "extolled *les harmonies économiques* of Soviet society under N.E.P. and prayed that nothing should disturb those harmonies."[46]

---

43   See Alexander Erlich, *The Soviet Industrialization Debate 1924-1928* (Cambridge, MA: Harvard UP 1960) for a summary of the discussion.

44   On "peasantist" programs versus pro-industrial neo-mercantilist programs in Eastern Europe between the world wars, see Mitrany 115-31. See also Alan Carlson, *Third Ways* (Wilmington, DE: ISI 2007) ch. 4 ("Green Rising").

45   N. Bukharin, "The Imperialist Pirate State," *The Bolsheviks and the World War*, ed. O. H. Gankin and H. H. Fisher (Stanford, CA: Stanford UP 1940) 236-9.

46   Isaac Deutscher, *The Prophet Unarmed, Trotsky: 1921-1929* (New York: Vintage 1959) 223-34. For more on Bukharin's views, see Alec Nove, *Political Economy and Soviet Socialism* (London: Allen 1979) 81-99; Nikolai Bukharin, "Notes of an Economist (the Problem of Planning)," *Krushchev and Stalin's Ghost: Text, Background and Meaning of Khrushchev's Secret Report to the Twentieth Congress on the Night of February 24-25, 1956*, ed. Bertram D. Wolfe (New York: Praeger 1957) 295-315; Nikolai Bukharin, "Organized Mismanagement in Modern Society," *Essential Works of Socialism*, ed. Irving Howe (New York: Bantam 1971) 190-4.

On the "left" (again, an obligatory term), Trotsky, Preobrazhensky and their ilk called for "primitive socialist accumulation" of capital to repeat the growth of early capitalism as set forth by Marx in *Capital*. They wanted to recreate this supposedly necessary stage of economic history under the aegis of the Bolshevik state and telescope the process into a few generations. As some wit has said, Trotsky wanted two stages of history for the price of one. They faced the implication that they would have to "exploit" the peasant majority to extract an economic surplus with which to build heavy industry, which to them was the essence of development (and would, incidentally, enlarge the proletariat, their supposed political base). Since they were Marxists, such "exploitation" was morally neutral, a tool in the building of socialism, and not at all the private exploitation of the bad old days. State control of agricultural prices would favor urban areas and heavy industry and build a modern economy as rapidly as possible. If the peasants didn't like new arrangements, they would be forced to. Trotsky had never shied away from using force.[47]

Unfortunately for both sides, Stalin gradually eased himself into control of the Party and state and purged them all. Once firmly in control, he adopted most of the Left's economic program, sending cadres of armed Party members into the countryside to divide the peasants and push them into collective farms as called for by ideology and interest. With all kinds of violence and dislocation necessary, the prosperous peasants, the kulaks, were eliminated as a class, many of them physically.[48] With their much-feared leaders eliminated by the Stalinist Terror, the peasants had little choice but to acquiesce in this bureaucratic enclosure movement. Only after Stalin's death could any debate on the direction of Soviet economic policy, however mild, reemerge.[49] The Soviet state itself had become the new landlord. It seems clear enough that the "right" program was viable.[50] Certainly, it did

---

47   On such "socialist exploitation" see Deutscher 43-6, 234-8, 415-6.

48   See M Lewin, *Russian Peasants and Soviet Power* (New York: W. W. Norton 1975) and Robert Conquest, *The Harvest of Sorrow* (New York: OUP 1986).

49   For a rather tepid debate, see the account in Sidney Ploss, *Conflict and Decision-Making in Soviet Russia: A Case Study of Agricultural Policy 1953-1963* (Princeton, NJ: Princeton UP 1965).

50   For an interesting defense of Bukharinism, see Micha Gisser and Paul Jonas, "Soviet Growth in Absence of Centralized Planning: A Hypothetical Alternative," *Journal of Political Economy* 82 (March-April 1974): 333-47, in which the authors allow that industrialization could have taken place "at the same rate or even a more impressive rate" without the Preobrazhensky-Stalin policies which "led to unnecessary sufferings on the part of the Soviet population and misallocation of resources" (348). Their argument, unfortunately, is

not entail the level of violence, death, and economic destruction required to carry through the Trotsky-Stalin model. But just as in the case of the English enclosures, political power decided the event, not necessarily in the interests of the peasants – short or long run. Perhaps the two cases, though they differ considerably, will shed light on some persistent fallacies concerning peasants, agriculture, and development.

## V. CONCLUSION: MERCANTILISM AND APPLIED GERMAN IDEALISM VERSUS PEASANTRIES, MARKETS, AND BALANCED DEVELOPMENT

The political success of the large estate system in England led many observers wrongly to conclude that large-scale agricultural enterprise was inherently efficient and progressive. Conversely, small-scale family-operated peasant farms came to be viewed as uneconomic, backward, reactionary obstacles to progress. Despite the obvious spectacular success of small farms in the non-slaveholding portions of the 19th-century United States – the model Bukharin came to embrace and extol – a curious alliance of Tories and technocrats (including the Marxists) asked nothing so much from progress as that peasants be swept away by large-scale enterprise, whether private or collectivist. Edward Gibbon Wakefield, for example, urged that the distribution of land in Britain's colonies be handled in such a way as to reproduce the class structure and concentration of capital characteristic of the mother country.[51] Marx, while critical of Wakefield as a "bourgeois thinker"[52] offered little or no quarter to small-scale farming, since as a form of "simple commodity production" it was doomed to succumb, first to bourgeois concentration of property, then to socialist organization of agricultural battalions. Strangely, he did seem to use the income which once went to small, direct producers as an implicit measure of exploitation and surplus value.[53]

It is perhaps unfortunate that the English experience became the basis of so much theorizing on economic growth. As Folke Dovring writes,

---

subject to the general methodological stricture that econometric models may not actually mean a great deal. For an endorsement of agriculture plus light industry, see John Kenneth Galbraith, "Ideology and Agriculture," *Harper's*, Feb. 1985, 15-6.

51    Bernard Semmel, "The Philosophic Radicals and Colonialism," *Journal of Economic History* 21 (Dec. 1961): 513-25.

52    Marx 1: 765-4 (Marx ignores the implications of his own argument).

53    Marx 1: pt. 7.

A principal origin of the myth of the large farm is clearly in the victory of the estate system in England through the enclosure movement from the sixteenth to the early nineteenth centuries. How mythical the beneficence of the English large estate was, has gradually become clear from research showing how little agricultural progress really was achieved in the eighteenth century.

Since the early socialists accepted the economic rationale of large-scale agricultural enterprise put forward by the defenders of Britain's landed elite, it is not surprising that they were hostile from the beginning to peasant aspirations. To quote Dovring again: "The parallel strands of ideology from English aristocracy and Marxist socialism have done much, over the years, to discredit small-scale peasant farming despite its successes in Europe and Asia."[54] This *mésalliance* still has much influence on the economic policies of the postcolonial Third World, where many governments prefer tax-intensive super-projects of capital investment in heavy industry (e.g. steel mills, nuclear power plants) in countries that barely feed themselves. Some economists are beginning to question this preferred model of development and are suggesting that the Jeffersonian/peasantist/Bukharinist program of letting small-scale farmers take the lead is the soundest path in agrarian societies with an abundance of labor and a shortage of everything else. Thus John Kenneth Galbraith writes that socialism "does not easily preempt the self-motivated farm proprietor" and urges the undeveloped countries to allow agricultural prices to rise to their natural level to stimulate production, rather than subsidizing city-dwellers at the expense of farmers.[55] Economist Sudha Shenoy argues that to achieve a working, integrated capital structure, Third World Governments should not pour investment into "higher order" goods for heavy industry, but should start where their economies are: "In these areas, the kinds of investment that would raise final output are more in the agricultural sector."[56] P. T. Bauer, longtime critic of Third World policies, says, "It is a crude error to equate capital formation with specific types of heavy industry."[57] Dovring observes that on the basis of family farming "a future, more broadly based cadre of business entrepreneurs"

---

54    Dovring 520 (both quotations).

55    Galbraith 16.

56    Sudha Shenoy, "Two Applications of Hayekian Capital Theory" (unpublished paper n.d.) 3. In fairness, it should be noted that the late Dr. Shenoy took a radically different view of Enclosures than the one proposed here.

57    P. T. Bauer, "Planning and Development: Ideology and Realities" (unpublished paper, n.d.) 7.

tends to emerge."[58] The belief in the superior efficiency of large-scale units as such and in all markets at all times extends far beyond the discussion on agriculture. Here too we can spy the same underlying ideological alliance of Marxists and the conservative and postclassical "liberal" thinkers who may best be understood as corporatists.[59] Noting the identity between the economic views of conservative corporatists like Theodore Roosevelt and the Marxists as regards economic concentration, Walter Karp writes that

"The political distortions engendered by class analysis [are] well illustrated in a common ideological treatment of America's small farmers. Since they, like small businessmen, were antimonopoly, they have often been categorized as 'capitalists.' One result of this is that the great Populist revolt against the party machines is often described as 'essentially conservative.' This is because 'small capitalists,' by ideological definition, are in the backwash of history trying to 'hold back social change,' a mealy-mouthed way of saying that the oligarchs were trying to get rid of them."

*Mutatis mutandis*, the same things could be said of the English yeomen or the Russian kulaks. According to Tories, neo-mercantilists and Marxists, peasants and petty bourgeois are doomed to be overrun by the Locomotive of History, whether in the name of efficiency, progress, or socialism. To quote Karp once more: "Ideological categories always describe as natural, inevitable or inherent what the wielders of corrupt power are actively trying to accomplish."[60] The obvious question is: Were other outcomes conceivable for England or Russia?

### A. Counterfactual England

The English Civil War of the 1640's provided perhaps the best opportunity for a measure of agrarian reform. For better or worse, the Revolution remained under the control of the men around Cromwell who were little disposed to unleash the forces that might destroy them. Even the Levellers, who were radical libertarians and not primitive socialists, largely shied away from raising any agrarian questions, although some effort was made to obtain freeholder status for copyholders.[61] At the height of the enclosures, one or two critics suggested alternative paths. We have already seen that

---

58   Dovring 519.

59   On corporatism, see R. Jeffrey Lustig, *Corporate Liberalism: The Origins of Modern American Political Economy, 1890-1920* (Berkeley, CA: University of California Press 1982).

60   Walter Karp, *Indispensable Enemies: The Politics of Misrule in America* (Baltimore: Penguin 1974) 179 (both quotes).

61   C. B. Macpherson, *The Political Theory of Possessive Individualism: Hobbes to Locke* (London: OUP 1962) 107-591.

Arthur Young, once an impatient advocate of enclosure, came to criticize the process. Among the most interesting proposals were those of the Reverend David Davies, who wrote *The Case of Labourers in Husbandry* (1795). Davies sought to get something for the small man out of the process of agrarian change:

"Allow to the cottager a little land about his dwelling for keeping a cow, for planting potatoes, for raising flax or hemp. Secondly, Convert the wastelands of the kingdom into small arable farms, a certain quantity every year, to be let on favourable terms to industrious families. 3rdly, restrain the engrossment and over-enlargement of farms."[62]

Such proposals, had they been implemented, might have slightly lessened the pace of industrialization while making the transition easier for cottagers and other poor farmers. Plans for agrarian reform became part of the English radical tradition from Paine and Shelley through Cobbett down to G. K. Chesterton and Hilaire Belloc (among others). As things actually happened, land-hungry Britons had to remove to North America and undertake their political and agrarian revolutions there – especially if we take the Homestead Acts as an attempt at land-reform-in-advance (despite its ultimate failure). But even the efficiency argument for the enclosures may not be conclusive. Writing of the continental experience, Dovring says, "the allegation often made that land consolidation is a pre-requisite of the use of modern crop rotations has not been borne out by experience, whatever damage fragmentation has done to the technical and economic efficiency of labour and capital."[63] Hence, a course of modernization more like that of France – though one could hope with less bureaucracy! – would not have been impossible for England. Newer writing on Enclosure strongly suggests a reopening the whole debate.[64]

---

62  Qtd. Hammond and Hammond 58.

63  Dovring 631. For migration out of the British Isles, see again Bailyn 43-9, 291, 375-6, 606-8.

64  See, for example, Jeffrey W. Bentley, "Economic and Ecological Approaches to Land Fragmentation: In Defense of a Much-Maligned Phenomenon," *Annual Review of Anthropology* (1967) 31-67; John Saville, "Primitive Accumulation and Early Industrialization in Britain," *Socialist Register* (London: Merlin 1969) 247-71; William Lazonick, "Karl Marx and Enclosures in England," *Review of Radical Political Economics* 6 (1974): 1-59; E. Thompson, *Customs in Common* (London: Penguin 1993); R. C. Allen, *Enclosure and the Yeoman* (Oxford: Clarendon-OUP 1992); M. E. Turner, *Enclosures in Britain, 1750-1830*, 2d ed. (London: Macmillan 1984); and J. M. Neeson, *Commoners: Common Right, Enclosure, and Social Change in England, 1700-1820* (Cambridge: CUP 1993).

## B. A Counterfactual Russia

Only a few die-hards would now defend the course of Soviet collectivization under Stalin. Even so, a great many economists and historians remain enamored of the notion that something like it was necessary to industrialize and modernize a backward peasant society. In the face of the growing critique of the centralized model of development this position no longer seems tenable. The emergence in the 1960s of "market socialism" and subsequent reforms from the 1970s onward in Eastern Europe, and later China, seemed partial vindications of Bukharin and foretold the eventual decision of purely economic issues in favor of the "right deviationists" of the 1920s.[65] A turn toward markets became inevitable, even if in practice internal gangsters and outside imperialists (NATO) reaped most of the gains. Unfortunately for Soviet society in the 1920s, sheer lack of experience with non-centralized economic management and Stalin's ability to seize the already dangerous political machinery created by Lenin combined to prevent a reasonable reform of Russia's agrarian economy. As with the Enclosures, political power proved decisive, although other outcomes would not have been impossible in principle.

## AFTERWORD ON ENCLOSURES: 2011

Accumulating evidence would seem to suggest new approaches to modern history. Instead of a simple "transition from feudalism to capitalism," we actually find considerable continuity between these supposedly opposed "systems," and along with that continuity, cumulative change yielding capitalism as we know it. Mercantilism and merchant capitalism flowed from the new forms of society and state, which conserved feudal land monopoly and certain feudal attitudes and behaviors while creating new commercial openings by which well-connected merchant adventurers and large landholders could profit from controlled trade, especially in overseas empires.[66]

65    See Wlodzimierz Brus, *The Market in a Socialist Economy* (London: Routledge 1972); Gary North, "The Crisis in Soviet Economic Planning," *Modern Age* 14 (Winter 1969-1970): 49-56; Gregory Grossman, ed., *Value and Plan: Economic Calculation and Organization in Eastern Europe* (Berkeley, CA: University of California Press 1960); V. V. Kusin, ed., *The Czechoslovak Reform Movement* (Oxford: OUP 1973) Radoslav Selucký, *Economic Reforms in Eastern Europe* (New York: Praeger 1972). Strangely, Stephen Cohen's *Bukharin and the Bolshevik Revolution* (New York: Knopf 1973) underestimates the value of Bukharin's economic program.

66    In addition to Mayer, Krishan Kumar, "Pre-capitalist and Non-Capitalist Factors in the Development of Capitalism: Fred Hirsch and Joseph Schum-

Thus, alongside Moore's three roads away from feudalism (where feudal *absolutism* is actually meant) – the Anglo-American ("democratic"), the Prussian ("revolution from above" as in Germany and Japan), and finally, mass-based peasant revolution followed by communist rule – there perhaps existed another route hinted at by Eric Hobsbawm: the "peasant road to capitalism," partially realized in North America,[67] if only for a season. (We may quarrel with Hobsbawm's choice of the word "capitalism" here.) Along with the new literature on Enclosures (referred to earlier), this reorientation threatens to undermine received Whiggish analyses of modern history in a way that should reinforce inquiry into Small Commodity Production as a potentially distinct mode of production and an alternate way of life.[68]

The bottom line seems to be this: in 1500 England had a large peasantry but by 1820 that class had virtually disappeared. Fear of conceding anything to Marx (who, after all, must occasionally be right) has blocked the vision of classical liberals investigating this disappearance. But 300 years of English agrarian history cannot easily squeeze themselves into a Whig story in which the forces of production demanded new relations of production, which done, everyone lived happily ever after – full stop. It might be added that improving landlords had many levers – and not just Enclosure – with which to rid themselves of unwanted peasants. (They did, however, *improve* their rent rolls.) Referring to the pre-Enclosure organization of English farming, Michael Turner writes: "If in so many ways the gains from enclosure are in doubt, yet the damage is plain to see, then we must ask ourselves – if it wasn't broken, why did we fix it?"[69] The question is best addressed to those classes that desired and brought about the new order of agrarian capitalism.

peter," *Dilemmas of Liberal Democracies* ed. Adrian Ellis and Krishan Kumar (London: Tavistock 1983) 151-66.

67    Moore; Hobsbawm, "Scottish Reformers" 21.

68    Geoff Kennedy, "Digger Radicalism and Agrarian Capitalism," *Historical Materialism* 14 (2006): 113-43, maintains that even the supposedly "proto-communist" Gerrard Winstanley was mainly interested in preventing the spread of wage labor where it did not already exist, in favor of small-scale production.

69    Michael Turner, "Enclosures Re-Opened," *Refresh* 26 (Spring 1998): 4.

## 40

The Freeman. Ideas on Liberty 60.2 (March
2010): 8-11.

# HEALTH CARE AND RADICAL MONOPOLY

## KEVIN A. CARSON
## (2010)

IN A RECENT ARTICLE FOR *TIKKUN*, DR. ARNOLD RELMAN ARGUED THAT THE VERSIONS OF health care reform currently proposed by "progressives" all primarily involve financing health care and expanding coverage to the uninsured rather than addressing the way current models of service delivery make it so expensive. Editing out all the pro forma tut-tutting of "private markets," the substance that's left is considerable:

> What are those inflationary forces?... [M]ost important among them are the incentives in the payment and organization of medical care that cause physicians, hospitals and other medical care facilities to focus at least as much on income and profit as on meeting the needs of patients... The incentives in such a system reward and stimulate the delivery of more services. That is why medical expenditures in the U.S. are so much higher than in any other country, and are rising more rapidly... Physicians, who supply the services, control most of the decisions to use medical resources...
>
> The economic incentives in the medical market are attracting the great majority of physicians into specialty practice,

and these incentives, combined with the continued introduction of new and more expensive technology, are a major factor in causing inflation of medical expenditures. Physicians and ambulatory care and diagnostic facilities are largely paid on a piecework basis for each item of service provided.

As a health care worker, I have personally witnessed this kind of mutual log-rolling between specialists and the never-ending addition of tests to the bill without any explanation to the patient. The patient simply lies in bed and watches an endless parade of unknown doctors poking their heads in the door for a microsecond, along with an endless series of lab techs drawing body fluids for one test after another that's "been ordered," with no further explanation. The post-discharge avalanche of bills includes duns from two or three dozen doctors, most of whom the patient couldn't pick out of a police lineup. It's the same kind of quid pro quo that takes place in academia, with professors assigning each other's (extremely expensive and copyrighted) texts and systematically citing each other's works in order to game their stats in the Social Sciences Citation Index. (I was also a grad assistant once.) You might also consider *Dilbert* creator Scott Adams's account of what happens when you pay programmers for the number of bugs they fix.

One solution to this particular problem is to have a one-to-one relationship between the patient and a general practitioner on retainer. That's how the old "lodge practice" worked.[1]

But that's illegal, you know. In New York City, John Muney recently introduced an updated version of lodge practice: the AMG Medical Group, which for a monthly premium of $79 and a flat office fee of $10 per visit provides a wide range of services (limited to what its own practitioners can perform in-house). But because AMG is a fixed-rate plan and doesn't charge more for "unplanned procedures," the New York Department of Insurance considers it an unlicensed insurance policy. Muney may agree, unwillingly, to a settlement arranged by his lawyer in which he charges more for unplanned procedures like treatment for a sudden ear infection. So the State is forcing a modern-day lodge practitioner to charge more, thereby keeping the medical and insurance cartels happy – all in the name of "protecting the public." How's that for irony?

Regarding expensive machinery, I wonder how much of the cost is embedded rent on patents or regulatorily mandated overhead. I'll bet if you

---

1    See David Beito, "Lodge Doctors and the Poor," *The Freeman: Ideas onf Liberty* 44.5 (May 1994): 220–5 <http://www.thefreemanonline.org/columns/lodge-doctors-and-the-poor> (March 13, 2011).

removed all the legal barriers that prevent a bunch of open-source hardware hackers from reverse-engineering a homebrew version of it, you could get an MRI machine with a twentyfold reduction in cost. I know that's the case in an area I'm more familiar with: micromanufacturing technology. For example, the RepRap – a homebrew, open-source 3-D printer – costs roughly $500 in materials to make, compared to tens of thousands for proprietary commercial versions.

More generally, the system is racked by artificial scarcity, as editor Sheldon Richman observed in an interview a few months back. For example, licensing systems limit the number of practitioners and arbitrarily impose levels of educational overhead beyond the requirements of the procedures actually being performed.

Libertarians sometimes – and rightly – use "grocery insurance" as an analogy to explain medical price inflation: If there were such a thing as grocery insurance, with low deductibles, to provide third-party payments at the checkout register, people would be buying a lot more rib-eye and porterhouse steaks and a lot less hamburger.

The problem is we've got a regulatory system that outlaws hamburger and compels you to buy porterhouse if you're going to buy anything at all. It's a multiple-tier finance system with one tier of service. Dental hygienists can't set up independent teeth-cleaning practices in most states, and nurse-practitioners are required to operate under a physician's "supervision" (when he's out golfing). No matter how simple and straightforward the procedure, you can't hire someone who's adequately trained just to perform the service you need; you've got to pay amortization on a full med school education and residency.

Drug patents have the same effect, increasing the cost per pill by up to 2,000 percent. They also have a perverse effect on drug development, diverting R&D money primarily into developing "me, too" drugs that tweak the formulas of drugs whose patents are about to expire just enough to allow repatenting. Drug-company propaganda about high R&D costs, as a justification for patents to recoup capital outlays, is highly misleading. A major part of the basic research for identifying therapeutic pathways is done in small biotech startups, or at taxpayer expense in university laboratories, and then bought up by big drug companies. The main expense of the drug companies is the FDA-imposed testing regimen – and most of that is not to test the version actually marketed, but to secure patent lockdown on other possible variants of the marketed version. In other words, gaming the patent system grossly inflates R&D spending.

The prescription medicine system, along with state licensing of pharmacists and Drug Enforcement Administration licensing of pharmacies, is another severe restraint on competition. At the local natural-foods cooperative I can buy foods in bulk, at a generic commodity price; even organic flour, sugar, and other items are usually cheaper than the name-brand conventional equivalent at the supermarket. Such food cooperatives have their origins in the food-buying clubs of the 1970s, which applied the principle of bulk purchasing. The pharmaceutical licensing system obviously prohibits such bulk purchasing (unless you can get a licensed pharmacist to cooperate).

I work with a nurse from a farming background who frequently buys veterinary-grade drugs to treat her family for common illnesses without paying either Big Pharma's markup or the price of an office visit. Veterinary supply catalogs are also quite popular in the homesteading and survivalist movements, as I understand. Two years ago I had a bad case of poison ivy and made an expensive office visit to get a prescription for prednisone. The next year the poison ivy came back; I'd been weeding the same area on the edge of my garden and had exactly the same symptoms as before. But the doctor's office refused to give me a new prescription without my first coming in for an office visit, at full price – for my own safety, of course. So I ordered prednisone from a foreign online pharmacy and got enough of the drug for half a dozen bouts of poison ivy – all for less money than that office visit would have cost me.

Of course people who resort to these kinds of measures are putting themselves at serious risk of harassment from law enforcement. But until 1914, as Sheldon Richman pointed out, "adult citizens could enter a pharmacy and buy any drug they wished, from headache powders to opium."[2]

The main impetus to creating the licensing systems on which artificial scarcity depends came from the medical profession early in the twentieth century. As described by Richman:

> Accreditation of medical schools regulated how many doctors would graduate each year. Licensing similarly metered the number of practitioners and prohibited competitors, such as nurses and paramedics, from performing services they were perfectly capable of performing. Finally, prescription laws guaranteed that people would have to see a doctor to obtain medicines they had previously been able to get on their own.

The medical licensing cartels were also the primary force behind the move to shut down lodge practice, mentioned above.

---

2   Sheldon Richman, "The Right to Self-Treatment," *Freedom Daily* (Future of Freedom Foundation, Jan. 1995) <http://www.fff.org/freedom/0195c.asp> (March 13, 2011).

In the case of all these forms of artificial scarcity, the government creates a "honey pot" by making some forms of practice artificially lucrative. It's only natural, under those circumstances, that health care business models gravitate to where the money is.

Health care is a classic example of what Ivan Illich, in *Tools for Conviviality*, called a "radical monopoly." State-sponsored crowding out makes other, cheaper (but often more appropriate) forms of treatment less usable, and renders cheaper (but adequate) treatments artificially scarce. Artificially centralized, high-tech, and skill-intensive ways of doing things make it harder for ordinary people to translate their skills and knowledge into use-value. The State's regulations put an artificial floor beneath overhead cost, so that there's a markup of several hundred percent to do anything; decent, comfortable poverty becomes impossible.

A good analogy is subsidies to freeways and urban sprawl, which make our feet less usable and raise living expenses by enforcing artificial dependence on cars. Local building codes primarily reflect the influence of building contractors, so competition from low-cost unconventional techniques (T-slot and other modular designs, vernacular materials like bales and papercrete, and so on) is artificially locked out of the market. Charles Johnson described the way governments erect barriers to people meeting their own needs and make comfortable subsistence artificially costly, in the specific case of homelessness, in "Scratching By: How the Government Creates Poverty as We Know It."[3]

The organizational culture of healthcare is a classic example of what Paul Goodman, in *People or Personnel*, called "the great kingdom of cost-plus."

> Their patents and rents, fixed prices, union scales, featherbedding, fringe benefits, status salaries, expense accounts, proliferating administration, paper work, permanent overhead, public relations and promotions, waste of time and skill by departmentalizing task-roles, bureaucratic thinking that is pennywise poundfoolish, inflexible procedure and tight scheduling that exaggerate congingencies and overtime.

Hospitals use the same Sloanist accounting system as the rest of corporate America, but in more extreme form. Sloanism treats labor as the only real variable or direct cost, and views inventory as an asset. Under this accounting system, fixed expenses like capital projects and administrative costs don't really matter, because they are passed onto the customer as a markup for general overhead. Under what the Sloanist management ac-

---

3    Ch. 41 (377-384), in this volume.

counting system, overhead is simply included in the cost of goods which are "sold" to inventory, and is thereby transformed into an asset. As practiced in hospitals, in particular, this means enormous markups for tests and patient supplies. So while administrators obsessively look for ways to reduce nursing staff and shave a few minutes here and there off of direct labor, they pour enormous sums of money down "capital improvement" ratholes and featherbed the organization with multiple layers of adminstrative bureaucracy without a qualm. These things don't count as costs, because they can be passed on to the patient in the form of $10 aspirins and $300 bags of saline. It's the same organizational culture of cost-plus markup that led to the Pentagon's $600 toilet seat.

The major proposals for health care "reform" that went before Congress would do little or nothing to address the institutional sources of high cost. As Jesse Walker argued at Reason.com, a 100 percent single-payer system, far from being a "radical" solution,

> would still accept the institutional premises of the present medical system. Consider the typical American health care transaction. On one side of the exchange you'll have one of an artificially limited number of providers, many of them concentrated in those enormous, faceless institutions called hospitals. On the other side, making the purchase, is not a patient but one of those enormous, faceless institutions called insurers. The insurers, some of which are actual arms of the government and some of which merely owe their customers to the government's tax incentives and shape their coverage to fit the government's mandates, are expected to pay all or a share of even routine medical expenses. The result is higher costs, less competition, less transparency, and, in general, a system where the consumer gets about as much autonomy and respect as the stethoscope. Radical reform would restore power to the patient. Instead, the issue on the table is whether the behemoths we answer to will be purely public or public-private partnerships.[4]

I'm a strong advocate of cooperative models of health care finance, like the Ithaca Health Alliance (created by the same people, including Paul Glover, who created the Ithaca Hours local currency system), or the friend-

---

4    Jesse Walker, "Obama is No Radical," *Reason* (Reason Foundation, Sep. 30, 2009) <http://reason.com/archives/2009/09/30/obama-is-no-radical> (March 13, 2011).

ly societies and mutuals of the nineteenth century described by writers like Pyotr Kropotkin and E. P. Thompson. But far more important than reforming finance is reforming the way delivery of service is organized.

Consider the libertarian alternatives that might exist. A neighborhood cooperative clinic might keep a doctor of family medicine or a nurse practitioner on retainer, along the lines of the lodge-practice system. The doctor might have his med school debt and his malpractice premiums assumed by the clinic in return for accepting a reasonable upper middle-class salary.

As an alternative to arbitrarily inflated educational mandates, on the other hand, there might be many competing tiers of professional training depending on the patient's needs and ability to pay. There might be a free-market equivalent of the Chinese "barefoot doctors." Such practitioners might attend school for a year and learn enough to identify and treat common infectious diseases, simple traumas, and so on. For example, the "barefoot doctor" at the neighborhood cooperative clinic might listen to your chest, do a sputum culture, and give you a round of Zithro for your pneumonia; he might stitch up a laceration or set a simple fracture. His training would include recognizing cases that were clearly beyond his competence and calling in a doctor for backup when necessary. He might provide most services at the cooperative clinic, with several clinics keeping a common M.D. on retainer for more serious cases. He would be certified by a professional association or guild of his choice, chosen from among competing guilds based on its market reputation for enforcing high standards. (That's how competing kosher certification bodies work today, without any government-defined standards). Such voluntary licensing bodies, unlike state licensing boards, would face competition – and hence, unlike state boards, would have a strong market incentive to police their memberships in order to maintain a reputation for quality.

The clinic would use generic medicines (of course, since that's all that would exist in a free market). Since local juries or arbitration bodies would likely take a much more common-sense view of the standards for reasonable care, there would be far less pressure for expensive CYA testing and far lower malpractice premiums.

Basic care could be financed by monthly membership dues, with additional catastrophic-care insurance (cheap and with a high deductible) available to those who wanted it. The monthly dues might be as cheap as or even cheaper than Dr. Muney's. It would be a no-frills, bare-bones system, true enough – but to the 40 million or so people who are currently uninsured, it would be a pretty damned good deal.

## 41

*The Freeman. Ideas on Liberty* 57.10 (Sep. 2007): 12-3.

# SCRATCHING BY
## How Government Creates Poverty as We Know It

*CHARLES W. JOHNSON*
*(2007)*

The experience of oppressed people is that the living of one's life is confined and shaped by forces and barriers which are not accidental or occasional and hence avoidable, but are systematically related to each other in such a way as to catch one between and among them and restrict or penalize motion in any direction. It is the experience of being caged in: all avenues, in every direction, are blocked or booby trapped.

    – Marilyn Frye, "Oppression," in *The Politics of Reality*

GOVERNMENTS — LOCAL, STATE, AND FEDERAL — SPEND A LOT OF TIME WRINGING THEIR hands about the plight of the urban poor. Look around any government agency and you'll never fail to find some know-it-all with a suit and a nameplate on his desk who has just the right government program to eliminate or ameliorate, or at least contain, the worst aspects of grinding poverty in American cities – especially as experienced by black people, immigrants, people with disabilities, and everyone else marked for the special observation and solicitude of the state bureaucracy. Depending on the bureaucrat's frame of mind, his pet programs might focus on doling out conditional charity to "deserving" poor people, or putting more "at-risk" poor people under the surveillance of social workers and medical experts, or beating up recalcitrant poor people and locking them in cages for several years.

But the one thing that the government and its managerial aid workers will never do is just get out of the way and let poor people do the things that poor people naturally do, and always have done, to scratch by.

Government anti-poverty programs are a classic case of the therapeutic state setting out to treat disorders created by the state itself. Urban poverty as we know it is, in fact, exclusively a creature of state intervention in consensual economic dealings. This claim may seem bold, even to most libertarians. But a lot turns on the phrase "as we know it." Even if absolute laissez faire reigned beginning tomorrow, there would still be people in big cities who are living paycheck to paycheck, heavily in debt, homeless, jobless, or otherwise at the bottom rungs of the socioeconomic ladder. These conditions may be persistent social problems, and it may be that free people in a free society will still have to come up with voluntary institutions and practices for addressing them. But in the state-regimented market that dominates today, the material predicament that poor people find themselves in – and the arrangements they must make within that predicament – are battered into their familiar shape, as if by an invisible fist, through the diffuse effects of pervasive, interlocking interventions.

## CONFINEMENT AND DEPENDENCE

Consider the commonplace phenomena of urban poverty. Livelihoods in American inner cities are typically extremely precarious: as Sudhir Alladi Venkatesh writes in *Off the Books*: "Conditions in neighborhoods of concentrated poverty can change quickly and in ways that can leave families unprepared and without much recourse." Fixed costs of living – rent, food, clothing, and so on – consume most or all of a family's income, with little or no access to credit, savings, or insurance to safeguard them from unexpected disasters.

Their poverty often leaves them dependent on other people. It pervades the lives of the employed and the unemployed alike: the jobless fall back on charity or help from family; those who live paycheck to paycheck, with little chance of finding any work elsewhere, depend on the good graces of a select few bosses and brokers. One woman quoted by Venkatesh explained why she continued to work through an exploitative labor shark rather than leaving for a steady job with a well-to-do family: "And what if that family gets rid of me? Where am I going next? See, I can't take that chance, you know… All I got is Johnnie and it took me the longest just to get him on my side."

The daily experience of the urban poor is shaped by geographical concentration in socially and culturally isolated ghetto neighborhoods within the larger city, which have their own characteristic features: housing is concentrated in dilapidated apartments and housing projects, owned by a select few absentee landlords; many abandoned buildings and vacant lots are scattered through the neighborhood, which remain unused for years at a time; the use of outside spaces is affected by large numbers of unemployed or homeless people.

The favorite solutions of the welfare state – government doles and "urban renewal" projects – mark no real improvement. Rather than freeing poor people from dependence on benefactors and bosses, they merely transfer the dependence to the state, leaving the least politically connected people at the mercy of the political process.

But in a free market – a truly free market, where individual poor people are just as free as established formal-economy players to use their own property, their own labor, their own know-how, and the resources that are available to them – the informal, enterprising actions by poor people themselves would do far more to systematically undermine, or completely eliminate, each of the stereotypical conditions that welfare statists deplore. Every day and in every culture from time out of mind, poor people have repeatedly shown remarkable intelligence, courage, persistence, and creativity in finding ways to put food on the table, save money, keep safe, raise families, live full lives, learn, enjoy themselves, and experience beauty, whenever, wherever, and to whatever degree they have been free to do so. The fault for despairing, dilapidated urban ghettoes lies not in the pressures of the market, nor in the character flaws of individual poor people, nor in the characteristics of ghetto subcultures. The fault lies in the state and its persistent interference with poor people's own efforts to get by through independent work, clever hustling, scratching together resources, and voluntary mutual aid.

## HOUSING CRISIS

Progressives routinely deplore the "affordable housing crisis" in American cities. In cities such as New York and Los Angeles, about 20 to 25 percent of low-income renters are spending more than half their incomes just on housing. But it is the very laws that Progressives favor – land-use policies, zoning codes, and building codes – that ratchet up housing costs, stand in the way of alternative housing options, and confine poor people to ghetto neighborhoods. Historically, when they have been free to do so, poor people have happily disregarded the ideals of political humanitarians and found their own ways to cut housing costs, even in bustling cities with tight housing markets.

One way was to get other families, or friends, or strangers, to move in and split the rent. Depending on the number of people sharing a home, this might mean a less-comfortable living situation; it might even mean one that is unhealthy. But decisions about health and comfort are best made by the individual people who bear the costs and reap the benefits. Unfortunately today the decisions are made ahead of time by city governments through zoning laws that prohibit or restrict sharing a home among people not related by blood or marriage, and building codes that limit the number of residents in a building.

Those who cannot make enough money to cover the rent on their own, and cannot split the rent enough due to zoning and building codes, are priced out of the housing market entirely. Once homeless, they are left exposed not only to the elements, but also to harassment or arrest by the police for "loitering" or "vagrancy," even on public property, in efforts to force them into overcrowded and dangerous institutional shelters. But while government laws make living on the streets even harder than it already is, government intervention also blocks homeless people's efforts to find themselves shelter outside the conventional housing market. One of the oldest and commonest survival strategies practiced by the urban poor is to find wild or abandoned land and build shanties on it out of salvageable scrap materials. Scrap materials are plentiful, and large portions of land in ghetto neighborhoods are typically left unused as condemned buildings or vacant lots. Formal title is very often seized by the city government or by quasi-governmental "development" corporations through the use of eminent domain. Lots are held out of use, often for years at a time, while they await government public-works projects or developers willing to buy up the land for large-scale building.

## URBAN HOMESTEADING

In a free market, vacant lots and abandoned buildings could eventually be homesteaded by anyone willing to do the work of occupying and using them. Poor people could use abandoned spaces within their own communities for setting up shop, for gardening, or for living space. In Miami, in October 2006, a group of community organizers and about 35 homeless people built Umoja Village, a shanty town, on an inner-city lot that the local government had kept vacant for years. They publicly stated to the local government that "We have only one demand... leave us alone."

That would be the end of the story in a free market: there would be no eminent domain, no government ownership, and thus also no political process of seizure and redevelopment; once-homeless people could establish property rights to abandoned land through their own sweat equity – without fear of the government's demolishing their work and selling their land out from under them. But back in Miami, the city attorney and city council took about a month to begin legal efforts to destroy the residents' homes and force them off the lot. In April 2007 the city police took advantage of an accidental fire to enforce its politically fabricated title to the land, clearing the lot, arresting 11 people, and erecting a fence to safeguard the once again vacant lot for professional "affordable housing" developers.

Had the city government not made use of its supposed title to the abandoned land, it no doubt could have made use of state and federal building codes to ensure that residents would be forced back into homelessness – for their own safety, of course. That is in fact what a county health commission in Indiana did to a 93-year-old man named Thelmon Green, who lived in his '86 Chevrolet van, which the local towing company allowed him to keep on its lot. Many people thrown into poverty by a sudden financial catastrophe live out of a car for weeks or months until they get back on their feet. Living in a car is cramped, but it beats living on the streets: a car means a place you can have to yourself, which holds your possessions, with doors you can lock, and sometimes even air conditioning and heating. But staying in a car over the long term is much harder to manage without running afoul of the law. Thelmon Green got by well enough in his van for ten years, but when the Indianapolis Star printed a human-interest story on him last December, the county health commission took notice and promptly ordered Green evicted from his own van, in the name of the local housing code.

Since government housing codes impose detailed requirements on the size, architecture, and building materials for new permanent housing, as well as on specialized and extremely expensive contract work for electricity, plumbing, and other luxuries, they effectively obstruct or destroy most efforts to create transitional, intermediate, or informal sorts of shelter that cost less than rented space in government-approved housing projects, but provide more safety and comfort than living on the street.

## CONSTRAINTS ON MAKING A LIVING

Turning from expenses to income, pervasive government regulation, passed in the so-called "public interest" at the behest of comfortable middle- and upper-class Progressives, creates endless constraints on poor people's ability to earn a living or make needed money on the side.

There are, to start out, the trades that the state has made entirely illegal: selling drugs outside of a state-authorized pharmacy, prostitution outside of the occasional state-authorized brothel "ranch," or running small-time gambling operations outside of a state-authorized corporate casino. These trades are often practiced by women and men facing desperate poverty; the state's efforts add the danger of fines, forfeitures, and lost years in prison.

Beyond the government-created black market, there are also countless jobs that could be done above ground, but from which the poor are systematically shut out by arbitrary regulation and licensure requirements. In principle, many women in black communities could make money braiding hair, with only their own craft, word of mouth, and the living room of an apartment. But in many states, anyone found braiding hair without having put down hundreds of dollars and days of her life to apply for a government-fabricated cosmetology or hair-care license will be fined hundreds or thousands of dollars.

In principle, anyone who knows how to cook can make money by laying out the cash for ingredients and some insulated containers, and taking the food from his own kitchen to a stand set up on the sidewalk or, with the landlord's permission, in a parking lot. But then there are business licenses to pay for (often hundreds of dollars) and the costs of complying with health-department regulations and inspections. The latter make it practically impossible to run a food-oriented business without buying or leasing property dedicated to preparing the food, at which point you may as well forget about it unless you already have a lot of start-up capital sitting around.

Every modern urban center has a tremendous demand for taxi cabs. In principle, anyone who needed to make some extra money could start a part-time "gypsy cab" service with a car she already has, a cell phone, and some word of mouth. She can make good money for honest labor, providing a useful service to willing customers – as a single independent worker, without needing to please a boss, who can set her own hours and put as much or as little into it as she wants in order to make the money she needs.

But in the United States, city governments routinely impose massive constraints and controls on taxi service. The worst offenders are often the cities with the highest demand for cabs, like New York City, where the government enforces an arbitrary cap on the number of taxi cabs through a system of government-created licenses, or "medallions." The total number of medallion taxis is capped at about 13,000 cabs for the entire city, with occasional government auctions for a handful of new medallions. The system requires anyone who wants to become an independent cab driver to purchase a medallion at monopoly prices from an existing holder or wait around for the city to auction off new ones. At the auction last November a total of 63 new medallions were made available for auction with a minimum bidding price of $189,000.

Besides the cost of a medallion, cab owners are also legally required to pay an annual licensing fee of $550 and to pay for three inspections by the city government each year, at a total annual cost of $150. The city government enforces a single fare structure, enforces a common paint job, and now is even forcing all city cabs to upgrade to high-cost, high-tech GPS and payment systems, whether or not the cabbie or her customer happens to want them. The primary beneficiary of this politically imposed squeeze on independent cabbies is VeriFone Holdings, the first firm approved to sell the electronic systems to a captive market. Doug Bergeron, VeriFone's CEO, crows that "Every year, we find a free ride on a new segment of the economy that is going electronic." In this case, VeriFone is enjoying a "free ride" indeed.

The practical consequence is that poor people who might otherwise be able to make easy money on their own are legally forced out of driving a taxi, or else forced to hire themselves out to an existing medallion-holder on his own terms. Either way, poor people are shoved out of flexible, independent work, which many would be willing and able to do using one of the few capital goods that they already have on hand. Lots of poor people have cars they could use; not a lot have a couple hundred thousand dollars to spend on a government-created license.

Government regimentation of land, housing, and labor creates and sustains the very structure of urban poverty. Government seizures create and reinforce the dilapidation of ghetto neighborhoods by constricting the housing market to a few landlords and keeping marginal lands out of use. Government regulations create homelessness and artificially make it worse for the homeless by driving up housing costs and by obstructing or destroying any intermediate informal living solutions between renting an apartment and living on the street. And having made the ghetto, government prohibitions keep poor people confined in it, by shutting them out of more affluent neighborhoods where many might be able to live if only they were able to share expenses.

## RATCHETING COSTS UP AND OPPORTUNITIES DOWN

Artificially limiting the alternative options for housing ratchets up the fixed costs of living for the urban poor. Artificially limiting the alternative options for independent work ratchets down the opportunities for increasing income. And the squeeze makes poor people dependent on – and thus vulnerable to negligent or unscrupulous treatment from – both landlords and bosses by constraining their ability to find other, better homes, or other, better livelihoods. The same squeeze puts many more poor people into the position of living "one paycheck away" from homelessness and makes that position all the more precarious by harassing and coercing and imposing artificial destitution on those who do end up on the street.

American state corporatism forcibly reshapes the world of work and business on the model of a commercial strip mall: sanitized, centralized, regimented, officious, and dominated by a few powerful proprietors and their short list of favored partners, to whom everyone else relates as either an employee or a consumer. A truly free market, without the pervasive control of state licensure requirements, regulation, inspections, paperwork, taxes, "fees," and the rest, has much more to do with the traditional image of a bazaar: messy, decentralized, diverse, informal, flexible, pervaded by haggling, and kept together by the spontaneous order of countless small-time independent operators, who quickly and easily shift between the roles of customer, merchant, contract laborer, and more. It is precisely because we have the strip mall rather than the bazaar that people living in poverty find themselves so often confined to ghettoes, caught in precarious situations, and dependent on others – either on the bum or caught in jobs they hate but cannot leave, while barely keeping a barely tolerable roof over their heads.

The poorer you are, the more you need access to informal and flexible alternatives, and the more you need opportunities to apply some creative hustling. When the state shuts that out, it shuts poor people into ghettoized poverty.

# PART EIGHT

Freed-Market Regulation: Social Activism and Spontaneous Order

# 42

The Goal is Freedom (Foundation for Economic Education, June 5, 2009) <http.//www.fee.org/articles/tgif/regulation-red-herring/> (Aug. 8, 2011).

# REGULATION RED HERRING
## Why There's No Such Thing as an Unregulated Market

*SHELDON RICHMAN*
*(2009)*

MOST PEOPLE BELIEVE THAT GOVERNMENT MUST REGULATE THE MARKETPLACE. THE ONLY alternative to a regulated market, the thinking goes, is an unregulated market. On first glance that makes sense. It's the law of excluded middle. A market is either regulated or it's not.

Cashing in on the common notion that anything unregulated is bad, advocates of government regulation argue that an unregulated market is to be abhorred. This view is captured by twin sculptures outside the Federal Trade Commission building in Washington, D.C. (One is on the Constitution Ave. side, the other on the Pennsylvania Ave. side.) The sculptures, which won an art contest sponsored by the U.S. government during the New Deal, depict a man using all his strength to keep a wild horse from going on a rampage.

The title? "Man Controlling Trade."

Since trade is not really a wild horse but rather a peaceful and mutually beneficial activity between people, the Roosevelt administration's propaganda purpose is clear. A more honest title would be "Government Controlling People." But that would have sounded a little authoritarian even in New Deal America, hence the wild horse metaphor.

What's overlooked – intentionally or not – is that the alternative to a government-regulated economy is not an unregulated one. As a matter of fact, "unregulated economy," like square circle, is a contradiction in terms. If it's truly unregulated it's not an economy, and if it's an economy, it's not unregulated. The term "free market" does not mean free of regulation. It means free of government interference.

Ludwig von Mises and F. A. Hayek pointed out years ago that the real issue regarding economic planning is not: To plan or not to plan? But rather: Who plans (centralized state officials or decentralized private individuals in the market)?

Likewise, the question is not: to regulate or not to regulate. It is, rather, who (or what) regulates?

All markets are regulated. In a free market we all know what would happen if someone charged, say, $100 per apple. He'd sell few apples because someone else would offer to sell them for less or, pending that, consumers would switch to alternative products. "The market" would not permit the seller to successfully charge $100.

Similarly, in a free market employers will not succeed in offering $1 an hour and workers will not succeed in demanding $20 an hour for a job that produces only $10 worth of output an hour. If they try, they will quickly see their mistake and learn.

And again, in a free market an employer who subjected his employees to perilous conditions without adequately compensating them to their satisfaction for the danger would lose them to competitors.

What regulates the conduct of these people? Market forces. (I keep specifying "in a free market" because in a state-regulated economy, market forces are diminished or suppressed.) Economically speaking, people cannot do whatever they want in a free market because other people are free to counteract them. Just because the government doesn't stop a seller from charging $100 for an apple doesn't mean he or she can get that amount. Market forces regulate the seller as strictly as any bureaucrat could – even more so, because a bureaucrat can be bribed. Whom would you have to bribe to be exempt from the law of supply and demand?

It is no matter of indifference whether state operatives or market forces do the regulating. Bureaucrats, who necessarily have limited knowledge and perverse incentives, regulate by threat of physical force. In contrast, market forces operate peacefully through millions of participants, each with intimate knowledge of his or her own personal circumstances, looking out for their own well-being. Bureaucratic regulation is likely to be irrelevant or inimical to what people in the market care about. Not so regulation by market forces.

If this is correct, there can be no unregulated, or unfettered, markets. We use those terms in referring to markets that are unregulated or unfettered by government. As long as we know what we mean, the expressions are unobjectionable.

But not everyone knows what we mean. Someone unfamiliar with the natural regularities of free markets can find the idea of an unregulated economy terrifying. So it behooves market advocates to be capable of articulately explaining the concept of spontaneous market order – that is, order (to use Adam Ferguson's felicitous phrase) that is the product of human action but not human design. This is counterintuitive, so it takes some patience to explain it.

Order grows from market forces. But where do impersonal market forces come from? These are the result of the nature of human action. Individuals select ends and act to achieve them by adopting suitable means. Since means are scarce and ends are abundant, individuals economize in order to accomplish more rather than less. And they always seek to exchange lower values for higher values (as they see them) and never the other way around. In a world of scarcity tradeoffs are unavoidable, so one aims to trade up rather than down. The result of this and other features of human action and the world at large is what we call market forces. But really, it is just men and women acting rationally in the world.

The natural social order greatly concerned Frederic Bastiat, the nineteenth-century French liberal economist. In *Economic Harmonies* he analyzed that order, but did not feel he needed to prove its existence – he needed only to point it out. "Habit has so familiarized us with these phenomena that we never notice them until, so to speak, something sharply discordant and abnormal about them forces them to our attention," he wrote.

> … So ingenious, so powerful, then, is the social mechanism that every man, even the humblest, obtains in one day more satisfactions than he could produce for himself in several centuries… We should be shutting our eyes to the facts if we refused to recognize that society cannot present such complicated combinations in which civil and criminal law play so little part without being subject to a prodigiously ingenious mechanism. This mechanism is the object of study of political

economy…

In truth, could all this have happened, could such extraordinary phenomena have occurred, unless there were in society a natural and wise order that operates without our knowledge?

This is the same lesson taught by FEE's founder, Leonard Read, in *I, Pencil*.

Most people value order. Chaos is inimical to human flourishing. Thus those who fail to grasp that, as Bastiat's contemporary Proudhon put it, liberty is not the daughter but the mother of order will be tempted to favor state-imposed order. How ironic, since the state is the greatest creator of disorder of all.

Those of us who understand Bastiat's teachings realize how urgent it is that others understand them, too.

## 43

"In a Freed Market, Who Will Stop Markets From Running Riot and Doing Crazy Things? And Who Will Stop the Rich and Powerful from Running Roughshod over Everyone Else?," *Rad Geek People's Daily* (n.p., June 12, 2009) <http.//radgeek. com/gt/2009/06/12/freed-market-regulation/> (Aug. 10, 2011).

# WE ARE MARKET FORCES

## *CHARLES W. JOHNSON*
## *(2009)*

IN A FREED MARKET, WHO WILL STOP MARKETS FROM RUNNING RIOT AND DOING CRAZY things? And who will stop the rich and powerful from running roughshod over everyone else?

We will.

Sheldon Richman recently wrote a nice piece for *"The Goal Is Freedom"* *(at The Freeman's website)* called "Regulation Red Herring: Why There's No Such Thing as an Unregulated Market."[1] Sheldon's point, which is well taken and important, is that if "regulation" is being used to mean "making a process orderly, or regular," then what radical free-marketeers advocate is not a completely unregulated market. For something to even count as a market, it has to be orderly and regular enough for people to conduct their

---

1  Sheldon Richman, "Regulation Red Herring," ch. 42 (387-390), in this volume. Emphasis added.

business and make their living in it and through it. Government interference only seems necessary to regulate a market, in the positive sense of the word "regulate," if you think that the only way to get social order is by means of social *control*, and the only way for to get to harmonious social interactions is by having the government coerce people into working together with each other. But, as Sheldon argues:

> [T]he question is not: to regulate or not to regulate. It is, rather, who (or what) regulates?
>
> All markets are regulated… What regulates the conduct of these people? Market forces… *Economically speaking, people cannot do whatever they want in a free market because other people are free to counteract them.* Just because the government doesn't stop a seller from charging $100 for an apple doesn't mean he or she can get that amount. Market forces regulate the seller as strictly as any bureaucrat could – even more so, because a bureaucrat can be bribed. Whom would you have to bribe to be exempt from the law of supply and demand?
>
> … [T]here can be no unregulated, or unfettered, markets. We use those terms in referring to markets that are unregulated or unfettered by government. As long as we know what we mean, the expressions are unobjectionable.
>
> But not everyone knows what we mean. Someone unfamiliar with the natural regularities of free markets can find the idea of an unregulated economy terrifying. So it behooves market advocates to be capable of articulately explaining the concept of spontaneous market order… that is the product of human action but not human design…
>
> Order grows from market forces. But where do impersonal market forces come from? These are the result of the nature of human action. Individuals select ends and act to achieve them by adopting suitable means… The result… is what we call market forces. *But really, it is just men and women acting rationally in the world.*

That last point is awfully important. It's convenient to talk about "market forces," but you need to remember that remember that those "market forces" are not supernatural entities that act on people from the outside. "Market forces" are a conveniently abstracted way of talking about the systematic patterns that emerge from people's economic choices. So if the question is, who will stop markets from running riot, the answer is: *We will*;

by peacefully choosing what to buy and what not to buy, where to work and where not to work, what to accept and what not to accept, we inevitably shape and order the market that surrounds us. When we argue about whether or not government should intervene in the economy in order to regiment markets, the question is not *whether* markets should be made orderly and regular, but rather whether the process of ordering is in the hands of the people making the trade, or by unaccountable third parties; and whether the means of ordering are going to be *consensual* or *coercive*.

The one thing that I would want to add to Sheldon's excellent point is that there are two ways in which we will do the regulating of our own economic affairs in a free society – because there are two different kinds of peaceful "spontaneous orders" in a self-regulating society.[2] There is the sort of spontaneity that Sheldon focuses on – the unplanned but orderly coordination that emerges as a byproduct of ordinary people's interactions. (This is spontaneity in the sense of achieving a goal without a prior blueprint for the goal.) But a self-regulating people can also engage in another kind of spontaneity – that is, achieving harmony and order through a *conscious* process of *voluntary* organizing and activism. (This is spontaneity in the sense of achieving a goal through means freely chosen, rather than through constraints imposed.) In a freed market, if someone in the market exploits workers or chisels costumers, if she produces things that are degrading or dangerous or uses methods that are environmentally destructive, it's vital to remember that you do not have to just "let the market take its course" – because the market is not something outside of us; *we are market forces*. And so a freed market includes not only individual buyers and sellers, looking to increase a bottom line, but also our shared projects, when people choose to work together, by means of *conscious but non-coercive* activism, alongside, indeed as a part of, the undesigned forms of spontaneous self-organization that emerge. We are market forces, and the regulating in a self-regulating market is done not only by us equilibrating our prices and bids, but also by deliberately working to *shift* the equilibrium point, by means of conscious entrepreneurial action – and one thing that libertarian principles clearly imply, even though actually-existing libertarians may not stress it often enough, is that entrepreneurship includes *social* entrepreneurship, working to achieve non-monetary social goals.

So when self-regulating workers rely on themselves and not on the state, abusive or exploitative or irresponsible bosses can be checked or plain run out of the market, by the threat or the practice of strikes, of boycotts, of

---

2   See Charles Johnson, "Women and the Invisible Fist," *Rad Geek People's Daily* (n.p., May 16, 2008) <http://www.radgeek.com/gt/2008/05/16/women_ and> (March 13, 2011).

divestiture, and of *competition* – competition from humane and sustainable alternatives, promoted by means of Fair Trade certifications, social investing, or other positive "pro-cott" measures. As long as the means are voluntary, based on free association and dissociation, the right to organize, the right to quit, and the right to put your money where your mouth is, these are all part of a freed market, no less than apple-carts or corporations. When liberals or Progressives wonder who will check the power of the capitalists and the bureaucratic corporations, their answer is – a politically-appointed, even less accountable bureaucracy. The libertarian answer is – the power of the people, organized with our fellow workers into fighting unions, strikes and slow-downs, organized boycotts, and working to develop alternative institutions like union hiring halls, grassroots mutual aid associations, free clinics, or worker and consumer co-ops. In other words, if you want regulations that check destructive corporate power, that put a stop to abuse or exploitation or the trashing of the environment, don't lobby – organize!

Where government regulators would take economic power out of the hands of the people, on the belief that social order only comes from social control, freed markets put economic power into the hands of the people, and they call on us to build a self-regulating order by means of free choice and grassroots organization. When I say that the libertarian Left is the real Left, I mean that, and it's not because I'm revising the meaning of the term "Left" to suit my own predilections or some obsolete French seating chart. It's because libertarianism, rightly understood, calls on the workers of the world to unite, and to solve the problems of social and economic regulation not by appealing to any external authority or privileged managerial planner, but rather by taking matters into their own hands and working together through grassroots community organizing to build the kind of world that we want to live in.

*All power to the people!*

# 44

*Austro-Athenian Empire* (n.p., Oct. 20,
2004) <http://praxeology.net/un-
blog10-04.htm#12> (Aug. 22, 2011).

# PLATONIC
# PRODUCTIVITY

## RODERICK T. LONG
## (2004)

Women on the job market make, on average, 75 cents for every dollar men make for the equivalent jobs.

What explains this wage gap? Various possibilities have been suggested. But some Austrians have argued that there is only one possible explanation: women are less productive than men.

The argument goes like this: If employers pay an employee more than the value of that worker's marginal revenue product, the company will lose money and so will be penalised by the market. If employers pay an employee less than the value of his or her marginal revenue product, then other companies can profit by offering more competitive wages and so luring the employee away. Hence wage rates that are set either above or below the employee's marginal revenue product will tend to get whittled away via competition. (See Mises and Rothbard for this argument.) The result is that any persistent disparity between men's and women's wages must be due to a corresponding disparity between their marginal productivities.

As Walter Block puts it:

396 | Roderick T. Long

Consider a man and a woman each with a productivity of $10 per hour, and suppose, because of discrimination or whatever, that the man is paid $10 per hour and the woman is paid $8 per hour. It is as if the woman had a little sign on her forehead saying, "Hire me and earn an extra $2 an hour." This makes her a desirable employee even for a sexist boss.

The fact that the wage gap does not get whittled away by competition in this fashion shows that the gap must be based, so the argument runs, on a real difference in productivity between the sexes. This does not necessarily point to any inherent difference in capacities, but might instead be due to the disproportionate burden of household work shouldered by women – which would also explain why the wage gap is greater for married women than for single women. (Walter Block makes this argument also.) Hence feminist worries about the wage gap are groundless.

I'm not sure why this argument, if successful, would show that worrying about the wage gap is a mistake, rather than showing that efforts to redress the gap should pay less attention to influencing employers and more attention to influencing marital norms. (Perhaps the response would be that since wives freely choose to abide by such norms, outsiders have no basis for condemning the norms. But since when can't freely chosen arrangements be criticised – on moral grounds, prudential grounds, or both?)

But anyway, I'm not persuaded by the argument, which strikes me as... more *neoclassical* than Austrian, in that it ignores imperfect information, the passage of time, etc. I certainly agree with Mises and Rothbard that there is a tendency for workers to be paid in accordance with their marginal revenue product, but the tendency doesn't realise itself instantaneously or without facing countervailing tendencies, and so, as I see it, does not license the inference that workers' wages are likely to approximate the value of their marginal revenue product – just as the existence of equilibrating tendencies doesn't mean the economy is going to be at or near equilibrium. I would apply to this case the observation Mises makes about the final state of rest – that although "the market at every instant is moving toward a final state of rest," nevertheless this state "will never be attained" because "new disturbing factors will emerge before it will be realized."

First of all, most employers do not know with any great precision their workers' marginal revenue product. Firms are, after all, islands of central planning – on a small enough scale that the gains from central coordination generally outweigh the losses, but still they are epistemically hampered by the absence of internal markets. (And I'm rather skeptical of attempts to simulate markets within the firm à la Koch Industries.) A firm confronts the test of profitability as a unit, not employee by employee, and so there is a fair bit of guesswork involved in paying workers according to their profitability. Precisely this point is made, in another context, by Block himself: "estimating the marginal-revenue product of actual and potential employees… is difficult to do: there are joint products; productivity depends upon how the worker 'fits in' with others; it is impossible to keep one's eye on a given person all day long; etc." But Block thinks this doesn't much matter, because "those entrepreneurs who can carry out such tasks prosper; those who cannot, do not." Well, true enough, but an entrepreneur doesn't have to solve those problems perfectly in order to prosper – as anyone who has spent any time in the frequently insane, Dilbert-like world of actual industry can testify. (The reason Dilbert is so popular is that it's so depressingly accurate.) A firm that doesn't pay adequate attention to profitability is doomed to failure, certainly; but precisely because we're not living in the world of neoclassical perfect competition, firms can survive and prosper without being profit-maximisers. They just have to be less crazy/stupid than their competitors. Indeed, it's one of the glories of the market that it can produce such marvelous results from such crooked timber.

Even if women are not generally less productive than men, then, there might still be a widespread presumption on the part of employers that they are, and in light of the difficulty of determining the productivity of specific individuals, this presumption would not be easily falsified, thus making any wage gap based on such a presumption more difficult for market forces to whittle away. (Similar presumptions could explain the wage gap between married and single women likewise.)

Hence a wage gap might persist even if employers are focused solely on profitability, have no interest in discrimination, and are doing the level best to pay salary on marginal productivity alone. But there is no reason to rule out the possibility of deliberate, profit-disregarding discrimination either. Discrimination can be a consumption good for managers, and this good can be treated as part of the manager's salary-and-benefits package; any costs to the company arising from the manager's discriminatory practices can thus be viewed as sheer payroll costs. Maybe some managers order fancy wood paneling for their offices, and other managers pay women less for reasons of sexism; if the former sort of behaviour can survive the market test, why not the latter?

I should add that I don't think my skepticism about the productivity theory of wages is any sort of criticism of the market. The tendency to which Austrians point is real, and it means that markets are likely to get us closer to wages-according-to-productivity than could any rival system. (Since neoclassical perfect competition is incoherent and impossible, it does not count as a relevant rival.) If employers have a hard time estimating their workers' productivity (the knowledge problem), or sometimes cannot be trusted to try (the incentive problem), that's no reason to suppose that government would do any better. Employers are certainly in a better (however imperfect) position to evaluate their employees' productivity than is some distant legislator or bureaucrat, and they likewise have more reason to care about their company's profitability (even if it's not all they care about) than would the government. So there's no reason to think that transferring decision-making authority from employers to the State would bring wages into any better alignment with productivity. People in government are crooked timber too, and (given economic democracy's superior efficiency in comparison with political democracy) they're even less constrained by any sort of accountability than private firms are.

Nothing I've said shows that men and women are equally productive; it's only meant to show that, given prevailing cultural norms and power relations, we might well expect to see a gap between men's and women's earnings even if they were equally productive (which is at least reason for skepticism about claims that they are not equally productive).

I would also add that even if there are persistent problems – non-governmental but nonetheless harmful power relations and the like – that market processes do not eliminate automatically, it does not follow that there is nothing to be done about these problems short of a resort to governmental force. That's one reason I'm more sympathetic to the labour movement and the feminist movement than many libertarians nowadays tend to be. In the 19th century, libertarians saw political oppression as one component in an interlocking system of political, economic, and cultural factors; they made neither the mistake of thinking that political power was the only problem nor the mistake of thinking that political power could be safely and effectively used to combat the other problems.

As I have written elsewhere:

> As students of Austrian economics (see, e.g., the writings of F. A. Hayek) we know that the free market, by coordinating the dispersed knowledge of market actors, has the ability to come up with solutions that no individual could have devised... [But as] students of Austrian economics (see, e.g., the writings of Israel Kirzner), we also know that the efficiency of markets depends in large part on the action of entrepreneurs; and on the Austrian theory entrepreneurs do not passively react to market prices (as they do in neoclassical economics), but instead are actively alert to profit opportunities and are constantly trying

to invent and market new solutions... [W]e should remember
to balance the Hayekian insight against the equally important
Kirznerian insight that the working of the market depends on
the creative ingenuity of individuals... I see our role... as that
of intellectual entrepreneurs; our coming up with solutions is
part of (though by no means the whole of) what it means for
the market to come up with solutions. We are the market. [1]

We know – independently of the existence of the wage gap – that there
is plenty of sexism in the business world. (Those who don't know this can
verify it for themselves by spending time in that world or talking with those
who have done so.) Once we see why the productivity theory of wages,
though correct as far as it goes, goes less far than its proponents often suppose, it does not seem implausible to suppose that this sexism plays some
role in explaining the wage gap, and such sexism needs to be combated.
(And even if the wage gap were based on a genuine productivity gap deriv-
ing from women's greater responsibility for household work, the cultural
expectations that lead women to assume such responsibility would then be
the sexism to combat.) But that's no reason to gripe about "market failure."
Such failure is merely our failure. Instead, we need to fight the power –
peacefully, but not quietly.

---

1    Roderick T. Long, "Defending a Free Nation," *Anarchy and Law: The Political Economy of Choice*, ed. Edward P. Stringham (New Brunswick, NJ: Transaction 2007) 152.

# 45

"The Goal is Freedom: Libertarianism = Anti-Racism," *The Freeman. Ideas on Liberty* (Foundation for Economic Education, Aug. 8, 2010) <http.//www.thefreemanonline.org/columns/tgif/libertarianism-antiracism/> (Aug. 8, 2011).

# LIBERTARIANISM AND ANTI-RACISM

## SHELDON RICHMAN
## (2010)

### INDIVIDUALISM ABHORS BIGOTRY.

RAND PAUL'S COMMENTS REGARDING THE FEDERAL BAN ON RACIAL DISCRIMINATION IN public accommodations (Civil Rights Act of 1964, Title II) have brought the libertarian position on civil rights to public attention. (This is odd because Paul insists, "I'm not a libertarian.")

It's not been an entirely comfortable experience for libertarians. For obvious reasons libertarians are committed to freedom of association, which of course includes the freedom not to associate, and the right of property owners to set the rules on their property. Yet libertarians don't want to be mistaken for racists, who have been known to (inconsistently) invoke property rights in defense of racial discrimination. (I say "inconsistently" because historically they did not object to laws requiring segregation.)

Evelyn Beatrice Hall could say, summarizing Voltaire's views, "I disapprove of what you say, but I will defend to the death your right to say it." But no libertarian I know relishes saying, "I disapprove of your bigotry, but I will defend to the death your right to live by it."

Yet that is the libertarian position, and we should not shrink from it. Defending the freedom of the virtuous is easy. The test is in defending it for the vicious. What I want to show here, however, is that this is not the entire libertarian position. There's more, and we do the philosophy – not to mention the cause of freedom – an injustice if we leave out the rest.

Let's start with a question of some controversy. Should a libertarian even care about racism? (By racism here I mean nonviolent racist acts only.) I am not asking if people who are libertarians should care about racism, but rather: Are there specifically libertarian grounds to care about it?

Some say no, arguing that since liberty is threatened only by the initiation of physical force (and fraud), nonviolent racist conduct – repugnant as it is – is not a libertarian concern. (This is not to say libertarians wouldn't have other reasons to object.)

But I and others disagree with that claim. I think there are good libertarian grounds to abhor racism – and not only that, but also to publicly object to it and even to take peaceful but vigorous nonstate actions to stop it.

## LIBERTARIANISM AND RACISM

What could be a libertarian reason to oppose nonviolent racism? Charles Johnson spelled it out in *The Freeman*. Libertarianism is a commitment to the nonaggression principle. That principle rests on some justification. Thus it is conceivable that a principle of nonviolent action, such as racism, though not involving the initiation of force and contradicting libertarianism per se, could nevertheless contradict the justification for one's libertarianism.

For example, a libertarian who holds his or her philosophy out of a conviction that all men and women are (or should be) equal in authority and thus none may subordinate another against his or her will (the most common justification) – that libertarian would naturally object to even nonviolent forms of subordination. Racism is just such a form (though not the only one), since existentially it entails at least an obligatory humiliating deference by members of one racial group to members of the dominant racial group. (The obligatory deference need not always be enforced by physical coercion.)

Seeing fellow human beings locked into a servile role – even if that role is not explicitly maintained by force – properly, reflexively summons in libertarians an urge to object. (I'm reminded of what H. L. Mencken said when asked what he thought of slavery: "I don't like slavery because I don't like slaves.")

## TOO CLOSE TO VIOLENCE

Another, related, libertarian reason to oppose nonviolent racism is that it all too easily metamorphoses from subtle intimidation into outright violence. Even in a culture where racial "places" have long been established by custom and require no coercive enforcement, members of a rising generation will sooner or later defiantly reject their assigned place and demand equality of authority. What happens then? It takes little imagination to envision members of the dominant race – even if they have professed a "thin" libertarianism to that point – turning to physical force to protect their "way of life."

It should go without saying that a libertarian protest of nonviolent racist conduct must not itself be violent. Thus a libertarian campaign against racism in public accommodations should take the form of boycotts, sit-ins, and the like, rather than assault and destruction of property. And if that's the case, it follows that State action is also beyond the pale, since government is force. Hence the libertarian objection to government bans on segregation in privately owned places.

It would be a mistake, however, to think that ruling out government action would severely limit the scope of protest. As I've written elsewhere,[1] lunch counters throughout the American south were being desegregated years before passage of the 1964 Act. How so? Through sit-ins, boycotts, and other kinds of nonviolent, nongovernmental confrontational social action.

Yes, people got worthwhile things done without government help. Amazing, isn't it?

Two more points in closing. First, libertarians lose credibility when they pretend to deny the obvious social distinction between a privately owned public place – such as a restaurant – and a privately owned private place – such as a home. We see this too often. A libertarian will challenge a "progressive" thus: "If you really believe there should be laws against whites-only restaurants, to be consistent you should also demand laws against whites-only house parties."

That's a lousy argument.

When I walk past a restaurant, in the back of my mind is the thought, "I can go in there." I have no such thought when I walk past a home. It's a

---

1    See Sheldon Richman, "Context-Keeping and Community Organizing," ch. 48 (421-424), this volume.

404 | Sheldon Richman

matter of expectations reasonably derived from the function of the place. Homes and restaurants are alike in some important respects – they're privately owned – but they're also different in some important respects. Why deny that?

Of course, it does not follow from this distinction that government should set the rules for the restaurant. The libertarian needs to challenge incorrect inferences from the distinction – not the distinction itself.

## SIT-INS AND TRESPASS

Finally, no doubt someone will have raised an eyebrow at my inclusion of sit-ins in the list of appropriate nonviolent forms of protest against racist conduct. Isn't a sit-in at a private lunch counter a trespass?

It is – and the students who staged the sit-ins did not resist when they were removed by police. (Sometimes they were beaten by thugs who themselves were not subjected to police action.) The students never forced their way into any establishment. They simply entered, sat well behaved at the counter, and waited to be served. When told they would not be served, they said through their actions, "You can remove me, but I will not help you." (Actually, blacks could shop at Woolworth's and similar stores; they just couldn't sit at the lunch counters. Boycotts hurt the stores' bottom lines.)

I could buttress this defense of sit-ins by pointing out that those stores were not operating in a free and competitive market. An entrepreneur who tried to open an integrated lunch counter across the street from Woolworth's would likely have been thwarted by zoning, licensing, and building-inspection officers. He would have had a hard time buying supplies and equipment because the local White Citizens' Council (the "respectable" white-collar bigots) would have "suggested" to wholesalers that doing business with the integrationist might be, shall we say, ill-advised. And if the message needed to be underscored, the Ku Klux Klan (with government's implicit sanction and even participation) was always available for late-night calls.

Did the beneficiaries of that oppressive system really have a good trespass case against the sit-in participants?

# 46

*Healing Our World in an Age of Aggression*, 3d ed. (Kalamazoo, MI. SunStar 2003).

# AGGRESSION AND THE ENVIRONMENT

## MARY RUWART
## (2003)

WE ARE MORE LIKELY TO PROTECT THE ENVIRONMENT WHEN WE OWN A PIECE OF IT and profit by nurturing it.

In this chapter, we'll learn how third-layer aggression harms the environment and increases costs of many important services. With third-layer aggression, we are forced – at gunpoint, if necessary – to *subsidize* the exclusive monopolies created by second layer aggression, even if we don't use them!

Of course, we can be forced to subsidize service providers who do not have an exclusive monopoly. In real life, the layers of aggression that create the Pyramid of Power may change order from time to time. What doesn't change is that each additional layer of aggression decreases our choices and increases our costs...

## ENCOURAGING WASTE

Whenever people do not pay the full cost of something they use, they have less incentive to conserve. For example, when people pay the same amount of taxes for solid waste disposal whether they recycle or not, fewer people are inclined to recycle. As a consequence, we have more waste and disposal problems.

Conversely, when subsidies decrease, conservation automatically follows. In Seattle, during the first year that customers were charged by the volume of trash they generated, 67% chose to become involved in the local recycling program.[1] Because about 18% of our yearly trash consists of leaves, grass, and other yard products,[2] composting coupled with recycling can dramatically lower a person's disposal bill. As less waste is generated, fewer resources are needed to dispose of it. What could be more natural?

## DISCOURAGING CONSERVATION

Water utilities are usually public monopolies subsidized by our tax dollars. In California's San Joaquin Valley, 4.5 million acres of once-desert farmland is irrigated by subsidized water. Taxes are used to construct dams for irrigators, pay many of their delivery costs, and support zero-interest loans to farmers who pay only a tenth of what residential customers do![3] These subsidies encourage wasteful over irrigation, resulting in soil erosion, salt buildup, and toxic levels of selenium in the runoff. Kesterson Wildlife Reservoir has been virtually destroyed by irrigation-induced selenium buildup, which now threatens San Francisco Bay as well.[4]

As long as our tax dollars subsidize the irrigators, however, they have little financial incentive to install drip sprinkler systems or other conservation devices. As a result, less water is available for other uses, so prices increase for everyone else. Without subsidies, irrigators would be motivated to conserve, making more water available for domestic use.

## DESTROYING THE ENVIRONMENT

The above examples of third-layer aggression deal solely with exclusive monopolies, where service is provided by a public works department, subsidized in whole or in part by taxes. Subsidies also go to maintain the federal and state lands which encompass over 40% of the U.S. landmass,[5] includ-

---

1   Lynn Scarlett, *Managing America's Garbage: Alternatives and Solutions*, Reason Foundation Policy Study 115 (Santa Monica, CA: Reason, Sep.1989).

2   Janet Marinelli, "Composting: From Backyards to Big Time," *Garbage*, July-Aug.1990: 44-51.

3   Randall R. Rucker and Price V. Fishback, "The Federal Reclamation Program: An Analysis of Rent-Seeking Behavior," in *Water Rights*, ed. Terry L. Anderson (San Francisco: Pacific 1983) 62-3.

4   Terry L. Anderson and Donald R. Leal, *Free Market Environmentalism: A Property Rights Approach* (San Francisco: Pacific 1990) 55-6.

5   John Baden, *Destroying the Environment: Government Mismanagement of Our*

ing nearly all of Alaska and Nevada.[6] Land ownership is not an exclusive government monopoly, but the sheer size of the government's holdings and the subsidies necessary for maintaining them, allow us to treat them as a product of third-layer aggression.

Rather than exclusive licensing, aggressionthrough-government takes the form of forcible prevention of homesteading. Lands in the United States were originally settled by homesteading, a time-honored way of creating wealth.

Individual or groups find unused land and clear it for agriculture, fence it for grazing, make paths for hiking, build a home, and so on. To own the new wealth (farm land, ranch land, etc.) that they have made, creators lay claim to the property on which it resides. When others settle nearby, they choose different property on which to stake their claim.

Government holds land by forcibly preventing homesteading. Sometimes we condone this aggression to protect rangeland, forests, and parks from abuse and destruction. By using aggression as our means, however, we endanger the ends that we seek.

### Overgrazing the Range

The incentives of the congressional representatives who oversee the U.S. Bureau of Land Management, are very different from individual land owners. The following imaginary conversation between a congressman and some of his constituents illustrates the dilemma that our sincere lawmakers have.

"Mr. Congressman, we represent the ranchers in your district. Things are pretty tough for us right now, but you can help us. Let us graze cattle on all that vacant rangeland the government has in this area. We'll be properly grateful when it comes time to contribute to your campaign. As a token of our goodwill, we'll make a substantial donation just as soon as we come to an agreement."

The congressman has twinges of conscience. He knows that the ranchers will overstock the government ranges, even though they carefully control the number of cattle on their own land. Since they can't be sure of having the same public range every year, however, they cannot profit by taking care of it. They cannot pass it on to their children. They profit most by letting their cattle eat every last blade of grass. When the congressman shares his concern with the ranchers, they respond with:

"Mr. Congressman, we will pay a small fee for 'renting' the land. Renters don't take as good care of property as owners do, it's true, but the land is just sitting there helping no one. People who want to save the land for their

*Natural Resources* (Dallas, TX: National Center for Policy Analysis 1986) 20-1.

6    Baden 38.

children and grandchildren must not have the problems we do just keeping our next generation fed. If you don't help us, sir, you'll have trouble putting food on your table too. We'll find someone to run against you who knows how to take care of the people he or she represents. We'll make sure that you're defeated."

The congressman sighs and gives in. After all, the ranchers gain immensely if allowed to graze cattle on the land he controls. They have every incentive to make good their threats and their promises. The person they help elect might not even try to protect the environment. The congressman reasons that he should give a little on this issue so that he, not some "yes man," can remain in office.

The congressman finds that his colleagues have constituents who want the government to build a dam on public land or harvest the national forests. He agrees to vote for these programs in return for their help in directing the Bureau of Land Management to rent the grazing land to his ranchers. Naturally, these changes set precedents for many of the resources controlled by the government, not just the ones in this congressman's district.

Because of these skewed incentives, almost half of our public rangelands are rented out to ranchers for grazing cattle at one-fifth to one-tenth the rate of private land.[7] By 1964, three million additional acres had been cleared with environmentally destructive practices, such as "chaining,"[8] to create more rentable rangeland. Because the ranchers and their representatives cannot profit by protecting the land, they have little incentive to do so. As early as 1925, studies demonstrated the inevitable result: on overgrazed public ranges, cattle were twice as likely to die and had half as many calves as animals raised on private lands.[9]

Are the ranchers and their representatives selfish others whom we should condemn for overgrazing the range? Not at all! Had ranchers been permitted to homestead these lands in the first place, the rangeland would now be receiving the better care characteristic of private grazing. Our willingness to use aggression to prevent homesteading has taken the profit out of caring for the environment. When this aggression is even partially removed, the environment greatly improves.

For example, in 1934, Congress passed the Taylor Grazing Act to encourage ranchers to care for the public grazing land. By allowing ten-year transferable leases, ranchers had control of the land for a decade. Ranchers

7    Ronald M. Latimer, "Chained to the Bottom," *Bureaucracy vs. Environment*, ed. John Baden and Richard L. Stroup (Ann Arbor, MI: University of Michigan Press 1981) 156.

8    Baden 18.

9    Gary D. Libecap, *Locking Up the Range* (San Francisco: Pacific 1981) 27.

who improved the land were given the positive feedback of good grazing or a good price when selling their lease. In essence, the lease gave them partial ownership. As a result, almost half of the rangeland classified as poor was upgraded.[10]

However, in 1966, leases were reduced to only one year, giving ranchers little incentive to make improvements. After all, they could not be sure that they would be able to renew their lease. As a result, private investment in wells and fences in the early 1970s dropped to less than a third of their 1960s level.[11]

When vast tracts of public property are misused, the environment can suffer great damage. Overgrazing of public rangeland was permanently destructive in many cases, contributing to the formation of a "dust bowl" in the midwestern states.[12]

### Logging the Forests

As subsidies increase, so does environmental destruction. Most of the trees in our national forests wouldn't be logged without subsidies, because the cost of building the roads necessary to transport the timber exceeds the value of the lumber. Once again, however, the special interests found a way to use the aggression of taxes to their own advantage. Let's listen to an imaginary conversation between the timber companies and their congresswoman.

"Ms. Congresswoman, the Forest Service has money in its budget for hiking trails. Now we're all for hiking; we just think we should get our fair share of the forest and our fair share of the subsidy. Some of that money for trails should be used to build logging roads. Consumers will benefit by increases in the supply of timber. We'd profit too and see that you got your 'fair share' for your campaign chest. We'd pay some money for replanting too, so the environmentalists will be happy."

The congresswoman considers their offer. She knows that the loggers, like the ranchers, have little incentive to log sustainably on public lands. She also knows that if the hikers complain, she can ask Congress for a larger subsidy so that the Forest Service can build more trails. Some of that subsidy can be siphoned off to build more logging roads. More logging roads mean more campaign contributions. Since hikers don't make money off of the forests, they won't help her out the way that loggers will.

The congresswoman won't protect the forests by fighting the loggers. Special interests reap high profits with subsidies, so they'll spend large

---

10    Libecap 46.

11    Libecap 76.

12    Murray N. Rothbard, *For a New Liberty* (New York: Macmillan 1973) 264.

amounts of money to protect them. If the congresswoman doesn't agree to the timber companies' demands, they'll put their considerable money and influence behind her opponent. The timber companies will be able to log the forests. The only question is which congressional representative will reap a share of the profits. The congresswoman sighs and agrees to fight for more logging subsidies.

As a result of subsidies' adverse influence, the Forest Service uses taxpayer dollars to log the national forests. By 1985, almost 350,000 miles of logging roads had been constructed in the national forests – eight times more than the total mileage of the U.S. interstate highway system![13] Construction of roads requires stripping mountainous terrain of its vegetation, causing massive erosion. In the northern Rockies, trout and salmon streams are threatened by the resulting silt. Fragile ecosystems are disturbed.[14]

The Forest Service typically receives 20 cents for every dollar spent on roads, logging, and timber management.[15] Even though the timber companies are charged for the cost of reforestation, 50% of these funds go for "overhead."[16] Between 1991 and 1994, $1 billion more in taxes were spent to log the national forests than the loggers paid.[17]

Although logging is encouraged, hiking is discouraged. The number of backpackers increased by a factor of 10 between the 1940s and the 1980s, but trails in the national forests dropped from 144,000 miles to under 100,000.[18]

Should we blame the timber companies and their congressional representatives for this travesty? Hardly! After all, if we sanction aggression to prevent homesteading, we take the profit out of protecting the forest.

While national forests are being depleted through special interest subsidies, trees on private property are flourishing. In the United States, 85% of new tree plantings are made on private lands; in Western Europe, private plantings increased forest cover by 30% between 1971 and 1990.[19]

---

13   Peter Kirby and William Arthur, *Our National Forests: Lands in Peril* (Washington, DC: Wilderness Society/Sierra Club 1985) 4.

14   Baden 10.

15   Thomas Barlow, Gloria E. Helfand, Trent W. Orr, and Thomas B. Stoel, Jr., *Giving Away the National Forests* (New York: NRDC 1980) Appendix 1.

16   Baden 14.

17   Edmund Contoski, *Makers and Takers: How Wealth and Progress Are Made and How They Are Taken Away or Prevented* (Minneapolis, MN: American Liberty 1997) 305.

18   Katherine Barton and Whit Fosburgh, *Audubon Wildlife Report 1986* (New York: Audubon 1986) 129.

19   Contoski 302.

The largest private U.S. landowner, International Paper, carefully balances public recreation (e.g., backpacking) with logging. In the Southeast, 25% of its profit is from recreation.[20] Industry grows 13% more timber than it cuts in order to prepare for future needs and increase future profits.[21] When we honor the choices of others, the desire for profit works hand-in-hand with sustainable environmental activities.

### Slaughtering Wildlife

Governments often prevent individuals from claiming wildlife just as they prevent homesteading on land. In essence, wildlife management has become a public monopoly.

Tax subsidies to "manage" wildlife give it the characteristics of third-layer aggression. Subsidies have often paid for the killing of wildlife, sometimes to the point of near extinction.

State governments encouraged the shooting of hawks. Some, like Pennsylvania paid hunters a tax-subsidized bounty. Aghast at this slaughter, Mrs. Rosalie Edge bought one of the hunters' favorite spot with voluntary contributions from like-minded people and turned it into a sanctuary. Hawk Mountain, in the Pennsylvania Appalachians, has been protecting hawks since 1934.[22]

In 1927, the owner of Sea Lion Caves, the only known mainland breeding and wintering area of the Stellar sea lion,[23] opened it to visitors as a naturalist attraction. Meanwhile, Oregon's tax dollars went to bounty hunters who were paid to shoot sea lions. The owners of Sea Lion Caves spent much of their time chasing hunters off their property. Although the owners of Sea Lion Caves and Hawk Mountain Sanctuary were protecting the wildlife on their land, they were also forced to pay the taxes that rewarded hunters who endangered it!

Not everyone in a group wants resources treated in the same way. When all people use their property as they think best, one owner's careless decision is unlikely to threaten the entire ecosystem. When bureaucrats control vast areas, however, one mistake can mean ecological disaster.

---

20   Terry L. Anderson and Donald R. Leal, "Rekindling the Privatization Fires: Political Lands Revisited," *Federal Privatization Project*, Issue Paper 108 (Santa Monica, CA: Reason 1989) 12.

21   Contoski 302.

22   "Special Report: The Public Benefits of Private Conservation," *Environmental Quality: 15th Annual Report of the Council on Environmental Quality Together with the President's Message to Congress* (Washington, DC: GPO1984) 387-94.

23   "Special Report" 394-8.

In addition, special interest groups struggle for control. For example, Yellowstone National Park, the crown jewel of the national park system, has been torn apart by conflicts of interest. In 1915, the Park Service decided to eradicate the Yellowstone wolves, which were deemed to be a menace to the elk, deer, antelope, and mountain sheep that visitors liked to see.[24] Park officials induced employees to trap wolves by allowing them to keep or sell the hides. Eventually, the fox, lynx, marten, and fisher were added to the list.[25] Without predators, the hoofed mammals flourished and began to compete with each other for food. The larger elk eventually drove out the white-tailed deer, the mule deer, the bighorn sheep, and the pronghorn. As their numbers increased, the elk ate the willow and aspen around the riverbanks and trampled the area so that seedlings could not regenerate.

Without the willow and aspen, the beaver population dwindled. Without the beavers and the ponds they created, water fowl, mink, and otter were threatened. The clear water needed by the trout disappeared along with the beaver dams. Without the ponds, the water table was lowered, decreasing the vegetation growth required to sustain many other species. When park officials realized their mistake, they began removing the elk (58,000 between 1935 and 1961).[26]

Meanwhile, the elk overgrazed, greatly reducing the shrubs and berries that fed the bear population. In addition, the destruction of willow and aspen destroyed the grizzly habitat, while road construction and beaver loss reduced the trout population on which the grizzlies fed. When the garbage dumps were closed in the 1960s to encourage the bears to feed naturally, little was left for them to eat. They began seeking out park visitors who brought food with them. Yellowstone management began a program to remove the problem bears as well. In the early 1970s, more than 100 bears were removed. Almost twice as many grizzlies were killed.[27]

Subsidies create tension between special interests with different views. Yellowstone visitors wanted to see deer and elk. Some naturalists would have preferred not to disturb the ecosystem, even if it meant limiting visitors and disappointing some of them. Since everyone is forced to subsidize the park, each person tries to impose his or her view as to how it should be run. The resulting compromise pleases no one.

---

24  Tom McNamee, "Yellowstone's Missing Element," *Audubon* 88.1 (1986): 12-9.

25  Alston Chase, *Playing God in Yellowstone: The Destruction of America's First National Park* (Boston: Mariner-Houghton 1987) 123-4.

26  Chase 12, 28, 29.

27  Chase 155, 173.

Contributors to private conservation organizations, in contrast, choose to donate to a group that shares their common purpose. For example, at Pine Butte Preserve, the Nature Conservancy replanted overgrazed areas with chokecherry shrubs for the grizzlies and fenced off sensitive areas from cattle, deer, and elk – animals that thrive in the absence of predators.[28] The Nature Conservancy has preserved more than 2.4 million acres of land since 1951.[29]

The Audubon Society also uses ownership to protect the environment. The Rainey Wildlife Sanctuary in Louisiana is home to marshland deer, armadillo, muskrat, otter, mink, and snow geese. Carefully managed natural gas wells and cattle herds create wealth without interfering with the native species.[30] Other private organizations investing in wilderness areas for their voluntary membership include Ducks Unlimited, the National Wild Turkey Federation, the National Wildlife Federation, Trout Unlimited, and Wings Over Wisconsin.

The story of Ravena Park, Seattle, illustrates how aggression compromises the care given to the environment. In 1887, a couple bought up the land on which some giant Douglas firs grew, added a pavilion for nature lectures, and made walking paths with benches and totems depicting Indian culture. Visitors were charged admission to support Ravena Park; up to 10,000 people came on the busiest days.

Some Seattle citizens weren't satisfied with this nonaggressive arrangement. They lobbied for the city to buy and operate the park with tax dollars – taken at gunpoint, if necessary. In 1911, the city took over the park, and one by one the giant fir trees began to disappear. Concerned citizens complained when they found that the trees were being cut into cordwood and sold. The superintendent, later charged with abuse of public funds, equipment, and personnel, told the citizens that the large "Roosevelt Tree" had posed a "threat to public safety." By 1925, all the giant fir trees were gone.[31] The superintendent could personally profit from the beautiful trees only by selling them, not by protecting them.

### Power Corrupts

The above example succinctly illustrates the dangers of third-layer aggression. Subsidies give few bureaucrats the *power* to trade public assets for

---

28  Tom Blood, "Men, Elk, and Wolves," *The Yellowstone Primer: Land and Resource Management in the Greater Yellowstone Ecosystem*, ed. John A. Baden and Donald Leal (San Francisco: Pacific 1990) 109.

29  "Special Report" 368.

30  Richard L. Stroup and John A. Baden, *Natural Resources: Bureaucratic Myths and Environmental Management* (San Francisco: Pacific 1983) 49-50.

31  Anderson and Leal 51-52.

personal gain. Unlike the personal power that comes from wisdom, inner growth, and hard work, this power comes from the point of a gun. This power of aggression corrupts those who use it, impoverishes those who have little, and destroys the earth that supports us...

Rad Geek People's Daily (n.p., May
17, 2010) <http://radgeek.com/
gt/2010/05/17/the-clean-water-act-vs-
clean-water/> (Aug. 22, 2011).

# THE CLEAN WATER ACT VERSUS CLEAN WATER

## CHARLES W. JOHNSON
## (2010)

M ARKET ANARCHISTS PROBABLY HAVEN'T WRITTEN ABOUT THE ENVIRONMENT AS MUCH
as we should. But not because we don't have anything to say about
it. When we do address environmental issues specifically, one of the things
that I think market Anarchists have really contributed to the discussion are
some key points about how *ex ante* environmental laws, intended to curb
pollution and other forms of environmental damage, make some superficial
reforms, but at the expense of creating a legal framework for big polluters to
*immunize* themselves from responsibility for the damage they continue to
cause to people's health and homes, or to the natural resources that people
use from day to day. And, also, how legislative environmentalism in general tends to crowd out freed-market methods for punishing polluters and
rewarding sustainable modes of production.[1] For a perfect illustration of

---

1    See, for example, Kevin A. Carson, "Monbiot: One Step Back," *Mutualist Blog: Free Market Anticapitalism* (n.p., Jan. 1, 2006) <http:/mutualist.
blogspot.com/2006/01/monbiot-one-step-back.html> (March 13, 2011);
Kevin A. Carson, "Fred Foldvary on Green Taxes," *Mutualist Blog: Free*

how legislative environmentalism is actively *hurting* environmental action, check out this short item in the Dispatches section of the May 2010 *Atlantic*. The story is about toxic mine runoff in Colorado, and describes how statist anti-pollution laws are *stopping* small, local environmental groups from actually taking direct, simple steps toward containing the lethal pollution that is constantly running into their communities' rivers. Also, how big national environmental groups are lobbying hard to make sure that the smaller, grassroots environmental groups keep getting blocked by the Feds.

> Near Silverton, the problem became bad enough to galvanize landowners, miners, environmentalists, and local officials into a volunteer effort to address the drainage... With a few relatively simple and inexpensive fixes, such as concrete plugs for mine portals and artificial wetlands that absorb mine waste, the Silverton volunteers say they could further reduce the amount of acid mine drainage flowing into local rivers. "In some cases, it would be simple enough just to go up there with a shovel and redirect the water," says William Simon, a former Berkeley ecology professor who has spent much of the past 15 years leading cleanup projects.
>
> But as these volunteers prepare to tackle the main source of the pollution, the mines themselves, they face an unexpected obstacle – the Clean Water Act. Under federal law, anyone wanting to clean up water flowing from a hard rock mine must bring it up to the act's stringent water-quality standards and take responsibility for containing the pollution – forever. Would-be do-gooders become the legal "operators" of abandoned mines like those near Silverton, and therefore liable for their condition.[2]

Under anything resembling principles of justice, people ought to be held responsible for the damage they *cause*, not for the problems that remain after they try to *repair* damage caused by somebody else, now long gone. But

*Market Anticapitalism* (n.p., Feb. 22, 2005) <http://mutualist.blogspot.com/2005/02/fred-foldvary-on-green-taxes.html> (March 13, 2011); Charles W. Johnson, "Left-Libertarian Engagement," *Rad Geek People's Daily* (n.p., Nov. 25, 2008) <http://www.radgeek.com/gt/2008/11/25/leftlibertarian_engagement> (March 13, 2011).

2   Michelle Nijhuis, "Shafted," *The Atlantic* (Atlantic Media Co., May 2010) <http://www.theatlantic.com/magazine/archive/2010/05/shafted/8025> (March 13, 2011).

the basic problem with the Clean Water Act, like all statist environmental regulations, is that it isn't about standards of justice; it's about *compliance with regulatory standards*, and from the standpoint of an environmental regulator the important thing is (1) that government has to be able to single out somebody or some group to pigeonhole as the People In Charge of the site; and (2) whoever gets tagged as "taking charge" of the site, *therefore*, gets put on the hook for meeting the predetermined standards, or for facing the predetermined penalties, no matter what the facts of the particular case and no matter the fact that they didn't do anything to cause the existing damage.[3]

The obvious response to this should be to repeal the clause of the Clean Water Act which creates this insane condition, and leave the people with a stake in the community free to take positive action. Unfortunately, the best that government legislators can think of is to pass a *new* law to *legalize it* – i.e., to create yet another damn bureaucratic "permit," so that shoestring-budget community groups can spend all their time filling out paperwork and reporting back to the EPA instead. Meanwhile, the State of the Debate being what it is, even this weak, hyperbureaucratic solution is being opposed by the lobbying arms of several national environmental groups:

> In mid-October, Senator Mark Udall of Colorado introduced a bill that would allow such "good Samaritans" to obtain, under the Clean Water Act, special mine-cleanup permits that would protect them from some liability. Previous good-Samaritan bills have met opposition from national environmental organizations, including the Sierra Club, the Natural Resources Defense Council, and even the American Bird Conservancy, for whom any weakening of Clean Water Act standards is anathema. Although Udall's bill is narrower in scope than past proposals, some environmental groups still say the

---

3   *Ex ante* regulation, by definition, isn't about looking at particular cases, and it isn't about looking back to who caused what; it's about identifying, licensing, controlling, and penalizing agents according to the situation *right now*. That sounds all progressive and forward-looking and practical, until you realize that the direct effect is to make sure that *nobody* who gives a damn about their community is able to afford to take responsibility for dealing with pre-existing damage; all kinds of positive action get burned out, and all that's left are cash-strapped, overworked government programs, which can proceed because government has made up the doctrine of sovereign immunity in order to protect its own enterprises from being held legally responsible for anything.

abandoned-mine problem should instead be solved with additional regulation of the mining industry and more federal money for cleanup projects. "If you support cleaning up the environment, why would you support cleaning up something halfway?" asks Natalie Roy, executive director of the Clean Water Network, a coalition of more than 1,250 environmental and other public-interest groups. "It makes no sense."[4]

All of which perfectly illustrates two of the points that I keep trying to make about Anarchy and practicality. Statists constantly tell us that, nice as airy-fairy Anarchist theory may be, we have to deal with the real world. But down in the real world, walloping on the tar baby of electoral politics constantly gets big Progressive lobbying groups stuck in ridiculous fights that elevate procedural details and purely symbolic victories above the practical success of the goals the politicking was supposedly for – to hell with *clean water* in Silverton, Colorado, when there's a federal Clean Water *Act* to be saved! And, secondly, how governmental politics systematically destroys any opportunity for progress on the margin – where positive direct action by people in the community could save a river from lethal toxins *tomorrow*, if government would just get its guns out of their faces, government action takes years to pass, years to implement, and never addresses *anything* until it's just about ready to address *everything*. Thus Executive Director Natalie Roy, on behalf of More Than 1,250 Environmental And Other Public-Interest Groups, is explicitly baffled by the notion that the people who live by these rivers might not have time to hold out for the decisive blow in winning some all-or-nothing struggle in the national legislature.

The near-term prospects of Udall's half-hearted legalization bill don't look good. The conclusion from the *Atlantic* is despair:

> The Silverton volunteers aren't expecting a federal windfall anytime soon – even Superfund-designated mine sites have waited years for cleanup funding, and Udall's bill has been held up in a Senate committee since last fall. Without a good-Samaritan provision to protect them from liability, they have few choices but to watch the Red and Bonita, and the rest of their local mines, continue to drain.[5]

But I think if you realize that the problem is built in, structurally, to electoral politics, the response doesn't need to be despair. It can be *motiva-*

4   Nijhuis.
5   Nijhuis.

*tion.* Instead of sitting around watching their rivers die and waiting for Senator Mark Udall Of Colorado to pass a bill to legalize their direct action, what I'd suggest is that the local environmental groups in Colorado stop caring so much about what's legal and what's illegal, consider some *countereconomic, direct action alternatives* to governmental politics, and perform some Guerrilla Public Service.

I mean, look, if there are places where it would be simple enough just to go up there with a shovel and redirect the water, then wait until nightfall, *get yourself a shovel and go up there.* Take a flashlight. And some bolt cutters, if you need them. Cement plugs no doubt take more time, but you'd be surprised what a dedicated crew can accomplish in a few hours, or a few nights running. If you do it yourself, *without identifying yourself and without asking for permission,* the EPA doesn't need to know about it and the Clean Water Act can't do anything to punish you for your "halfway" clean up.

The Colorado rivers don't need political parties, permits, or Public-Interest Groups. What they need are some good honest outlaws, and some Black-and-Green Market entrepreneurship.

# 48

Cato Unbound (Cato Institute, June 18,
2010) <http://www.cato-unbound.
org/2010/06/18/sheldon-richman/
context-keeping-and-community-organiz-
ing/> (Aug. 8, 2011).

# CONTEXT-KEEPING AND COMMUNITY ORGANIZING

## SHELDON RICHMAN
## (2010)

THE STRONGEST LIBERTARIAN CASE I CAN IMAGINE FOR TITLE II OF THE CIVIL RIGHTS ACT of 1964, the provision against racial discrimination in public accommo- dations, rests on the key point – which I fully embrace – that the Southern states operated the equivalent of a "white supremacist cartel" in restaurants and hotels. Before explaining my criticism of Title II, I'd like to elaborate on this point.

Standard libertarian criticism of Title II appears to treat the targeted res- taurants and hotels as purely private businesses that, however odious their racial policies, were unjustifiably imposed on by government policies that violated private property rights. But this account misses something crucial. Outwardly those businesses looked like private enterprises, but the sub- stance was different. The social-legal environment in the pre-1964 South, when Jim Crow reigned, was hardly what any libertarian would envision as a laissez-faire environment. Rather, the region was in the grip of a pervasive social system based on white supremacy – one enforced by formal government rules, discretionary official decision-making, and extralegal measures, ranging from social pressure all the way to violence that was countenanced and even participated in by government officials.

A racially liberal entrepreneur who sought to compete next door to a segregated restaurant in the downtown of a Southern city would have been in for a difficult time. How would the city's zoning, licensing, and building-code authorities have reacted? How inclined would they have been to find myriad reasons why that restaurant wasn't qualified to operate? Assuming the restaurateur overcame those obstacles, mightn't he have had trouble buying equipment and food from suppliers once they had been visited by the local White Citizens' Council, sometimes known as the "white-collar Klan"? The WCC might also have had something to say to prospective employees. If that form of persuasion didn't suffice, the actual Ku Klux Klan would have been available for nocturnal assignments. Property damage and physical intimidation might have been used to persuade the agitator not to upset the town's "way of life," which, up until then, was perfectly satisfactory. No need to call the cops; they were probably there already.

Any libertarian would object if a municipal fire department had a policy of ignoring burning homes in the black part of town. If the municipality contracted out its firefighting services to a "private" company with the same racial policy, libertarians would similarly object on grounds of equality under the law. They would not be fooled by the mere façade of private enterprise. Form does not alter substance. But that would also be true for the white-supremacist cartels that operated public accommodations throughout the South. So libertarians should not regard those businesses as mere private enterprises.

The key to understanding this matter is what libertarian scholar Chris Matthew Sciabarra calls dialectics, or context-keeping. As he wrote in *The Freeman*, "Society is not some ineffable organism; it is a complex nexus of interrelated institutions and processes, of volitionally conscious, purposeful, interacting individuals – and the unintended consequences they generate." Thus dialectics "counsels us to study the object of our inquiry from a variety of perspectives and levels of generality, so as to gain a more comprehensive picture of it. That study often requires that we grasp the object in terms of the larger system within which it is situated, as well as its development across time. (Emphasis added.)

Applying Sciabarra's principle, we can see that racial discrimination at particular "private" Southern lunch counters and hotels before 1964 cannot be judged apart from the "larger system within which it is situated." The full context must be kept in view.

Ironically, an example of dialectical thinking, albeit applied to bank regulation, is provided by Rep. Ron Paul, father of Rand Paul, whose rejection (before his acceptance) of Title II prompted the recent controversy. In 1999 the elder Paul opposed repeal of a key section of the New Deal-era Glass-Steagall Act, which separated commercial from investment banking. Considering Ron Paul's commitment to a free market, his opposition to repeal of an intervention might seem illogical. Yet he opposed it because "This increased indication of the government's eagerness to bail out highly-leveraged, risky and largely unregulated financial institutions bodes ill for the... future as far as limiting taxpayer liability is concerned." Paul was thinking dialectically: Removing a restriction from a form of business that enjoys government privileges is not necessarily a libertarian move. Context is crucial.

By the same token, imposing a restriction on a form of business that enjoys government privileges is not necessarily an unlibertarian move. Again, context is crucial.

So does this mean that Professor Bernstein is right that libertarians ought to have supported Title II in 1964? I don't think so.

Professor David Bernstein of George Mason University Law School is one libertarian who accepts Title II only because a "massive federal takeover of local government to prevent violence and threats against, and extralegal harassment of, those who chose to integrate" would have been "completely impractical."[1] Undoubtedly so.

But why does that exhaust the options? Why assume government is the only salvation? That's an odd position, indeed, for a libertarian. Professor Bernstein does not so much as mention another strategy for ending racial discrimination in public accommodations: direct nonviolent social action by the people affected and those in sympathy with them.

We can't dismiss that as impractical because it had been working several years before Title II was enacted. Beginning in 1960 sit-ins and other Gandhi-style confrontations were desegregating department-store lunch counters throughout the South. No laws had to be passed or repealed. Social pressure – the public shaming of bigots – was working.

Even earlier, during the 1950s, David Beito and Linda Royster Beito report in *Black Maverick*, black entrepreneur T.R.M. Howard led a boycott of national gasoline companies that forced their franchisees to allow blacks to use the restrooms from which they had long been barred.

It is sometimes argued that Title II was an efficient remedy because it affected all businesses in one fell swoop. But the social movement was also

---

1    David E. Bernstein, "Context Matters: A Better Libertarian Approach to Antidiscrimination Law," *Cato Unbound* (Cato Institute, June 16, 2010) <http://tinyurl.com/2wupdfv> (March 13, 2011).

efficient: whole groups of offenders would relent at one time after an intense sit-in campaign. There was no need to win over one lunch counter at a time.

Title II, in other words, was unnecessary. But worse, it was detrimental. History's greatest victories for liberty were achieved not through lobbying, legislation, and litigation – not through legal briefs and philosophical treatises – but through the sort of direct "people's" struggle that marked the Middle Ages and beyond. As a mentor of mine says, what is given like a gift can be more easily taken away, while what one secures for oneself by facing down power is less easily lost.

The social campaign for equality that was desegregating the South was transmogrified when it was diverted to Washington. Focus then shifted from the grassroots to a patronizing white political elite in Washington that had scurried to the front of the march and claimed leadership. Recall Hillary Clinton's belittling of the grassroots movement when she ran against Barack Obama: "Dr. King's dream began to be realized when President Lyndon Johnson passed the Civil Rights Act of 1964... It took a president to get it done."

We will never know how the original movement would have evolved – what independent mutual-aid institutions would have emerged – had that diversion not occurred.

We do know, as Professor Bernstein reminds us, that Title II became a precedent for laws forbidding all types of private "discrimination" that were in no way rooted in government-sanctioned cartels. Bernstein may see the South's social system as providing a "limiting principle" for when antidiscrimination laws are permissible, but this overlooks the perverse dynamic of the political world. Simply put, after 1964 there just was no way that antidiscrimination laws were going to be confined to Jim Crow-type cases.

Libertarians need not shy away from the question, "Do you mean that whites should have been allowed to exclude blacks from their lunch counters?" Libertarians can answer proudly, "No. They should not have been allowed to do that. They should have been stopped – not by the State, which can't be trusted, but by nonviolent social action on behalf of equality."

The libertarian answer to bigotry is community organizing.

# CONTRIBUTORS

**Benjamin Tucker** was the dean of nineteenth-century American individualist anarchists. He served as editor of the influential anarchist periodical *Liberty*; many of his essays are collected in *Instead of a Book: By a Man Too Busy to Write One* (1897). The text of *Liberty* is available on-line; see <http://travellinginliberty.blogspot.com> for an index.

**Brad Spangler** is the director of the Center for a Stateless Society <http://www.c4ss.org>.

**Charles Johnson** is an individualist anarchist living and working in Auburn, Alabama. He is a Research Associate at the Molinari Institute, a member of the Industrial Workers of the World, and an alumnus of Auburn University. He has published the *Rad Geek People's Daily* weblog at radgeek.com since 2001 and is a frequent speaker and columnist on topics in market anarchism, stateless social activism, and the philosophy of anarchism. He can be reached through his website, <http://charleswjonhson.name>.

**Dyer Lum** was an anarchist theorist and campaigner. He briefly edited *The Alarm* (1892-3). A radical labor activist and sometime partner of Voltairine de Cleyre, he was the author of books on Mormonism, trade unionism, and anarchism, notably *The Economics of Anarchy* (1890).

**Gary Chartier** is Associate Dean of the School of Business and Associate Professor of Law and Business Ethics at La Sierra University. He holds a PhD from the University of Cambridge and a JD from the University of California at Los Angeles. He is the author of over thirty scholarly articles in publications including the *Oxford Journal of Legal Studies*, *Legal Theory*, the *Canadian Journal of Law and Jurisprudence*, and the *Law and Philosophy*, and of three books: *The Analogy of Love* (2007); *Economic Justice and Natural Law* (2009); and *The Conscience of an Anarchist* (2011). He is a member of the Alliance of the Libertarian Left and of the advisory boards of the Center for a Stateless Society and the Moorfield Storey Institute. He blogs at <http://www.liberalaw.blogspot.com>.

**Jeremy Weiland** is a software developer and activist in Richmond, VA. He holds a bachelor's degree in computer science and German from Mary Washington College and maintains the websites <http://socialmemory-complex.net> and <http://leftlibertarian.org>.

**Joe Peacott** is a contemporary individualist anarchist. Formerly an active member of the Boston Anarchist Drinking Brigade, he now resides in Alaska.

**Joseph R. Stromberg** is an independent historian whose work is concerned with a broad range of issues related to state power.

**Karl Hess** was an influential anarchist theorist and activist and a vocal proponent of local empowerment. A former speechwriter for US senator Barry Goldwater, he became associated with the New Left in the mid-1960s. He was the author or co-author of books including *Dear America* (1975), *The End of the Draft: The Feasibility of Freedom* (1970), *Neighborhood Power: The New Localism* (1975), *Community Technology* (1979), *A Common Sense Strategy for Survivalists* (1981), and *Mostly on the Edge* (1999).

**Kevin A. Carson** is Research Associate at the Center for a Stateless Society. He is the author of *Organization Theory: A Libertarian Perspective* (2008); *Studies in Mutualist Political Economy* (2007) – the focus of a symposium published in the *Journal of Libertarian Studies* – and *The Homebrew Industrial Revolution* (2009), as well as of the pamphlets *Austrian and Marxist Theories of Monopoly-Capital*; *Contract Feudalism: A Critique of Employer Power Over Employees*; *The Ethics of Labor Struggle*; and *The Iron Fist behind the Invisible Hand: Corporate Capitalism As a State-Guaranteed System of Privilege*. His writing has also appeared in *Just Things, Any Time Now, The Freeman: Ideas on Liberty*, and *Land and Liberty*, as well as on the P2P Foundation blog. A member of the Industrial Workers of the World, the Voluntary Cooperation Movement, and the Alliance of the Libertarian Left, and a leader in the contemporary revival of Proudhonian mutualist anarchism, he maintains the site *Mutualist Blog: Free Market Anticapitalism* at <http://mutualist.blogspot.com> and a set of resources related to mutu-alism at <http://www.mutualist.org>.

**Mary Ruwart** is an anarchist activist, author, and scientist. She is perhaps best known as the author of *Healing Our World in an Age of Aggression* (3d ed., 2005). She earned a BS in biochemistry and a PhD in biophys-ics at Michigan State University before serving as a faculty member at St. Louis University and as a research scientist at The Upjohn Company. She has worked extensively with the poor through her decade-long efforts to rehabilitate low-income housing in the Kalamazoo area and was an active member of the Kalamazoo Rainforest Action Committee. She currently serves as chair of a for-profit independent review board based in Austin. Her Internet column, "Short Answers to the Tough Questions" is a popular feature on the Advocates for Self-Government website – <http://www.self-gov.org>.

**Murray N. Rothbard** was an economist, political theorist, and historian. He was the author of such books as *Man, Economy, and State, with Power and Market* (2009), *The Ethics of Liberty* (1982), and *An Austrian Perspective on the History of Economic Thought* (1995). He played a key role in efforts during the mid-1960s to link the anti-interventionist, anti-authoritarian "Old Right" with the New Left in opposition to the Vietnam War and the draft.

**Pierre-Joseph Proudhon** was a philosopher, social theorist, activist, and member of the French Parliament. Arguably the first person to use the self-description "anarchist," Proudhon was the author of many influential books, including *What is Property?* (1840), *The System of Economic Contra-dictions or the Philosophy of Misery* (1846), *General Idea of the Revolution in the Nineteenth Century* (1851), *Theory of Property* (1866), and *Of the Principle of Art* (1875).

**Roderick T. Long** is a senior fellow of the Mises Institute. He is currently Professor of Philosophy at Auburn University and president of both the Molinari Institute and Molinari Society. He holds a PhD from Cornell University and a BA from Harvard. He is the author of *Reason and Value* (2000) and *Wittgenstein, Austrian Economics, and the Logic of Action* (2011) and the co-editor (with Tibor Machan) of *Anarchism/Minarchism: Is a Gov-ernment Part of a Free Country?* (2008). He blogs at <http://www.aaeblog.com/>.

**"Rosa Slobodinsky"** was the pen-name of Rachelle Slobodinsky-Yarros, a nineteenth- and twentieth-century physician and activist who was involved at various points in feminist and anarchist struggles. Her partner was the sometime anarchist theoretician Victor Yarros. She was the author of *Women and Sex* (1933).

**Roy A. Childs, Jr.,** was a political theorist, historian, and journalist who served as the editor of the *Libertarian Review* from 1977-81. He was especially well known as an incisive book reviewer. Many of his essays are available in a posthumous collection, *Liberty against Power* (1994).

**Shawn P. Wilbur** is an anarchist theorist, historian, publisher, and bookseller. He blogs at <http://libertarian-labyrinth.blogspot.com> and maintains an enormous array of resources related to the history of anarchism at <http://www.libertarian-labyrinth.org>.

**Sheldon Richman** is the editor of *The Freeman: Ideas on Liberty* and the author of books including *Tethered Citizens* (2001) and *Separating School and State* (1994). He blogs at <http://sheldonfreeassociation.blogspot.com>.

**Voltairine De Cleyre** was a feminist and anarchist writer and speaker who defended "anarchism without adjectives." Collections of her essays and speeches include *The Voltairine de Cleyre Reader* (2004); *Exquisite Rebel: The Essays of Voltairine De Cleyre – Anarchist, Feminist, Genius* (2005); and *Gates of Freedom: Voltairine De Cleyre and the Revolution of the Mind* (2005).

**William Gillis** is an anarchist activist and theoretician in Portland, Oregon. He holds a bachelor's degree from Macalester College.

# Minor Compositions

Other titles in the series:
*Precarious Rhapsody* – Franco "Bifo" Berardi
*Imaginal Machines* – Stevphen Shukaitis
*New Lines of Alliance, New Spaces of Liberty* – Felix Guattari and Antonio Negri
*The Occupation Cookbook*
*User's Guide to (Demanding) the Impossible* – Laboratory of Insurrectionary Imagination
*Spectacular Capitalism* – Richard Gilman-Opalsky


## Forthcoming:

*A Very Careful Strike* – Precarias a la Deriva
*Punkademics* – Ed. Zack Furness
*Communization & its Discontents* – Ed. Benjamin Noys
*Revolutions in Reverse* – David Graeber
*19 & 20* – Colectivo Situaciones
*Art, Production and Social Movement* – Ed. Gavin Grindon

As well as a multitude to come…

CPSIA information can be obtained
at www.ICGtesting.com
Printed in the USA
FFOW02n1903301115
18939FF

9 781570 272424